The Ways of Confucianism

The Ways of Confucianism

Investigations in Chinese Philosophy

David S. Nivison

Edited with an Introduction by
Bryan W. Van Norden

Nivison, David S.
The ways of Confucianism : investigations
in Chinese philosophy
BL1840 .N56 1996

RSN=00025348

OPEN COURT
Chicago and La Salle, Illinois

Cover calligraphy by Chin Yin-lien.

Open Court Publishing Company is a division of Carus Publishing Company.

Copyright © 1996 by Carus Publishing Company

First printing 1996

Printed and bound in the United States of America.

Library of Congress Cataloging-in-Publication Data

Nivison, David S.
    The ways of Confucianism : investigations in Chinese philosophy /
David S. Nivison ; edited with an introduction by Bryan W. Van
Norden
        p.   cm.
    Includes bibliographical references and index.
    ISBN 0–8126–9339–6 (alk. paper). — ISBN 0–8126–9340–X (pbk. :
alk. paper)
    1. Confucianism   2. Philosophy, Chinese   I. Van Norden, Bryan W.
(Bryan William)   II. Title.
BL1840.N56   1996
181'.112—dc20
                                            96–39050
                                            CIP

In memory of Paul Desjardins (1921–1991), *junzi*
D.S.N.

In memory of Helen Kwiecinski Van Norden (1917–1994)
B.V.N.

為政以德譬如北辰

居其所而眾星共之

Contents

Acknowledgments

Van Norden

I would like to thank Lois Jerke for typing Nivison's manuscripts, including some quite hard to read nth-generation dittos, onto the computer; our editor at Open Court, Kerri Mommer, who has shown almost infinite patience; and my wife, Becky Thomas, for humoring what she has described as my "expensive hobby."

Nivison

The articles and papers that make up this volume extend, if I include substantial rewriting and revisions, over forty years, and I am conscious of debts I owe that go back much farther, to persons living and dead. Any list would be sure to be far from complete. I wish here to emphasize my gratitude to the American Council of Learned Societies and to the John Simon Guggenheim Foundation, for support during an extended period of research in 1973 and 1974 on the problem of weakness of will, especially in Chinese philosophy. I learned much from Donald Davidson at this time, and earlier. This is a theme pursued especially in chapters 6, 7, and 9. Later, in 1977, a generous grant from the American Council of Learned Societies enabled P. J. Ivanhoe and me to complete a four-volume set of concordances of important Neo-Confucian texts, by Zhu Xi, Wang Yangming, and Dai Zhen. Most of the work was Ivanhoe's, but the project led me more deeply into the philosophy of Dai Zhen, and chapter 17 would not have been possible without this. My long interest in Zhang Xuecheng shows itself in this and several other papers, and it is with pride that I remind myself that my late teacher William Hung introduced me to Zhang's writings; and I continue to be grateful to Professor J. Robert Hightower of Harvard for his patience with my work on Zhang that led, ultimately, to a book. Chapters 2, 3, 4, and 5 might not have come into being had not the late Professor William Clebsch of Stanford and Stanford's Department of Religious Studies invited me to give the Walter Y. Evans-Wentz Lectures in 1980 and 1984. I owe a like debt to Henry Rosemont, for asking me for a review article on translations of Mencius, generously giving me six months to do it, and silently holding his peace while I then proceeded to take eight years to write, ultimately, what appears here as chapter 12. The first paper (chapter 2) allows me to play with material drawn from very ancient inscriptions, and I will always be conscious of my debt to Professor David N. Keightley and to Father Paul L-M Serruys for their guidance into this dark subject. The cluster of related themes woven into all of the papers—"virtue," self-cultivation, voluntaristic ethics, anxieties about commitments and performance—I can trace back to historical interests I was pursuing in the 1950s, writing on "knowledge" and "action" in late Neo-Confucianism and on coercive persuasion in what one has to call "ethics" under the Communists; my friendship with the late Arthur and Mary Wright was especially valuable to me then. Also very important at this time to my developing understanding of Chinese philosophy was my work with colleagues in the "Committee on Chinese Thought" of the Association for Asian Studies, which held five conferences between 1952 and 1960. In addition, from time to time, I have had reason to be grateful to Fred Brandauer, Francis Gramlich, Kathleen Hartnett, Sidney Rosen, and Lee Yearley.

Finally and not least, emerging from the past and looking at the book in front of me, I want to thank Bryan Van Norden for help that has gone far beyond what might be expected of an editor. The notes marked as his do not begin to show what he has done for me. In particular, his reworking of "Motivation and Moral Action in Mencius" makes that chapter partly his, and significantly more valuable than it might otherwise have been.

Introduction

The study of Chinese philosophy requires an unusual combination of talents. First, one must be a philosopher at heart (if not of academic department), for the issues that Mencius, Zhuāngzǐ 莊子, Zhū Xī 朱熹, Wáng Yángmíng 王陽明, and other Chinese thinkers address are living philosophic issues. Just as it took someone with a genuine understanding of science—Joseph Needham—to first appreciate Chinese science, so it takes a genuine philosopher to fully engage Chinese philosophy. Second, one must be a Sinologist, for even modern Chinese are separated by wide linguistic and cultural barriers from their predecessors. And to study Chinese philosophy without the tools to overcome those barriers is merely to project one's own preoccupations and concerns onto an alien culture, thereby robbing oneself of the opportunity for a genuine "fusing of horizons."

Among the generation of scholars who came to intellectual maturity following the second world war, several stand out for their knowledge of both philosophy and Sinology. Among these are A. C. Graham, D. C. Lau, Donald Munro, and David S. Nivison. Of these four, Nivison's work is the least well known. Although highly respected in Sinological circles and among us "happy few" who study Chinese philosophy, Nivison has remained a philosopher's philosopher, and his work is not commonly cited. Consider two outstanding recent histories of ancient Chinese philosophy—Benjamin Schwartz's *The World of Thought in Ancient China* (1985) and A. C. Graham's *Disputers of the Tao* (1989). Schwartz cites only two papers by Nivison—one dating the conquest of the Shang by the Zhou (1983), and one a highly technical bit of philology analyzing Shang Dynasty oracle bone inscriptions (1978–1979). Graham, on the other hand, cites three articles by Nivison, only one of which is on philosophy (1980a), the other two essays dealing with chronological issues (1982–1983, 1983).

There are several reasons for this unfortunate neglect of Nivison's work. One is that, unlike Lau and Graham, Nivison has not published any popular translations which keep him in the public eye. Furthermore, until now, many of Nivison's best papers have been available only in manuscript form to a few students and colleagues.[1] And those papers of Nivison's that are published are strewn across various academic journals. Before the publication of this volume, one would have had to look in *The Proceedings and Addresses of the American Philosophical Association* and in a supplemental volume to *The Journal of the American Academy of Religions*, and to have attended the 1977 "Asilomar Conference on Early Ch'ing Thought," in order to have encountered some of the papers here reproduced.

The ignorance of Nivison's work is especially distressing given its timeliness. To begin with, there is currently a surge in interest in Chinese philosophy. Mainstream philosophers such as Martha Nussbaum (1988, 1993), Alasdair MacIntyre (1991), and David Wong (1989, 1991) have started to seriously address Chinese philosophy. Furthermore, virtue ethics are being taken seriously again. And while Graham, for example, is a devotee of Zhuangzi, the classic Chinese anti-ethician, much of Nivison's work focuses on Mencius, whose virtue ethic provides a radical alternative to the Aristotelian and Thomistic paradigms most often invoked.[2]

In another essay (Van Norden, 1996), I discuss how Nivison's work fits into the context of contemporary comparative philosophy as a whole. In this introduction, I shall discuss what is distinctive of Nivison's work, and then provide brief summaries of the papers included in this collection.

1.1 Characteristics of Nivison's Work

One distinctive aspect of Nivison's work is his ability to illuminate the relationships between Chinese thought and contemporary Anglo-American philosophy. Three philosophical themes are especially prominent in Nivison's work: *akrasia* (or weakness of will); internalism (or prescriptivism); and the "management of one's moral motivations." The first two positions are related, and have received extensive treatment in contemporary Western philosophy. *Akrasia* occurs when one performs an action that one knows to be wrong. For example, I know that smoking is bad for me, yet I smoke anyway. Or, I know I should be grading my students' papers, but I watch TV instead. Some philosophers would further distinguish between two sorts of failure to act on moral knowledge: *akrasia* and *acedia*. *Akrasia* occurs when one is overcome by some temptation (desire for sex, wealth, etc.) that conflicts with one's moral knowledge, while *acedia* occurs when one simply cannot muster sufficient motivation to do what one knows is right, even though no particular strong desire tempts one. Consider my failure to grade my students' papers: this is *akrasia* if I do it because I succumb to the desire to spend a night out on the town with my friends; it is *acedia* if I am not tempted by anything else in particular, but simply cannot get myself to grade. (Perhaps I just "channel-surf" without even finding anything fun to watch.)[3]

That weakness of will occurs seems an undeniable part of our experience, yet some philosophers in ancient Greece, the more recent West, and China have apparently denied that it could occur. Why? The answer has to do with internalism (or prescriptivism), the doctrine that to judge that something has value is to be proportionately motivated in favor of that thing.[4] Thus, according to internalism, if I judge that A is more valuable than B, then I am motivated in favor of A more than I am motivated in favor of B. Many philosophers in the West have thought that internalism is required in order to make sense of a basic aspect of our moral experience: as David Hume (1978, 457) put it, moral judgments are "practical" rather than purely "speculative"; that is, they necessarily "have an influence on the actions and affections." But if we assume internalism, then *akrasia* becomes paradoxical. If I know that A is better than B (i.e., judge that A is more valuable than B), then (by internalism) I am motivated in favor of A more strongly than I am motivated in favor of B. But then it seems impossible that I should do B instead of A (i.e., *akrasia* is impossible).

One of the basic themes of Nivison's work is the changing attitudes toward weakness of will and internalism in the Confucian tradition. Confucius and Mencius were painfully aware of the possibility of weakness of will, for they faced it in their students and in political leaders whom they tried to motivate. Nivison argues that the particular form of it that was most prominent for them was *acedia*, and that this reflects (in part) the social situation of early Confucians. They were typically dependent upon gifts or stipends from rulers. However, accepting gifts from unworthy rulers helped to legitimize them. Consequently, improperly accepting an inappropriate gift is a favorite Confucian paradigm of moral weakness. When offered a gift I am initially in a passive state, the object of someone else's action, and the temptation to be avoided is to remain passive—to be unable to summon the moral stamina to refuse the gift—an instance of *acedia*.

Whereas Confucius and Mencius acknowledged the existence of weakness of will, Xúnzǐ 荀子, the next major Confucian, held what might be described as an "intellectualist" position: Confucianism can be justified with almost mathematical certainty, and knowledge guarantees right action. Centuries later, on the basis of a very different (and Buddhist-influenced) metaphysical picture, Wang Yangming denied the possibility of *akrasia*. Wang's doctrine of "the unity of knowledge and action" is essentially an assertion of internalism.[5] Then, in the last flowering of traditional Confucianism in the Qing Dynasty, philosophers like Zhāng Xuéchéng 章學誠 and Dài Zhèn 戴震 rediscovered, and defended, Xunzian intellectualism.

What these earlier and later Confucians have in common, and what distinguishes them from most Western philosophers, is a concern with ethical cultivation. For those like Confucius and Mencius who recognized that weakness of will *is* possible, a major concern becomes *how* it happens and *how* to overcome it, both in others and in oneself. For Wang Yangming it is important to stress "the unity of knowledge and action" precisely because otherwise students will fail to see the inherent connection between their study and their moral activities. Consequently, both earlier and later Confucians see adults as responsible for "the management of their moral motivations." In this, they differ from almost all the major figures in the Western tradition. For example, Aristotle thought that proper feeling was crucial for genuine virtue, but he held that the only way to acquire proper feeling is through the inculcation of good habits as a child and adolescent.[6] Kant explicitly denied that we are responsible for our emotions. This is what led him to see reason as a better foundation for morality than emotion.[7] As Nivison observes, the contrasting Confucian position on this topic is certainly defensible, and may just be right.

Another distinctive aspect of Nivison's work is his fastidious and dogged attention to particular passages, phrases, and even individual words.[8] Instead of assuming that he understands the meaning of some key term or phrase, Nivison employs a methodology, illustrated in several essays in this volume, with the following steps: (1) Read the commentaries on the text, both classic and contemporary. As Nivison illustrates, one often finds substantive disagreements among these commentaries,[9] which suggest a variety of possible interpretive strategies. (2) Read different translations of the text. This also helps clarify interpretive issues, by forcing one to ask how other translators arrived at their conclusions, and whether they are defensible. (3a) In the case of a key term, look for glosses of the word in commentaries and translations, and occurrences of the word in other contexts. The glosses will provide hypotheses about how to understand the term. Other occurrences of the word can provide evidence for its meaning, since we should prefer (all else being equal) translations of the term that make sense of its use in a variety of different contexts. (3b) In the case of key phrases, look for paraphrases in commentaries, and sentences with parallel syntax in other contexts. Once again, the commentaries provide new interpretive hypotheses, and syntactic parallels provide evidence for interpretations. (4) Having assembled a variety of interpretive hypotheses and pieces of evidence, prefer (all else being equal) interpretations that *attribute a sensible meaning to the text*.[10] In other words, when considering a possible interpretation, ask yourself, "Do I understand why an intelligent human being, in that culture, and in that concrete situation, would say this?" Consider an example. In *Mèngzǐ* 孟子 2A6.3, Mencius offers what philosophers today would call a "thought-experiment" to illustrate what he means by the virtue of benevolence. One sentence reads, *Jīn rén zhà jiàn rúzǐ jiāng rù yú jǐng* 今人乍見孺子 將入於井. The correct translation (I submit) is something like the following: "Suppose a person were, all of a sudden, to see a baby on the verge of falling into a well."[11] A student in a classical Chinese course once asked why this piece of text could not be understood to mean, "Suppose a person were, all of a sudden, to see a baby. He or she would jump into a well."[12] It seems to me that the student's interpretation *cannot* be ruled out on syntactic or lexical grounds alone. What does rule it out, however, is the fact that it fails to *make sense of the text*. Why would Mencius say *that*? How could it help to illustrate benevolence that someone jumps into a well when she sees a baby?

The final aspect of Nivisonian methodology is to (5) prefer (all else being equal) interpretations that are *holistic*, in that they make sense of a given piece of text in the light of both the individual thinker's corpus, and also the thinker's intellectual context as a whole.[13]

One last aspect of Nivison's work is suggested by the title of this collection: "The Ways of Confucianism." For Nivison has long stressed that there is no one thing that is "Confucianism" as an intellectual movement. Rather, Confucian philosophy is a cluster of problems and themes that develop over time, as particular Confucian thinkers choose to emphasize certain key concepts over others and integrate outside influences. Thus, although critical of Mohism, Mencius assimilates vocabulary and forms of argument from the later followers of Mòzǐ 墨子. Xunzi learns from both Mohists and Daoists.[14] Much later, "Neo-Confucians" like Zhu Xi and Wang Yangming inherit from Buddhism a metaphysical picture completely different from anything in pre-Buddhist China.[15]

1.2 Paper Summaries

1.2.1 Investigations in Chinese Philosophy

Part I of this collection, "Investigations in Chinese Philosophy," consists of a series of lectures that Nivison gave at Stanford in 1980 and 1984. The first three of these chapters provide an excellent overview of the themes and issues of Nivison's historical work as a whole. The essays in parts II and III of this volume develop in more detail, and provide sustained argumentation for, the positions sketched in chapters 2, 3, and 4.

"'Virtue' in Bone and Bronze" begins with what seems, at first, an unpromising starting point for philosophical discussion: the cryptic pronouncements on the "oracle bones" used for divination in China some three thousand years ago.[16] However, Nivison uses this, and other early sources, to construct and defend a powerful interpretation of one of the key terms in early Chinese philosophy: *dé* 德. *De* is the "power" or "charisma" by which a king rules without needing to resort to force or violence. *De* is also related to what Western philosophers would call "virtue."[17] What is the connection? Humans typically feel gratitude for gifts. However, in some societies, this feeling becomes magnified, so that my gratitude to you comes to seem like a force you exert over me.[18] *De* was originally this "force," which the Chinese kings acquired through their willingness to make "sacrifices" to the spirits of their ancestors and for their subjects. However, there is an important difference between a gift given sincerely, and one given with the intention of gaining control over another. Consequently, *de* became connected with humility, generosity, and (in general) the "virtues." Furthermore, it became clear that others besides the king could sincerely sacrifice themselves for others. At that point, *de* was no longer the king's prerogative alone.

But what if I wish to be virtuous, but am not so already? To be virtuous involves, among other things, performing acts of kindness toward others. But in order to be genuine acts of *virtue*, these actions must not be performed with the (self-interested) intent of gaining favor with you by my (supposed) kindness. So it seems that I cannot perform a genuinely virtuous act, unless I already have virtuous inclinations—in other words, unless I am virtuous already. Nivison calls this "The Paradox of 'Virtue'," and argues that it is central to understanding the development of early Chinese philosophy. Many passages in the *Analects*, for example, illustrate the problem, as Confucius tries to deal with disciples of varying degrees of moral development. Mozi, founder of an anti-Confucian "consequentialist" school, apparently takes an extreme "voluntarist" position, assuming that humans can simply adopt emotions and motivations at will.[19] Mencius's view of human nature and the "four sprouts" can be seen as an attempted solution to this paradox: all humans already are virtuous (albeit incipiently), so we all can perform genuinely virtuous actions. Nivison also contrasts Mencius with Aristotle, who apparently held that one can become a more virtuous person by (at least initially) performing virtuous actions without the appropriate virtuous motivations.

Mencius's view of human nature seems to imply that he must answer "Yes" to the question, "Can Virtue Be Self-Taught?" The next major Confucian, Xunzi, criticized Mencius on this ground, claiming that such a position leads to a very un-Confucian denigration of the importance of education, teachers, and tradition. Nivison argues that Xunzi, and all Confucians over the next two millennia of Chinese history, struggle (unsuccessfully) to come up with a view of the development of morality that validates the essential importance of the great sages of antiquity and the tradition that arises from them, but also makes clear how any human could, in principle, discover (or invent) morality.[20] Xunzi himself seems torn between two positions (each of which does better with one of the two desiderata than the other): (1) anyone who is capable of "doing arithmetic" can see that it is in one's self-interest to undergo the Confucian process of education and cultivation; (2) the Confucian tradition is the result of a process of historical "accumulation." The former answer explains how the sages (being mere humans like us) could discover morality, but it makes it unclear why we need the sages or their tradition. The latter answer makes clear why we need tradition, but it makes it more mysterious how the sages managed to come up with that tradition in the first place. In the remainder of this chapter, Nivison sketches how later Confucians develop Mencian and Xunzian positions: Wang Yangming is led (by a Buddhist-influenced reading of Mencius) to an extreme antinomian (and, in principle, anti-intellectual) philosophy; Dai Zhen and Zhang Xuecheng each emphasize one of the two views suggested by Xunzi.

In the last of the essays in part I, "Golden Rule Arguments in Chinese Moral Philosophy," Nivison examines the particular form this near-universal moral principle takes in the Chinese tradition. He argues that, in early Chinese philosophy, the golden rule is associated with two key virtues, *zhōng* 忠 and *shù* 恕, which apply the golden rule to different hierarchical relationships. *Zhong* is the virtue of those who, mindful of what they would expect of their own subordinates, provide good service to their superiors. *Shu* is the virtue of those who are empathetic and flexible in dealing with their subordinates, because they think about how they would want their superiors to treat them. Later in the Chinese tradition, different thinkers emphasize different apsects of these concepts. Thus, Zhu Xi (ever mindful of the danger of selfish desires) stresses the need to be stern with oneself, while Wang Yangming, Zhang Xuecheng, and Dai Zhen (in very different ways) stress the importance of sharing the feelings of others.

1.2.1 Ancient Philosophy

Most of the essays in part II of the present volume focus on particular thinkers or even particular passages. The one exception is "Weakness of Will in Ancient Chinese Philosophy," which provides an overview of this problem as it surfaces in the thought of Confucius, Mozi, Mencius, Xunzi, and Wang Yangming (with sideways glances at Plato and Aristotle). The problem arises first in connection with rulers. The good king has *de*, which means first the political charisma born of virtue, and later refers to that virtue itself. The bad king needs *de*, and the instruction of those who would inculcate *de* in him. But a bad king is precisely the one who is motivated neither to seek *de*, nor to listen to the advice of wise ministers. Such a king manifests what Western philosophers call "weakness of will" or *akrasia*: he knows what he should do, but does not do it. And, as Nivison notes, "the concept of the moral instruction of a king" becomes "the model of later conceptions of the role of a teacher in moral education."[21] So the problem of *akrasia* enters Chinese moral philosophy in general. Although the general problem is found in both ancient Greece and ancient China, the precise understanding of that problem differs importantly. Aristotle's model of *akrasia* is that of "the drunken rhapsode" blindly reciting poetry: real moral knowledge properly motivates, but one who succumbs to *akrasia* merely recites things ("Stealing is wrong") she does not (at the moment) really know to be true, because she is overcome by passion. In contrast, for Mencius, moral knowledge will not motivate without an additional *act*. Moral knowledge will not motivate unless we maneuver a proper moral motivation into place.[22]

"Motivation and Moral Action in Mencius" is one of the most ambitious papers in this collection. In sections 7.1 through 7.3, Nivison sketches Mencius's view of moral motivation, and contrasts it with several contemporary Chinese alternatives. Focusing on Mencius's intriguing (and often underemphasized) dialogue with King Xuān of Qí 齊宣王 in *Mengzi* 1A7,

Nivison shows that in the background of Mencius's thought is the original Mohist picture, according to which humans can simply "adopt" feelings and attitudes. Mencius rejects Mohism strongly, but as Nivison shows, he adopted much of the vocabulary and technique of Mohist dialectics. Mencius's own view is that, for every human, there are paradigmatic cases in which one will have virtuous reactions. The process of moral cultivation is one of extending our reactions from the paradigmatic cases to other, relevantly similar, situations in which one does not yet have these reactions. This model can be understood in at least two ways, though, which Mencius refers to as "one root" and "two root" models. According to "two root" models, our natural reactions can be extended in a variety of ways. We might, therefore, choose to steer the development of our natural reactions in accordance with some moral doctrine. Mencius attacks this position in a debate with the neo-Mohist, Yí Zhī 夷之. A second kind of "two root" position holds that some of our virtuous reactions are innate (or "internal"), while others are acquired (or "external"). Mencius criticizes the rival philosopher Gàozǐ 告子 for holding this position. Nivison presents more detailed defenses for these positions in several of the following papers in part II. But in sections 7.4 and 7.5 he discusses some of the philosophical problems raised by the Mencian conception of "extension." Finally, in section 7.6, Nivison briefly compares Mencius's position with that of several other philosophers from the Western and Chinese traditions.

"Philosophical Voluntarism in Fourth-Century China" is an effort to unravel the meaning of one sixteen-character expression in *Mengzi* 2A2.9. Literally, "not get from words, don't seek in heart; not get from heart, don't seek in *qì* 氣." As Nivison shows, the task is surprisingly difficult. However, the payoff from the quest is rich, for we learn along the way how a variety of early Chinese philosophers thought about the relationships among moral doctrine, our innate moral sense (if any), human nature, and self-cultivation. At the one extreme, Mozi seems to assume that human nature is a tabula rasa that can be molded to fit any ethical doctrine. The philosopher Gaozi, although critical of Mozi in certain respects, came under Mozi's influence and later explicitly asserted the malleability of human nature in debate with Mencius. Mencius, in contrast, thinks that human nature has active dispositions in the direction of virtue. Furthermore, while recognizing the importance of the doctrines of the sages for self-cultivation, he holds that our innate moral feelings and dispositions (our "heart" *xīn* 心) are also an indispensable source of guidance. Finally, Zhuangzi rejects both moral doctrines and the heart as sources of guidance, preferring to rely instead on the *qi*.

"Two Roots or One?" takes as its starting point a debate between Mencius and the Mohist Yi Zhi in *Mengzi* 3A5. Nivison shows that this passage is concerned, among other issues, with the proper relationship between human motivation and moral obligation. Yi Zhi holds that humans have feelings of concern for their kin (the first "root" of morality) which must be redirected in

Part I

Investigations in Chinese Philosophy

accordance with Mohist doctrines (the second "root") to be universal and impartial. Mencius, in contrast, holds that there is only one "root": our innate moral heart-mind, which both tells us what we ought to do and provides the motivation to do it. The notion of "one root" can be cashed out in various ways, however, and Nivison notes that some later Mencians such as Wang Yangming and Dai Zhen understood it in a way that ruled out *akrasia*, or weakness of will. For Wang and Dai, to recognize something as a motivation is to be appropriately motivated. In this respect, Wang and Dai are like many twentieth-century Anglo-American philosophers, and unlike Mencius himself. For, despite his adherence to the "one root" doctrine, Mencius recognized that *akrasia* was possible. In the last part of this paper, Nivison offers his own reflections on the philosophic issues raised by these thinkers.

"Problems in the *Mengzi*: 6A3–5" is a detailed examination of a debate between Mencius and the rival philosopher Gaozi. At issue is whether "righteousness" is "internal" or "external." Nivison examines various possibilities about what these key terms mean in the context of fourth-century B.C. philosophy, and concludes that Mencius successfully exploits a crucial ambiguity in Gaozi's position.

"Problems in the *Mengzi*: 7A17" discusses one seventeen-character passage in the text. It is a nice example of Nivison's methodology of carefully studying previous translations and commentaries to uncover interpretive hypotheses. However, he also shows that one need not be a slave to previous scholarship, for Nivison's own view is that all previous interpretations miss the meaning of this passage.

"On Translating Mencius" is a critical review of the present translations of the *Mengzi* into English. (Nivison also discusses many of the classic Chinese commentaries, and several translations into other languages.) The *Mengzi* includes both stretches of relatively straightforward classical Chinese, and very "problematic" sections. Nivison examines how the translators and commentators handle samples of each. Nivison's discussion reflects his intense involvement with this text over decades of teaching and research, and incorporates many of the insights that resulted from earlier papers in this volume. One can learn an immense amount about classical Chinese through a careful reading of this chapter, which is essential reading for anyone translating the *Mengzi*, or seeking to understand any of the numerous passages Nivison covers.

In "Xunzi on 'Human Nature'" Nivison addresses an apparent tension in the thought of the next major Confucian philosopher after Mencius. Xunzi is perhaps best known for claiming that human nature is evil. This is an explicit swipe at Mencius, who argued that human nature is good. Nonetheless, Xunzi also says that what distinguishes humans from "birds and beasts" is that humans have *yì* 義 (normally rendered "a sense of righteousness"). But if humans, qua humans, have a sense of righteousness, then isn't Xunzi really saying that human nature is good after all?

Nivison first considers the possibility that *yi* is not best thought of as "a sense of righteousness." To examine this possibility, Nivison outlines Xunzi's justification of ethics. It turns out to be a rather interesting one, combining both consequentialist and deontological elements. Essentially, Xunzi argues that humans, although naturally selfish, have prudential reasons for undergoing an ethical transformation that will turn them into altruists: given human nature and our "environment" (broadly construed), pure egoists cannot satisfy their desires; humans can only find satisfaction as members of a community of altruists. Xunzi's justification of ethics is interestingly different from the Neo-Kantian and Neo-Hobbesian justifications more familiar to contemporary philosophers, and deserves further critical discussion. However, Nivison focuses on the implications relevant to his original question. For it seems that Xunzi's justification requires that humans have a capacity to *learn* to value "righteousness" for its own sake. So not only does Xunzi refer to "a sense of righteousness," but the logic of his position seems to require that humans have such a sense.

The second possibility Nivison considers is a version of the "complementarian strategy." Complementarian interpreters of Xunzi argue that his position is not fundamentally different from that of Mencius. Instead, the two philosophers merely emphasize different things. Consider an individual who longs to be virtuous. Mencius, Nivison suggests, focuses on the longing for virtue as a sign of the goodness of the person's nature. Xunzi, on the other hand, focuses on the lack of virtue, without which there would be no longing.

1.2.3 Recent Centuries

Part III includes Nivison's papers on Confucianism in the Song, Ming, and Qing dynasties. "The Philosophy of Wang Yangming" provides a general introduction to the thought of this extremely influential Neo-Confucian. Wang was a philosopher, with a Buddhist-influenced metaphysical picture very different from that of earlier Confucians like Mencius. However, Wang was like earlier Confucians in being concerned with more than abstract theory; Wang had a profound concern with moral cultivation. Wang's metaphysical and "soteriological" concerns join to influence his particular conception of the nature and goal of moral cultivation. For Wang, self-cultivation is a matter of escaping the "obscuration" of "selfish desires," and attending instead to the voice of one's true self. Because one's true self is ultimately identical with the universe, successful self-cultivation results in a recognition (that is both theoretical and practical) of the unity of all things.

"Moral Decision in Wang Yangming: The Problem of Chinese 'Existentialism'" critiques the provocative thesis that Wang and his followers were philosophical existentialists. Nivison argues that the similarities between Wang's philosophy and existentialism are largely superficial. Like Western existentialists, Wang descibes the self as being "nothing." But Wang's "nothing" is not the existentialist's radical freedom to create value, but rather the openness of the self to the normative-descriptive "principles" of things. Like Western existentialists, Wang rejects reliance on rigid moral rules. But this is not because reliance on rules is "inauthentic," but rather because moral facts are radically situational and must be perceived in each context. Like Western existentialists, Wang talks of "suffering." But the best life for Wang is not one of continual *angst*, but rather one of joy that persists even in mourning. Like Western existentialists, Wang talks of "spontaneity," but this is not an unconstrained freedom to choose, but rather the unrestrained action of one's true self.

The heyday of Western existentialism is already past, but the points Nivison makes in this chapter are still important. For existentialism is a member of a family of positions that make normative facts dependent upon individual choice, and this family, like the mafia, will probably always be with us. Consequently, one occasionally still sees efforts to read Wang Yangming and other Confucians as subjectivists or relativists of some variety. This chapter is a good antidote to this tendency.

One of Nivison's contributions as a scholar has been to stress the philosophical interest and importance of an often-overlooked figure, Zhang Xuecheng. "The Philosophy of Zhang Xuecheng" presents Zhang's philosophy as a response to trends in Neo-Confucianism initiated by Wang Yangming. In the Ming Dynasty, Wang encouraged people to trust their "innate intuition" over "empty words"—even the words of the Confucian Classics! As a result, Confucians in the Qing Dynasty began to reject metaphysical speculation, and even philosophical speculation in general, as empty words. Nonetheless, being Confucian scholars, they felt a need to be engaged with the classical texts. Consequently, they turned to a sort of detailed philology that avoided grand generalizations in favor of precise work on linguistic details. Thus, paradoxically, Wang Yangming's intense personal commitment to moral development led to arid and morally sterile philology. Zhang, according to Nivison, accepted Wang's rejection of empty words, but thought there was an important moral role for the words of the Classics. The Classics were not empty philosophical generalizations, but were the "traces" of the concrete actions of the historical sages in specific contexts. Studying these "traces" can help one to acquire the sound situational judgment of the sages.

Interesting comparisons can be made between the thought of both Wang and Zhang, and some recent trends in Western ethics. For example, like Zhang, Martha Nussbaum emphasizes the importance of moral perceptiveness in concrete situations. However, Nussbaum (1990) argues that novels are an especially good tool for cultivating this perceptiveness, while Zhang recommends study of the Confucian Classics. This cross-cultural ethical disagreement merits further investigation.

"Two Kinds of 'Naturalism': Dai Zhen and Zhang Xuecheng" showcases Nivison's skill at both detailed philological work and broader intellectual history.

In section 17.2 of this chapter, Nivison presents a hypothesis about the historical relationship and mutual influence of Dai and Zhang. In section 17.3, Nivison discusses the solutions offered by Dai and Zhang to the following problem:

> [H]ow can we give a rational account of the human world of value—human norms and goals—in terms of an abstract picture of the world as a whole in which norms and "virtue" are not explicitly posited—in such a way as to explain and justify our study and veneration of the Confucian classics? And conversely, how can we give a plausible natural account of the origin and nature of the Classics such that, given the respect we have for them, they in turn justify the personal values and goals we do have?[23]

This problem is far from academic. If we substitute "Aristotelian" for "Confucian," we can see that the issue Nivison explores is also a problem for contemporary Western philosophers, such as Alasdair MacIntyre (1988, 1990), who argue that appeal to an intellectual tradition helps provide a justification for their own beliefs. In addition, the issues raised by Nivison's discussion of Dai and Zhang are of general interest regardless of whether one believes in the importance of Classics and tradition. As Nivison observes, "we could as well put 'generally accepted moral order' for 'Classics'."[24]

So what solutions do Dai and Zhang propose? Briefly, Dai seems to present a sort of ideal-observer theory, which relies upon a universalizability test. Zhang presents a historical justification for ethics as the cumulative wisdom of the past. (Hence, Zhang has been compared to both Burke and Hegel.)[25]

1.3 Editorial Issues

The editor chose to convert all romanizations in these essays to Pinyin, and to supply characters and tone marks for at least the first occurrences of Chinese expressions in each chapter. Citations were standardized and supplied where lacking. In some cases, text that was originally in the body of an essay has been moved to the notes. The editor occasionally requested, or made suggestions for, partial rewriting for the sake of clarity.[26] Every note (or parenthetical comment within a note) that is an addition by the editor (other than supplying citations for works referred to) has been marked as "[Editor.]" The reference listings include annotations by both Dr. Nivison (mostly drawn from his 1980b) and the editor. Dr. Nivison has read the revised manuscript, and (with the exception of some formatting issues), the editor has not knowingly diverged from his wishes. In a work so wide-ranging, some typographical errors or mistaken citations may remain. Readers are invited to report any to the publisher for correction in future editions.

One other issue perhaps deserves special mention. The use of gender-neutral language presents special problems in dealing with traditional texts (whether Eastern or Western). Since its pronouns are genderless, and grammatical subjects are often assumed rather than stated, classical Chinese does not require one to specify the gender of an indefinite person. Nonetheless, it is true that classical Chinese philosophers would have (like their Greek counterparts) taken the "generic person" to be male. In addition, Dr. Nivison wrote most of these essays before it became common to use gender-neutral language in scholarly writing. Consequently, while the editor occasionally rephrased in the direction of gender-neutrality, this volume is not consistent in this regard. I hope readers will remember that no solution to this problem will satisfy everyone, and will not allow disagreement on this issue to distract them from the substance of Nivison's essays.

"Virtue" in Bone and Bronze[1]

This and the following two lectures are on what I shall baldly call the Chinese concept of virtue. I will be told at once by some that there is no such concept, and by others that there are not one but many; and by yet others that what I am talking about is not one of them. To each I must reply that I think I have understood you.

Let me say more exactly what I think I am doing.

You will have noticed that the titles of these three lectures play a game with quotation marks: In this one I am talking about "virtue"—double quotes; in the next (chapter 3), about 'virtue'—single quotes; and in the last (chapter 4) I am talking (I think) about virtue. I shall first be talking about uses, in early inscriptions, of a word that we now pronounce *dé* 德 in the Mandarin dialect, and that most of us uneasily translate "virtue," or leave untranslated. In the next lecture ("The Paradox of 'Virtue'"), I will show that the concept represented by this word, in an easy and natural extension of its scope, comes in the high classical moral philosophers to include the qualities that a good person would have to have to be morally good, and so collectively one's 'virtue'. But the word *de* seems to have other senses too. Arthur Waley (1958), translating the Daoist classic *Dào dé jīng* 道德經, uses for the title "The Way and Its Power"—"power" being Waley's translation for *de*; and Waley had good reasons. When he encounters the word *de* used to name a moral quality, as it sometimes is in the Confucian *Analects* (*Lún yǔ* 論語), he combines these senses, translating it "moral force" (1938). Indeed, I think it is common knowledge that *de* as a moral-making property of a person was conceived as giving the person psychic power or influence over others, and sometimes even over one's nonhuman surroundings. This aspect of the concept, too, has its explanation in the very earliest usage of the word; and it has implications, not easily analyzed, that make mature and sophisticated moral-philosophical discussion by the Chinese philosophers complex and fascinating—even when the word and syllable *de* has been left behind, and these philosophers are talking about *rén* 仁 ("benevolence"), *yì* 義 ("duty"), *xìn* 信 ("trust"), *lǐ* 禮 ("propriety"), *liáng zhī* 良知 ("moral intuition"), etc. I will get into some of these complexities in "The Paradox of 'Virtue'," and will pursue one of them farther in "Can Virtue Be Self-Taught?"

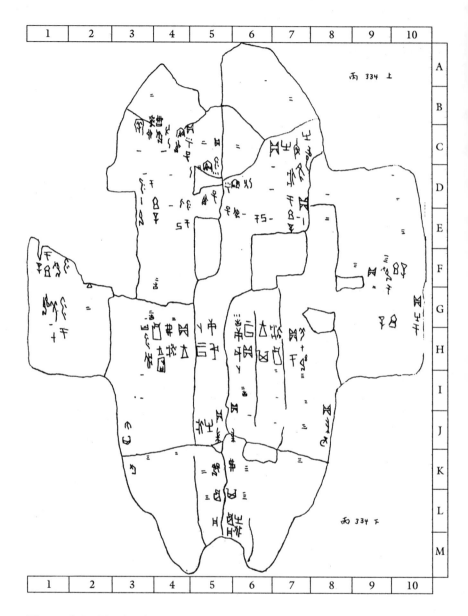

Figure 2.1: Turtle Plastron (*Bing bian* 334)

By that time, I think I will be talking about problems that are quite universal, for all their peculiar origin and local color, and that are as much a part of your experience and mine as of the great Chinese moralists and their students.

But for this evening, I invite you to join me in looking at another world, long past, that will seem strange, and sometimes amazing. I am going to try to show you how I find and interpret things in this archaic world. This may be enlightening. It is also lots of fun.

Figure 2.1 is a hand-traced copy, reduced to about half size, of the smooth (exterior) side of the plastron (ventral shell) of a large turtle, in which numbers of inscriptions are carved.[2] This piece is referred to as *Bǐng biān* 丙編 334. It was assembled from smaller pieces, and is among many excavated ca. 1928–1932 at Xiǎotún 小屯 village near Ānyáng 安陽, in Hénán 河南 province. Ink-squeeze copies of these were published by Academia Sinica (in Taiwan) in the 1950s and 1960s. This one is from the third series of these publications, which totals six volumes, edited by Zhāng Bǐngquán 張秉權 (1957–1972), who has supplied some tentative transcriptions into modern graphs and a limited amount of other interpretation. But this interpretive work one must always do over for oneself—the reason being that in 1967, with a revision in 1971, there was published in Japan a concordance of most of the collections of such inscriptions that had been published since these inscriptions first began to come to light in 1899. Intelligent use of this tool, which took ten years to compile (under the direction of the late Shima Kunio 鳥邦男 [1971]), enables even newcomers like me to make discoveries that would have been impossible for even the best of earlier scholars.

Some of these inscriptions are not on shells but on scraped shoulder-blade bones of cattle—hence "bone and bronze" in my title, for simplicity; but the one I am examining is on a shell. This one dates from about 1200 B.C., and like all of them, shell or bone, it had a religious purpose. The Chinese king of the time, whose posthumous name is Wǔ Dīng 武丁, had as his capital "the great city Shāng 商," near the site from which this piece came, and so we call him one of the kings of the Shang Dynasty. This dynasty was replaced by another, the Zhōu 周, whose ruler King Wǔ 武王 defeated the last Shang king Dì Xīn 帝辛 in (I believe) early 1040 B.C.[3] The Shang king's power and functions were both military and religious. He maintained an elaborate ritual-sacrificial ancestor cult, and his ancestors were very powerful. He was also a diviner, and in addition had in his service a large corps of professional diviners. It was the task of these court diviners to find out what sacrifices needed to be made to ancestors and other spirits, to make sure that these spirits would help the king and his people in their undertakings—hunting, growing crops, fighting battles—and to make equally sure that the spirits did not harm the living—which they were frequently doing, typically by afflicting a living person, the king himself or someone close to him, with toothaches, headaches, eye and foot ailments, and other miseries, all too often fatal.

When someone got sick, therefore, the court diviners or the king had to use their arts to find out what ancestor spirit was causing the mischief, and what sacrificial steps were needed to stop it. This happens to be what this particular shell was for. The divination procedure was to take a shell or bone such as this one, which had been prepared by chiseling almond-shaped hollows in geometrical arrangements on the back side, and then applying a burning stick to the hollow, cracking the shell on the front side in a "T" shape. As the diviner did this, he had in hand or in his head, or declaimed, a statement he was testing—e.g., "It is ancestress so-and-so who is doing it." Examining the crack, he could interpret it and tell whether this statement was true. At times the king himself would be the officiating diviner. But sometimes he would come into the act at a second stage: after the diviner had done his work, the king would reexamine the crack and pronounce his evaluation of it. After all was done, the test sentence and evaluations would be inscribed beside the crack. The cracks were numbered in sequence.

Now look at our shell. My copy does not show the cracks—only numbers and inscriptions. Notice the inscription consisting of seven graphs at top right, C–D/7–8. It reads down and to the right: "Testing: 'There is an ailment in her pregnant womb, because she is being afflicted by an ancestral spirit.'" Looking down now, to two inscriptions on either side of the axis of the shell at the bottom, at J–M/5–6, we find out who is in trouble. These are a positive-negative pair, reading down and away from the axis, in opposite directions: (1) "Testing: 'Lady Hǎo 婦好 will successfully recover from her illness.'" (2) "Testing: 'Lady Hao will not successfully recover from her illness.'"

There are many other inscriptions, on other shells and bones, about Lady Hao (perhaps the graph that I read "Hao" should be read "Zi"), who was apparently one of King Wu Ding's consorts. All of the inscriptions on this shell—there are others on the back too—are about her present problem, directly or indirectly. The two short ones on the lower edges retest the sentences I have just read: "Testing: 'The Lady will get better'" (right edge); "'She won't get better'" (left edge). On the bridges and at top left are inscriptions proposing sacrifices to various ancestors who might be responsible, or at least might help.

And in the lower center are two that are very interesting—again, reading away from the axis:

(1) G–H/6–7: "Crack on day *gēngxū* 庚戌, diviner Xuān 亘 testing: 'The king will get sick in his bones.'"

(2) G–H/4–5: "Crack on day *gengxu*, diviner Xuan testing: 'The king will not get sick in his bones.'"

And then, at the end, five words: *Wáng zhān yuē wù jí* 王占曰勿疾 "The king read the crack and said, 'Let him not get sick.'"

What is going on here? I had said that everything on this shell revolves around the royal consort's present illness. Why, then, inscriptions about a possible future illness of the king? And what is the king himself doing in his "crack reading"?

For enlightenment, we must turn the shell over (to *Bing bian* 335). On the reverse side are more inscriptions, too rough to copy, again all, I think, on the one problem of this shell: Will Lady Hao get well? (Yes—another royal crack reading.) Whom do we sacrifice to on her behalf? And, directly back of the two inscriptions on the front side concerning the king and his "bones," two more that are quite puzzling: should the king offer, or not, a certain sacrifice—involving a human victim—to ancestress Bǐ Gēng 妣庚 (possibly a deceased consort of the king's father; sacrifices to her would be appropriate on *gengxu* day) lest the king get a certain illness which I will call *kǔ* 苦—the later word "pain," though the graph on the shell has no obvious later form.

We know something about this illness. It is indeed an ailment of the bones, or perhaps the joints (one suspects arthritis). And it is an ailment that almost nobody gets but the king (fifty-two out of fifty-four inscriptions containing this word in Shima's concordance, in which there is a named sufferer, out of a total of about a hundred inscriptions concerning this ailment). Furthermore the word *kǔ* has another meaning, apparently completely unrelated to this one: it is the name of a sacrificial rite in which the object is an animal—a dog or pig; after the ritual, whatever it is, the animal is buried in a pit. As a feared royal disease, it is associated on another shell too (*Bing bian* 90) with inscriptions about the recovery of some other person. One more detail: There are over sixty inscriptions in Shima's concordance concerning hoped-for recovery of someone from an illness, using just the formula used for Lady Hao: the person "will (will not) successfully recover from" his or her illness. Persons being helped by this use of the royal divination technology include other consorts, generals and feudal vassals, princes of the blood—but never the king himself. Not that he doesn't get sick; Wu himself has to make his way back to health by other means.

We can now put some of this together. (This will be guesswork; you must judge for yourselves whether it is good guesswork.) The king's lady is ill. The king is concerned. Rites are put in motion. In these rites, the king offers himself in the sick person's place—as a royal scapegoat, like the poor dog or pig—saying in effect to the offended spirit, "Don't take her, take me." Only, of course, the king can hardly invite upon himself a pregnancy disorder. What he does is to invite upon himself an attack of *kǔ*. And having thus put himself ritually at risk, he then takes steps to protect himself—first by divining to determine whether the offer of self-sacrifice will be taken up, and then by using rites to ward off the attack if it should threaten to come: proffered sacrifices, on the back of the shell; and on the front, a command, "Let the king not get sick." It appears that in the crack-reading rite—we have over two dozen examples—the

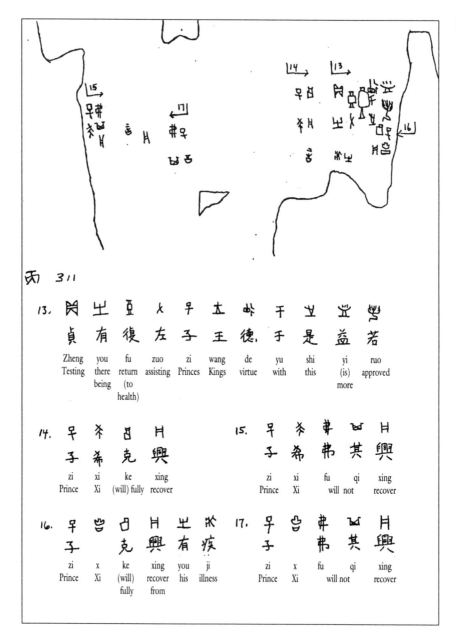

Figure 2.2: Inscription on *Bing bian* 311

king acquires supernormal powers, and can issue commands to spirits, even of ancestors.

But what has all this to do with *de*, "virtue"? I have talked for ten minutes without mentioning the concept. To see, turn to figure 2.2, my tracing of a part of *Bing bian* 311. Here we have another illness problem. Test is made twice each for two named princes, using the same formula found on the "Lady Hao" shell: "N will (will not) successfully recover from his (her) illness."[4]

Then, as part of this group of inscriptions and almost entangled with them, there is another, about the king (numbered 13 by Zhang Bingquan), which I think should be translated as follows: "Testing: 'The assisting princes having been restored [to health]; the king's *de* ("virtue") is with this [event] even more approved [by the ancestors].'"

The immediate inference I make is this: In this rite in which the king as diviner-intermediary assists another person to get well, the king's offer of self-sacrifice, ideally, has this result: not only does the sick person get well; further, the king does not himself get sick; and more, because of his willingness to put himself in danger on behalf of another, his *de*, "virtue," is magnified.

Can we find other support for this inference?

Indeed yes. There is a famous story in chapter 26 of the *Shàng shū* 尚書 (*Classic of History*), concerning King Wu, founder of the Zhou Dynasty, and his younger brother Dàn 旦, known as the Duke of Zhōu 周公.[5] The king has suddenly been taken dangerously ill; the time is the second year following the conquest of Shang; the king's death would be disastrous. So the Duke of Zhou—secretly—performs a divination rite. Using the turtle shell, he addresses the king's ancestors. "If you must take someone," he tells them, "then take me, and allow the king to recover." The cracks indicate a favorable response. The record of the event is stored in a sealed box and the attendants sworn to silence. The king does recover, and the Duke of Zhou remains in good health. Years later, perhaps after the Duke's death, there is a wild storm, causing the high court ministers to open and scrutinize old divination records, and the matter comes to light. We are told at the end that Heaven sent the storm, "to display the virtue of the Duke of Zhou."

This story is a myth, and the account was probably written several centuries after the supposed events. In fact, the myth exists in more than one form: another still later but more primitive version (in the "Lǔ shìjiā" 魯世家 section of the *Shǐjì* 史記, *Records of the Historian*) has the Duke offering himself to the irate god of the Yellow River on behalf of the ill King Chéng 成王, Wu's young successor, for whom the Duke served as regent. "The king is still young and unintelligent," he tells the god in his prayer; "the one who has disobeyed your commands is really I myself." And as a pledge he then cuts off his finger-nails and throws them into the water. As before, all goes well, and the Duke's "virtue" is enhanced. Myth, indeed. But more important for being myth. For a people cannot afford to allow an idea as important as this one to wait upon chance historical happenings for its dramatization. The importance of these stories, I would suggest, goes beyond my immediate purpose in retelling them—which was the parallel with what I see Wu Ding to have been doing in his curing rites. The Duke of Zhou was not a king. *De* in one in a subordinate political position, established by one's demonstrated willingness to sacrifice one's life in loyalty, gives one moral independence and the right to be heeded with respect.

But back to Shang and Wu Ding's oracle inscriptions. An obvious next move is to look for other uses of the graph *de*, to see if we can fill in more of the early shape of this concept.

In Shima's concordance we find about 150 examples, most of them short fragments. Most of these are of two kinds. Those in the largest group appear to concern proposed military campaigns—e.g., "This spring the king will *de* the Tǔ Fāng 土方" (an enemy border people), or "will *de*-attack the Fang," using the word, apparently, as a verb denoting some kind of military action. This seems so strange that for many decades, until the late 1970s, almost all scholars doubted that the graph I am pursuing could correctly be identified as *de* at all, and they gave it other readings—e.g., *xún* 循, to "make a [military] tour of inspection." The other major group of inscriptions concerns sacrifices to ancestral spirits—e.g., "The king should *de*-sacrifice to ancestor so-and-so." And here too, though "tour of inspection" hardly fits, most have doubted the word could really be *de*.

But *de* it surely is, in both cases. The graphic evidence is compelling: the Shang graph is almost exactly like some instances of the Zhou graph, in Zhou inscriptions where context leaves no doubt that the word is *de*. Certain of the Shang sacrifice inscriptions make the identity unmistakable. We find one very much like *Bing bian* 311, except that it is the king's having performed a certain sacrifice that now causes the spirits to "approve the king's *de*." So "*de*-sacrifice" perhaps means simply "sacrifice in order to enhance the royal *de*." Once we find it said that "the fragrance of the king's *de* is approved" by the spirits. The phrase is important just because the idea seems so strange that the savor of the royal *de* might be pleasing to the nostrils of the ancestors. Such an odd phrase can't be an accident of speech; and we find precisely the same phrase, rarely, in later literature (such as the *Shang shu*) telling us, for example, that it isn't the burnt offerings themselves, but the fragrance of the king's *de* that is pleasing to the spirits.[6]

These sacrifice contexts tell us more already about what *de* is: it appears to be a quality or psychic energy in the king that the spirits can perceive and are pleased to see in him; and it appears to be something he gets, or something that becomes more evident in him when he denies or risks himself, does something for another—for another human being, in the medical cases we looked at, or for a spirit, in offering sacrifice.

But what is going on in the military inscriptions? Here too, later literature helps. For example, the *Zuǒ zhuàn* 左傳, under the year 656 B.C., describes the confrontation between the forces of Chǔ 楚 (the big Chángjiāng 長江 Valley state, originally independent of the Chinese king) and the northern alliance under Duke Huán of Qí 齊桓公 and his minister Guǎn Zhòng 管仲. Chu sends an envoy of their royal family, Qū Wán 屈完, to parley. Each side combines modesty with boasting and defiance. Huan denies credit for gathering the combined armies under himself; the allied states are continuing traditional friendship with Qi cultivated by his predecessors. Would not Chu like to join them? But, he adds, if this army were used in anger, no one could withstand it. The Chu envoy replies, "If your lordship . . . by your virtue (*de*) seeks the tranquillity of the states, who will dare not to submit to you? But if you depend on your strength, our state of Chu has the mountains of Fāngchéng 方城 for a wall and the Hàn River 漢水 for a moat. Great as your multitudes are, you could not use them."[7]

In the end, of course, there is an accommodation, and Chu is drawn within the Chinese orbit. So, military *de* is not, really, military. It is the combined impact of awe, perceived prestige, fear, and gratitude for the leader's restraint; and this impact, as a felt force, actually makes his using military measures unnecessary. I would offer this as a paradigm of a "*de*-campaign": part of the Shang king's function, revealed in these inscriptions, seems to have been to lead his forces forth each fighting season to overawe the borders, showing the flag, and doubly impressing the border peoples by his restraint in not showing his weapons' edges.

One more inscription gets us to the root of what is really going on. It is one of the "sacrificial" group:

> Oracle on the day *jiǎ-wǔ* 甲午, the king officiating: "We have *de* with royal ancestor Tài Yǐ 大乙. Let there be a *you*-sacrifice 酒 on the next *yǐ-wèi* day 乙未."[8]

The test sentence contains an example of a simple idiom common in classical Chinese, and in the archaic Chinese of the Western Zhou bronze inscriptions: for example, "A has merit with (in the regard of) B," "A has favor with B," etc. And we also find, as here, "A has *de* with B." This is an ancient colloquial idiom with a simple meaning: A has done something for B, and B consequently feels a debt of gratitude to A. We might say, "A has gratitude credit with B."

Simple, but not so simple. The feeling of a debt of gratitude for a kindness or gift or service is something we all know. It is part of being human. But in some societies it is greatly magnified, in countless ways, by socialization and social pressure, until it comes to seem to be an ambient psychological force. Chinese society is like this. I think it is now, and I think it has been, for as far back as I have been able to study it. In this kind of society, the compulsion I feel to respond appropriately, now or sometime, when you do something for me or give me something, is a compulsion I feel so strongly that I come to think of it not as a psychic configuration in myself, but as a psychic power emanating from you, causing me to orient myself toward you. That power is your *de*—your "virtue" or "moral force."[9]

Our materials—so far—are by their nature focused on the king. But his kinghood is not, if this analysis is right, a part of the definition of *de*. It is just that the king's *de* is, potentially, both extraordinarily important and extremely powerful. For he, by his position, is able to generate this relationship between himself and others in all directions—vis-à-vis members of his family, ministers in his court, his many subjects, his enemies, the spirits above, future generations. It will come to be felt that this is what he must do if he is to be a genuine king, and that there is something terribly wrong with him if he doesn't.

The relation of king to spirit powers can be taken as paradigmatic. I, as king, perform my sacrificial duties and the spirit is grateful. "I have *de* with—from—ancestor Tai Yi." Looked at in this way, my *de* is something I get from the spirit. But a spirit may not accept a sacrifice. (This is an ever-present anxiety in the oracles.) Surely it will not accept, if I am making the sacrifice in order to get a hold on the spirit. I must be, really, generous and dutiful; the sacrifice is the external embodiment of these qualities, which are just the qualities I am regarded as having in having *de*. From this point of view, the favorable response of the spirit is approval of *de* I already have, and my religious performances are acts of maintenance. And it would seem that they cannot be mere performances: they must have an inner aspect. So, also, with every *de*-engendering or *de*-reinforcing relationship with other persons and groups. Maintaining his *de* comes to be the king's most important duty. Already in the oracles there is one example (if I interpret the inscription right) of an idea repeated over and over in Zhou bronze inscriptions and in early literature: the king must "reverently care for his 'virtue'"—*jìng dé* 敬德 (Nivison 1978–1979).[10] We have here more than an oddity. The king must seek to occupy a role defined as a *de*-manifesting role. As one adviser to a king in a *Shang shu* chapter tells him, "as king you must rest your position in the primacy of your 'virtue'."[11] And yet the king is to do this in all religious humility, with no pride in being "virtuous."

Time has not arranged for the survival of inscriptional material to suit the convenience of such investigations as mine. Already I have been leaning on matter in the literary tradition, which begins at the earliest probably two centuries after that stratum of the oracles that speaks of *de*. We can narrow the gap a little by looking at bronze inscriptions of the beginning of the Western Zhou Dynasty. This dynasty, replacing the Shang, lasted with effective power for almost three centuries, and had a nominal existence for five centuries more as the so-called "Eastern Zhou"—a period encompassing the great ancient Chinese philosophers Confucius, Mencius, Zhuāngzǐ 莊子, and the rest. It began with a conquest by a west Chinese people. The date has been in dispute for the past two thousand years, different dates defended ranging over more than a century. Recent work indicates that this event occurred a little after the middle of the eleventh century B.C.[12] It follows that from here on inscriptions too can sometimes be dated.

The inscriptions I speak of now are cast on the insides of bronze ritual vessels (or on the outsides of bronze bells)—wine cups, jugs, tripods, platters—intended to be used in sacrifices to family ancestors. Typically, an inscription will announce that the vessel is dedicated to a named ancestor—usually father or grandfather—and it may begin by describing an event in which the dedicator received some gift or honor, perhaps from the king. Figure 2.3 shows an inscription found inside one of these vessels, together with a chart that highlights the ten words in it that are important for my argument.

This vessel was made by a man named He 何 (that is, he had it made and paid for it). This He describes himself as one of a group of young noblemen who listened to an address in Luòyáng 洛陽, the newly founded eastern capital, by King Cheng, the second king of the dynasty, as we can infer from the content. It is dated the king's fifth year, fourth month, day *bǐngxū* 丙戌.[13] The inscription was discovered—you will see that it is a vessel with a very deep throat—during a careful cleaning ten years later.[14]

My translation will show you at once why I have put it before you:

> When the king first moved his residence to Chéng Zhōu 成周 [i.e., Luoyang], he resumed the practice of King Wu and performed rituals seeking blessings from Heaven. In the fourth month, on the day *bingxu*, the king made an address to the junior princes of royal ancestry in the principium hall, speaking as follows: "In past times, when your late fathers, the heads of your noble families, were alive, they ably came to the support of King Wen; and so King Wen received this great [commission, to rule the world]. When King Wu had conquered the Great City Shang, then in the court he made an announcement to Heaven, saying 'I will reside in this middle country, and from this place govern the people.' Oh! Even though you are only junior princes, surely we can expect that you will emulate [your] princely [fathers] in the noble status they earned in Heaven's regard, attending dutifully to Heaven's bidding and caring reverently for the sacrifices! Help [me] the king to uphold [my] virtue, so that Heaven will make me compliant when I am not earnest." The king concluded his lecture. I, He, was given thirty strings of cowrie shells, and with this I make for Duke X this precious *zūn* 尊 vessel—this being the king's fifth cult year.[15]

Obviously, I am interested in the words "Help [me] the king to uphold [my] virtue, so that Heaven will make me compliant when I am not earnest"—and in the fact that a king would say this in this situation. We should appreciate the fact that King Cheng was probably at this time only a very young man (he had succeeded as a minor). The accents of humility are likely to be as genuine as they are appropriate; and they say something about the concept of "virtue":

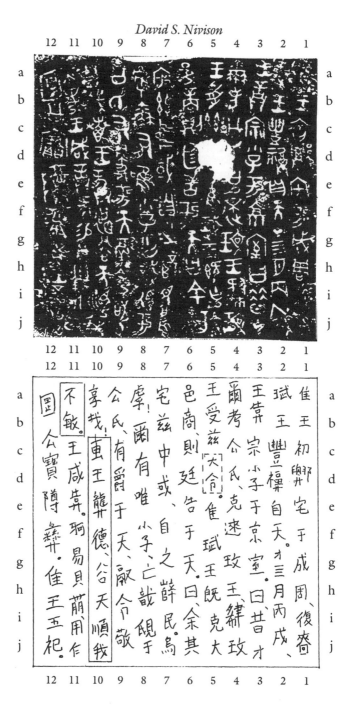

Figure 2.3: Bronze Vessel Inscription

Again it is the king's duty to nourish and care for his "virtue," a duty it is even appropriate for him to ask for help in performing. And having "virtue" makes him open to correction in future failings—makes him, in a word, morally teachable. It even seems to be a prerequisite for his being morally teachable.

This dimension of the royal "virtue" is amply filled in in the *Shang shu* and other archaic literature. A king with "virtue" listens to advice; wise counselors are attracted to his service. A king without "virtue" spurns advice. Again, a "virtuous" king is self-denying—in this case ego-denying—and so is self-restrained. A king without "virtue" is self-assertive, arrogant, and guilty of other forms of unrestraint, including violence, lust, and cruelty. The *Shang shu* shows that quickly after the conquest a picture developed of the last Shang king as living a life of self-indulgence, of drunkenness, of heeding only his female favorites, of unfeeling cruelty. It seems we are to see this as both cause, substance, and consequence of his lack of "virtue."[16]

Others of these bronze inscriptions mention "virtue" often enough to be informative. Not to attempt a catalog of occurrences, I would point to three things that become apparent.

(1) "Virtue," *de*, is clearly some kind of inner mental entity. One recently discovered inscription of the ninth century B.C. mentions the dedicator's father and ancestors as having been "able to make their hearts shine," and he says that "I do not dare not to follow the shining virtue (*míng dé* 明德) maintained by my grandfather and my father."[17] The word *de* is now written (as it had not been in the Shang) with the element "heart" (*xīn* 心) as part of the graph.

(2) As here, we see it explicit that not just kings have "virtue". The king may be a model, but my parents and ancestors have it too, and by implication so can I. It seems to be a property of the filially pious good person.

(3) Another inscription (of the same period and authorship)[18] begins with a historical paean on the dynastic ur-founder King Wen: "Of old . . . God on High (*Shàngdì* 上帝) sent him down good virtue, and greatly helped him, so that he spread his influence over all the lands." Here is explicit what my analysis posited, that virtue is both given and rewarded by the divine powers.

To recapitulate (selectively):

(1) "Virtue" is a property of a good king; but really, of any good person.

(2) It is generated, or given in reward for, acts of generosity, self-restraint, and self-sacrifice, and for an attitude of humility.

(3) It is at the same time constitutive of such behavior and of such an attitude.

(4) It is something good to have, not just for itself but for its consequences for the possessor. A king, for example, cannot function without it. It gives him prestige (consider its military dimension) and influence.

(5) And since it involves being (a) generous, (b) not self-indulgent, (c) self-sacrificing, (d) dutiful (at least in a religious sense), (e) humble and polite, etc., it must obviously be granted that whatever else may be said, it is proper to call it "virtue"—indeed, it seems to be a collection of virtues.

But, I now want to ask, is this a logically consis tent list of characteristics? And if I have been describing the earliest Chinese concept we can describe of what it is that makes a good person good, what is a moral-philosophical tradition going to look like that evolves as an elaboration of such a concept as this? These questions I pursue in my next lecture, "The Paradox of 'Virtue'."

The Paradox of 'Virtue'[1]

上德不德是以有德
下德不失德是以無德
Shàng dé bù dé, shì yǐ yǒu dé;
xià dé bù shī dé, shì yǐ wú dé.

This is the opening line of the second half of the *Lǎozǐ* 老子, also known as the *Dào dé jīng* 道德經, the "Classic of the Way and Virtue."[2] D. C. Lau (1963a, 99) renders this line as follows:

> A man of the highest virtue does not keep to virtue and that is why he has virtue. A man of the lowest virtue never strays from virtue and that is why he is without virtue.

And the translation is acceptable, if taken as suggestive only, even though the text doesn't contain the word "man."

I quote it at the beginning, fearing that perhaps half of you have come here expecting that this is my "paradox of virtue." Actually, this is not quite what I had in mind, though perhaps it will fall into place if my overall analysis is successful. I am pursuing some problems in moral philosophy that require me to put the Confucians, not the Daoists, in the center of the stage. But I shall give Daoism and other such intoxicating ideas a nod before really getting down to it.

Recall my characterization (in chapter 2) of the *dé* 德 of a king: the ideal king has qualities we would call moral ones:

- He is dutiful in regard to his religious obligations, attending to the rituals and the sacrifices to his ancestors, etc.
- He lives a life of personal self-restraint.
- He is generous, kind, even self-sacrificing (as in the curing of illness).
- He avoids force, if he can, in his military functions and in his administration: he is gentle.

- He is humble: while "resting his position in the primacy of his virtue" (*wèi zài dé yuán* 位在德元),[3] he yet doesn't take personal credit for his "virtue" but asks others to help him, so that Heaven will guide him out of error.[4]

- And so, he is nonassertive, opens his mind to instruction; he listens, then responds.

At the same time, as I tried to show, the king's *de* really is "moral force": the source of the concept seems to be what we might call gratitude credit—a compulsion felt by the benefited person to respond favorably to the benefactor, felt so strongly that it seems to be a psychic power emanating from the benefactor (the king) to orient those around him favorably in his direction.

We might compare the "moral force" relationship in *de*/"virtue" to the relation between a mass of matter and the gravitational field of which it is the center: there cannot be the one without there also being the other. Interestingly, Confucius (without benefit of the scientific law of inverse squares) uses almost this metaphor: "One who rules with moral force (*de*) is like the polestar, which remains in its place while all the lesser stars do homage to it."[5] Confucius of course couldn't know that the apparent motion of the stars around the polestar is not caused by the polestar. A more accurate metaphor for his purpose might have been a planetary system; that he didn't understand either; but if he had had the concept of a planetary system he probably would have used it.

The *de* of the king thus automatically produces a complementary response within his field of "moral force." To the extent that his character, his *de* such as it is, has the quality of good order, this *de* will affect those around him, in such a way that their behavior will be smoothly and functionally related to his, effortlessly and naturally on both sides. This character and its producing of effects are his *de*-as-king.

It is a simple extension from this idea to a concept of the *de* of a person—or of any kind of entity—as being its fixed character, thought of as both the configuration of the thing itself and all of its sympathetic causal relationships—for good or ill, active or passive—with the world around that thing. To stay still within the realm of the political we have Confucius again: To Jì Kāng Zǐ 季康子 he counsels, there is no need for capital punishment in your government. "If you desire what is good, the people will at once be good." This is *de*, of course; but Confucius in the next breath uses the very word in the newly derived sense: "The *de* of the superior is wind. The *de* of the people is grass. Let the wind be over the grass and it must bend."[6] These are more than metaphors. If Confucius (making a different point) had wished to say, as does an old proverb, that the ruler's very existence depends on there being people to support him, like a wooden boat floating on a river,[7] he might have said "the *de* of the ruler is wood; that of the people is water"—and he would have been, while using the same idiom, now using the systematized metaphor of the so-called "Five Phases" theory (and its complementary concept of "resonant causality") of the late Zhou and Han Dynasties, and all subsequent Chinese metaphysical thought. The theory was in fact called by its popularizer Zōu Yǎn 騶衍 in the late fourth century B.C. "the Five *De*"—"powers" or natural tendencies.[8] (Here I note—and for now firmly turn my back on—a whole library shelf of doctoral dissertations to be.)

Yet another example of *de* as inherent character together with field of resonant causal force: the sexual attractiveness of a young woman is her *de*. Under the year 636 B.C., the *Zuǒ zhuàn* 左傳 has a story about the then reigning Eastern Zhou king. The text reports that the Di (a "barbarian" tribe) provided military assistance to the king. "The king felt grateful to the Di people" (*wáng dé dí rén* 王德狄人), and proposed (unwisely) to enter into a marriage with a Di princess. Good advice—to desist—was offered by a minister, who quoted what seems to be a proverb: *nǚ dé wú jí; fù yuàn wú zhōng* 女德無極婦怨無終: "A girl's [i.e., young unmarried woman's] *de* is limitless; but a married woman's resentment is without end." (So, a woman is like the polestar, and all the young men . . .) It's always too late when such advice gets offered. The king went ahead, and lost his throne.[9]

In the full flower of philosophical Daoism the notion of *de* is given studied metaphysical statement. What had been the *de* of the king now becomes, one might say, the character of *dào* 道 (the "Way") itself, as the center of gravity of all nature: the *dao* allows and enables everything to be what it is; it claims no credit, does no pushing, and all is ordered. *De* now becomes a concept standing in a certain contrast to *dao*: it is said to be the "localization" of the *dao* in a particular thing; but it retains its *dao*-character—it enables that thing to be what it is, alive, intelligent, causally interconnected with other things, as the case may be. *De* thus is what the thing "gets" from the *dao* to be itself. Here is a curious bit of philosophical philology of very early date. The words *dé* 德, "virtue," and *dé* 得, "get," are (and were) exact homophones; so "virtue" must be a metaphysical "getting."[10]

The two words probably *are* cognates. One finds occasional puns on the two in the Confucian moral texts; but the connection sensed there seems to be quite different: if a ruler is kind to the people, the ruler "gets" their hearts.[11] But, of course, the ruler's doing so is a manifestation of *de* in the sense of (virtuous) generosity. If the ruler does this they will *de* the ruler—regard the ruler as generous, be grateful; and the word in this sense can be written as *dé* 得 "get."[12]

But we need not pursue this speculation. It is time to close this sampling of semantic taxonomy and get back to work. Let us return to the basic *de* situation: person A does some generous or considerate thing for B, in a sense sacrificing him- or herself. B feels compelled to respond. B feels this compulsion, by a sort of transference, as a "moral force" emanating from A. From this, I have argued, flows the rest.

We now can notice not one but two oddities to *de* situations so conceived:

(a) When I deny or sacrifice my self or my own good or interest for some-
    one else, and so literally "have *de* with" the other, I acquire a hold on
    this person, and so gain an advantage over him or her. So, it seems, I
    am enhancing my own interest by denying it. But then, one would
    think, I am not really denying it but pursuing it, and by the same
    token ought to be losing *de* rather than gaining it.

(b) From the model of the good king, it would seem that we must con-
    clude that one must already have *de* if one is to do the things that
    would get it; and in particular one must have "virtue" already if one is
    to heed the instruction that would lead one to it.

Should I be talking, then, about two paradoxes of virtue, not one? Yes, and no.

Yes, in that each of these puzzles has its own history, its own paradigmatic
exemplifications and its own consequences in the shaping of developing Chinese moral philosophy. No, in that, as I think I can show, the two are but
opposite sides of the same coin.

For, if I do something for you, with the intention of "having *de*" with you,
I am seeking to benefit myself—even, in fact, at your expense—and so am
doing something just the opposite of generous. The only way, then, that I can
do a generous thing is to do it for its own sake, which is to say, really want to
be generous. It looks as though this must mean that I cannot perform *de*
acts—which would give me *de* in its "moral force" aspect—unless I have *de*
already.

Nor, since *de* is something very advantageous to have, can I seek *de* in any
de-engendering way unless I seek it for its own sake, not for myself. But this
would be to have *de* already. And in particular, if my seeking *de* takes the form
of going to you and asking you to be my moral teacher, I can't do this unless I
am positively inclined toward virtue for itself, and to this extent virtuous already. Notice, now, that the student-teacher relationship could be simply an
instance of the basic *de* situation. Perhaps I go to you, pretending to humble
myself, asking for your instruction. You could refuse, seeing my insincerity (a
common situation). But if you want to teach me, you have the second form of
the paradox, and can only ask, "What can I do?"[13]

In the first form of the paradox, where I do a self-denying act in order to
serve myself and so would be losing virtue rather than gaining it, what is wrong
is not that I would if successful improve my situation in fact, but that I intend
to do so. So perhaps one should so act that one can't improve one's position in
any gainful sense—in power, substance, or repute. There are several solutions
conceivable along this line.

Solution (1): secrecy. Keep the benefited person, and everyone else, from
knowing of the virtuous act; or else go and hide after you've done it. The

behavior of the Duke of Zhōu 周公, swearing the divination staff to secrecy after he had offered his own life to the royal ancestors in place of his brother King Wǔ 武王, is an obvious example of the first tactic.[14] The paradigm of the second is Tài Bó 泰伯, eldest son of the "old duke."[15] Although entitled by primogeniture to the throne, Tai Bo was aware of his father's esteem for the merit of his younger brother's son—the later King Wén 文王. Consequently, Tai Bo ran off into the wilds of the south, and thereby, says Confucius, "attained to the very highest pitch of moral power"—of *de*: not only was his renunciation the greatest possible short of life itself, but also he made it "impossible for the people to praise him for it" (*mín wú dé ér chēng yān* 民無得而稱焉).[16]

Solution (2): excess. Though this is illustrated along with secrecy in the two preceding cases, it has its special logic: one must make the virtuous act so extreme that anyone positively oriented toward you as a result could never do anything that could match it.

Here is how things could go: person A does something for B, or shows B extraordinary courtesy. Because of the *de*-effect, B is disadvantaged. B must defend him- or herself by doing something for A. One sacrifice B can always make to A is to capitulate—perhaps even callously, thereby sacrificing B's own *de* to enhance A's *de*. Just this drama structures the story of Hòu Yíng 候嬴, ascetic gate-keeper of the eastern city gate of Dàliáng 大梁, at first ignoring the repeated invitations and gifts of Prince Wújì 無忌 of Wèi 魏, only in the end to accept with deliberate impoliteness. More, he does so contriving to cause the unruffled prince maximum inconvenience and embarrassment, and goes out of the way to make it obvious to all. Thus he sacrifices for the prince, totally, the one thing he has that is precious to him, his own *de*, in order to demonstrate the prince's patience and politeness, and thus to demonstrate and increase the prince's *de*. By this Hou Ying lifts his own *de* beyond reach among all in the prince's circle: he becomes *shàng kè* 上客, highest ranking retainer. (*Shang de bu de . . .*)[17]

Solution (3): in acting virtuously, cut yourself free even from the intention to do something virtuous. This is bound to be tricky. Here I merely point to the possibility. It will find its place later.

In considering the second form of the paradox—how can the teacher teach virtue unless the student is already virtuous—examples will be helpful, and the *Analects* is full of them. "Zǎi Yú 宰予 used to sleep during the day. The Master said, 'Rotten wood cannot be carved, nor a wall of dried dung be trowelled. What use is there in my scolding him any more?'"[18] "Rǎn Qiú 冉求 said, 'It is not that your Way does not commend itself to me, but that it demands powers I do not possess.' The Master said, 'He whose strength gives out collapses during the course of the journey [literally, the Way]; but you deliberately draw the line.'"[19] We need, of course, to distinguish between *de* as (a) "virtue" in the sense of knowing what is right and doing it, and *de* as (b) "moral force." They are aspects of the same thing: I have (a) if and only if I have (b). But it is a simple sub-distinction of (a) that the Ran Qiu case forces out: we must distinguish between

(i) knowing what the right things to do are; and

(ii) being moved, and moved in the right way, to do them.

A Plato-type paradox of knowledge would apply to (i): to be taught, one must recognize the thing taught as something to be learned, and this requires that in some sense one already know it.[20] But the "paradox of virtue," as I have explained it, applies to (ii). This means that the Chinese paradox is equivalent to the Chinese form of the problem of moral weakness. The unmoved person is, by hypothesis, sufficiently aware of the world of moral obligations, known and unknown, so that he or she could do something about it—act, or seek instruction; but the person doesn't care. This is Ran Qiu's problem, which he disguises self-deceptively by telling himself and others that he lacks ability to do the right; so this is what we might call *acedia*, rather than *akrasia*.[21]

Aristotle's ways of talking about virtue (*aretē*) are worth examining. He has thought carefully and hard about the matter, and he may either show us things we hadn't noticed about virtue and how it is acquired and imparted, or else show by contrast more clearly what the Chinese concepts are, by enabling us to see more clearly what they are not. In the second book of the *Nicomachean Ethics* he talks for quite a space of virtues as like skill in an art or craft (though the comparison is eventually carefully qualified). Two points stand out:

(1) We are not born virtuous. But nature gives us the capacity to become so. This capacity is fulfilled by habit. Therefore, we become virtuous by doing virtuous acts:

> For we learn a craft by producing the same product that we must produce when we have learned it, becoming builders, e.g., by building and harpists by playing the harp; so also, then, we become just by doing just actions, temperate by doing temperate actions, brave by doing brave actions. (Aristotle 1985, 34, 1103a30–1103b5)

(2) We must be trained from childhood in virtuous habits. The Philosopher stresses this a number of times, and admits that this is "very important, indeed all-important." (1985, 35, 1103b25)

Aristotle perceives a possible difficulty in this apparent "practice makes perfect" concept of training in virtue:

> However, someone might raise this puzzle: "What do you mean by saying that to become just we must first do just actions and to become temperate we

must first do temperate actions? For if we do what is grammatical or musical, we must already be grammarians or musicians. In the same way, then, if we do what is just or temperate, we must already be just or temperate." (1985, 39, 1105a15–25)

Has Aristotle put his finger on my "paradox of virtue"? His solution shows that he hasn't, and that he must be making assumptions that keep my paradox from being a paradox for him. His solution is to make a distinction between a just action and acting justly. Acting justly requires both knowing how to act, and choosing the act for its own sake, out of "a firm and unchanging state" of character (1985, 40, 1105a30–1105b1). But a just act, like a correct spelling, need be only the sort of act that a just person would do (as a correct spelling would be the spelling a good speller would give me—though you might in a single case give me a correct spelling even though you are a bad speller).

Now this suggests immediately a connection between Aristotle's concept of virtue as quasi-"craft" in which "practice makes perfect" and his insistence that we must start the training in childhood—"get 'em young," we might say. For the learner must be naive, in the best sense. It will hardly do if one has reached that age of intelligence that would make it all too likely that one might do a just act in order to ingratiate oneself with one's teachers, or in order to enhance one's reputation, or worse, in order to induce a prospective victim of contemplated injustice to drop his or her guard. In this situation, one would have to add the proviso that the just act, to avoid having a deleterious effect on one's character, let alone to have an educative effect, must be done out of a proper motive.

This would put us "back in the problem area." And that is where the Chinese are. For the Eastern Zhou Dynasty moral philosophers do not, except parenthetically, talk about childhood education. The standard learning situation is assumed to be one in which a master is surrounded by students ("disciples") who are already adults. There is no *paideia*—though the *later* Chinese literature on pedagogy is rich.

Suppose it seems baffling—as I argue it did for Confucius—how one starting cold, even if one sees what the *dao* is, can be gotten to be sufficiently aroused about it to have a behavior-determining commitment to the *dao* as right, and to *rén* 仁 "benevolence" as good.

Consider *Analects* HY 7:30:

仁遠乎哉。我欲仁斯仁至矣。

Rén yuǎn hū zāi? Wǒ yù rén, sī rén zhì yǐ.

"Is benevolence so far away? If I want benevolence, then benevolence is here!"

One way of taking this—suggested by Fingarette (1972, 38, 49–52)—is that the problem is easy. Just want it! There can be a voluntary act of heart-mind (*xīn* 心). Though Confucius is usually not this optimistic, perhaps he does think this way at this point.

But if loving the good for itself is something I can do just by deciding to, the problem is mischievously simplified. Suppose that (as seems all too reasonable) anyone can be got to do something if that thing is simple enough, and it is in one's immediate material interest, and that fact is made sufficiently obvious to one. Then, it would seem, a moral teacher can move anyone to morality if the teacher can just show that person, by a clear argument (or by clearly announced sanctions) that one will be materially better off if one is so moved: if one loves (really loves) the people one is told one should love, accepts (really accepts) as right the principles one is told one should, and accepts as obligatory—morally obligatory—the duties one is told one should accept; and even, perhaps, believes (really believes) in the existence and power of supernatural beings one is told one should believe in for one's own and others' benefit.

Weird as this sounds, it is a view that has been held in many parts of the world—including parts of it that we think of as our own. And it is, I will argue, precisely the view held by the next major Chinese philosopher after Confucius, whose name was Mòzǐ 墨子.

To cite only two examples: Mozi saw that the world about him was a sorry mess, and that the immediate and obvious cause was that people fought with one another, individually and in groups—my family against yours, my city against yours, my state against yours. This would cease if people would love one another, without being prejudiced in favor of their own families or cities or states. They would obviously be better off if they did so. So, they should start "loving impartially" forthwith. How? Not difficult at all. Some things are difficult—for example, picking up a mountain and jumping over the ocean. But this is easy. Just do it.[22]

Again, in another analysis of strife-engendering human dispositions and what to do about them, Mozi concludes that at a deeper level people don't agree on what one ought to do. The solution is to set up a state structure in which everyone is commanded to accept the same set of "ought's," the same standard of what is right, and one is rewarded if one does and punished if one doesn't. And Mozi assumes that if the people, who are perhaps a bit weak on philosophy, are given this obvious extra material incentive, there will be no further difficulty. The command will be obeyed. One will think to be right what one's superiors tell one to think to be right.[23]

If Mozi were merely a flash in the philosophical pan, we might note him as a curiosity and forget about him. He wasn't. His movement thrived for several centuries. And since people are a bit more complex than he was inclined to picture them, problems developed that led to more stages in the dialectic engendered by the "paradox of virtue."

The next step was probably taken within the ranks of Mozi's followers, perhaps in the generation after his death. It would be natural for a disciple of Mozi to ask, when the master argues for "universal love," "Yes, but how can I love impartially, indeed love at all, just because I see it is in my (enlightened) selfish interest to do so? Isn't the self-directed wanting which is stimulated by awareness of interest simply different in kind from the other-directed caring that loving a person involves? Where does love come from? If I don't have this attitude already, how can simply following an argument to self-interest enable me to love?"

In the texts, we do not have the question. We do have the answer. And it is found, interestingly enough, not in the *Mozi*, but in the *Mèngzǐ* 孟子—the sayings of Mencius—the Confucian moral philosopher of most enduring influence after Confucius himself. Mencius was probably born about 390 B.C., perhaps a decade before Mozi died. The influence of Mozi on Mencius was deep, and Mencius also argued with philosophers of many kinds—in an age of philosophers that was, to use a modern metaphor, producing hundreds of flowers. Some of the people he argued with were Mohists.

One of these was a man named Yí Zhī 夷之. Mencius criticizes Yi Zhi for giving his parents lavish burials—favored, indeed, by Confucians as a natural expression of filial piety, but in conflict with the teachings of Mozi, who argued that elaborate rituals waste material goods and interfere with production, and so generate want, greed, quarrelling, and warfare. Further, elaborate funerals for one's own parents are not consistent with the principle that I should love your parents as much as my own. Yi Zhi defends himself against the charge of inconsistency by arguing that there should in principle be no gradations in love, but the practice of it must begin with one's parents.[24]

So here, in the mouth of a Mohist, is the answer to the hypothetical objection I put to Mozi. Where does love come from? We all have it already, naturally manifested and developed in family relationships. But then reason—for Mohists, a completely enlightened self-interest turned into Mohist doctrine—should direct how we use or focus this capacity for love; and what we ought to do in the long run is spread it out evenly over everybody. But in the short run it is justifiable to nurture the capacity for loving in the way Yi Zhi did.

In brief, I have a natural emotional capacity for loving, nurturable in a quantitative way; but I also separately have principles which tell me how to use this capacity. Curiously, Mencius often thinks this way himself. He does so, for example, in his long conversation with King Xuān of Qí 齊宣王, in 319 or 318 B.C. Adroitly, Mencius shows King Xuan that he has a natural feeling of sympathy—drawn into play by a mere animal, an ox being led to sacrifice. So just use it, Mencius says to the king. Pick it up, so to speak, and put it down over there: extend it to your people, who surely you can see are a much more appropriate object for it than a mere sacrificial ox. We touch base here, for this conversation follows upon the king's question to Mencius, "What kind of *de* — 'virtue'—do I need to become king of the world?" The quality you need, says

Mencius, is a quality you already have. Just use it. There is no difficulty if you will just do it. There are difficult things to do—taking a mountain under your arm and jumping over the ocean with it, for example—but this, using your compassion, is surely easy.[25]

I retell the story so as to bring out Mencius's Mohist accent. Nonetheless, here a Mohist solution to a Mohist problem has become a Confucian solution to a Confucian one. What is to be done with the person who just doesn't care? Mencius's answer here is that everyone cares, really. How can the teacher teach the student to be moral unless the student already is moral?—in which case the teacher's task is the trivial one of giving the student some information merely; and the real problem, the unmotivated, or those who approve only in a blood-less and cerebral way, are given up in despair.[26] Mencius's solution is that we all have genuine moral motivation. The teacher's job is to perform a sort of moral psychoanalysis, get one to catch oneself in a moral-making response—characteristically, in Mencius's examples, of spontaneous sympathy—so that one notices one's real "heart."

What Mencius says to King Xuan—a Mozi-like "just do it," just extend your sympathy-capacity to the kind of object (the people) that the *de*-concept calls for—is not typical of his view of what happens from here on. He offers a much more sophisticated program in his long conversation with Gōngsūn Chǒu 公孫丑 and elsewhere: the process of "extending" (*tuī* 推) is not just like ex-tending one's arm, by act of will. It requires self-development, in which one nurtures but does not force the moral sprouts in the heart. Paradigmatically, these are impulses to affection and respect in family relation situations—affec-tion for parents, respect for elders—which Mencius supposes to be natural. As one expresses these impulses in appropriate behavior in so far as that behavior feels natural, a feeling of satisfaction follows, and the impulse becomes stronger by reinforcement. As this happens, Mencius thinks, one's capacity for natural unforced moral action expands: more action is possible, with more reinforce-ment, and so on. As he puts it cryptically, one "extends what one does to what one doesn't."[27]

But, we must ask, what control is there on the direction of the expression of moral capacity? Could one come to feel an enabling moral satisfaction in doing just anything, perhaps wrong things, if one chose that course of self-development? Not surprisingly, there are two possible answers to this question, yes and no.

If one answers "no," one will be supposing that there is built into the moral psyche a "deep structure" that in the natural course of the development of moral personality can be articulated in "surface structure" in essentially only one way.

If one answers "yes," then simply cultivating (strengthening) potentially moral-making capacities is not going to be sufficient to make one a moral person. Even if one has the given set of "sprouts" that Mencius supposes, one must also identify the right objects of the moral-making attitudes of sympathy, affection, dutifulness, courteousness, etc. And this identification must come from outside the process of cultivation itself. Perhaps it will come from a body of traditional rules such as the Confucians defended, or a moral theory that generates such rules, such as the Mohists developed and defended. In either case, one seems to be back on essentially Mohist voluntarist ground; one has a developing moral capacity of potential motivatedness, which the will must then use as intellect and doctrine show may be appropriate.

This was the position of Mencius's rival Gàozǐ 告子.[28] For Gaozi, human moral capacity is inherently directionless. The direction has to come from "outside," from doctrines, moral maxims, or as he puts it "words"—"What you do not get from words, do not seek for in your heart."

This position Mencius explicitly rejects: the heart-mind, cultivated, takes a natural direction that leads one just to the right things. Mencius puts the matter in two different ways:

(a) We all have natural tastes, that are more or less alike because we are all human. We tend to agree on what is beautiful to see, beautiful to hear, and delicious to eat. Similarly, our hearts tend to like the same things, viz., *lǐ* 理 and *yì* 義, "what is orderly and right." Tradition gives us standards about this—in the language of Mencius's world view, the civilization-creating sage kings have left us their teachings. But this simply means that the sages got there first. Just as a famous cook of past time might have written a cookbook to which we prudently turn for good recipes—since this cook, with his or her excellent taste, has anticipated what we are all going to find we like—so also the teachings of the sages can be thought of as moral cookbooks. We can ask, doesn't this mean that what is right is so, in the last analysis, simply because we like it? I think that Mencius would not have seen this inference as a problem because, I suspect, he would have denied its premise. Some things really are delicious, and if I don't think so there is something wrong with me. In the same way, some things just are good and right, and since I am human, if there is nothing wrong with me I will just see this, if my moral taste is sufficiently developed.[29]

(b) Sometimes Mencius talks in a different way. There are basic human situations—in the bosom of the family—that arouse the basic morality-making impulses of caring for and respecting others. There are many other situations significantly like these—in the same "category" (*lèi* 類)—though the resemblance may at first be unobvious. When I come to see the resemblance, I will, or can, "extend" (*tuī*) my basic moral impulses to these cases too. It is difficult not to see Mencius beginning to slip back into a Mozi-esque way of talking here: even though the judgment "this is like that" is given me by my own understanding—

it's something I just see—still, it seems to be something other than the emotion of sympathy or respect itself. The latter, it seems, is something I am now to use, as my recognition of similarity directs. It is worth noting that the very language of analysis is Mohist: *tuī lèi* 推類, "extend the category," or "extend to a similar category," means "make an inference." And *tui* is defined in the Mohist logical texts as a type of argument in which one forces an opponent to "extend" a judgment one has made to an analogous case.[30]

Perhaps what Mencius would say here is that he covers this point in ascribing to the heart a basic disposition—on a par with obviously emotional dispositions—to "see the right as right and the wrong as wrong."[31] For couldn't this mean that there *isn't* first a cognitive judgment "this is like that," and then an act of extending my love or respect from that to this. On the contrary, there is just a seeing, which is at the same time a feeling. This, at least, is what is said on this point by Wáng Yángmíng 王陽明—and in mentioning him I am jumping lightly over eighteen centuries—who in saying it thinks he is articulating Mencius's philosophy.[32]

We can now go back to where we left the Mohist Yi Zhi, caught in inconsistency between his tenets and his acts. Yi Zhi makes Gaozi's mistake, of not seeking in his heart for what he thinks he has to get from "words"—his false Mohist doctrines. And so he lands in a tangle of self-deception. He should have seen, Mencius goes on to suggest, that the heart all by itself provides guidance that starts with primitive revulsion at the sight of the rotting corpses of one's parents, and leads from there all the way to validation of the rich and beautiful funeral rituals Yi Zhi has performed.

In thus insisting that the heart alone is the "source" of being moral, Mencius goes rather far. His position is not going to allow him to grant that I can be moral simply by seeing that X is the right thing to do and then doing X because it's right. I must on the contrary do X because it is the completely natural thing to do, if my doing X is to be a moral act. In modern jargon, he would say that the "pro-attitude" constitutive of my judgment-from-principle, "X is right," even if it is strong enough to allow me to form and carry out an intention to do X, still is not the sort of attitude that can lead to my doing X as a genuinely moral act.[33] I would be "putting morality into practice" (4B19) instead of acting morally. I must not do the thing "because" it's moral, in a purposive sense of "because." I must do it because I am moral, in a causative sense of "because." I must be "acting out my respect" (6A5.2), or whatever the feeling is, as the case may be.

Why does Mencius think this way? "So long as one is good, it's all right," says the *xiāng yuàn* 鄉原, the "village worthy"—the one, says Mencius, whom Confucius detests "for fear that he might confuse virtue" (7B37). In contrast the "great person" is one who "does not make a point of being true to one's word or of carrying through one's acts" (4B11). This is not to describe the morally great person (*dà zhàng fū* 大丈夫, 3B2) as beyond ordinary rules. It is just that, like the sage emperor Shun, such a person "acts morally, rather than doing moral acts" (4B19). In yet another sense, *shang de bu de, shi yi you de.*

But we must also, here, look back to the "pragmatic" aspect of the "paradox of virtue." Doing moral things is a way of building up *de* in the "moral force" sense—and so, of being self-serving, and so on. One possible way out of the conundrum, as I noted without exploring it, would be to cut the moral act loose from the intention to do a moral act just because it is "right." In the shadows is the fear of being self-servingly "moral" in a morally withering way. A paradigmatic situation of moral weakness, in Mencius, is the *de* situation in which I am offered a gift by a person I know to be unworthy of my respect or service—and, wanting the gift, I accept it anyway, thereby tying myself to the unworthy person. So, often it is right to refuse gifts. Suppose I refuse—not because I "desire the right" more than the thing (6A10), but in order to do the "right" thing (and perhaps be known for so doing). Then, says Mencius, if one is "not the person to do such a thing, it will show in one's face, even if all that is refused is a basket of food or a bowl of soup" (7B11).

Mencius does seem to have done a fair job of resolving the "magisterial" form of the paradox: he meets the challenge of a Zai Yu and shows how moral teaching is possible: the student of morality does have to be moral already; but then, we all are. The teacher's task then becomes one of skillfully calling one's attention to one's moral "sprouts," and then coaching one in nurturing them. Of course, the student may deny perception and say at the first lesson, "No, I can't; I don't have it"—like Ran Qiu. This problem has no solution, except the standard solution for unsolvable problems: building up a shock-effect by giving it a snappy name. Mencius scathingly dubs the attitude "self-rejection" (*zì qì* 自棄, HY 4A11).

But hasn't Mencius actually done too well? For you may now ask, perhaps Mencius shows how moral education, in a sense, is possible. But doesn't he, in effect, show that moral education is unnecessary? Granted we are not completely moral to start with. But everything Mencius's teacher is described as doing looks like something I could do for myself; even the "sages" have only "anticipated" (6A7) what my heart and others' hearts "have in common."

So we reach the question of the next lecture: couldn't virtue be self-taught? One valid and rewarding way of reading the next major moralist, Xúnzǐ 荀子, is to see him as reacting to just this problem.

Can Virtue
Be Self-Taught?[1]

4

What would it be like for virtue to be self-taught?

What would it be like for *anything* to be self-taught?

There are many kinds of things. Let me try one that isn't virtue:

More than twenty-eight years ago, I was in Professor John D. Goheen's office.[2] While a long phone call interrupted our conversation, I picked up a book out of the clutter on the table in the middle of the room and started scanning it. When the phone call ended, I asked, "Is this a good book?" John said that he thought so—that its author had a blossoming reputation.

A half hour later I was in the bookstore. The book was in stock. I bought it. It was Quine's *Methods of Logic*. In the course of the next two months, I read it with the rigor it demanded, not passing from one sentence to the next until I was certain that I understood the relation of that sentence to everything that had preceded, and putting myself through every one of the frequent and never trivial exercises. At the beginning of the next term, I invited myself to be an auditor-participant in Patrick Suppes' intermediate course in logic.

Did I teach myself logic?

In an obvious sense, yes. But of course, I didn't write the *book*. Willard Van Orman Quine did that. So, in another obvious sense, Quine taught me logic. Was Quine's part in the story a necessary one? In an obvious sense, yes. But perhaps there is a sense that allows us to wonder.

An author's part in such a story might be necessary for *some* kinds of things. If the book were an autobiography, perhaps. Is virtue one of those kinds of things? Whatever the answer to *that* question, how does the virtue case fit other aspects of the story?

After two months on Quine, I knew a lot "of" logic. I knew some facts and had acquired some skills. Had I *become* logical?

Suppose the book had been the *Nicomachean Ethics*, and that after two months on Aristotle I "knew a lot of morality": knew some facts about what people have thought, and perhaps had acquired new skill in seeing the connections between certain ideas. Would I have *become virtuous*?

The concept of moral learning I have been exploring in the previous two lectures supposes that one *becomes virtuous*. One is moved to *do* the virtuous things for their own sake, and out of the right kind of motivation or character. At least, this will characterize the last philosopher discussed, Mencius.

In Mencius one is not to do the virtuous thing out of selfishness. (Though one might be moved to become virtuous out of selfishness.) What kind of "pro-attitude" toward virtue-doing does count as virtue-constituting?[3] Not, in Mencius apparently, just a feeling that one *ought* to (of being *commanded*, *mìng* 命). But apparently it *is*, as some Western philosophers would put it, *under the description* "order and right" (*lǐ yì* 理義) that the heart (*xīn* 心) favors morality.

4.1 A Review of Mencius

I noted in Mencius that

(a) He solves the "paradox of virtue" by arguing that we all have moral motivatedness to start with, and it has an inherent *direction* toward what is in fact right and good.

(b) Further, if it is cultivated in the right way (normally), it will grow into the right shape: we become morally stronger through the self-reinforcement of "satisfaction in the heart" when the act is a right one.

(c) As Mencius says, we all have the same moral "tastes." The sages, authors of our moral rules, simply "anticipated what all hearts have in common."

I then raise the questions:

(i) Once I see what I am like, do I need a *teacher* leading me by the hand?

(ii) And since the sages have only anticipated *my* heart, do I need *them* as my teachers, in the sense of authors of rules that I learn? Couldn't I write my own book?

So, couldn't virtue be self-taught, on Mencius's account?

True, Mencius himself respected his "sages" and their rules.[4] But all around him, other moralists and political thinkers by the scores *were* writing their own rule-books. And even Mencius can look at a saying or belief or text in his own tradition and, sometimes, just see—with rocklike certainty—that it must be rejected. And when he does this, he is not turning philologist or historian and giving some scholarly argument; rather, he just sees that what it says is *morally abhorrent*—"the statement of a wild person from eastern Qi," as he puts it once— and so must be rejected as not being the words and records of the sages.[5]

This potential in Mencius must have been alarming to moral philosophers who looked at the sea of speculation around them and believed (with Mòzǐ 墨

子) that the anarchy must be reduced to order, and believed (if they were Confucians) that that order must be one in which the authority of the traditional *Confucian* moral rules is safely established.

4.2 Xunzi

Xúnzǐ 荀子 (ca. 300–215 B.C.) was such a philosopher.[6] Over and over, he inveighs against the wild-minded philosophers of his age. And over and over he hammers on the theme that the guidance of teachers and the models and rules of the "sages and early kings" are essential to the person who would become morally perfected:

> The sage has complete mastery of all moral principles; the king has complete mastery of all regulations of society. Those who possess these two kinds of mastery are worthy to be called the pinnacles of the world. Hence scholars should take the sage and the king as their teachers. They should take their regulations as their model and, on the basis of this model, seek to penetrate their reasoning and work to become like them.[7]

And of the necessity for teachers in the more usual sense, he holds,

> Ritual [i.e., the traditional rules of conduct] is the means by which to make yourself correct; the teacher is the means by which ritual is seen to be correct. If you are without ritual, how can you make yourself correct? If you have no teacher, how can you understand the correctness of ritual?[8]

So, Xunzi must reject Mencius's natural-leaning-toward-virtue theory of human nature, and does so, firmly. And this will require him to find another solution to the paradox of virtue.

For Xunzi, it works out this way:

(1) We have a natural tendency to be selfish, greedy, and quarrelsome. This is our "nature" (*xìng* 性).

(2) We also have a given ability to think, choose the most advantageous course, and act. This capacity for intelligent intentional action he calls *wèi* 偽.

(3) The first tendency in us, running unchecked, would result in a miserable existence for all (here he follows Mozi). Our *wei* capacity enables us to see this, see that rules and roles are needed, and then to formulate them. The sages were the formulators; and the origin of authority is simply posited: the sages were kings, and made these rules and roles the law.

This "moral" order is really moral, and can be grasped as a set of moral obligations, not just a set of utilitarian rules of prudence, for two reasons:

(1) As humans, in contrast to animals, we have a characteristic Xunzi calls *yì* 義. The word meant "what is right" and also "sense of what is right" for Mencius. For Xunzi it seems to be an unfunded[9] capacity to feel a "must"—perhaps in origin consequentialist—as a *moral* "must." This faculty makes human society *possible*.

(2) The set of rules that optimizes human satisfaction and minimizes conflict can be worked out essentially in only one way—the way the sages did it. It thus can be thought of as (we might say) an overflowing into the human social order of the necessity of the order of the universe as a whole. The person of understanding, seeing this, will have the same perception of beauty in it, the same sense of awe and respect for it, that one has for the order of nature (*tiān* 天) as a whole.[10]

One who is philosophically reflective can so to speak *think* one's way into this social-cultural-moral order and eventually become a completely socialized member of it, as follows:

(1) One sees, simply by "doing arithmetic,"[11] that although one is a desiring being who never satisfies all one's desires, this system optimizes satisfaction. Even if one had more than one's share, enjoyment of this would be nullified by anxiety.

(2) So one "approves" (*kě* 可) it (the *dào* 道, Way) and "follows" (*cóng* 從) it.[12] But this requires one to learn the rules and make them one's own— i.e., it requires moral education.

(3) So enlightened self-interest directs me to choose a life of moral learning. I proceed by studying the Classics—the teachings of the sages—under the guidance of teachers. The latter are useful as present models, and are necessary to bridge the interpretive gap between traditional written teachings in the Classics and present situations: "Ritual and music present us with models but no explanations; the *Odes* and *Documents* deal with ancient matters and are not always pertinent; the *Spring and Autumn Annals* is terse and cannot be quickly understood."[13]

Choosing to cause myself to be saturated in this educative milieu, I will arrive ideally at a *total* result: "The learning of noble persons enters their ears, clings to their minds, spreads through their four limbs, and manifests itself in their actions."[14] Notice that while the result is moral behavior, the *route* is through *understanding*, through the "ear" and the "mind."[15]

But attending to a teacher and the teacher's lessons requires love and respect, for the teacher and for the rites, the teachings of the sages. How are these attitudes acquired? Xunzi is weak here. He talks in two ways—sometimes, like Mozi, talking as if these attitudes can be acquired at will, though this may take time.[16] Love and hate can be turned on and off at will, notably in the criticism of self; note the imperative use: "When you find good in yourself, steadfastly approve it; when you find evil in yourself, then always hate it as something loathsome."[17] Sometimes he argues that constancy in behavior necessarily means that the appropriate inner attitude has come to be: "If you do as ritual prescribes, it means that your emotions have found rest in ritual. If you speak as your teacher speaks, it means that your understanding has become like that of your teacher."[18] These really aren't very satisfactory statements.

A more serious difficulty is Xunzi's problem of accounting for the unique position of the "sages." He says they are humans like anyone else. He follows Mencius in this; but he would be led to this view anyway by his rejection of everything supernatural, and by his persistent attempt to put values on a naturalistic basis. Obviously we want to ask, if the sages, with faculties I share, could figure all this out, why can't I?

We can do some filling in: If *I* did it, and *you*, and so on, we would, most of us, be likely to make mistakes; and then the purpose, of getting us all into a *uniform* system of rules, would be compromised. But it does seem as if Xunzi would be committed to allowing that a *king* might do it—*if* he had completed his moral education and has the *dé* 德, "virtue," of a sage. (But why *de*? Why not simply perfect *wei*?) And if he did it all afresh, the result, it would seem, might be very different in detail if not in substance from the teachings of the sages; for Xunzi admits that those teachings are not always on their face applicable to the present and require "explanation" by teachers.

This is just where a Xunzi-type ethics is headed; and we find this step taken explicitly in the *Zhōngyōng* 中庸:[19] if one has both *de* and *wèi* 位 ("virtue" and a "position" of authority) then (but only then) one may "make rites and music." So, only the "son of Heaven" may "order ceremonies, fix the measures, and determine the writing system."[20] But *he*, it seems, may do it afresh in the present age, superseding the authority of the sages.

4.3 Neo-Confucianism

Xunzi's position can be viewed as an intellectualistic reaction against a moral philosophy headed toward surrendering the authority of tradition to individual intuition, a philosophy that, in Mencius, would seem in principle to allow me to "teach myself virtue."

The sequel in Confucian moral thinking is an intriguing history of contradictions. Tradition continued to be honored fiercely (and in simple self-defense) by the state, the social establishment, and its teachers. But Mencius was gradually accorded more and more respect, until the collection of his sayings and dialogues with others, the *Mèngzǐ* 孟子, was accorded the status of a Classic;[21] while Xunzi's repute steadily faded. Allow me now to vault over a dozen centuries—no mean feat: the whole of the rise, flourishing, and decay of Buddhist China passes beneath me.[22]

A strong and progressively stronger revival of a Mencian type of moral philosophy, commonly labeled "Neo-Confucianism," characterizes the centuries from A.D. 1000 on. There is one effect that must be noted, however, that the Buddhist centuries had produced. The goal of Confucian moral education and self-development had always been partly a religious one. Mencius's innate tendencies to virtue were Heaven's "patents of nobility" (*jué* 爵) in my heart.[23] For Confucius it was Heaven that "produced the *de* in me."[24] Xunzi's Heaven was not divine in theory; but religion does not require divinity. The rites—including those of ancestor "worship"—remained intact for Xunzi, and his goal of moral self-perfection for the "noble person" has the appeal of a religious personal goal.

Now, it was different. Or, the same only more so. A life of moral "learning" had as before the goal of "sagehood"—moral self-perfection; but the goal now was also thought of as a Buddhist would have thought of it—a final, total, world-and-outlook-transforming *enlightenment*, although still a form of moral perfection. This meant two things for my subject: oddly, what students of virtue were doing was something they could do only, in the last analysis, *alone*; yet they were very often, we feel, compulsively teacher-dependent.

The *shūyuàn* 書院, local "academies" (literally "book halls"), were the institutional seed beds of moral philosophy and metaphysical speculation in Song, Yuan, and Ming Dynasty China; and the students in them, around the local charismatic teacher, were indeed engaged in some forms of study that obviously sometimes require the help of a teacher. They were reading and puzzling over the Classics—especially a repertoire of fewer and fewer challenging passages from the *Four Books* and the "Great Appendix" (*Dà zhuàn* 大傳) to the *Yìjīng* 易經, on moral self-cultivation.[25] They were constantly putting questions to their teachers about these. Some were—guiltily—practicing the art of examination essay writing, using these texts as sources, and would need criticism of their efforts.[26] But more and more, as time went on—as one must judge from the "collected conversations" (*yǔlù* 語錄) of the philosophers or their commentaries on the favorite Classics—such students were engaged in something one has to do oneself: monitoring their own inner lives in an exercise of "self-watching" (*shèn dú* 慎獨) directed toward their goal of inner moral perfection and self-understanding;[27] noticing every "selfish impulse" (*sī yì* 私意) that surfaces in the mind and saying "no" to it, for example. This came to be called *gōngfu* (功夫 or 工夫), the "task," or "moral effort," and could be virtually, for the ardent, tantamount to a constant life of silent prayer. The final morally purifying goal of understanding could, depending on your school, be furthered by "study" in the ordinary sense: by reading books—the Classics, the histories—and thereby increasing the mind's by nature incomplete grasp of the *li* 理 of things and events, their normative and also causally determining "principles." (This was the form of the "task" for the Song Dynasty philosophers Chéng Yí 程頤 and Zhū Xī 朱熹.)[28] But progress and success were necessarily personal even here.

4.3.1 Wang Yangming

Wáng Yángmíng 王陽明 (1472–1529), the most popular philosopher of the later "school of mind" (*Xīn xué* 心學), carried the subjective implications of Mencian self-education in virtue much farther.[29] For him, and the many students who hung on his words, there are no "principles" or moral rules that can be abstracted from concrete situations. One has to learn to let the mind, with a mirror-like total lack of prejudice in favor of a past concept or present twinge of selfishness, confront each problem in life as it arises. Ideally the *li* or "principle" of that situation just is such a mind's reaction to it, given in a self-evident moral intuition that Wang called *liáng zhī* 良知, "pure knowing"—a term taken, of course, from *Mengzi* 7A15. But Wang's picture of the process of self-development differs from that of Mencius: with him as with other Neo-Confucians, inner monitoring of "selfish desires" is very important, whereas the point of Mencian inner "nourishment" is the positive reinforcement effect of the feeling of satisfaction in right action. And for Mencius, real moral capacity, a kind of energy, *grows*; whereas for Wang this capacity is a capacity of *understanding*, which is always there. Wang's "task" aims at breaking through a veil of "be-clouding" selfish impulse that keeps one from utilizing it.

But the rather veiled implications in Mencius that one can "get it" oneself if one just "thinks" (*sī zé dé zhī* 思則得之, 6A15) are much more explicit in Wang. He will, he says boldly in a letter to one powerful official, even criticize Confucius if he finds him wrong. (He never does.) As for the "sages" in general—without in fact ever withdrawing his respect—he says of them, "the thousand sages are all passing shadows; it is pure knowing alone that is my teacher" (*qiān shèng jiē guò yǐng; liáng zhī nǎi wǒ shī* 千聖皆過影良知乃我師) (1933, sec. 20, p. 133).

Yet with this—for students of such a man: he himself did it alone—there is teacher-dependence. One student, recording an exchange of question and answer that left all present "sweating with fright," says that "our teacher" is always giving us such skillful help in getting us by our mental blocks (Chan 1963, 216, no. 260; 239–41, no. 313). Another, in difficulties, says to Wang that he has trouble "overcoming my selfish desires." Wang replies sweetly, "Give me your selfish desires and I will overcome them for you" (Chan 1963, 79, no. 122). This is ridiculous, of course—only you can do it—but that was the point; and a demonstration of Wang's skill in administering a salutary shock. This seems to imply that virtue *must* be self-taught, but also that one must be carefully taught how to teach oneself.

The age after Wang was another epoch of great intellectual variety in China. We can count two centuries of it. Having got thoroughly unstuck in time, I shall jump lightly over them.

4.4 The Qing Dynasty

As Xunzi's intellectualist reaction followed on the perceived threat of a world of great philosophical variety, and, I have suggested, of Mencian subjectivism, so after the Manchu Conquest that began the Qing Dynasty (1644–1911) the preoccupation I have been describing with self-cultivationist Mencian moral philosophy gave way to a new "intellectualism"—to use Yü Ying-shih's term (1976, chap. 3) for a change of temper many have described. The "fashion" of the age was "solid learning," and intellectual excitement lay in discoveries in history and philology by scholars who performed marvels of library-wide reading and annotating, in lifelong research.[30]

It is possible to notice that at a deeper level, life orientations don't change quite so radically quite so quickly. The Song and Ming Confucian moralists did become controversial; the classical ones did not. Moral "effort," *gongfu*, remained a preoccupation of certain almost eccentric moral perfectionists. For the writers and scholars of great and little reputation, it was replaced by the philologist's eternal chimera: If I can add one brick more today, one more polished fact tomorrow, then someday truth's edifice will take its own shape—the one brick, the polished fact, are then my own contribution to the vision of the *dao*.[31]

I turn my attention now to two men of the eighteenth century, who did their philosophy in the disguise of scholarship. Both can be read as confronting a problem like Xunzi's: how to secure the Confucian tradition of moral rules and values against a variety of voices in recent centuries whom they saw as putting forward their own subjective intuitions as truth; and how to do this in a nonarbitrary way. Not just to say "the sages were right and the Classics authoritative, and through them alone can we get to the truth," but to give a plausible account of the world in time such that this or something like it turns out to follow necessarily from seemingly self-evident assumptions. They did poorly at this; it's a losing game. But one of them did better than Xunzi did.

How did the "sages" create a moral order if they were not moral supermen—assuming that *I* couldn't do it? Xunzi gets the *authority* into their "ritual rules and principles of right" (*lǐ yì* 禮義) by stipulating that they were rulers. Where did the *rightness* come from?

4.4.1 Zhang Xuecheng

The solution (perhaps indicated by Xunzi himself, but not developed by him) could be to reason that just as the student depends on teachers to interpret the Classics and show how they bear on the present, so we can say that a sage just couldn't have written a book of rules that would unproblematically fit the whole of subsequent history, prescribing for all its unfolding detail. In fact the Classics can't be moral cookbooks at all. They are not *written* by a "sage" but are the residues of a long process of history.

If a "sage" participates in this process, and so contributes to the production of a "Classic" text, it is not conceivable that he (or she, if Confucians had acknowledged any female sages) could anticipate a whole societal set of needs not yet come to be. Therefore,

(a) The sage must do this legislating piecemeal, attending to problems as they arise.

(b) It is reasonable to suppose that this process of *jī wèi* 積僞 (Xunzi's term: literally, "accumulation of [the results of] intelligent action")[32] will take not just one lifetime but centuries (and the work of many "sages").

(c) Even if a "sage" could do it all at once (pull a whole moral order, in principle sufficient for all time, out of one's head), this wouldn't be the product of *necessity*, and so couldn't command the respect that the moral order, thought of as an overflowing of the necessity of the natural world into the human, does command in a Xunzi-type of thought. It would be just "empty words," and probably merely the product of vanity; its author wouldn't be a sage at all.

(d) Here is a neat solution to one Xunzi problem: If the sages could do it at all, why can't I? The mistake in the question is that I shouldn't be comparing myself with some person or persons in the past, but with a (perhaps still continuing) *historical process. It* may have something to teach me that I can learn in no other way, even if a single person doesn't.

(e) This also seems to solve another Xunzi problem: How could one (even a sage) conceivably lift oneself by one's moral bootstraps—invent some rules, which have pragmatic utility, and then say *to oneself as well as to others*, "we will now all feel *morally* obligated to obey these rules"? The answer is that it didn't happen this way. The process reaches back beyond memory, and when it "started" nobody was aware of what was happening. Any "sage" would have been as much embedded in a historically given moral order as I am, and what the sage creates in response to a particular perceived need seems to the sage and others simply as a reasonable extension of that order, as something the sage *must* do.

There is a price to be paid for a view like this:

(1) The positive moral order is a historical product, perhaps still unfolding, not final.

(2) A present-day person or ruler in the right "position" can keep on creating, if a need exists and it is that person's function to meet it. But so
can I; and another person is as much bound by the past as I am.

This seems to be a decent revision of Xunzi's version of Confucian ethics.
Ironically, the person who thought it out wasn't a moral philosopher, in any
special sense. The person was Zhāng Xuéchéng 章學誠 (1738–1801), and the
foregoing is part of what he says in his monograph "Yuán Dào" 原道 (literally,
"tracing the Way back to its source"), which he wrote in Ānhuī 安徽 in the
spring of 1789, after years of pondering and previous trials. Zhang was interested in *history*, in the thing itself, in how you think about it and study it, and
in how you write about it.

Zhang did not represent himself as critically revising Xunzi, nor, probably,
even think of himself as doing that. He *was*, I think, consciously critically revising the position of another man, older, and much better known (then, not
now) than himself: Dài Zhèn 戴震 (1724–1777).[33] And read in this way Zhang
does a good job. But I must leave him now for Dai himself, who is very interesting in his own right.

4.4.2 Dai Zhen

Dai Zhen is one of those philosophers who spends his whole life rewriting the
same book—at least, this is true if we consider his explicitly philosophical work.
Dai was known primarily as a philologist, a scholar of ancient mathematics,
astronomy, and geography. But his real love was moral philosophy—an embarrassment to his nonphilosophical friends, who thought he was wasting his
time on it. The book he wrote, in its final form finished a year before he died,
was on its face another piece of philological scholarship: he called it "an explanation of the meaning of terms in the *Mengzi*" 孟子字義疏證.

Where Mencius had said that we humans naturally enjoy "order and right"
(*li yi*), Dai reduces moral norms *to* human desires: it is from human desires
that we *get* our system of norms originally. (This is actually like Xunzi, though
perhaps Dai did not see this.) Further (like Mencius) what our norms say we
ought to do is what we really *want*. And we are able to *understand* what is right
only because we are desiring beings. Dai appears to think thus:

(a) To find out what is right, one notices what one wants (compare *Mengzi*
6A7), and then makes sure this is *yi*, "right," and not just *yìjiàn* 意見,
"personal opinion," by testing it with Confucius's maxim of "reciprocity" (恕 *shù*): "Do not do to others what you do not want done to
yourself."[34] The point is that one cannot even begin to think this out
unless one knows what it is like to *want* something.

(b) What we want, in the beginning, is what it is natural for us to want:

This Dai calls *zìrán* 自然, "the natural." When this is tested out by thought (seen to be "universalizable," we might say), so that we are sure of it, it becomes *bìrán* 必然, "the necessary," in the sense both that we will always do it or honor it, and also that it is objective, valid for all, "an unchanging standard" (*bú yì zhī zé* 不易之則).

(c) If our minds were perfectly clear—"unclouded"—we could do this perfectly. But only the sages' minds were perfectly unclouded. Dai as far as I can see gives no reason for saying this; and if so he dodges right here the crucial problem; and notice that it is precisely the problem that Zhang Xuecheng concentrates on.

(d) So, we are dependent on the sages for our knowledge of "the necessary," i.e., for being sure that it is necessary and really right. In *this* sense, for Dai, we do need teachers of morality, i.e., we need the "sages."

(e) But to understand the words of the sages, philology is enough; and we apparently don't need a *moral* teacher for this.

(f) And *cognitive* understanding of "the necessary" appears to be enough, for Dai. There is no need for separate cultivation of the "moral will" (*zhì* 志) or "heart-mind" (*xin*). The "approval" (*ke*) involved in *seeing that* a candidate principle really is a universalizable principle would be sufficient for me to act morally, out of conviction; for Dai treats this intellectual approval as a form of our natural liking for the right, along with Mencius's pleasurable satisfaction in doing the right.

But Dai's interest is not, perhaps, primarily in how I can become virtuous: He doesn't, one senses, sweat over philology in the same way and with the same desperation that Wang Yangming's students sweated over *gongfu*. His interest is in giving a theoretical account of the right and the good that will enable us to expose *yijian*, "opinion," so that it cannot pose as genuine moral principle.

When Dai does talk about the cultivation of virtue, he sees it as an intellectual process, and we can see it as of a kind that I could perfectly well do myself. It is a process of adding to the content of the understanding until—he is confident—the understanding becomes transformed (here he seems to me like Zhu Xi, whom he tirelessly denounces):

> The physical form is initially young and immature, but becomes full-grown; the moral nature (*déxìng* 德性) is initially wrapped in childish ignorance, but becomes sagely and wise. The maturation of the physical form depends on the nourishment of food and drink and is a matter of daily growth, not of restoring its initial condition; and when the moral nature, nourished by learning, advances to sageness and wisdom, it is clear that this (also) is not a matter of restoring its initial condition.[35]

4.5 Summary

What do I think I have been doing? I began, two lectures ago, examining an archaic concept, the *de* or "virtue" of the king—appropriately and necessarily as an archaeological inquiry. One concern suggests itself immediately: is the value, such as it may be, of the idea of *de* as *virtue* in a moral sense (and not "virtue") undermined by thus being traced back to primitive concepts, which (as I have shown) even include sexual attractiveness and something like magic? (Perhaps this thought is part of some of the objections to the "mana thesis" about *de*.)[36] But there is a name for such an assumption: it is called the genetic fallacy. On the genetic fallacy, let me pause to say something obvious.

(a) Consider this situation: I encounter, first, information about the author of a book I have *not* read. I see he is a fool, motivated in absurd ways, etc. Someone now asks me to read the book and tells me I am narrowminded if I refuse. I brush the argument aside, quite properly: the book may be good, but probability is against it, I read slowly, and life is short.

(b) Now consider this situation: I have read something I find insightful, or inspiring, or beautiful. I now come upon, or investigate and discover, information about who wrote it, his purposes, etc. and find that he was a fool, his purposes such as I could never share, etc. This tells me *nothing directly* about the value of what I was first reading. It might lead me toward a discovery that I was mistaken in my interpretation of it, and so valuing something that just isn't there; but this does not *have* to be so. Barring such reinterpretation, if I thought it good to begin with, that judgment is untouched.

In situations of the second kind—deducing the value of the effect from the value of the cause—the genetic fallacy is indeed a fallacy. This is why I must insist that it is quite possible for us to see—as I have seen in this study—a rich and broadly human moral point of view, with its difficulties but also with universal value, evolving step by step out of archaic primitive beginnings. Indeed, the idea that we are morally responsible for our motives, implicit very early in this tradition, seems to me to have much more to recommend it than many philosophers have thought. Yet we begin to suspect that the Chinese might well not have come to explore it had they not earlier held beliefs about *de* that we may want to call intrinsically worthless.

How did this come about? The structure of the primitive concept turned out to generate a paradox: Apparently, to acquire this "virtue" one has to have it already. Worse, to *seek* this "virtue" is to seek an advantage, which is *un*virtuous.

This led me to Mencius, and toward what we easily recognize as *virtue*, and

I find that Mencius solves the problem in effect by saying that we all *are* virtuous already.

But this solution, for the Chinese, generated another problem: Moral teaching, including the instruction we draw from the past, begins to appear unnecessary.

So Xunzi rejects Mencius's solution, to try to show that virtue *can't* be self-taught. But this requires him to find another solution to the paradox. How *do* human beings gain entry into a virtuous orientation? Somehow, he thought, by the exercise of enlightened *intellect*. (This much anticipates Dai Zhen, who seems not to recognize his debt.)[37] But this by itself seems not only not to give Xunzi what he wants, but also to lead, in Dai, to another question.

Can one, by sitting down by oneself and doing some reading and thinking about it, become virtuous? Can one in this way so nourish the mind and the "moral nature" that one not only knows what the right things are, knows them to be right, but also chooses to do them for their own sake, and out of a fixed disposition of character, a fully nourished "moral nature"? This is what Dai seems to say, and one may very well be doubtful; for my own intuition tells me firmly that I can sometimes see clearly what I ought to do and why, and—particularly if the obligation is a moral one, but not only then—proceed deliberately to do something else. Must I set this intuition aside? Or simply conclude that I am not, myself, virtuous?

Once again I end with a question. But this time I do not promise a follow-up lecture in which to wrestle with my concluding question. Perhaps, in that, I have shown wisdom, if not virtue.

Golden Rule Arguments in Chinese Moral Philosophy[1]

By "golden rule" I shall mean the idea, expressed in many different ways, that my behavior or attitude affecting another person should in some sense be the kind of thing that I would find acceptable if I were the person affected. Most of what I have to say will be describing what some Chinese philosophers have said, and attempting to analyze it. I will seldom be talking about actual "arguments" (except the sort that we silently address to ourselves). And I will not cover the subject: I lack the knowledge, and you could accord me neither the patience nor the time to go through what little I do know.

5.1 Examples and Distinctions

The "golden rule" has not been the subject of a very large literature of philosophical analysis, though it is very close to some basic problems in ethics. In contrast, if we are liberal in interpreting the term, we find it very widely exemplified in the wisdom, inspirational and religious literatures, and folk traditions of the world. I will content myself with two random examples.

To a Stanford doctoral dissertation by Bruce Alton (1966) I am indebted for the intelligence that the Ba-Congo of tropical Africa have the following proverb:

> If you see a jackal in your neighbor's garden, drive it out; one may get into yours one day, and you would like the same done for you.

And from the seminal book, *The Theory of Morality*, by the late Alan Donagan, I glean the following:

> According to the Babylonian *Talmud*, a gentile once demanded of Hillel that he be taught the whole law while he stood on one foot. "Do not do to your fellow what you hate to have done to you," Hillel told him. "This is the whole law entire; the rest is explanation." (1977, 57)

Assuming a bipedal posture myself, I shall proceed.

The expression "golden rule," for many, refers to one or more formulations gotten directly or indirectly from Christian scripture. There are many formulations to be found there, but the following (from the King James version) are especially memorable:

> (i) Matthew 7:12: Therefore all things whatsoever ye would that men should do to you, do ye even so to them.
>
> (ii) Luke 6:31: And as ye would that men should do to you, do ye also to them likewise.
>
> (iii) Matthew 22:39: Thou shalt love thy neighbour as thyself.[2]

These examples will serve as the basis for several simple formal distinctions:

> (a) The criterion for one's treatment of others can be explicitly how one would want others to treat oneself—as in the first two formulations; or it can be explicitly one's own concern for oneself (and, perhaps, how one would treat oneself)—as in the last formulation.
>
> (b) The rule could be taken as a general rule about what acts to perform affecting others, as in the first formulation; or it could be taken as a meta-rule about what kinds of acts to perform, i.e., about what (first-order) rules of action to adopt—as perhaps in the last two formulations.
>
> (c) The rule could be unqualified—as it appears to be in the first formulation: ". . . all things whatsoever . . ."; or it could allow or invite qualification (e.g., taking into account how the needs and desires of the other person may differ from one's own; or taking into account some independent standard of what is right; etc.).
>
> (d) The rule can be stated positively, as it is in all three formulations above; or it might be stated negatively: e.g., "as ye would that men should *not* do to you, likewise do *not* do these things to them."

I offer this list of possible differences in formulation as suggestive, not as exhaustive. Another kind of differentiation can be got if we ask what the rule is supposed to be for:

> (A) We might take it as an attempt to clarify what it is to act morally; e.g., with Kant, we might say that a moral act ought to be one that would conform to a law applying universally, without respect to persons; the greatest temptation to make exceptions favoring a particular person is to make an exception favoring oneself, and the rule points out that this must not be done. The rule thus gives part of the formal meaning of "morally right," so that as long as one wants to be moral it would be irrational not to follow it.

(B) The rule could be offered and understood simply as a counsel of prudence: it is in your best interest to treat others as you would want to be treated, because, e.g.,

    (i) In this way you dispose others to treat you well, or at least you do not provoke them to treat you ill; among Chinese philosophers, there are examples of this view in both the *Mòzǐ* 墨子 (in the essay, "Universal Love") and *Mèngzǐ* 孟子 (book 1B, passim).

    (ii) If everybody acts this way, all will be better off (as Mozi also argues).

    (iii) The rule is favored by higher authority, e.g., God, or Heaven, or the state; and if we follow it then this higher authority will approve of us and treat us well (again, one can look at Mozi for this position).

(C) The rule might be simply a convenient rule of thumb for checking to see whether something I contemplate doing is a just act. (Perhaps this is like (A), except that here my interest is a simple practical one. Furthermore, viewed in this way, the rule is a "hypothetical imperative" and not a "categorical imperative.")[3]

(D) The rule could be taken as an effective rule to follow if I want to be, or to become, an ideally morally good person: it is a guide for morally cultivating oneself. (Again, the rule so conceived is a "hypothetical imperative." And it is not necessarily limited to acts that would be "just" in the sense of being required by one's moral code.)

5.2 *Shu* in the *Analects*

Let us now consider some Chinese examples. The earliest one that I know of is found in the *Lúnyǔ* 論語 (*Analects* of Confucius), in book 5:[4]

> Zǐgòng 子貢 said, "If I do not desire other people to do something to me, then I also desire not to (*wú* 無) do it to others."[5] The Master [i.e., Confucius] said, "Oh, Sì 賜![6] This is not something you have attained to."[7]

A better-known example also involves Confucius's disciple Zigong; it is found in book 15, probably added to the *Analects* a century and a half later, at the end of the fourth century B.C.:[8]

> Zigong asked, "Is there one maxim that can be practiced throughout one's life?" The Master replied, "Surely, it is *shù* 恕 (consideration)! 'What you do not wish for yourself, do not (*wù* 勿) do to others.'"[9]

What is going on here is not meta-ethical analysis but practical guidance: the rule or rules appear to be thought of as a guide to becoming a good person, or as something one can "attain" to only if one has become a sufficiently good person. The formulations are negative. They appear to apply directly to acts rather than being a criterion for rules of action. The first formulation explicitly makes my imagining what another might do to me the test of what I should do to that person; in the second, the test could be either what I imagine another might do to me, or how I might want to treat myself.

In neither case are qualifications mentioned. But they are not ruled out either. And it may be argued (as does Fingarette 1980) that the closely self-referential form "as I would want myself" (in 15:24) takes care of this: by calling on me to put myself, as myself, in the place of the other, thus becoming the other's "I," it effectively draws on my intuition to see things as that person would see them, and at the same time to use my own judgment. Thus the necessary qualifications (given the other's preferences, but not allowing them to dictate an act that that person ought not to want, etc.) don't need to be stated. If this is true, it is philosophical good fortune; for the qualification problem is notorious. If we state it without any "if's," the golden rule is immediately subject to counterexamples that make nonsense of it. (Should I kill you, if I desire to commit suicide—or to have someone save me the trouble?) But if we try to spell out the needed qualifications, we quickly find that there is no end to it.

How significant are the other taxonomic features I have noted in these two early examples from the *Analects*? In particular, what about the fact that the Chinese formulations (so far) tell us *not* to do things to others that we would *not* want done to us?

Sometimes negative formulations of the golden rule are invidiously dubbed the "silver rule." The critical literature has much along this line, especially when written or inspired by Christian divines: We are asked to acknowledge that Jesus' warmly positive attitude of love and compassion can hardly be said to have an equivalent in Confucius's sour "don't."

Such talk overlooks certain facts: (1) There are more Chinese formulations, even in early books of the *Analects*, and some of these, that I will look at presently, are positive. (2) Very early Christian literature abounds in both positive and negative forms, and it is quite evident that the early Christian divines never thought of these as being significantly different. Thus, Tertullian (Adversus Marcionem), "Even as you wish it to be done to you by other men, so also do you to them." And in the next breath, "Even as you wish it not to be done to you by other men, so also let you not do to them."[10] (3) Further, it is obvious that these gentlemen were right. If, having promised to appear this evening, I had not done so, I still would have done something, namely, breaking a promise. Not doing something to another is always, under another description, doing something to that person, and conversely.

So in one sense the issue is trivial. (This is a standard point.) But it is true that negative formulations are much more prominent in the Chinese literature, and this may be significant: it may indicate (and I think it does indicate) a difference in intent that is yet to be uncovered. Pursuing this matter will lead to a much finer understanding of what the Chinese moralists thought they were saying.

5.3 Fung Yu-lan on *Zhong* and *Shu*

Among the defenders of Confucius and the early Confucians, one scholar who maintains that they did, after all, have both a positive and a negative formulation of the golden rule is Fung Yu-lan, well-known historian of Chinese philosophy. What Fung says on this matter will serve to introduce an intricate problem of exegesis that has a rich history through many centuries.

In brief what he says is this (Fung 1953, 43–44). There are positive formulations of the rule in early Confucian moral literature. One of these is in the *Analects*, book 6 (possibly mid-fifth century B.C.), chapter 30:

> The term *rén* 仁 (benevolence) means that when you desire getting established [i.e., being received at court] for yourself, you help others to get established; and when you desire success for yourself you help others to succeed. The ability to make a comparison [sc. with the other person] from what is near at hand [sc. from your own case] can simply be called the method of [attaining] benevolence.

Here the rule is explicitly a program for self-development, and the statement is positive.

Another Confucian moral text, later but still quite early, is the *Zhōngyōng* 中庸.[11] It contains something more explicit:

> *Zhōng* 忠 and *shù* 恕 are not far from the *dào* 道 (Way). If you would not be willing to have something done to yourself, then don't do it to others. The ways of the noble person are four, and I [Confucius] have not yet mastered even one of them: What you would require of your son, use in serving your father; . . . what you would require of your subordinate, use in serving your prince; . . . what you would require of your younger brother, use in serving your elder brother; . . . what you would require of your friend, first apply in your treatment of your friend.[12]

Here Fung notes that first we have Confucius naming two virtues (or virtuous practices), *zhong* and *shu*. The second, *shu* (which I, with many others, translate "consideration"—some use "reciprocity," or even "altruism"), is what Confucius defined for Zigong in *Analects* 15:24 with the classic negative formulation; and in the *Zhongyong* text just quoted, a close paraphrase of this negative formulation follows immediately after the mention of *zhong* and *shu*. What comes next ("what you would require of your son . . . ," etc.) is obviously a way of saying—positively—"treat others the way you would want them to treat you." This, then, must be *zhong*, which must be simply the name for the positive counterpart of the negative *shu*.

And there is more direct evidence that the (apparently negative) *shu* had a correlate in what was called *zhong*. It is found in the oldest book of the *Analects*, book 4, in chapter 15:

> The master said, "Shēn 參! My Way has one [thread] running through it." Zēngzǐ 曾子 replied, "Quite so."[13] The Master went out. The other disciples asked, "What did he mean?" Zengzi replied, "Our Master's Way consists simply of *zhong* and *shu*."

This has to be an interpolation in book 4, done by the followers of Zengzi, to give the idea prominence, and to appropriate it for their own master.[14] It expands *Analects* 15:3, where Zigong, not Zengzi, is involved, and Confucius is quoted as saying, without explanation, that his (Confucius's) Way has "one thread running through it." Book 15 is the book that also has the definition of *shu*; so the idea that the essence of the Confucian moral Way is *zhong* and *shu* appears to date to about 300 B.C.

But dates, though comforting, are not in themselves explanatory. *Shu* has been defined—though this can hardly be the end of the matter. What is *zhong*? If *zhong* and *shu* are a pair of concepts that are matched in some way, we sense at once that we will understand each better if we understand them both, and see how they are related. This is what Fung was trying to do, and what commentators through the centuries have tried to do. Was Fung right?

5.4 An Alternative Interpretation

Fung was right, I will argue, in pointing to the *Zhongyong* text as an important key to the problem, but not in taking *zhong* and *shu* to be positive and negative correlates. Another ancient locus (Fung quotes this too) should show that there is trouble with this idea. It is found in the *Dàxué* 大學, a short but very important Confucian moral text from about the same time as the *Zhongyong*:[15]

> What you would dislike in your superior, do not use in employing your inferior; what you would dislike in your inferior, do not use in serving your superior; what you would dislike in the one who precedes you, do not use in dealing with the one who comes after you; what you would dislike in the one who comes after you, do not use in dealing with the one who precedes you.[16]

The *Daxue* calls this the moral "measuring square" (*xié jǔ* 絜矩). The striking thing about it, I think, is that it has the same kind of social-political-hierarchical explicitness as the second part of the *Zhongyong* text. This feature of Confucian moral philosophy exasperated Immanuel Kant, who lectured on Chinese philosophy in Königsberg (but only in his courses on "physical geography"). It led him to dismiss Confucius as having no concept of genuine morality at all: "Their teacher Confucius teaches in his writings nothing outside a moral doctrine designed for the princes." He concludes, "a concept of virtue and morality never entered the heads of the Chinese."[17]

But it is precisely the concreteness of the Chinese that shows what is going on: The second part of the first pair of injunctions seems to say exactly what the *Zhongyong* text had said: serve your superiors as you would have your inferiors serve you; but here the statement is forcefully negative, not positive.

Further, there is something formal to be appreciated here: The Chinese Golden Rule as here stated—and so perhaps as always intended—does not say "treat another as you would have that other treat you," but "treat another as you would have anyone else related to you as you are to that other treat you."

A closer look at the language in which these ideas are expressed reinforces the impression that both *zhong* and *shu* are conceived quite concretely in terms of familiar social, familial, and political relationships, in which distinctions of precedence and authority are taken for granted. Consider again *shu*: "Do not do to others what you would not want yourself"—the word for "do," *shī* 施, is normally used of doings that are givings (or inflictings) directed downward toward one's inferiors in status, or at most toward equals. On the other hand, the ordinary meaning of the word *zhong* is "loyalty"—and the meaning is so ordinary that it would be very strange (though this hasn't bothered the dominant tradition of commentary) if its meaning when paired with *shu* were utterly different; and *zhong* as "loyalty" is always directed toward superiors, or at most toward equals.

One should see at once that this is what is going on when one looks at the other text in the *Analects* containing the *shu* formula "Do not do to others what you do not want yourself." It is found in book 12 (perhaps twenty years earlier than book 15), chapter 2:

> Zhònggōng 仲弓 asked about *ren*. The Master said, "When you are out of your house behave as though you were conducting a great reception [i.e., by a ruler or official "hosting" vassals or subordinates]. When employing the common people behave as if you were conducting a great ritual sacrifice. What you do not want for yourself, do not do to others. In this way you will be free from ill will whether [serving] in the state or in a noble family."

Here the application of *shu* (the word itself is not used, but the formula used to explicate *shu* in 15:24 *is* used) is explicitly toward inferiors; and just as interesting, it assumes that you must treat your inferiors not callously and harshly but with decorum and civility, or, in Confucian language, "according to the rites." Further, this is all offered as an explanation of what "benevolence" (*rén* 仁) is.[18]

Analects 12:2 linked *shu* and benevolence; now what about *zhong* and benevolence? An example is supplied in book 5 (one of the early books), chapter 19:

> Zǐzhāng 子張 asked the following question: "Prime Minister Zǐwén 子文 was three times appointed Prime Minister, and showed no sign of delight. He was three times dismissed, and showed no sign of resentment. He always informed the incoming Prime Minister of the past administrative business of the Prime Minister's office. What would you say of him?" The Master replied, "He was indeed *zhong*." Zizhang continued, "But was he *ren*?" Confucius answered, "I do not know yet [from what you have said] how he would qualify as *ren*."

Here we have a man clearly described as "using what he would require of the person coming before him in his dealing with the person coming after," not letting any personal feeling interfere, and qualifying as *zhong* thereby. In so doing he is "loyal" in the real sense, as Xúnzǐ 荀子 has Confucius define it: one does not follow one's ruler no matter what; one follows the Way—the requirements of public morality of a person in one's role.[19]

Zhong, then, is the quality of reliably following one's duties, toward superiors or equals. *Shu* on the other hand is a quasi-supererogatory virtue—that is, it has to do with things that are not strictly required of one;[20] it will mean that in dealing with equals or inferiors as our respective roles may require, I will be polite and considerate. The distinction is implicit again in a familiar early text, *Analects* 3:19, not usually brought into this discussion: "A ruler employs subordinates according to the rites; subordinates serve their ruler with *zhong*."

Other things now fall into place: The early Confucian texts, as often the *Analects* do, frequently conjoin *zhong* and *xìn* 信 as a moral compound, *zhōngxìn* 忠信; *xin*, "good faith," "being true to one's word," is to hold oneself to responsibilities generated by one's own personal commitments and promises; *zhong* is to hold oneself to responsibilities implied by public morality. *Zhong* is paired with *xin* in one way, and with *shu* in another: *shu* is to show as much favor to another, in an equal or lower position, as one would want oneself if the roles were reversed, in so far as rules allow, when it is a matter of going beyond rules or tempering and humanizing their application; *zhong* is to be just as strict with oneself in one's responsibilities to a superior or equal as one would be with another in one's position, if roles were reversed.

So as the Chinese concepts are more explicitly revealed, we see that there is a rich structure of qualification assumed in them. Still, they are "universalizability" (or reversibility) rules. It may therefore be instructive to compare them with a form of the "Categorical Imperative." (Though Kant himself dismissed the "Golden Rule" as merely derivative, and scorned such comparison.)[21]

If the Categorical Imperative says in effect that one's acts should be describable as instances of laws that one can, or does, "will to be universal," then if I find myself hesitating to perform an act that would be an instance of a law I think I should accept, logical pressure can fall at either of two points: I can say to myself, the fact that I hesitate shows that the law ought to be inter-preted flexibly here, or that it ought to be amended so as to make this an exception, etc. Or I can say to myself, the fact that I think the law should be a law, i.e., universally applying, shows that I ought to stop hesitating, and ought to toughen myself.

Let us try applying this to *shu* and *zhong* respectively. *Shu* directs me to notice, when someone else "down there" is to be hurt by my act, whether I would be willing to accept the hurt myself; if I would not, I am to hold off, if I can. Thus *shu* is a directive for amending or suspending rules, or applying them flexibly; hence its association with *lǐ* 禮, "rites," which are rules that are flexible and humane, in contrast to *fǎ* 法, "laws," which are neither.

Zhong, on the other hand, if I am right about it, directs me to notice, when I find myself hesitating to follow a rule governing my behavior toward someone "up there," that would be unpleasant for me, that it is a rule I would expect all to follow no matter what. Noticing this, I am to go ahead, and if necessary straighten myself. Thus *zhong* is a directive for self-discipline, and for holding rules firm.

5.5 Later Chinese Interpretations

That the Chinese "golden rule" family of concepts has these two aspects is seen clearly by the Song Dynasty Confucian moral philosopher Zhāng Zài 張 載 (1020–1077):

> If one holds oneself responsible just as one is disposed to hold others re-sponsible, then one realizes the Way completely. This is illustrated by the words "The Ways of the noble person are four; and I, Confucius, have not yet been able to attain even one of them." If one loves others just as one is disposed to love oneself, then one realizes benevolence completely. This is illustrated by the words "If something is done to you and you don't want it, then for your part don't do it to others."[22]

Obviously Zhang is commenting on *Zhongyong*, chapter 13. He does not use the words *zhong* and *shu* here, nor do I know whether he would have. But his "holding oneself responsible" and "loving (i.e., being considerate to) others" are the *zhong* and *shu* concepts, respectively, as I have described them.

The major Song philosophers Chéng Yí 程頤 (1033–1108) and Zhū Xī 朱 熹 (1130–1200), though Zhu quotes Zhang respectfully, took a different line, one that strongly emphasizes the self-discipline aspect of *zhong-shu*. And one must grant that they had reason to; for one finds this emphasis also in Xunzi, already in late antiquity (third century B.C.). In the *Fǎ xíng* 法行 (an essay in the *Xunzi* that is perhaps later than the man Xunzi, but written by someone who thought as he did) we read this:

> Confucius said, "The noble person has three [rules of] *shu*: (1) To have a ruler one cannot serve, and yet to have a subject one seeks to employ, is not *shu*. (2) To have parents one cannot repay, and yet to have a son and to require filial piety of him, is not *shu*. (3) To have an elder brother and be unable to give him proper respect, and yet to have a younger brother and require obedience of him, is not *shu*."
> If scholars understand these three [kinds of] *shu*, then they will be able to straighten themselves.[23]

I have left *"shu"* untranslated. Obviously it cannot be "consideration" here. In a distant sense it is, in that it seems wrong to expect one's son, e.g., to be filial toward oneself if one backslides on one's own filial obligations. But we can hardly imagine Confucius recommending a suspension of the rules here. It would be absurd to interpret him as saying that one who is morally weak ought therefore to be lax as well. In a closer sense the idea is *shu*: I should have the same "consideration" for my father that I want my son to have for me; but now the "consideration" is directed upward, and directs me not to lenience with the other person, but to firmness with myself. The idea, explicitly, is that one should "straighten oneself." *Shu* here has assumed the meaning I had assigned to *zhong*. If Zhang Zai too was thinking this way, then both of his paired formulations are about *shu*, which has two aspects: self-discipline and benevolence; and *zhong* therefore would have to be something else.

And this is just the way that Cheng Yi and Zhu Xi think about it. Where Zengzi in *Analects* 4:15 identifies *zhong* and *shu* as Confucius's "one thread," Zhu has a long comment, with multiple definitions:

> Fully realizing the self is called *zhong*; extending the self (*tuī jǐ* 推己) is called *shu*. . . . Hence, someone has said that inner disposition (*zhōng xīn* 中心) is *zhōng* 忠; congruent disposition (*rú xīn* 如心) is *shù* 恕.

Some translators have tried to get Zhu's definition of *zhong* here to imply that *zhong*, like *shu*, is an aspect of other-directedness, by rendering the word as "conscientiousness to others."[24] But it seems to be for Zhu just a total conscientiousness, an "inner" (*zhōng* 中) perfection of self (rather than—as I might have suggested—a disposition [*xin*] to stay on target, or in the middle [*zhōng* 中] of the moral Way). The idea of other-directedness ("extending the self") upward or downward, is all in *shu* (concern [*xin*] for "likeness" [*ru*]), which suggests the universality of morals. (I might have suggested in contrast, the etymology, concern for the other person's being after all like (*ru*) oneself, and so appropriately regarded with sympathy.)[25]

So far, it remains unclear how *zhong* and *shu* are connected for Zhu. He continues, quoting "Master Cheng" (presumably Cheng Yi):

> *Zhong* is the Way of Heaven; *shu* is the Way of humans. *Zhong* means absence of error; *shu* is how we put *zhong* into practice. *Zhong* is *tǐ* 體 (substance); *shu* is *yòng* 用 (function).[26] The one is the great root; the other is the realized Way.

Neo-Confucian metaphysics has taken over: *shu* is outer manifestation in behavior of *zhong* as inner reality.

The ideal is the fully cultivated moral person who always does the right, effortlessly, because it is what he or she naturally wants; and the word *rén* (仁 "benevolence," but now perhaps perfect moral goodness) is used of this. But *ren*, Confucius had implied (*Analects* 6:30) is the end result of the practice of *shu* (qua "method" of getting *ren*). If so, *shu* must be something requiring effort, a self-disciplining *encratic* virtue.[27]

This is just what Zhu is led to say when he comments on the two formulations of the Confucian golden rule with which I began, at *Analects* 5:12 and 15:24. These are different in a way I did not develop, and it is a difference that would have to disturb a man like Zhu Xi, pious exegete within the tradition. In book 15 Zigong requests instruction and Confucius gives him the rule. In book 5 Zigong offers unasked a formulation of the rule as a description of his own moral attitude, and Confucius says, "You haven't attained to that yet." I see this as two different stages in the articulation, at different times, of an evolving concept, and the historically earlier one an instance of Confucius gently and humorously pricking a bubble of self-importance in a disciple he is obviously fond of.

Zhu couldn't be expected to see it this way: The text is a *Classic*, the *ipsissima verba* of the Master; and the Master is the Master: it is unthinkable that he could be less than serious, even instructively so. So there must be a difference between the two formulations. Zhu finds it in an ingenious bit of linguistic analysis. First, 15:24:

> Confucius tells him the method of seeking *ren*. If we extend this to the extreme, then even a sage's selflessness (*wú wǒ* 無我) does not go beyond this.

This implies that *shu*, short of "the extreme," itself falls short of true sage-like selflessness; and so it requires of us effort against inner resistance. Now 5:12:

> Master Cheng says, ". . . *shu* was something that Zigong perhaps was capable of with effort, but *ren* was something he had not attained to." As I [Zhu Xi] see it, the word *wú* 無[28] implies that it is naturally so. But the word *wù* 勿[29] has the meaning of forbidding. This is the distinction between *ren* and *shu*.

Zhu Xi's analytical point is that in *Analects* 5:12, Zigong's *wú* 無 is *descriptive* of his *disposition* (as Zigong claims): "I desire (*wú* 無 that *there shall not be any* =) not to be [doing it to others]"; whereas in *Analects* 15:24 (and 12:2) Confucius formulates a *prescriptive rule*: (*wù* 勿 =) *do not* [do it to others]." Thus, where Confucius in 12:2 had been represented as offering the golden rule as part of an explication of *ren*, Zhu sees a crucial difference: the golden rule *shu* is a *rule* for *getting to ren*; in *shu*, we are still at the stage of *making* ourselves do the right thing, to which we are not yet completely inclined.

The point is restated by the Ming Dynasty philosopher Wáng Yángmíng 王陽明, in a letter in 1511 to a disciple:

> [N]ow, [the words] "[other people] doing something to me" refer to what I do not desire; and [the words] "not doing it to other people" [in *Analects* 5:12] refer to what I do desire. [The latter] comes from what the heart desires, "just as it is naturally," without any forcing. [On the other hand, the words] "one must not do it to others" [*Analects* 15:24] refer to what one can do only if one tries. This is "the distinction between *ren* and *shu*." (1933, sec. 4, p. 53)

The quotations in this text that I have not identified are from Zhu Xi's commentary; and Zhu there (as I have shown) made his point by analyzing two negatives. Does this mean that the negative statement of the Chinese golden rule is, after all, important? Not yet: for the distinction between a virtue that requires effort (is *encratic*) and one that is effortless (*sophrosynic*) could have been made anyway, in either a positive or negative formulation.

This is not the end of the story. But in continuing, I must admit that I cannot be as precise as I have been, and perhaps what I have to say should be thought of as a program for investigation only. In Song and Ming Dynasty philosophy, among certain moralists, the moral ideal of "benevolence" (*ren*) has an aspect not yet brought out; and yet it has firm Classical roots. The Song philosopher Chéng Hào 程顥 (Cheng Yi's elder brother) points out a common *medical* use of the term "*ren*": one says that a finger is "*bù rén* 不仁" if it is numb. Just so, one may be said to be "not *ren*" if one is morally "unfeeling," insensitive to the feelings and sufferings of others. In reverse this implies that "others," for the benevolent or sensitive (*ren*) person, are thought of as extensions of oneself; instead of "no self" (*wu wo*) the ideal moral attitude is "pan-self."[30] In Wang Yangming, this is expressed in the idea that for the perfect moral person "all things are one body." In Wang's more excited moments, "all things" include even the inanimate and nonliving. One who is truly good winces even when seeing a tile broken.[31]

The result is a sympathetic identification with others that leads one to see others fully as individuals, in their own situations and with their own viewpoints, and to draw back from rigid application of ready-made concepts and judgments. The result is a blossoming of the "consideration" and rule-soften-ing aspects of the *zhong-shu* idea. Following are some examples, of quite diverse kinds.

Jīn Shèngtàn 金聖歎 was a literary critic of the mid-seventeenth century who wrote a famous critique and revision of the classic Chinese novel, *The Water Margin*.[32] In the course of his work Jin turns his attention to the question, how is it that the characters in a novel, if it is a good one, are so lifelike and individualized—even though some or all are admittedly fictional, and even though the whole account is the product of a single man's mind. Jin concludes that this is so because the author is capable of *shu*, putting himself in the place, imaginatively, of even an imaginary character, doing this so successfully that the character takes on a life of its own. *Shu* as a critical-methodological concept comes to refer to a sensitivity that enables the author to feel one's character as unique, as this individual in this situation, different from all others.

Zhāng Xuéchéng 章學誠 (1738–1801) was a historian and a literary man, and was a very intelligent person who thought carefully about history and literature, and so was also a philosopher.[33] He is known now chiefly for his philosophical essays and letters. In 1796 Zhang wrote a short essay he called "Wén dé" 文德 (which means literally "literary virtues"). In it he argues that a writer who like himself is also a critic of others' writings must be careful about two things in particular:

(1) One's literary output may flow freely from one's hand, perhaps one knows not how. One should respect this source of creativity in oneself and not block it; but at the same time one should remember that one has a duty of self-criticism, and must not let go of what one produces until one has done one's best to determine that it is genuine and of high quality. Zhang calls this "literary virtue" *jìng* 敬, self-respect.

(2) When one is engaged in writing that could involve passing judgment on what other writers have written in the past—Zhang's examples are all of earlier historians, but his point is a general one—one should not make hasty or biased judgments (perhaps one shouldn't make judgments at all), but should carefully try to see what the writer's situation and constraints were. One should "put oneself in the other's place" imaginatively; and this will probably lead one to withhold judgment, or at least to be deeply sympathetic toward someone who has written something one would not have written oneself. This attitude is the other of Zhang's two "literary virtues," and needless to say he calls it *shu*, consideration.

This second idea runs deep in his thinking. I cite only one other of many forms of it. In 1797 Zhang wrote a long letter to another scholar named Sūn Xīngyǎn 孫星衍; it contained some rather blunt criticisms of what he took to be defects in Sun's scholarship, one of which was Sun's tendency to unrestrainedly sharp criticism of certain other writers. Zhang counsels Sun to stop it, and writes, "Remember that a century from now you and I too will be 'people of old'—so just put yourself in their place."

We already sense that Zhang may have felt the importance of *shu* as "literary virtue" because he himself had need of it. An older acquaintance who was the object of some of his stiffest criticism (as well as warm praise) was the classical scholar and moral philosopher Dài Zhèn 戴震 (1724–1777).

Dai as philosopher was one of those who spends his life rewriting the same book.[34] The final version (1777)—the longest and clearest—was his *Mèngzǐ zìyì shūzhèng* 孟子字義疏證, *An Explication of the Meaning of Terms in the Mengzi*. I will try to distill an extended argument near the beginning of it.

Dai sets himself to refute Zhu Xi's version of Confucian moral philosophy, or what he sees as the central ideas of Zhu. Zhu's basic mistake was to divide us in two, making us consist of a morality-tending "good" nature versus a set of animal appetites and passions pushing us into evil. This duality leads Zhu to suppose that our "good" nature "is a quasi-thing implanted in our heart-mind by Heaven," this "thing" being a representation of or direct insight into eternal moral truths. On the contrary, if we take this view of ourselves, Dai thinks, we are in danger of mistaking our arbitrary subjective (quite possibly emotional and selfish) judgments for true moral "principles" (*lǐ* 理).

The correct view is to see that our appetitive and passionate nature is not bad; on the contrary if we didn't have it we would be unable to appreciate values, including moral values, at all, or to appreciate what others value. The problem is to distinguish between those of our judgments of value that are purely subjective and those that are not. At this point Dai turns to Mencius. Mencius had argued (*Mengzi* 6A7) that we all tend to appreciate similar flavors, sounds, and sights, using our mouths, ears, and eyes; and that it is reasonable to suppose that our minds work the same way: that we all have the same moral "taste" for "good order and rightness" (*lǐ yì* 理義). Therefore, Dai suggests, genuine moral "principles" must be just those among what appear to us to be "principles" that not just our own but all minds are inclined to assent to. To sort out and discard our merely subjective and selfish judgments, so that what is left will be genuine moral "principles"—that is, what Dai calls the morally "necessary" (*bìrán* 必然)—we must apply Confucius's method of *shu*, asking, if I were X or Y or Z, would I then also accept this judgment?

Notice that for Dai *shu* is not a virtue but a method of thinking. Dai tends to think we will be virtuous if we can just think clearly—so far is he from Zhu Xi's assumption that we need stern self-discipline, Zhu's view being, of course, that we are always in danger of being subverted by the "selfish desires" of our material nature. Also notice that this method is in effect a sieve: it eliminates impostor "principles." The whole thrust of Dai's thinking is to see to it that persons with power and influence, who are in a position to hurt the rest of us, cannot invest their mere "subjective opinions" (*yìjiàn* 意見) with the sanctity of being genuine "principles" (*lǐ*).

Both Dai and Zhang, then, in quite different ways, use the *shu* idea not to determine what we should do, what critical judgments we should make, or what principles we should accept, but rather what ones we should not. Perhaps, then, it *is* significant that the Confucian golden rule is usually stated negatively.

5.6 Concluding Reflections

Let me summarize what I think I have been doing.

Probably all human societies have, at least at the level of folk wisdom, formulated the idea that one's actions affecting another ought to be reversible — that the act ought to be one that it would be right for the other person to do if your positions were exchanged.

In ancient China this idea has a dual formulation:

(1) What I do *to* you, if I am in a *superior* position, should be what I would find it acceptable for you to do to me, if our positions were reversed. I should be kind, lenient, considerate; if I am following a rule of action that would lead me to hurt you, I should relax the rule if possible. This I identified as *shu*.

(2) What I do *for* you, if I am in an *inferior* position, should be what I would expect you to do for me, if our positions were reversed. I should be "loyal," and so should be strict with myself even when what I am doing might hurt me, observing rules to the best of my ability. This I identified as *zhong*.

In the intellectual history of later China, I allowed myself to suggest, these two aspects of reversibility are emphasized in turn: the self-disciplinary aspect in the Confucian moralists of the Song, who take even *shu* as something one must make oneself do; and the leniency aspect in moralists such as Wang Yangming and early Qing Dynasty thinkers.

I was able to point to examples, and they do have to be noticed. But the actual picture of later intellectual history is much more complex than this.[35] There was great variety in thought; and the disciplinary accent in Confucian morality was in the Ming and Qing Dynasties vigorously promoted not only as state orthodoxy, but also by many moralists who avoided any identification with that orthodoxy. One cannot derive a really workable schema for actual history through an exercise in philosophical analysis.

Nor am I confident that I have the analysis right. Consider, for example, a famous line from one of the late Zhou Dynasty Confucians:

> All things are already in me. There is no greater joy than to look into oneself and find that one is complete (*chéng* 誠). There is no quicker way to seek to attain benevolence than to try hard to be considerate (*shu*).[36]

This seems to conjoin the idea of self-identification with everything—in which I had seen spontaneous "consideration" in its farthest reach—with an explicit statement of just that *encratic* concept of *shu* that I found in Zhu Xi; and the speaker here is none other than Mencius. Gentleness in dealing with others, Mencius appears to suggest, may well require firmness in dealing with ourselves, at least for a while.

We can imaginatively question other nuances of *zhong* and *shu* as I have painted them. Why, for example, couldn't there be *shu*—"consideration"— toward superiors? Might not my being dutifully filial in my behavior and demeanor toward my father flow from my schooling myself in sympathy— reflecting how hurt and disappointed I would be if my own son were unfilial toward me? (Rather than saying to myself, "I would insist on my son's doing thus and so, so it's only fair that I do likewise.")

Or take the aspect of *zhong*, "loyalty," that requires one if necessary to criti- cize a superior courageously and forthrightly: Rather than saying to myself (as I enter the dean's office), "I see it's my duty to speak plainly, and I would condemn anyone else in my position who didn't do so; so speak plainly I must"—instead I might say, "I know it's going to embarrass the dean unless I'm tactful." This is not far from the point made in a story in the *Zuǒ zhuàn* 左 傳 under the date 550 B.C., of a certain Zāng Wǔzhòng 藏武仲, who has an interview with the Duke of Qí 齊公 and is blunt with him about his recent dealings with the state of Jìn 晉, actually saying to the Duke that he had be- haved like a rat.[37] A comment attributed to Confucius is quoted: Zang, "in acting for others, was not accommodating (*shùn* 順), and in dealing with others was not considerate (*shu*)." Confucius concludes with the admonition, "Be accommodating in serving others and considerate in dealing with others."[38]

Likewise, one can exercise one's wits thinking of cases in which one is prompted to "consideration" (*shu*), in the deviant sense of doing one's duty, for someone beneath oneself in status: Instead of being moved by a lively imaginative sympathy for the weaker position of the other, there might be cases where one would sternly address oneself to one's duty, if duty it were, reflecting that one would condemn anyone in one's place if that person be- haved callously toward the other. The large literature of moral tales probably does illustrate all of these delicately shaded situations. It is one thing, how- ever, to find sensitivity to such distinctions in the practice of the storyteller, and quite another to find the distinctions abstracted and talked about by the moralist.[39] As far as I have discovered, the way the moralist talks about *zhong* and *shu* is as I have described it.

There seems to me to be another aspect of the *shu* concept, however, that I have not yet brought out, and that my attention is drawn to when I notice what I have been led to say about it in examining the Chinese data, and then compare this with things that are said about the golden rule by certain con- temporary philosophers.

I turn again to Alan Donagan. He invites us to consider "a characteristic of the Golden Rule which not only exposes its inadequacy as a first principle but also explains its ubiquity":

> For it is ubiquitous. The earliest known version of it . . . is credited to Confucius; and others appear in all the major religions. It is a proverb in many languages. Nor does the evidence suggest that it was diffused from a single source. The explanation is simple. What a man would or would not have another do to him is in part a function of the mores he has made his own. Hence in cultures whose mores differ radically, what the Golden Rule is taken to *require or forbid* will differ radically too. And so any system of conduct that can be put forward as rational can include it. (1977, 58, emphasis added)

Obviously I must be at ease with the view that the golden rule—if Confucian versions are examples of it—cannot be the first principle of morality as such. What set me to thinking anew here was the suggestion that in any local morality that includes it, the golden rule "is taken to require or forbid" things. As I had interpreted the *shu* half of the Confucian concept—which is after all what one quotes as Confucius's "golden rule"—it is not really a "rule" at all, but a maxim to guide one in shaping and cultivating a character of ideal human kindliness in oneself. That is, it describes a *virtue* in persons rather than a quality of correctness in *acts*.

And as for the acts that one aspiring to such perfection does, they are on my analysis as likely as not to be acts that go beyond what moral rules ordinarily require.[40] But if this is so, then to be guided by the *shu* maxim is not simply to affirm the universality of the mores one has made one's own. What is *shu*, then?

What it is is perhaps indicated by a way of talking that we find already in Confucius that might seem to validate Donagan's observation: the linking of *shu* with observing *li* 禮, "ritual," in one's conduct. *Li*, for Confucius, did include to a large extent doing things it would be wrong not to do. But it included a great deal more. And even to the extent that it was right-doing, one could do the right without observing *li*. It is one's plain obligation to provide the means of life and reasonable comfort for an aged and dependent parent. But one does not satisfy "ritual" (or filial piety) by merely doing that. It would be wrong for me deliberately to bump into you when I pass. But I am not showing politeness (*li*) and consideration (*shu*) just by avoiding doing that. And there are all sorts of things we do, in common politeness—extending the hand in greeting, for example—that it would not be wrong not to do. This is in large part the sort of thing Confucian *li* is, although the word is a religious term become metaphor, retaining something of its religious flavor.

Here I am grateful to Herbert Fingarette for his insights in his book *Confucius—The Secular as Sacred* (1972); but I want to stress one aspect of his idea. *Li* involves countless gestures and acts that, whether required or simply available to me, serve as signals to you and invite response from you in such a way as to reassure both of us that you and I are "we"; and of course it serves this function most effectively when these acts are expected and "traditional." As such it is premoral, indeed perhaps prehuman. (The grooming behavior of chimpanzees leaps to mind; though perhaps partly instinctive, this is the function it seems to serve.) This is what Zǐxià 子夏 was talking about (in *Analects* 12:5) when he consoled Sīmǎ Niú 司馬牛, who lamented that he had no living brothers. The noble person, said Zixia, acts according to *li*, with the appropriate attitude of respect for others, and finds that "all within the four seas are one's brothers."

Shu, I want to suggest, was the articulation of the ideal attitude that should be expressed in this kind of behavior. If we can learn from this something about the golden rule in other forms and places, perhaps we should say that the golden rule is not an affirmation of one's particular mores, nor the "summary of the law," nor "the whole of the law and the prophets"; neither is it the basic "principle" of morality.

It is something more basic than this: It is the very ground of community, without which no morality could develop at all: it is the attitude that the other person is not just a physical object, or a (possibly hostile) animal, that I might use or manipulate, and that might shove back or bite, but a person like myself, whom I should treat accordingly even in trivial ways, thereby reassuring both that person and myself of our common humanity.

That stirring thought closes what I have to say. But I have left out much more than I have covered, of course. I mentioned the Chinese philosophers Mozi and Mencius only in passing, for example, and that is not pardonable. I said little more about Kant, and that is an outrage. Nor, if I had seriously attended to fine points, could I have gotten away with the meager analyses I have offered. If we count the so-called "law of love" as one paradigm, i.e., "Love thy neighbor as thyself," we would want to ask which of the many senses of "love" is understood—the Chinese themselves have several "love" words—and who counts as my "neighbor"—a problem that has particularly worried Jewish moral philosophers.

The fact is that when I picked my subject for tonight's lecture, I thought merely that some simple ideas I had that I had been sharing with my students for a dozen years, and that no one else seemed to have thought of, might be worked up into something appropriate for the three departments—Asian Languages, Philosophy, and Religious Studies—that have claims on me. The subject has opened up into something far larger, and far more interesting to me, than I had imagined, and I expect that I am not done with it.

Part II
Ancient Philosophy

Weakness of Will in Ancient Chinese Philosophy[1]

I shall begin, as nearly as I can, at the beginning.

Some time ago I set about to gain some knowledge of the earliest examples of Chinese writing. These are (as far as we now know) inscriptions on pieces of bovid shoulder blades and turtle shells that record communications between the Chinese king and gods, nature spirits, and deceased royal ancestors.[2] One inscription that I found, possibly dating from about 1200 B.C., reads as follows, as I interpret it:

> 甲午卜王貞我有德于大乙
> 酒翌乙未
> Oracle on the day *jiǎwǔ*, the king officiating: "We have gained favor with royal ancestor Tài Yǐ. Let there be a *you*-sacrifice on the next *yǐwèi* day."[3]

Not much, perhaps. But what kind of favor is the king talking about? His language and ideas can be recognized in writings of seven or eight centuries later; and if we can from this later usage infer the king's meaning, he is saying this: in my actions or offerings I have done something that greatly pleases my ancestor, and he now feels for me a debt of gratitude. "Favor" here is "gratitude"—the kind of hold that in the Chinese social "way" one comes to have on another when one gives another something, shows another special courtesy, or renders another some service, creating in that person thereby a psychic compulsion to respond later in the same way.[4]

The word the king uses I identify as the word *dé* 德, which in somewhat later material we would have to translate as "royal virtue."[5] The inscription appears to show how that very important concept has its beginning. In the religious-political ideology of the beginning of the Zhou Dynasty—1040 B.C.— the king's occupation of his role as king is justified by his having this quality, which by this time has come to be a psychic power with both moral and supernatural aspects.[6] Having it, he attracts the favorable attention of Heaven and the spirits. His having it shows itself in the harmony and well-being of the world under his rule, and the approval of those around him. If he lacks it—? I leave this to your imagination. But there is a danger that he will lose it, through immoral conduct, or that he does not have enough of it and should strengthen it through being a better person. So the king needs wise advisors who can guide him so that he can grow in virtue—and now we have the word in close to its ordinary sense for us.

Royal virtue itself supplies the need. Having it, among other things, has this effect: wise and good people throughout the world will want to come to the king's court and serve him. And the king, having "virtue," will be able to and eager to recognize them, distinguish them at once from selfish flatterers, and respectfully listen to their advice. And if a king lacks virtue? Again, I leave this to your imagination.

But now there is a problem, and it is this: it seems that a king who is able to enjoy and heed the instruction of the wise and good is the king who already has virtue, and so already has what they could give him. While the king who lacks virtue—not the knowledge of his role and its obligations, for that is public knowledge, but the inner quality and disposition that would make him a good king in that role—such a king finds that the wise and good have given up on him and are hiding in the hills; furthermore, he doesn't care. If a good person *were* to come to his court and try to reform him he would not listen to that person, would be offended, or even worse. Such is the king who lacks virtue. Yet *he* is just the one who needs the instruction a teacher could offer. This problem is so important that it deserves a name. I propose that we call it "the paradox of virtue."

Just as the concept of the good king is the model for the concept of a good person in later Chinese moral philosophy, so the concept of the moral instruction of a king is at least in important measure the model of later conceptions of the role of a teacher in moral education. We now see that at the core of that concept there is a paradox: the most important thing—perhaps the only important thing—that moral teachers can teach their students is to *want* to be moral. For, especially in a society in which concrete obligations, e.g., of filial piety, are role-defined and clear even if sometimes complex, *wanting* to be moral—being disposed or being sufficiently disposed to perform the role that you and everyone else knows you should perform—is the essential part of *being* moral. But if the teacher is to teach this disposition, to impart it, the student must already be disposed to accept the instruction, and so, apparently, must already have it. The problem is structured like Socrates' paradox of learning in the *Meno* (to be taught, one must recognize the thing taught as something to be learned, and this requires that in some sense one already know it); but in the Chinese moral education form it is far more convincingly and distressingly real.[7]

6.1 Confucius

Confucius puts his finger deftly on the problem when he says, "Is Goodness indeed so far away? If we really wanted Goodness, we should find that it was at our very side."[8] I shall not stay to argue with those who wish to say that Confucius was a sage. Anyone who thinks he was able to deal with all moral questions he faced has not read him with open eyes. The problem I am now pointing to baffled him from beginning to end. The problem arises not just with those who know what they should do but are cold to this "ought," but also with those who are warmed, but not, apparently, warmed enough. Confucius may have just assumed that if I *know* I ought to do a thing I am in *some* degree moved to do it; and this makes my failure all the more culpable and exasperating:

> The words of the *Model Sayings* cannot fail to stir us. But what matters it that they should change us. . . . For those who approve but do not carry out, who are stirred but do not change, I can do nothing at all.[9]

We can, I think, see two problems which may for Confucius have been essentially the same. There are the people who know what they should *do* and do something else. They know what their roles are, but they do not live up to them; or perhaps they have made a promise they don't keep. (Western philosophers refer to this as the problem of *akrasia* or "weakness of will." I discuss this more below.) And there are those who perform as they should—for example, a mourning rite—but don't have the feeling or disposition that should go with it ("the forms of mourning observed without grief . . ").[10] Confucius seems to see both as pretending. Guǎn Zhòng 管仲 let us keep on thinking he knew the rites. Yet he used a cup-mound, and only the ruler of a state may do that.[11] Those who fail to act could do what they fail to do if they just would:

> Just as to sacrifice to ancestors other than one's own is presumptuous, so to see what is right and not do it is cowardice.[12]

But so, also, with the person who fails to feel. When Confucius says, "People who are not Good—what can they have to do with ritual?"[13] or "ritual performed without reverence, the forms of mourning observed without grief— these are things I cannot bear to see!"[14] he is exhorting, not just scorning. If so, perhaps he assumes that our feelings as well as our actions are under the control of our will, and this is a view that I think most Chinese moral philosophers have had.

This helps, perhaps, to provide a kind of entree into the paradox problem. Common sense will say, surely I might *want* to be a better person than I am. Wanting *this*, I am already to some extent good, and so am disposed to accept the help of a teacher, who will make me still better, or guide me in making myself better. So sometimes there *is* something for a moral teacher to do. There is, but only if I can, in the last analysis, accept direction (perhaps from myself) and carry out a resolve to change my dispositions, for example to strengthen my enthusiasm another notch for the good, and to deepen, make a bit more sincere, my feeling of respect when I bow—even if many years and subtle self-management are needed. Here we have the concept of *self-cultivation*, the guiding Chinese concept of moral learning. So Confucius says of himself that "at fifteen I set my heart upon learning [to be a good person] . . ." and after a series of stages "at seventy I followed my heart's desires without overstepping the boundaries [of right]."[15]

But what if, halfway, I just stop, or begin to drag my feet? What is my teacher to do with me? Confucius had no solution, in theory or in practice. "Only one who bursts with eagerness do I instruct, only one who bubbles with excitement do I enlighten."[16] A student who stayed abed in the morning provoked a burst of exasperation: "Rotten wood cannot be carved, nor a wall of dried dung be trowelled. What use is there in my scolding him any more?"[17]

The *Analects* of Confucius is finite in length, and this mine has a bottom, but I will not try to plumb it. I do want to look at one more passage:

> Rǎn Qiú 冉求 said, "It is not that I do not delight in your Way (*dào* 道), but my strength is insufficient." The Master said, "One whose strength is insufficient collapses during the course of the journey [lit., the Way], but you deliberately draw the line."[18]

What does *this* say? Not quite what we had before. Here the *teacher's* position (Confucius's) is this:

(i) Perhaps a person just might *not* have the inner dispositional resources needed to go all the way to perfection; perhaps this is not culpable moral weakness. But

(ii) the resources one *does* have one may *choose* to use or not to use, and one *is* responsible for this. *You* have chosen not to.

And the student's position is the same, that is, Ran Qiu makes the same assumptions about the human psyche; he simply insists that he has done his best—one can't after all, simply by sheer strength of will, pick up a mountain.

That image is mine here, but only by theft. I stole it from Mencius (Mèngzǐ 孟子), which is fair enough, for Mencius himself stole it from Mòzǐ 墨子. Study of their use of it will lead us deeper into the problem of moral weakness.

6.2 Mozi and Mencius

In his essay on universal love, Mozi develops most fully his position that we all ought to adopt an attitude of impartial rational altruism, and that to do so would produce a human state of affairs in which all human needs would be optimally satisfied, and dangers (the chiefest being human violence against other humans) minimized.[19] Here and everywhere in the so-called "synoptic chapters," probably the earliest stratum of material in the *Mozi*, Mò Dí 墨翟[20] reveals an assumption about the relationship of thought to action strikingly in contrast to that of Confucius and virtually all Confucians. There is, for him, at this stage of his thought, *no* problem of inner psychic restructuring or nurturing needed to make a person morally perfect. In effect he assumes this: a person is a kind of rational calculator, unless he or she is just *intellectually* mixed up. The good is the will of Heaven. But Heaven desires the well-being of humankind. Therefore the good is the prudent. Right action is the most reasonable action for people to take, in their own interests, and they will always see this clearly if you can lead them through a properly constructed argument.

Mozi is obviously aware that it would be impractical for the political reformer to use this approach on all human beings. If rulers can be persuaded, they have their means of simplifying the decision problem of the masses by instituting a suitable structure of constraints and inducements, and this is what is proposed in the chapter on authority, "Identifying with the Superior": at each level of political organization, starting with the lowest, the officers in charge are to order those below them to adopt the standard of right, the *yì* 義, of the next higher authority.[21] But in neither context, that of persuasion *simpliciter* or of structured "persuasion," is there any sense in Mo that there is anything more complex or subtle inside people than an ability to think out, or follow your thinking out, where their interests lie. There is no virtue or moral sense to be got hold of or developed, no motivation to be utilized other than the desire to optimize material satisfaction.

Nonetheless—and this is what is almost bizarre in Mozi—persuasion is directed toward altering more than just overt behavior. Mozi appeared to think that if you can get people to follow an argument implying that it would be in their rational interest for them to have certain affections (and beliefs, for that matter), then they will conclude that they should have those affections, and can at that point if they will (and they are simply perverse if they don't) proceed to adopt them, just as one might decide, on persuasion, to move one's limbs or adopt a certain physical posture.

Here we will find a comparison instructive. Mencius teaches King Xuān of Qí 齊宣王 the distinction between just not doing something and not being able to do it (1A7.11). The latter is exemplified by the impossible task of taking Mt. Tai under one's arm and jumping over the North Sea, the former by the quite possible task of ruling with kindness. The figure Mencius uses comes from Mozi's discussion of universal love.[22] Is universal love just impossible, like "carrying Mt. Tai and leaping over rivers"? Hardly. But Mencius carefully shows the king that he really has in himself all the time the disposition needed to be really kind. Mozi merely counters, "you *can* practice universal love. The six Sage Kings did it." For him, all you have to do is make up your mind to *do* it, and there's no further problem.

But what about this "making up the mind to do it"? Could there be a failure here? That is, when I, by some argument, show you that you *should* and *can* do a thing, that you *should* act and *can* adopt (as perhaps in Mozi) or *can utilize* (as in Mencius) the dispositions needed to power the act, is it automatic that you will do so? I think the answer for both Mo and Meng is, No. Mozi seems clearly to envisage the possibility of sheer perversity intervening—somehow—to prevent argument from having its desired effect, at least when he is directing his attention not to the mass of people but to thinking persons. We find as a refrain in the "universal love" essay, after each developed argument, the words: "I cannot understand how the worthies of the world can hear about universality and still criticize it! And yet there is no end to the words of the worthies of the world criticizing universality."[23] And Mo's arguments grind on.

And of course in Mencius's very distinguishing between not being able to do something (in the sense of one's strength being insufficient, in Ran Qiu's words) on the one hand, and on the other hand just not doing it, Mencius implies that it is possible that one will just not use one's resources. One may in the end just refuse to lift the feather, just close one's eyes to the wagon-load of firewood, just balk at massaging the old man's joints (1A7.10-11).[24]

I suggest that Confucius, Mozi, and Mencius are in one way all heading in the same direction. All seem to assume that various sorts of things one could do—pursue the Way, practice universal love, govern benevolently—require appropriate dispositions, and that one can simply choose to use (effectively have) these dispositions or not. So, if we think of these dispositions as part of ourselves, we must also think of there being in the self, so to speak, a sort of control tower that can activate them, perhaps as one might flip a switch—a core of the self that is radically free to choose. Mencius is the first philosopher who begins to think carefully about this, though he does not have a lot to say about it; and along with this increase in sophistication there is another one. Confucius's problem, about how to get at the unmotivated student, which he never solved, led among his immediate disciples (as is well known) to active speculation about human nature (*xìng* 性) and whether it has any built-in moral direction. In taking the position that human nature is "good," i.e., that in various specific ways we are predisposed to accept the rules and ideals of received morality, Mencius is inheriting this interest and in a way solving Confucius's problem.

In theory, the teacher now does have a possibility of getting at the unmotivated student, perhaps through a kind of moral psychoanalysis such as Mencius applies to King Xuan that brings the student to an awareness of his or her real nature. (Mencius is doing more in taking this position, of course. For example, he is also defending Confucianism against the attack of Daoist-like philosophers who argue that morality painfully distorts human nature.) Perhaps, then, one might say that the Mencian theory of human nature functions within

Confucian moral theory like Plato's theory of recollection in Platonic episte-mology.

But in thinking further about how the whole human moral personality works, Mencius begins to expose another problem. The four innate moral "sprouts" (*duān* 端) or "minds" (dispositions, *xīn* 心) are things we "have" like our "four limbs." This says more than that they are in and of us. It reiter-ates dramatically the idea that just as I can choose, for example, to lift my arm, so I can choose to activate (or cultivate), for example, my disposition to *lǐ* 禮 (ritual activity). This, of course, is from 2A6. In book 6A Mencius is more explicit about this inner mental autonomy. We note there that the mind is a kind of inner-directed sense: Mencius says he likes fish, bears' paws, and "righ-teousness" (*yì* 義, 6A10). And *yi*, he repeatedly says, is "inside us." And in 6A7 he says, just as flavors are the objects of the sense of taste, sounds of the sense of hearing, and beauty of the sense of sight, so "good order and rightness" (*lǐ yì* 理義) are the objects of the mind. But Mencius notices a sharp distinction between the ordinary physical senses and the mind (heart). The former (6A15) we see are directed toward *outside* objects, the latter toward *inside* objects. Mencius further thinks that the outer-directed senses are automatic and gov-erned by necessity in their operation, while the inner-directed sense (the mind) is free and autonomous:

> It is not the function of the ears and eyes to think (*sī* 思), and they are obscured (*bì* 蔽) by [external] things. When one thing interacts with another,[25] as a matter of course it leads it away. The function of the heart is to think. If it thinks then it will get it.[26] If it does not think, then it will not get it. (6A15)

The picture could be reinforced by other passages, but this should be enough to show that Mencius makes *these* assumptions: we naturally have a liking for and an impulse to seek certain things—the beautiful, the delicious, etc., and also the good and right. We will automatically seek objects of the former, physi-cal kind if they are within reach, unless we *choose* not to (if we see that to do so would be wrong). But our natural "pro-attitude" toward the good and right in no way guarantees that we will seek them.[27] We will not unless we focus our thought on them and seek them voluntarily, performing this inner act of thought, so to speak, as we would perform any other voluntary act.

Mencius, like Confucius, of course wants it to be the case that we will always choose the good and right when we recognize it, and that we will al-ways recognize it. This, as in Confucius, requires a life of self-cultivation, con-ceived by Mencius as one in which we recognize and "nourish" the beginnings of moral impulse in ourselves as we might nourish and cultivate a plant. But in the light of Mencius's analysis of mind and sense as such, it would seem that the moral acting of perfected individuals remains act, and does not become reflex. They do it freely, not automatically, and remain moral *agents*.

6.3 Xunzi

I will return to Mencius, but any account of ancient Chinese approaches to moral weakness would be truncated without at least a review of Xúnzǐ 荀子, for in him we find the most articulate analysis of the whole problem, though not the most influential.[28] I believe that Xunzi saw his scheme of mind and choice as solving problems he recognized in both Mozi and Mencius. Mencius is in the position of needing to explain why, if we all have the ability to become sages, most of us don't. Xunzi tries to handle this in two different ways, first by giving a different account of human moral directedness, locating it not in our innate dispositions, which he provocatively calls "evil," but in our capacity for intelligent choice; and further by introducing a distinction, that I and others have trouble with, between two senses of "being able."[29] (These moves we find in his essay on human nature.) Mozi had seen the possibility of a person seeing what is best and yet perversely and inexplicably refusing to accept, favor, or do it; and he seems to have had the view that I can just adopt, by deciding to do so, an affection or belief.

Xunzi rejects both of these possibilities while retaining other important elements in both Mo's and Meng's thinking. He retains Mo's view that humans are, in the last analysis, moved by their wants and a calculation of their own interests. He retains Mencius's assumption that cultivation of the self and education are necessary for living a good and satisfactory life, which must be a social life. And he retains essentially Mencius's view of the relation of mind to sense: the senses' seeking of their objects is automatic and will go forward unless the faculty of intelligent decision in us brings it to a stop or slows or redirects it. The intelligence is free to do this or not, but it always will choose the best deal for the senses, all things considered, if it succeeds in considering all things. For Xunzi the *dao*—it's a Confucian *dao*—is a moral life, that is, a life lived in society accepting social rules, norms, and restraints, and with one's appetites given their due but kept under control.

Such a life and only such a life gives the optimum satisfaction of human desire, and one who has thought this out clearly—who knows how to do arithmetic, as Xunzi puts it—will see this.[30] When one sees it, one's decision and course of action can be counted on. Xun says:

> Now in general people never fail to follow a course they approve and to reject what they disapprove. There has never been anyone who has failed to follow the Way when understanding that there is nothing to compare to it.[31]

Here at last the problem of weakness of will is brought fully into view, and the possibility of it explicitly rejected. But there is more to this, Xunzi says, than a person's simply deciding simpliciter that the life of the *dao* is best. If prudent and intelligent one will see that one must be conditioned and changed in education before one can live that life, and will submit oneself to the necessary conditioning.

So for Xunzi, in the end, the good is good because it is satisfying, and we are predisposed to seek satisfaction; whereas for Mencius, the good is satisfying because it is good, and we are predisposed to like the good. But for both, completed cultivation is total commitment to the good, so that one is willing to die for it. Does this make nonsense of Xunzi, whose ethic is grounded in individual satisfaction? Note that for Mencius, the satisfaction I derive from the good does *not* constitute the value of the good. For Xunzi, however, in a different sense, it does. So Xunzi's *cultivated person* has apparently acquired an affection for the good, for its own sake, inconsistent with the view of Xunzi's *enlightened philosopher*, who values it for what he or she sees it will do (namely, provide a satisfying life). The paradox is perhaps resolved by the fact that philosophers, understanding that the good is in fact the "best" for them and all people, thereby give themselves reason to love it.

6.4 Models of Mind and Desire

I return now to this model of mind and sense which I think both Mencius and Xunzi share. The mind is free, the senses are bound. Our responding to objects of sensual desire is automatic unless stopped, but our pro-attitude toward something we recognize as morally good does not result in active appropriation of or acting out that good unless we "think" (*si*). "If the mind thinks it will get it," Mencius says (6A15). What does Mencius mean by "think"?[32]

I assume that the meaning must include in some way cognitively focusing attention on the mind's moral object, but it is more than this. We see this in another Mencius text, in 7A3. I need only quote part of it:

"If you seek it you get it; if you neglect it you lose it." In this case seeking is of use in getting, for it is a case of seeking within ourselves.

The similarity of this to the picture of mind in 6A15 is obvious enough, but here instead of *si* 思, "think," we have *qiú* 求, "seek." So Mencius's thinking is a voluntary seeking as well as cognitive focusing on the good.

Many Western philosophers, from earliest times, have been puzzled about how it can happen that I might both (a) see that I ought to do a certain kind of thing, and (b) see that to take a particular option now open to me would be doing that kind of thing, yet (c) not do it, perhaps do the exact opposite. I have a glass of paint in my hand. I know that paint is bad for me to drink, and I know that this is paint, not milk. Nonetheless, down it goes. Could this ever happen? The problem is this. Suppose I do have an urge to drink some paint (just this once). If that urge is stronger than my desire to preserve my health, it seems I will down it. But what then has happened? Apparently my judgment has been overridden by some kind of compulsion, so that *either* (a) we can't say that at the time I drank the paint I really knew that I shouldn't, *or* (b) we just can't say that at the time I drank it I was really free not to. Yet if we shift to a different, but logically similar, kind of example (you may not have this peculiar taste)—perhaps a moral one where I see that I ought, for example, to do something for a friend who has put himself out for me in the past, even though helping him in his need now would be very unpleasant for me—it is easy to imagine oneself failing to do the thing one sees one ought to do. Intuition and introspection tell us these things happen. Intellect tells us they can't. Why?

A reason for this puzzle seems to me to be this.[33] We assume, in setting up such an example, that the attraction for us in doing something because we see it to be right is an attraction of the same kind as the attraction we feel toward doing something that we believe, for example, would give us sensual pleasure. The assimilation goes both ways. We assume that if we actually do the right, it is because our favorable attitude toward it as right has *caused* us to do it; on the other hand, we assume that if we actually do the wrong, it is because in our being more strongly attracted to *it* we, in effect, judged it to be the right-for-us. The first assumption leads many philosophers in accounting for weakness of will to try to drive a wedge between motivation and knowledge of obligation. The second we summarize in the cliché that one must infer others' moral beliefs from their acts, not from their words.

I think indeed that I can find this point of view in Aristotle himself. (I say this with trepidation, because my knowledge of him is meager.) In the first half of book 7 of the *Nicomachean Ethics*, Aristotle tries to account for moral weakness in terms of his analysis of practical reasoning. When we act, we in effect know or believe to be true a universal and a minor premise; these together *imply* that we should do the act, and the knowledge of them together *causes* us to do the act, so that an act is (in a certain sense) the "conclusion" of our practical reasoning:

> One belief (a) is universal; the other (b) is about particulars, and because they are particulars perception controls them. And in the cases where these two beliefs result in (c) one belief, it is necessary in purely theoretical beliefs for the soul to affirm what has been concluded, and in beliefs about production (d) to act at once on what has been concluded.
>
> If, e.g., (a) everything sweet must be tasted, and (b) this, some one particular thing, is sweet, it is necessary (d) for someone who is able and unhindered also to act on this at the same time. (1985, 180–81, 1147a25–31)

In weakness of will what happens is that an unruly desire or appetite lurking in the wings of ourself, so to speak, makes a raid on our syllogism and steals the minor premise to set up a syllogism of its own. The old one implied, "Don't do this." The new one implies, "Do this," and we do it from the same necessity, but in doing it we are in temporary ignorance of the major moral premise, and not really in possession of the minor premise either—we are in effect possessed. We might utter the latter, but only "as the drunk says the words of Empedocles" (181, 1147b10–15). "For," Aristotle concludes, "the knowledge that is present when someone is affected by weakness of will . . . is not the sort that seems to be knowledge to the full extent." (182, 1147b15–20).[34]

Now I've argued that Mencius—and, I think, all his descendents in Confucian moral philosophy, including almost every Chinese philosopher in the past thousand years—just does not make such assumptions. On Mencius's model of mind, I may be attracted to some delicious food but know that eating it would be theft, and wrong. Knowing this, I have a disposition not to eat it (in this case under the description of avoiding thievery). But for that disposition toward the moral to be interposed between sense and object requires an *act* of mind-heart. It is not automatic. Since an act is required, I may fail to perform it in any of the ways in which one may fail to perform an act.

Now this, it seems to me, opens the way for completely different analyses of weakness of will. It would seem that I might know that I ought not to eat the food, and knowing this have a strong moral disposition not to, but still fail to use this disposition to block illicit satisfactions of my appetite because I believe mistakenly that my disposition is not strong enough to block that appetite. On a charitable interpretation this was the situation of Ran Qiu and of King Xuan. On a subtler and not so charitable interpretation, we might suppose that they had deceived themselves into supposing that they lacked sufficient strength of disposition.

Another kind of impasse might be this. I might know *that* refraining is my moral duty and know *that* I have a disposition to refrain, and not *know how* to employ that disposition, so to speak not know how to maneuver it into position between sense desire and object. This may seem implausible, but I think it is just the situation moral students in the course of self-cultivation "efforts" often see themselves to be in. Perhaps in some measure it is advice to this kind of problem Mencius is giving in the Gōngsūn Chǒu 公孫丑 dialogue (2A2.9–16) when he says things like, "hold the will firm but don't do violence to the *qì* 氣," or "you must work at it but not correct it; don't let the mind lose it but don't help it to grow either," etc.—though here Mencius is speaking to the long-term rather than case-by-case problems of inner self-management.[35]

The Mencian language is also suggestive rather than literal, and it has to be. One cannot literally "take hold of" something in the mind-heart. Such a teacher and student are confronted with a problem that seems to me to be like that of the piano teacher and student, the teacher trying to get the student to have his or her hands in proper posture and in complete control of the keys yet relaxed so that he or she can play freely. The student is likely to come to see what is wanted, and yet not be able to do it, and the teacher may say, "imagine all the weight of your arm draining down to your fingers," or "shake your arms like this and try again," or "you're getting cramped, go soak your hands in warm water. Not too long! Not too hot!" Wáng Yángmíng 王陽明 seems to be doing something like this in his letter replying to Oūyáng Dé 歐陽德 in the *Chuán xí lù* 傳習錄. The student pleads that the moral "work" (*shì* 事) of self-monitoring is often utterly exhausting (Chan 1963, 153–55, no. 170).[36] Wouldn't it be all right if when it gets like this he breaks off and meditates? Wang doesn't absolutely forbid this, but advises that the student is thinking about his task of mind-cleaning in the wrong way. He quotes the *Dàxué* 大學: making the thoughts sincere "is like hating a bad odor, like loving a beautiful color."[37] Wang adds, "Have you ever seen a person hating a bad odor or loving a beautiful color rouse himself in order to hold on, or getting completely exhausted when the work is done? . . . From this you can know where the trouble comes from" (Chan (1963, 155, no. 170).

In place of Aristotle's model of moral weakness — essentially, I would suggest that of the drunken rhapsode — in the Mencian tradition we are going to need other, quite different models. One that seems not far off to me is the problem of a muscle cramp. In what Mencius and Wang Yangming call "obscuration" (*bì* 蔽), an otherwise harmless natural desire runs out of control, the mind fixes on it and makes it worse. In the case of the cramp, one can see the muscle shouldn't behave this way, but one does not know how to get it to stop. One can forcibly control it, of course, but this can simply start up a secondary cramp. This situation, too, has its parallel in the danger that the effort of self-cultivation will itself become an obsession.

I cannot begin to explore all the possibilities that the Mencian model of mind opens up for analysis of weakness of will. One, certainly, is Wang Yangming's notion of the kind of inertia that results from students' misconceiving the problem of moral learning in the way they must if they follow Zhū Xī 朱熹 (who, Wang thinks, treats as two separate stages of moral learning (1) learning what the moral norms are, and (2) subjectively appropriating them as one's own). Another, perhaps, will be the problem of writer's block, a crude description of what Hán Yù 韓愈 is talking about in his letter to Lǐ Yì 李翊 — inability to release one's energies in desired creative performance.[38] It is conceivable to me that this kind of situation may in turn be a model for a kind of problem of moral blockage, since, for example, for Wang Yangming every moral situation is in some sense unique and the moral act thus in a sense creative. The theory of pedagogy is yet another area that needs investigation.

As I continue to investigate these problems I mean continually to play the Chinese tradition against the Western. It seems obvious to me that these problems are of central importance in both traditions of moral philosophy, and I suspect that each can throw light on the other.

Motivation and Moral Action in Mencius[1]

In what follows I am going to examine an important cluster of ideas in the fourth-century B.C. philosopher Mencius. I think these ideas probably seemed to him to be one idea; but I believe I can, in different ways, distinguish several non-equivalent things that he is saying. The first few sections of this chapter (7.1 to 7.3) will be descriptive, and partly historical. When the description is done, it may seem (section 7.4) that I have made Mencius out as saying something quite bizarre. I do not think what he says is bizarre, and in section 7.5 of this chapter, I will argue that an important part of what he says is at least plausible, even quite reasonable, and perhaps right. Finally, in section 7.6, I shall compare Mencius, first, to two other Chinese philosophers of the Eastern Zhou Dynasty, and then to several Western philosophers.

The slice of matter in Mencius that I am looking at has not, as far as I know, been examined as a unit before, and important things I find in it have not been noticed by sinologists, even though they have talked a great deal about some of it. There are at least two reasons for this. One is that the cluster of ideas I am after cannot be identified in the usual way, by tracking down the use of some loaded term like "human nature" (*xìng* 性) or "benevolence" (*rén* 仁). The connecting language cues are much more subtle; and in fact Mencius has at least six different ways of saying what chiefly interests me, and uses no one of them very much. The second reason is that what ties this material together and shows it to be a whole is its being Mencius's treatment of a problem that had been vexing moral philosophers for several "generations" of teaching and debate. But students of Chinese philosophy have usually seen their subject as a succession of people who lived, acted, taught, and died, rather than a weaving of strands any one of which may be a subtle dialectic of question and answer.

7.1 "Self-Rejection" as a Form of Action Failure

The problem that concerns me is closely related to two problems (many will prefer to call them one problem) that have agitated Western moral philosophy from Socrates to the present time. Sometimes it seems that I judge I should do something yet cannot or do not control temptations which move me not to. Socrates, Plato, and Aristotle call this *akrasia*. Sometimes it seems that I judge I should do something yet just do not, or perhaps cannot, care enough about it to act. This condition (chiefly analyzed in the tradition of Western religious psychology) is called *acedia*.[2] I agree with Donald Davidson (1982b: 29–30) that we deal here with problems of action, not morality per se; but they arise naturally in discussions of morality—the kind of action that seems to us to matter most—and this has been true in the Chinese philosophical tradition too.[3] I think that *acedia* rather than *akrasia* is the form of this problem that typically concerns Chinese moral philosophers in early times (and that may have an importance).[4]

It is, of course, debatable whether these sorts of what we might neutrally call "action-failure" ever really occur. Perhaps when you want to say I *don't* do what I see I should, I really *can't*, am really psychologically powerless to do so, as R. M. Hare suggests of St. Paul and Medea (1963, 77–79).[5] But now, suppose that *I* am the one who makes this judgment about *myself*; and suppose further that as long as I do make it I *am* immobilized, but if I did not I would not be. This sort of self-fulfilling mistake (perhaps a self-deceptive mistake) in self-analysis is explicitly and frequently recognized by Mencius. Sometimes he colorfully says of those who make such a mistake that they "rob" or "mutilate" themselves (*zì zéi* 自賊, e.g. 2A6). But I shall use, for convenience, a different, less passionate expression he uses. At one point (HY 4A11) he speaks of such people as "rejecting themselves" (*zì qì* 自棄);[6] and I shall hereafter speak of "self-rejection" to refer to this problem, without thereby assuming Mencian optimism about the nature of the self that is rejected.

The problem of self-rejection surfaces first in Confucius (traditionally dated 551–479 B.C.). Here is one of many examples:

> Rǎn Qiú 冉求 said, "It is not that your Way does not commend itself to me, but that it demands powers I do not possess." The Master said, "He whose strength gives out collapses during the course of the journey [lit., the Way]; but you deliberately draw the line."[7]

Confucius, it is said, had other reasons to be displeased with this disciple (*Analects* 11:17, *Mèngzǐ* 孟子 4A15).[8] But if he is put down firmly here, his problem is not. Confucius elsewhere (*Analects* 9:24) despairs of "those who approve but do not carry out, who are stirred, but do not change." He concludes that he will try to teach "only one who bursts with eagerness" (*Analects* 7:8). Of a student who slept through the day, he said testily, "Rotten wood cannot be carved or a wall of dried dung be trowelled. What use is there in my scolding him anymore?" (*Analects* 5:10). But Ran Qiu presents a sharper problem to the moral teacher than the mere slug-abed. It's not just that he seems not to care enough to live and learn and practice the moral "way." He consciously represents his *acedia* as a genuine lack of requisite inner "powers." How does one cure such a person? It seems that he will respond to reproaches only if he is not really ill. This of course is true of the slug-abed too. But a Ran Qiu has found a view of himself that protects him from even hearing reproaches. Well, then, correct his view of himself. Confucius tries to; but the attempt sounds merely like another reproach.

This is the route that Mencius will take nearly two centuries later, more effectively, in the context of a moral psychology. ("It's not that you can't. You just don't," he paraphrases the Master in 1A7.10.) Meanwhile there is the anti-Confucian Mòzǐ 墨子, living and teaching (and organizing a save-the-world movement) during the century between the death of Confucius and the birth of Mencius.

Oversimplifying, I take Mozi's differences with the early Confucians, as far as those differences are of significance to this inquiry, to be these: (1) He is not concerned with the moral cultivation of individual people (except for the hardening of his cadre of followers who have to be selfless and fearless). What people *are* is not important. All that matters is what they *do*. (2) Good government (and a good world) will result, he thinks, from the adoption of the right policies and programs of action, not from getting good people into office. (Adopting such policies is what Mohists *mean* when they speak of a ruler being "benevolent and righteous." And a "worthy" official is simply one who does his job well.) (3) To get these policies adopted, one must construct conclusive arguments showing that adopting them is in the material interest of the person to whom the argument is addressed. There is no appeal to a person's moral better nature. (4) The supposition that a person might follow such an argument, see its point, yet reject its conclusion and not act on it, is unintelligible. (5) Our emotions, preferences, and even our beliefs, are under our voluntary control: so that, e.g., if I am persuaded that following a certain course is best, or am commanded to follow it, and doing so involves my having certain emotions, preferences, or beliefs, I can adopt them at will, as easily as I can act.

The last point sounds extraordinary. Several things need saying about it: first, Mozi nowhere *says* this explicitly; but he seems to me clearly to imply it (most clearly in *Mozi* chapters 11–13, "Identifying with Superiors," where subordinates are to be commanded to adopt the standards of right of their superiors). Second, Mohists are not totally different from Confucians on this matter: every Confucian moralist urges that one *ought* to have certain emotions (genuine grief at a funeral, for example—*Analects* 3:26); but Confucians from the start pay close attention to the problem of developing the desired dispositions in a person, and Mohists seem not to (which was point [1] above).

In regard to one of their tenets this element of Mohist thinking became a disturbing and confusing problem for them. Mohists argued that material interests of human beings are maximized if each person "loves" all others equally:

I am to love other people's fathers as I love my own, other people's children as I love my own, etc.; and as a corollary, a ruler is to love all of his subjects equally and have no favorites among them. But is this really possible? it was objected. Suppose, for example, there are infinitely many human beings in the world. How can I love them all?[9] Or, is executing criminals consistent with universal love?[10] Or, is loving all equally really *psychologically* possible?

This last challenge is taken note of and dealt with already in one of the earliest Mohist texts, the one that initially puts forward the doctrine of universal love:

> This doctrine of universality is benevolent and righteous. And yet how can it be carried out? As we see it, one can no more put it into practice than one can pick up Mount Tai and leap over a river with it! Thus universality is only something to be longed for, not something that can be put into practice.
>
> Mozi said: "As for picking up Mount Tai and leaping over rivers with it, no one from ancient times to the present, from the beginning of mankind to now has ever succeeded in doing that! But universal love and mutual aid were actually practiced by four sage kings of antiquity."[11]

And Mozi goes into the relevant ancient texts about various sage kings. The objection is like Ran Qiu's to Confucius; but the reply is not "this might be a problem for some people but not for you: you're mistaken about yourself or self-deceived." The reply of Mozi is in effect "This just isn't a problem at all." But of course it was a problem, and the Mohist position was eventually modified, as will be seen.

Confucians too had a problem of a sort, about whether their own program was a possible one. But there is a subtle yet important difference. For them, the challenge "How can I?" comes usually not to an exhortation "Do thus and so" (where the doing has both a behavioral and an affective component). Rather, it is to the exhortation "Become the sort of person who will always, naturally and effectively, do thus and so" (where being such a person involves having the right feelings and dispositions). In particular, the Confucian position was that only in this way would a ruler be a really satisfactory (and successful) one.

Sometimes Mencius finds himself apparently engaged in the simpler case. In one exchange with King Xuān of Qí 齊宣王 in 1B5 (there are several conversations like it), Mencius urges Xuan to practice the "kingly government" of King Wén 文王, founder of the Zhou Dynasty, who provided for the people's needs, taxed them little, cared for the destitute, etc.

> "Well spoken," commented the king.
> "If you consider my words well spoken, then why do you not put them into practice?"
> "I have a weakness (*jí* 疾).[12] I am fond of wealth."

Mencius replies adroitly that this "weakness" can be turned to advantage: let his majesty simply see that his subjects have enough, so that "you share this fondness with the people."[13]

So the dialectic is really not so simple. To be able to do as he sees he should, and really be moved to, the king needs "merely" to put a disposition he already has to a different kind of use.

Mencius here shows himself a clever court persuader. (The same rhetorical tactics Mencius uses are noted and recommended by the Machiavellian Hánfēizǐ 韓非子 in his essay, "Difficulties of Persuasion," perhaps seventy years later.)[14] He is a better philosopher (though a rather strange one) in a much longer conversation with the same king, which like the foregoing probably took place in 319. The story is well known, but its relevance has been obscured by clumsy translation. Mencius steers Xuan—"king" of the former dukedom of Qi—into the question, What sort of "virtue" must he acquire to become the sort of ruler who will, as the natural result of the way he will be naturally disposed to act, eventually become king in fact, i.e., of all China. Mencius replies that Xuan has this quality already, and points out to him that recently when he had watched men leading an ox to a sacrifice he had suddenly felt sorry for it and had ordered that they substitute a sheep (which he hadn't seen and so didn't feel sorry for). The very senselessness of this act (why feel sorry for the ox but not the sheep?), Mencius went on, showed that the king acted out of spontaneous compassion. This means that Xuan really has already the emotional capacity to be a real king, and in saying he can't he is like a man who says he can't lift a feather or see a cartload of firewood: "Your compassion (ēn 恩) is sufficient to reach animals," yet you do nothing for your people.

> [I]f a feather isn't lifted, it is because one does not use one's strength. If a cartload of firewood is not seen, it is because one does not use one's eyesight. And if the people are not cared for, it is because you do not use your compassion. So, the reason why you do not become a real king is that you do not act, not that you cannot (*Gù wáng zhī bú wàng, bù wéi yě, fēi bù néng yě* 故王之不王不爲也非不能也).[15]

Asked to elucidate this distinction between "not doing it" and "not being able to do it" Mencius allows that the latter concept would apply if it were a question of "striding over the North Sea with Mount Tai under your arm"—and we see, if we hadn't, that we are back with Mozi and his "universal love."

Note also that the ox incident is *itself* a (happy) case of action failure. Perhaps the significance of the sparing of the ox in 1A7, qua action failure, is this: if we think of action failure as, sometimes, failure to adhere to one's judgment or conception of what is the thing to do, caused by the prompting of an inner *moral* emotion, then for Mencius the possibility of *akrasia* has positive as well as negative value; it can save us from rigid adherence to a doctrine or program that may be wrong-headed. Yí Zhī 夷之 (see below, pages 102–3) exhibits this: his Mohist tenets are wrong; but because of his natural (and good) feelings for his parents, he backslides in failing to adhere to Mohist "economy" in burying them. He then tries to deceive himself by an ad hoc rationalization, making it possible for Mencius to detach him from his tenets by showing him what he is doing.[16]

7.2 How Is Moral Action Possible?
The Concept of "Extending"

Despite Mencius's use of Mohist metaphors, there is an important difference. Mozi had paid no attention to the problem of my ability to feel the way I would have to to be genuinely moved to do what his utilitarian argument tells me it would be sensible for me to do. (This has led most of his interpreters to assume that his "universal love" isn't love at all, but mere expedient behavior.) He simply assumed, apparently, that I can adopt an attitude as easily as I can move my arm. By Mencius's time, some Mohists were more careful: one after all has the capacity of caring for others, they said. Consider how everyone naturally feels about their parents. Well then, now that you see you have this capacity to care, just apply it to everyone. (So argues, in effect, the Mohist Yi Zhi, with whom Mencius had an argument I shall return to.) In his discussion with King Xuan Mencius thinks in just this way: "all you have to do is take up this heart (*xīn* 心)"—i.e., this capacity for compassion we've discovered you have, in your reaction to the ox—"and apply it to what is over there"—i.e., to your people.

> Hence one who extends one's compassion (*tuī ēn* 推恩) can take care of all people within the Four Seas. One who does not cannot even care for one's own family. There is just one thing in which the ancients greatly surpassed others, and that was in being good at extending what they did (*tuī qí suǒ wéi* 推其所爲). Why is it then your compassion is sufficient to reach animals yet you do no good acts that reach the people?[17]

This passage contains important technical phrases. The expression *tui en*, literally "pushing out compassion," has a limited use among later Confucians, but the word *tuī* 推 alone is an important technical term for the later Mohist dialecticians, and there can be little doubt that Mencius here is consciously appropriating that use. It is defined in chapter 45 of the *Mozi*:

> Extending (*tui*) is getting someone to grant what that person has not accepted when it is the same as something that that person does accept.[18]

This definition occurs in a series of definitions of four types of analogical inference that are rhetorically distinct but can (I think) be shown to be equivalent, in that any argument of one type could be reformulated as of another type.

Briefly, the Mohist dialectician distinguishes between (1) a material mode— "analogy," i.e., comparing things; (2) a formal mode—"parallel," i.e., comparing sentences; (3) a defensive mode—"supporting," i.e., insisting on my right to make a judgment like one you make; and (4) an aggressive mode—insisting on your obligation to make a judgment like another you make, this last being "extending." The point of the whole chapter is defensive and metalogical, aimed at showing that certain kinds of arguments used against the Mohists are invalid.[19] Among examples that follow, one used against the Mohists that I take to fall both into the "parallel" and "extending" categories would be this: Mohists urge loving all humans equally; but they dislike robbers and favor executing them. But surely a robber is a human; if so, then if (1) they dislike a robber, they must admit that (2) they dislike a human; and this is inconsistent with loving all humans equally. This argument actually has to be inferred from the refutation given, which is a combination of "parallel" and "supporting," and is an argument about arguments: interpreting and simplifying, the Mohist can be described as saying in effect that the argument fails because the common element, "disliking," would have to be asserted for different reasons: I can admit "I dislike that robber" without admitting "I dislike that human" (for, as we would say, I do not dislike the robber *as* a human). This is seen at once if one compares the inference with another formally like it: that since a robber is a human, there being many robbers here implies there are many humans here. The opponent would reject this latter argument as ridiculous, so the opponent must let the Mohist reject the former argument.[20]

Sometimes (e.g., 6A3–4 and perhaps 3A5) we see Mencius showing his familiarity with the Mohist method of undermining an argument. In 1A7 the important point is simply that he is applying a Mohist concept of inference. But how? He is, after all, talking with the king not about moving from accepting this proposition to accepting that one—"extending acceptance" from this to that, so to speak—but about "extending compassion" from this to that, "taking this heart" and "applying it to what is over there." *We* could, however, construct a logical sideshow to bring out how "extending compassion" could be thought of as "logical"; Mencius has pointed out that the compassion-capacity exists, and asserts it *can* be moved from "this" to "that." He allows that it was good—an "artifice of benevolence" (1A7.8, Legge's translation)—for the king to feel the way he did about the ox but implies that it would be even better for him to feel this way toward his people. Without forcing more logic into Mencius's persuasion than is there, we might represent him as urging the king to think as follows:

(1) I ought to be compassionate toward my people if I can be; but I just can't.

But, (2) it is easier to be compassionate toward human beings than toward animals.

And (3) here I am, compassionate toward this animal.

Thus, (4) I can be compassionate toward animals.

Thus, (5) I can be compassionate toward my people.

Thus, (6) I ought to be compassionate toward my people. I have no excuse for not being.

This is not, on its face, in the form of practical reasoning as it is usually discussed, i.e., showing that a normative principle applies in a particular case. But it is not hard to twist it into standard form: (1) I ought to do A (apply my compassion to my people) if condition C obtains (I am able to do so); but (2) I *am* able to do so; therefore. . . .

It will be useful to have another example before us, because the focus, in Mencius's conversation with King Xuan, on "being able" probably obscures the way Mencius typically thinks of "extending" a motivating disposition.

> Mencius said, "Bó Yí 伯夷 would serve only the right prince and befriend only the right person. He would not take his place at the court of an evil person, nor would he converse with such people. For him to do so would be like sitting in mud and pitch wearing a court cap and gown. He extended (*tui*) his heart (*xin*) of disliking evil to the extent that, if a fellow-villager in his company had his cap awry, he would walk away without even a backward look, as if afraid of being defiled. Hence even when a feudal lord made advances in the politest language, he would repel them. He repelled them simply because it was beneath him to go to the feudal lord."[21]

Here we are not told what might be a basic case in which Bo Yi's "heart of disliking evil" (*wù è zhī xīn* 惡惡之心) would automatically reveal itself (as in King Xuan's pitying the ox). If we assume there was one, then Bo Yi's "extending his heart of disliking evil" will be for him to "take up this heart"—revealed in the basic case—"and apply it to what is over there," as Mencius said to Xuan, i.e., apply it to other things he also sees to be evil—an evil ruler, evil person, even a villager whose cap isn't on straight. The logic of "extending" one's "heart" (i.e., one's disposition to "dislike," in this example) will go like this:

i. Paradigm case (1) of "evil": My disliking "heart" is applied (and appropriately applied) here.

ii. Case (2) (involving perhaps an evil person) is like case (1) in also being evil.

iii. So, I should apply my "disliking heart" to case (2) (by not speaking with that person).

And so on to other "conclusions" (as we might style them) of Bo Yi's "extending," even the case of the mere clumsy villager.

In either example, according to one conception of what goes on in practical reasoning (that of Aristotle and his modern followers), when the king sees that he both ought and can, or when Bo Yi sees that case (2) is relevantly like case (1), the form the acceptance of this conclusion takes is that the one who "extends" forthwith actually does "apply one's heart" to the case in question (that is, assuming—as Aristotle would not—that "extending one's heart" is something one can *do* at all). And then, "extending" in the logical sense will be *identical* with "extending compassion" or "extending one's heart of disliking evil."[22]

For Mencius, I think, this is not the way it goes. Once the horse has been led to water, there is still the problem of getting it to drink. Mencius was fully aware that although he may have gotten the king to *see* something, he hadn't gotten him to *do* anything yet, even to himself; and he eventually had to give up on Xuan in disgust. He makes a commonsense distinction between judging or believing that one should do something and actually doing it, and given his view of motivation perhaps he must. For consider how Mencius would have to respond to a sophist who said, "Look, Mencius, if King Xuan *really* concluded that he *ought* to do that, the 'pro-attitude' toward doing it that constitutes his judgment that he ought to would effectively *move* him to do it."[23] To this, Mencius might reply as follows: "You just don't understand my concept of 'benevolent government' (*rén zhèng* 仁政). What I'm trying to get the king to do is not just to issue some orders that will result in lightening the hardships of his people, but to do this with a particular *motivation*, namely, a lively and animated concern for their suffering. And this kind of motive just isn't the same as your 'pro-attitude' constituting a judgment of obligation." More than this, I think Mencius in effect holds that this distinction carries over into what is observably done. If opening the granaries in a famine would be an act of benevolence, he distinguishes invidiously between benevolence (doing it from benevolent motivation) and "benevolence" (doing it because one feels one ought to do benevolent things, because it's virtuous to do so):

> Slight is the difference between humans and the brutes. The common person loses this distinguishing feature, while the noble person retains it. Shùn 舜 understood the way of things and had a keen insight into the norms of human relationships. He acted through benevolence and rightness. It was not that he put into action benevolence and rightness (*yóu rén yì xíng, fēi xíng rén yì yě* 由仁義行非行仁義也). (*Mengzi* 4B19)

In the same vein, Mencius says (4B6) "the propriety that is not propriety, the rightness that is not rightness—these things the great person does not do."

Mencius thinks of a capacity to feel a certain way toward others, or toward doing something, as a faculty in oneself that one *can* use, or (as he told the king) *just not* use. This is strikingly borne out in one of the most familiar sections of the *Mengzi*, the enumeration in 2A6 of the four innate "sprouts" (*duān* 端) of the moral virtues, namely benevolence (*rén* 仁), righteousness (*yì* 義), propriety (*lǐ* 禮), and moral wisdom (*zhì* 智)—the first, the sprout of "benevolence," illustrated by the spontaneous feeling of alarm one would have if one saw an infant about to fall into a well. Mencius adds, "humans have these four sprouts just as they have four limbs. For one possessing these four sprouts to deny one's own abilities is to mutilate oneself." But while here, as in King Xuan's pulling the ox out of the procession, the paradigmatic response that reveals one's "ability" just *happens*, further use of the "ability" seems to be, from this way of talking, something one *does*, just as one might use one's legs. It will be objected that what must be understood by "using one's compassion" is not just feeling a certain way but acting in the ordinary sense—say, opening the granaries during a famine. And *that* act, it will be said, is one you will just do forthwith, once you really are persuaded you should and see that you can. But the point is that, even if "using compassion" has a behavioral component, in Mencius's "act" of "using" or "applying" one's "heart," the act as behavior and the "applied" motivating feeling have to be taken together.

But let us follow up another cue offered in 1A7—Mencius's notion of "extending what one does." Mencius uses this puzzlingly bare "what one does" way of speaking again in a short aphorism (7A17) which no translator or commentator known to me has interpreted correctly. Literally, it is

Do not do what you do not do; do not want what you do not want. That is all.

In "Problems in the *Mengzi*: 7A17," in this volume, I critically discuss various possibilities for interpreting this passage. Here I shall merely summarize what I think is the most plausible reading: there are simple paradigm cases where I just naturally shrink back, would be appalled at the thought of doing or wanting something; and these are in fact cases where I obviously *should* not do or want the thing. There are other sorts of cases where it is not so immediately obvious that I ought not to, but which are in the same "category" (*lèi* 類) as one or another of the basic cases. The *whole* problem of moral action is to get the disposition that manifests itself in the basic case to "break through" into the others that are in the same category, to "fully develop" (*chōng* 充) it, or as Mencius sometimes says, to "fill the category" (*chōng qí lèi* 充其類) in question (e.g. 3B10). And this of course involves "understanding categories" (*zhī lèi* 知類, 6A12). "Do not do what you do not do" will therefore mean "Do not do things of essentially the same kind as things you just wouldn't do—and be moved, in so refraining, by an extension of the same basic impulse"; in other words, "extend what you do *not* do," to revert to the language of the King Xuan dialogue. And so, also, for what you do or do not allow yourself to desire.

In the locutions "what you do," "what you do not do," Mencius refers to the paradigmatic behavior (as expressive of basic moral feeling) rather than the paradigmatic feeling or "heart" (with presumed expression in act). Sometimes, as in 7B31, in the same sense, he speaks of the "actuality" (*shí* 實), i.e., the paradigmatic "what you do" as expressive of "heart." (So, also, in 7B25 and 4A27; and in 7A37 where the "actuality" is not necessarily paradigmatic.) There are new words for "extending" here, with nuances that are important for Mencius: he sees me as having a reservoir of moral energy that will carry all obstacles if I can tap it, "expand and fill it out" (2A6), "get it to break through into the whole world" (7A15). But we can separate this enthusiastic picture of human nature from the structure of Mencius's concept of motivation and action. Even in these passionate statements he is still thinking of the management of motivations as a kind of para-logical occupation. The ordinary term for "inference" came to be *tuī lèi* 推類, "extend [to another case in the same] category."[24]

7.3 One-Source and Two-Source Moralities

Now, what is the status of these "categories"? Mencius's theory of moral life as a quasi-logical extension of basic dispositions, which everyone can be counted on to have some of, was in part a solution to the problem of "self-rejection" in people like Ran Qiu, who had held that however well we may come to *see* what is good and right, some of us (including himself) just aren't and can't become morally competent. But if one deals with this annoying stance as Mencius does with his concept of quasi-logical "extension" of basic motivating feelings, what is the relation of the "conclusion" of one's "extending" to what one starts with? Are we to think of the acts of a fully socialized individual as "implied" by the character of one's basic feelings? Or do they need merely to be compatible with those feelings? Mencius was a Confucian, and as such was committed to a particular highly specific code of rules of moral behavior, and lots of people weren't. Is the theory of extending basic dispositions compatible with any moral code that anyone may think up?

The matter may be put a bit differently. D. C. Lau (1953, 561) suggests that for Xunzi, becoming morally socialized (one might say) is like learning a language, whereas for Mencius it is something that happens naturally under normally favorable conditions, like sexual maturation. That was before the age of Chomskyan linguistics. It is now less easy to think of developing language competence as radically unlike developing sexual competence. Let us then try thinking of Mencius's picture of developing moral competence as (contra Lau) like developing language competence. We must ask, how is the moral "deep structure" of self-revealing affections and motivations articulated into the "surface structure" of developed morality?[25]

Mencius says one "fills the categories." But categories can be drawn in various ways. And even if one thinks there is one objectively right way of drawing them, which one could think of perhaps as something one could write down in some ideal rule book, perhaps it has little or nothing to do with the shape of one's natural reservoir of moral motivation, which in so far as it has a "shape" just happens to be consistent with the rules one considers right, although perhaps also with others. In such a case we would have to think of morality as having two sources, one formal and public, set out in words and doctrines, which one would have to learn; and the other motivational but relatively amorphous, "inside" ourselves so to speak, or we might say in our "hearts." We might compare this situation to the relationship between the rules of various games on the one hand, such as tennis, and our muscular strength, enjoyment of exercise, and zest for competition on the other. An alternative view would be that, so to speak, all of the morally significant features of any moral surface structure are determined by the moral deep structure; so that even if there are genuine moralities that are different, they would have to be in essential respects the same: there would be "moral universals"; and morality as a whole could be said to have one source, which is our "hearts."[26]

I have mentioned Mencius's argument with the Mohist Yi Zhi (otherwise unknown) which is found in *Mengzi* 3A5.[27] Mencius criticizes Yi Zhi for having given his parents lavish funerals, thereby acting inconsistently with his Mohist tenet that funerals should be simple. Yi replies

> The Confucians praised the ancient rulers for acting "as if they were guarding a newborn baby."[28] What does this saying mean? In my opinion it means there should be no gradations in love, the practice of it beginning with one's family.

(So, Yi suggests, I am justified in this manifestation of caring for my parents because this caring capacity is what makes it possible to carry out a more basic element in the Mohist program.) Here again is the fundamental idea of "extending compassion." I have a *basic affection-capacity* which reveals itself in a basic way—in this case as parental and familial affection.[29] Having this capacity, I then am to apply it to others, in accordance with my *beliefs* about how it should be focused—i.e., in accordance with the doctrines to which I adhere or my moral reasoning from those doctrines. Morality on this view depends on two things, which are independent of each other: what I *think* I should do, and could state in *words* and reason about; and my capacity to feel certain emotions, which I can steer and shape so as to be *moved* to do what my principles tell me I should. It is now clear that this was what we might call the Mohist philosophy of action as it must have evolved by Mencius's time.

And for all one can see in Mencius's dialogue with King Xuan, it was Mencius's position too. But it was not quite Mencius's position, and we must assume that perhaps Mencius saw no point in going into philosophical subtleties with a mere king; the practical problem after all was merely to soften him up a bit. But Mencius needs to make his differences with Yi Zhi clear, and does. He replies (the argument is carried on through a third party):

> Does Master Yi truly believe that one feels no closer to one's brother's son than to one's neighbor's newborn baby? It's just that for that [i.e., the "newborn baby" model of caring for everyone] there is a special reason for accepting it: when a newborn baby creeps toward a well it is not its fault. Moreover, whenever Heaven produces anything, it makes it have one root (*běn* 本) yet Master Yi has two roots. This accounts for his mistake.

This rejoinder reveals several interesting things: (1) Mencius shows again his close familiarity with Mohist dialectic in the form and wording of his refutation. Chapter 45 of the *Mozi* cautions against misuse of the "extending" form of argument in these words: "When one accepts something, there is a special reason for accepting it. One may accept the same thing [in regard to two cases] but one's reasons for accepting it may be different."[30] The point is that the "ancient rulers" in caring for their people as if they were "newborn babies" were thinking of them not as objects of familial love but as needing protection from undeserved harm. (2) The fact that Mencius just assumes Yi Zhi's familiarity with the child-crawling-into-the-well paradigm (best known to us today from *Mengzi* 2A6) suggests that this paradigm may have been as much a Mohist as a Confucian one. And (3), while we must be cautious about what Mencius meant by "one root" and "two roots" (the commentators and translators have various suggestions) it seems entirely possible that he is talking about the basis of Yi Zhi's moral system, which he is criticizing as being double, insisting that, morally considered, a human as one of Heaven's creatures has just one "root." And that root for him has to be, of course, the "heart" in its different aspects as dispositional "hearts." He argues elsewhere (6A10), for example, that if one accepts a gift without caring whether it is right to do so one has "lost one's root heart" (*běn xīn* 本心). Yi Zhi's trouble, then, would be that he has gotten into a mess by accepting guidance both from his "heart" and from a set of doctrines that are unconnected with the "heart."

Mencius confronts and rejects a much more explicit statement (universally misunderstood) of a "two sources" theory of morality in another short dialogue in *Mengzi* 2A2.[31] Here Mencius is talking with a disciple, Gōngsūn Chǒu 公孫丑 (identified as a native of Qi) about doctrines of another rival philosopher, Gàozǐ 告子, possibly by this time deceased, and possibly at one time in early life a disciple of Mozi. Mencius quotes and discusses a double maxim of Gaozi's which he represents as Gaozi's formula for moral self-development:

(1) What you do not get from words (*yán* 言) do not seek in the heart (*xīn* 心).

(2) What you do not get from the heart do not seek in *qì* 氣.[32]

Mencius summarily rejects (1) and cautiously accepts (2). Much of the discussion of this has centered on the meaning of *qi*. It is "animal energy," perhaps, but the word is the focus of much mystification in early Daoist literature, and Gao here is probably simply firmly rejecting any kind of mystical view of self-development.[33] A more important question is what Gaozi is talking about in speaking here of "words." It can be shown, I think, that he has to mean "doctrines" or philosophical "maxims."[34] This is, after all, just what one should expect a moral philosopher with a Mohist background to be saying. One can think of what are in effect Gaozi's two "sources"—in his words what you "get it from," i.e., "words" and the "heart"—as respectively independent of myself and so "external" to me, and in myself and so "internal." Gaozi uses this way of talking in book 6, where he and Mencius engage in a much studied debate over the question whether "rightness" (*yì* 義) is "external" (as Gao and his disciples hold) or "internal" (as Mencius and his followers insist). The two use recognizable Mohist techniques of argument and refutation, and here again one can see how familiar Mencius was with the use of Mohist dialectical concepts.[35]

Now, the two-sources picture has an interesting bearing on the question whether I might see that there are things I ought to do yet feel I do not "possess the powers" to do them, which was Ran Qiu's problem. I have represented this picture as coming into being in response to felt difficulties in naive Mohism. But in a way a position like Gaozi's is even worse. It does allow that I have capacities for moral motivation, but it *systematically* separates those capacities from "what I get from words," i.e., what I can come to apprehend cognitively as my obligations. It must now seem that, having learned what the rules are, I can get myself to follow them and marshal my dispositions into line only by a sheer act of will (and the possibility even of that must remain dark). I think this was what Mencius was criticizing in Gaozi in 2A2, in cautioning obscurely that the "will" (*zhì* 志, directed "heart") must not "bully one's *qi*," and in caricaturing Gaozi's method of "cultivation" with the absurd picture of a farmer who tugs at his plants in order to make them grow faster. Essentially the same criticism of Gaozi is advanced by Wáng Yángmíng 王陽明, the Mencian philosopher of the early sixteenth century, and Wang finds the same difficulty in his twelfth-century rival Zhū Xī 朱熹: this kind of philosophy systematically introduces a gap between what I know to be my duty and my dispositions to act, a gap that can't in any comprehensible way be bridged.[36]

7.4 How Is "Extending" Possible?

There is an obvious problem in all of this that by now I may be accused of pretending I don't even see: on *either* the "one source" *or* the "two sources" account, how is one to go about "extending" one's feelings of love, hate, compassion, latent self-respect, or whatever so that they "fill the categories," adequately and effectively motivate one to do the things one sees, or should come to see, one should do. "I have these four sprouts as I have my four limbs," Mencius tells me, and cries "shame" if I deny it. Suppose I admit it. I "just know" how to use my arms and legs. But I do not "just know" how to use my emotions; or if I do, at least I don't "just know" that I do. Isn't the idea that one can control one's emotions basically absurd?

I do not think it would seem absurd to a good actor. I questioned a very good one once about this. Oh, he replied, it's really not hard. If I'm playing a part that calls for crying in a certain scene, I just think about sad things for a while and soon I'm crying. Not "crying," but crying. But is the performance of an actor—even a very good one, with his quotation marks off—just the model one wants for Mencian moral agency? In any case Mencius no less than his opponents owes an answer to this question. What is it, or what would it be?

What seems wrong with my actor friend is that to get himself to cry the actor has to think of something he really feels to be sad, and to that extent his activated emotion is unrelated to what he is engaged in, viz., the play. And if he can do it by thinking of aspects of the play itself, to that extent we want to say he is not crying but "crying." Well then, let the play be real. Confucius could not bear to see "the forms of mourning conducted without real grief" (*Analects* 3:26). It seems plausible to suggest that one could, and should, approach one's participation in a funeral by getting oneself into the right frame of mind and feeling—recalling the personality of the deceased and one's relationship with this person, reflecting sympathetically on the sadness of the survivors, etc.—so that as one takes one's part in the ritual, one does what one does from genuine feelings of sadness, respect, sense of doing a last service to an acquaintance, perhaps. Now, try thinking of everything one does in life as participation in ritual, in this sense. "Behave in public business as though you were in the presence of an important guest. Deal with the people as though you were officiating at an important sacrifice" (*Analects* 12:2). In this, Mencius agreed with Confucius. The Confucian concept of "ritual" (*lǐ* 禮, "propriety," proper action in a role) was broad enough easily to include the actions of a King Xuan that, done from a proper compassion, would constitute his *being* king—his really occupying this role.

Thinking of "extending" as orienting oneself toward role-filling helps to make Mencius plausible, and I suspect it is the way he himself unconsciously takes it. But Mencius does say more about how the process of maturing and applying embryonic dispositions proceeds, and more importantly, how one keeps this process on track.

It is not just a matter (as with the "total" actor) of dwelling on emotion-arousing aspects of the situation in which one acts one's role. Cognitively one knows what one *should* do. In certain paradigm areas of activity—for Mencius, typically caring for parents and obeying elders—one does the right or good thing naturally and easily, *enjoying* the doing of it. This doesn't mean that

morality for Mencius is grounded in pleasure. (He gives an earlier moral hedonism—that of Zǐhuàzǐ 子華子—a quick twist here.)[37] Rather, the natural
enjoyability of morality is what makes it *possible*. In *Mengzi* 4A27 we read that
caring for parents is the core activity (*shí* 實), so to speak, of what Mencius
calls *ren* (benevolence, kindness) and obeying elders (literally, elder brothers)
the core of *yi* (rightness or dutifulness). And when we do these things *enjoying*
them, the dispositions *grow*, and eventually become spontaneous and irrepress-
ible—and (I think it could be shown Mencius thinks) in gradually expanding
application.[38]

This model of how one is to cultivate one's virtues suggests the way we
actually do go about *cultivating tastes* for things we see to be worthy of our
attention, such as good literature or good wine or good philosophy. But one
doesn't just do these things because they are "good" things to do—this is the
surest way to put oneself to sleep, or make oneself sick, or drive oneself crazy.
On the moral plane, this would be to "put into action benevolence and rightness" rather than "acting through benevolence and rightness."[39] You would
move yourself back rather than forward. (Compare 2A2.16: one mustn't "forget" the development of one's moral feelings, but one also must not "help" the
process.)

7.5 A Limited Defense of Mencius

Can Mencius be taken seriously in all of this? Or if not in all of it, in some of it?
I shall raise three problems for Mencius, and discuss possible solutions to each.

7.5.1 Deontology or Consequentialism?

Is Mencius (in passages such as 1A1, 1A7, and 6B4) in the logically unlovely
situation of offering a utilitarian (consequentialist) argument for a deontological
commitment to morality for its own sake?[40] It will not suffice to say of such
arguments, "This criticism is unfair, because Mencius was simply trying to get
rulers to behave better in an age when they were doing all sorts of terrible
things." Such a defense doesn't touch the question whether Mencius's argument is *coherent*.

So suppose I am persuaded for some ulterior reason (e.g., my own political interest) that it would be best for me to "extend my compassion" in the
full-blooded sense of both refocusing it on a new object *and* doing a compassionate act for that new object, and doing this out of compassion. Mencius
appears not to see inappropriateness or incongruence in having such an ulterior
motive for "extending." After all, he is arguing to get King Xuan to "extend his
compassion" because that is the way to become a real king: "One who extends
his compassion can take care of all people in the world; one who does not
cannot even take care of his own family" (1A7.12). Perhaps Mencius perceives
that although

(1) Doing A from motive C.
   — where A is a compassionate act and C is a focused feeling of compassion—is not the same as

(2) Doing A from motive O.
   —where O is my bloodless feeling that I ought to do A—nonetheless in

(3) (Doing A from motive C) from motive S.
   —where S is my desire for political success, I am after all still doing (1).

I find this unlovely, but Mencius often engages in this kind of persuasion when talking to eminent persons.

But it does seem that motive S, the desire for political success, and motive C, disinterested compassion, must coalesce so that the former fatally infects the latter if I am to do it now, at once[41]—that is, if Mencius has remained close enough to Mohism to think of using a capacity to be moved (or to act-with-motivation) as really being simply like lifting one's arm.

There is, it seems to me, an analysis that removes the incoherence from Mencius's *argument* in 1A7. In fact, I can offer three.

Solution 1

Mencius's hierarchic picture of the self requires a hierarchy in the languages of moral analysis for one accepting it:

Level 1: I ought to *do* A because it's simply *right* to do so.

Level 2: I ought to be *motivated* by morality because this will have good *consequences*.

(And perhaps the levels go on.) This is *not* to offer two *overlapping*—and so possibly conflicting—reasons *for doing A*, one deontological and one consequentialist. It is not required here that I even be *aware*, when *doing* A, of the consequentialist argument for being *motivated* in a certain way in general. And even if I were, we have to take "good consequences" at level 2 in a sense that would conflict at most with "it's simply *right*" if this expression were to be used *in the language of level 2*, which it is not.

Solution 2

If you feel there's an element of hocus-pocus somewhere in the foregoing argument, here is another: Mencius argues—with King Huì 惠王, and with King Xuan—that the king should govern benevolently (and let us agree that "benevolently"—rather than "'benevolently'"—means "moved by genuine compassion")—and that a reason, or *the* reason, for doing so is that in this way he will *wàng* 王—become a real king. But what Mencius means in saying this—in fact what he *says* in 1A7—is that the king really already has the virtue or *de* necessary and sufficient for being a "real king," if he will just use it. But of course, as everybody knew, it is a ruler's *duty* to govern with *de*, if he has the *de* to use; and being a "real king" just *is* doing that. Of course, this being a real king is going to involve being a *successful* ruler, bringing peace and order to the world; but *that* is a ruler's duty too: it is only in that way that a ruler can bring the greatest benefit to the people.

So, Mencius is not urging his kinglets to be good to their people in order to succeed in the general military-political competition. He is urging them to govern compassionately—i.e., to govern with *de*—because that just is a ruler's *duty*, and the way, the only way, for him to realize the *ideal* of true "kingship." Of course Mencius knows that a ruler becoming "a real king" will involve becoming "king in fact," i.e., beating his rivals, and he knows his royal hosts will understand this. But at the time of these conversations (320–318 B.C.) the notion of several different local "kings" having equal legitimacy was scarcely two decades old, and still had only a precarious existence at the level of inter-state diplomacy. Within the context of a "royal" audience, a "king" had no rivals; there were only other lords who had not yet accepted the king's rightful authority. Mencius had to talk according to these rules if he were to talk at all.

So the incoherence of Mencius's position is not in his argument. It is con-centrated entirely in the semantic ambiguity of the word *wang*, "be king." And this is an ambiguity for which he is not responsible. It is simply given in the politics of his time.

Solution 3

Even if parts of the *Mengzi* do suggest a sort of extreme Mohist position, there are indications, even in 1A7 itself, that Mencius is less of a "voluntarist" than I have been assuming. He says there that "the ancients" were better than we are "in being good at extending what they did"; and this still needs interpret-ing. It would be surprising if "extending what one does" did not have the same meaning as, or at least include, "extending one's compassion." And the ancient Chinese, like ourselves, spoke ordinarily of "being good at" (*shàn* 善) doing something only if doing it involves skill it takes time to use, even if not much time, and probably still more time to acquire. That is, whether my prob-lem is to get myself *now* to "extend" my feeling so as to be moved effectively to do some immediately projected act, or, to bring about a long-term change in myself so that normally my presently recognized feeling-capacity does "ex-tend" to do the sorts of things I see now I ought to do, Mencius is led from the over-simple "you *can* do it" position of 1A7 to a more sophisticated concep-tion that one will need to "cultivate" (*yǎng* 養) oneself carefully. The most memorable discussion of this is in 2A2.[42]

7.5.2 The Problem of Immediate Action

Thus, when he talks to somebody like King Xuan, Mencius seems to want immediate action, and seems to see no reason why he shouldn't get it. And I

think one can without difficulty find other examples. Doing it—acting appropriately from "extended" compassion—is just a matter of "picking up" this "heart"
and putting it down over there, as one might move a chess piece. Yet we also
see him talking very differently in passages such as 2A2: becoming morally
developed takes delicate self-cultivating. Forcing the development, doing something you're not ready to do, will actually hurt you. There are two positions
here, and both seem to be things Mencius wants to say, and this should arouse
suspicion. Could there be a difficulty in each that the other compensates for?

(i) If I say, "It isn't that you can't, you just don't!" I seem to oversimplify
the problem of moral action absurdly. For, doesn't doing something require
that I be *moved* to do it? If Mencius is (as he is) saying, "You have the capacity
to feel strongly enough about this to act. Just apply that capacity and act!" he
seems to be overlooking the fact that even if (as many would not grant at all)
it is possible for me deliberately to reshape myself emotionally, surely I can't
do this just as I might lift a feather in the air. If I try simply to force myself to
do the "right" thing, I may simply incur all of the cost of being moral without
attaining the substance of it. Thus, Mencius observes (7B11) that it will be
possible for someone who is interested only in gaining a reputation for being
a person who is indifferent to mere possessions "to give away a state of a thousand chariots." But "if one is not the sort of person to do it, reluctance would
be written all over one's face if one had to give away merely a basketful of rice
and a bowlful of soup." Becoming this sort of person may take some time and
skill in self-management.

This leads to (ii) the view that acting rightly requires a process, which may
take much time, of "extending" my embryonic emotions in directions that are
delimited by their (hence my) nature. Meanwhile simply forcing myself to do
the act because it is "right" may injure my self-development. But doesn't *this*
mean I may be in the situation of having to say to myself and others, "I see
that this is the right thing to do, but I'm not ready yet—so let me do what I
can but not all of it"? Mencius takes note of this attitude, and his response is an
exasperated "If you can see that it's right, *do* it *now*, *all* of it!" So he speaks,
when someone asks if it would be a good idea to reduce taxes a bit this year,
and next year drop all the way to the ten percent urged by Mencius (3B8):

> Here is someone who appropriates one of his neighbor's chickens every
> day. Someone tells him, "This is not the Way of a noble person." He responds,
> "May I reduce it to one chicken every month and wait until next year to stop?"
> When one realizes that something is morally wrong, one stops at once. Why
> wait till next year?

So the suspicion is borne out. One might argue that this shouldn't embarrass Mencius. Does not this shifting of position mirror a genuine perennial
dilemma of moral life? Sometimes we *aren't* ready: yet the obligation on its
face *can't* be denied or put off.[43]

A related misgiving is suggested by a penetrating passage from Iris Murdoch (1962):

> One must perform the lower act which one can manage and sustain: not the higher act which one bungles. . . .
> Self-knowledge will lead us to avoid occasions of temptation rather than to rely on naked strength to overcome them. We must not arrogate to ourselves actions which belong to those whose spiritual vision is higher or other than ours. From this attempt, only disaster will come.[44] (201, 204)

In contrast with Murdoch, Mencius *just assumes* that the person who looks at an obligation and says "I can't, so I needn't try" is always *wrong*—making a very limited exception of the case where he feels one would be mismanaging *oneself* in forcing oneself to do right acts just because they are acts of "rightness." Consider, for example, 7A39, where Mencius excoriates King Xuan's desire to observe less than the ritually prescribed period of mourning, yet condones a similar request from a certain "prince whose mother died." But this case is different, he argues: the prince *wanted* to do the thing right, but was not going to be able to. Mencius concludes, "What I said the other day referred to those who failed to act even when there were no obstacles." Mencius cannot admit that there could be an exculpating *internal* obstacle; for, he insists, *every* person can become a sage. But, suppose we agree. Even so, on Mencius's own admission, the process takes time. (In 2A2.1 he allows that it took *him* forty years to attain a degree of perfection that he will not allow to be called "sagehood.") In the meantime, if I have any moral obligations of self-appraisal and self-management at all, it would seem that I might *sometimes* have a *moral* obligation to make the best of what I recognize to be a (temporarily) less than ideal state of my character. But if Mencius were to admit this, he would have hard work preserving the moral opprobrium of his concept of "self-rejection" and its applicability to persons such as King Xuan (or Ran Qiu).[45]

The ruler who is hesitant about slashing his tax rate right off might of course be *right* in a much more disturbing way: He might size himself up, conclude that the kind of ruler-role Mencius urges on him is one *he* would in the end make a mess of, with the result that not just he but *everyone* would be worse off. It is to be regretted that Mencius, and other Confucians, do not seem to have the sophistication to consider problems of this kind—which are thus abandoned to Daoists and a very different treatment.[46]

7.5.3 Am I Responsible for How I Feel?

There will be deeper objections; and it will be useful here to notice that Mencius's position as I have presented it is a composition of several distinguishable views:

(1) There is a sort of innate moral "deep structure" in a person, that can be fully developed, without forcing, in only one way.

(2) I can choose the feelings I shall have, to a significant extent: either (a) I can simply *use* my basic emotional capacities as I use my physical ones, or (b) I can over time *develop* them in desired ways. This last is Mencius's characteristic view, and he thinks of either the using or the developing of noticed emotional capacities as a matter of "extending" them into what I see to be appropriate "categories" of possible motivated action. This is independent of (1), because I *could* hold that you and I have different root motivational capacities, or none at all to start with, or acquire them in various ways.

(3) I can judge I ought to do something without ipso facto being moved to do it: This is independent of (1) and (2), because I could deny it and still insist that I could come to do the thing from a different motive, e.g., genuine compassion rather than simply doing-what-I-ought; and this requires "extending."

(4) There is a significant moral difference between doing something because it's commanded by a rule I accept as a rule of right conduct and doing it because of my fully involved sensibility to the aspects of the case that make it right for me to do it. Only the latter sort of act is morally satisfactory.

All of this implies that for Mencius a moral person is a hierarchic structure of faculties such that I both can and should notice, evaluate, choose among, and often modify different dispositions that I may have. This itself is a view many will reject.[47] Point (1), which is Mencius's theory that "human nature is good" (6A6), is the aspect of his thought that has received nearly all the attention of students of China and Chinese philosophers. But the others seem to me to be, though controversial enough, both more plausible and more interesting, and more worth attention.

An objector will hold, perhaps, that (1) feelings can't be chosen. (Or, the objector may go along with half of Mencius and admit they can be *changed*, even though not chosen-and-assumed-in-the-choosing.)

But then the objector will say (2) even if they could be, it would never be *right* or *needful* to do it. (a) Never *needful* because whenever I *really* judge that a course is best, I am (or come to be), in the judging, disposed to follow it. And (b) never *right*, because the only *honest* and non-self-deceptive way to come to a judgment that a course is the right one for *me* is to see how I *do* feel about it, and to start manipulating my feelings will be, so to speak, to tamper with the evidence.

Now rather than saying that it is wrong—not the course of "emotional honesty," we might say—ever to try to modify our affections and attitudes, one really has to be arguing that one can't. For if one can, then it would seem one must, in some cases, be responsible for what one's feelings are. And it seems unfair for you to tell me that I am forbidden to change what I am to be held responsible for, even though I can. And I think examples like the funeral case show that one can. The foregoing argument works also for beliefs, of course, and that should give one pause. Perhaps the thing to say is that there are some ways of going about modifying one's feelings or beliefs that would be proper and others that would not be, and that these ways differ for the two. In any case, one doesn't have to go all the way with William James to see that often one does have the ability to focus and refocus one's attention on particular aspects of a contemplated act, and this may well affect how one feels about doing it.[48]

One could still take the position that this is never going to make any difference in what one does, but only at most in the shape or color of one's motive for doing it. This would be to slight one of the points I made about Mencius earlier—that just this for him is a morally significant difference in *what* one does. But it is also quite plausibly denied. For a try at making Mencius look more reasonable here, consider some examples (I shall deliberately exclude anything suggesting Mencius's notion of extending innate feelings):

(1) I buy a new compact car, impulsively. Should I have done so? Well, I'm stuck with it, and consciously or subconsciously I "make the best of it"—I direct my attention to desirable features of my car (I can, after all, almost get into the driver's seat without getting my legs stuck—and that's a lot better than many other brands of car), and away from their undesirable features (not enough headroom for me, etc.). I reflect that I'm going to get fair mileage; I remind myself that I could have spent a lot more (and I try not to think about how much I *did* spend). Soon I feel better about it.

(2) I sign a promissory note for Jones who is borrowing five-hundred dollars from the bank. It develops that Jones can't pay it, and I have to. Again I'm stuck, this time with an *obligation* I don't think I like too much. So I try to be philosophical. I reflect that Jones really needed the money and is using it to good purpose, and is a decent chap and will try to pay me later, and it isn't really hurting me much anyway, and so on. Soon I feel better about it.

(3) I promise Jones—verbally and privately—that if he doesn't make enough on some land he is selling to cover his wife's hospital expenses, I will *give* him five-hundred dollars. It turns out he doesn't. He's too decent to bring the matter up, but he knows, and I know, that I've promised. It doesn't happen to be very convenient, but it seems to me I mustn't go back on my word. So I try to be philosophical about *this*.

Jones really needs it. He'd do as much for me if I were in his fix. I see how I can manage, by cutting here and there, say, by dropping a few of my professional subscriptions, etc. Soon I feel better about it.

(4) The last example I propose is just like the preceding one, except that in this case the strength of my "moral" motivation to keep my word is at best in an even balance with my distress about the difficulty it will cost me to do so. I reflect on the matter as before, and as before, soon I feel better about it. But in this case, if I hadn't come to feel better about it, I wouldn't have kept my promise, even though I judged that I ought to.

Shall I say that the first three examples are plausible enough, but the last one just isn't? Mencius's objection to those who like Ran Qiu "reject themselves" is in significant part precisely that they see no such utility in "reflecting."[49]

But, one may ask—and quite properly—doesn't this simply move the problem up one level? What account should be given of the relation between (1) my full understanding of myself, as well as the problem before me, and (2) my being effectively moved to embark on a course of emotional self-management and self-change—supposing that we accept hypothetically Mencius's implicit picture of a person as a structure, such that *I* have emotional *powers* that I can *use*. Or to put it another way, perhaps Mencius ought to admit an "internal" relationship (in current philosophical terms, not Mencius's) between *this* judgment[50]—that I *ought* to "extend" my root-motivation into the problem-area of moral action—and my being *moved* to *do that*, or to embark on and pursue the course of self-cultivation that will have that result. Mencius's poor results, already noted, with royal patrons such as King Xuan do not encourage one to suppose Mencius would have agreed. But he does seem almost to say this elsewhere.

To return to the example given: I judge that I ought to keep my promise to give Jones five-hundred dollars. I measure the strength of my motivation to do what I judge I ought to do and see that it is not strong enough to carry against my reluctance, unless I take steps, i.e., *focus my attention for a while* on aspects of the case that make this the right thing to do and that mitigate the difficulty of doing it; and I see, further, that if I do take these steps, I'm going to become effectively disposed to keep my promise.

Ex hypothesi, engaging in the indicated line of attending is both necessary and sufficient for my keeping my promise. The question is not about that now, but whether on the level of deciding how to handle myself, the same stand-off between morality and self-interest might be repeated: my moral half might say, since reflecting is necessary and sufficient for you to keep your promise, and since you ought to keep your promise, you ought therefore to reflect. And self-interest will say, better not tamper with yourself; you'll end doing something you don't like. What happens now?

At this point, if I understand him, Mencius is like Bishop Butler in holding that I *ought* to heed "the greater part" of myself, that it has right of place over "the lesser part."[51] But he also seems to think sometimes that if only I do reflect carefully enough to get this far—to take complete inventory of myself—I just *will*: "It is the common disposition of people to desire nobility. But everyone has nobility in oneself. It's just that one doesn't think (*sī* 思)" (6A17). Sense appetites automatically seek their objects; they "don't think," don't act, but simply respond. "It is the function of the heart to think; if it thinks it will get it" (compare Gaozi, "what you do not get from words . . . from the heart . . ."); and "If it doesn't think it will not" (6A15).

7.5.4 The Regress Problem

"It's just that I don't think." But why don't I? "Thinking"—not a purely cognitive activity for Mencius but the heart's reflective attending to and even savoring of its own inner dispositions—is something I *do*, can be *urged* to do, and so, apparently, can *resist* doing. What kind of judgment or perception about myself would I have to reach to see that I *ought to think*? And how would I reach it, except by thinking?

To say, as Mencius seems always to assume, that I am morally responsible for my moral dispositions seems to lead to a regress: if I ought to do A, then I ought to come to want to do A, and so, I ought to come to want to come to want to do A, and so on. If I accept Mencius's view, I have to find some way of stopping the regress without destroying the point, or else show that the regress is acceptable without embarrassment. Without going into great detail, a possible resolution of the problem, I would suspect, goes as follows: it is indeed true that if I *ought* to do A, then I *ought* to be motivated to do it, if I am not; and so ought to be motivated to be motivated, etc. At every step, there is the *possibility* that I will not see my obligation; and the further *possibility* that even if I see it I will do nothing. This is quite different from saying what would be quite absurd: that to do A intentionally, I *must adopt* a motive to do it; but to do this I must adopt a motive to adopt this motive, and so on, and so can never do anything. This is not to say there is no problem at all. Mencius is very much involved in this part of ethics in 6A15. Why are some people "greater" than others? Some follow the "greater part" of themselves. But why do some do *that*? Well, one has to *think*. . . . And of course sometimes we don't or won't, or somehow can't. A certain sixteenth-century gentleman is in this part of the woods, too, when he asks his teacher "Why is effort not earnest?"[52] Sometimes of course it just *is*, and this should not be forgotten. If it isn't, there may be times when, though I can understand the problem, the only way for my teacher to *deal* with it is to reach for the proverbial dust whisk—seeing that my itch to understand the problem (rather than thinking what to do) is paralyzing me by directing me to each of infinitely many acts of attention.[53]

But this is a pathological case. Normally such a regress would be self-terminating. When I notice that I *ought* to do the thing, *and* that I am insufficiently *moved*, I then have an obligation *and a motive* to work on myself. And this motive does not depend, for its existence, on an anterior motive to be motivated. It may, of course, be insufficient; it may be sufficiently strong to get me to try as hard as I can and I may *still* fail; but then, I might be adequately moved to try as hard as I can to do the thing in the first place and still fail. It is part of the concept of *trying* that success is problematic. Mencius, and Mencians, have not been willing to say this. Not only do they insist (rightly) that trying *helps* (求有益於得, 7A3); they want also to insist that it must *succeed* (求則得之, 6A6).

This is, after all, what makes them Mencians.

7.6 Comparisons

7.6.1 The Problem in Zhuangzi and Xunzi

The dialectic that I have been pursuing from Confucius through the Mohists into Mencius can at this point be continued into Zhuāngzǐ 莊子 (late fourth century B.C.) and Xúnzǐ 荀子 (third century B.C.).

Zhuangzi is of course completely unsympathetic with the specific moral objectives of the Confucians, but he does have his own concept of the "perfect person." And he recognizes that, whatever one may think of the possibility of human perfectibility in the abstract, whether a particular person can be straightened out or not, even with the best of masters, is in effect a matter of grace. There is, for example, the amusing story of "No-Toes" telling Lǎozǐ 老子 about Confucius:

> "Confucius certainly hasn't reached the stage of a Perfect Man, has he? What does he mean coming around so obsequiously to study with you? He is after the sham illusion of fame and reputation and doesn't know that the Perfect Man looks on these as so many handcuffs and fetters!"
>
> Lǎo Tān [老聃] said, "Why don't you just make him see that life and death are the same story, that acceptable and unacceptable are on a single string? Wouldn't it be well to free him from his handcuffs and fetters?"
>
> No-Toes said, "When Heaven has punished him, how can you set him free?"[54]

Moreover, where a Confucian cannot conceive of choosing less than the best moral objective, the Daoist feels no discomfort. Such a one will typically transvalue the "best" as less than best, and the less than best as best—seeing, for example, a relaxed acceptance of existence, including one's own less than beautiful impulses, as higher "virtue"—as does Zhuangzi, in talking of the "true person of old."[55] The attitude can even reach to recommending an amoral hedonism as a way of life, lest one hurt one's spirit.[56]

Xunzi is a classic example of a two-sources moralist: we have a nature, and all that is good in human life results from applying to it the direction of the intellect.[57] "Extending compassion (*tui en*) without order does not achieve benevolence."[58] He takes a straight Socratic position at the level of the (for him nonmoral) choice of a moral way of life: "All people abide by what they approve and reject what they disapprove. For one to know that there is nothing comparable to the Way, and yet not abide by it, has never happened."[59] It is clear from the context of this chapter ("Rectifying Names") that "abide by (*cóng* 從, "follow") the Way" cannot mean do the right thing in each particular, but refers to the choice of a way of life and of the kind of person to be, if one is to be optimally satisfied. Wise people submit themselves to proper training and so become moral. At this stage whether one always acts according to the Way one is committed to is simply a matter of how far one's conditioning has progressed.

There remains, however, the problem how one *sees* that the "Way" is incomparable. This is a matter of "doing arithmetic," Xunzi suggests;[60] but one can be confused, "obsessed" by a single seductive idea; and Xunzi devotes another essay to this problem.[61] In it one learns much about the value of dispassionate thinking and much about what a clear-headed person is like, but little about how one could see the need to become this sort of person if one were not one already.

7.6.2 A Sampling of Western Views

Aristotle

Comparing Aristotle and Mencius, we find what my colleague Lee Yearley (1990a) would describe as "differences in similarities." Aristotle, like Mencius, is normally (not always) interested in the shape of character, rather than in facing up to individual choices and acts. However, there is a sharp contrast between Mencius and Aristotle on the "internality" of virtuous acts. For Mencius, one cannot perform a (genuinely) virtuous act unless one acts out of the appropriate motivation. In contrast, for Aristotle, a virtuous act need be only the sort of act that a virtuous person would perform (just as a correct spelling would be the spelling a good speller would give me). Thus, according to Aristotle (but not Mencius) you *can* perform a virtuous act, even if you *lack* the motivations that would make you really virtuous (just as you might, in a single case, give me a correct spelling even though you are in general a bad speller).

Although both philosophers assign great importance to human nature, Mencius and Aristotle disagree over whether virtue is "natural."[62] While Mencius is explicit that our capacity for virtue is guaranteed by the goodness of our nature (6A6), Aristotle remarks that "the virtues arise in us neither by nature nor against nature, but we are by nature able to acquire them, and reach our complete perfection through habit" (1985, 33–34, 1103a20–30).

Mencius and Aristotle agree that one becomes a virtuous person by performing virtuous actions. However, their differing attitudes on human nature and the "internality" of virtuous acts lead to a further difference on the connection between actions and moral cultivation. Aristotle discusses a paradox posed for his view that we become virtuous by performing virtuous actions:

> What do you mean by saying that to become just we must first do just actions and to become temperate we must first do temperate actions? For if we do what is grammatical or musical, we must already be grammarians or musicians. In the same way, then, if we do what is just or temperate, we must already be just or temperate. (1985, 39, 1105a15–25)

This is very similar to what I have called the "paradox of virtue" in early Chinese thought (see chapter 3 of this volume). However, since Aristotle does not make the connection between performing a virtuous act and having virtuous motives as tight as does Mencius, there is a resolution of this paradox that is available to Aristotle but unavailable to Mencius. Aristotle believes we become just and temperate by doing just and temperate acts so that these become habitual in us. But if we are not just or temperate already, we will not behave thus unless we are obliged to. Therefore we must be obliged to, necessarily *in youth*, when character is formed (1985, book 10, chapter 9). If a person has not had a satisfactory moral education when young the situation is hopeless; but when an adult, one is responsible for one's moral dispositions, for one may lose one's virtues through slackness and profligacy (book 3, chapters 4–5). Nonetheless, Aristotle notes that "this does not mean that if [someone] is unjust and wishes to stop, he will stop and will be just. For neither does a sick person recover his health" simply by wishing (68, 1114a13–15). Therefore the essential moral "task" (*gōngfu* 功夫 or 工夫, the later Confucians would call it) is to fight off such slackness, i.e., to avoid *akrasia*, which is characteristically *confusion* of reason by the passions (here Aristotle is Socratic). I assume that is why a conceptual investigation such as that provided by the *Nicomachean Ethics* can have *practical* moral value: it can help us to be *clear* about being moral.

But these Aristotelian moves are not open to Mencius: being forced or forcing oneself to do a thing that leaves one unsatisfied in one's heart (*bú qiè yú xīn* 不慊於心) will be counterproductive (2A2.15). Now we see why Mencius *must* hold that (pace Aristotle) human nature is good, in the sense of having natural tendencies toward virtue (i.e., the sprouts). For given the assumptions that (1) a virtuous act *does* have to be virtuously motivated, and (2) it is by acting rightly that virtue is developed, then (3) only one who is, really, virtuous already will be moved (or can move oneself, or even, can effectively respond to instruction) to develop or strengthen virtue in him- or herself. Thus, without these natural tendencies it would be impossible (on the Mencian picture) for humans to become virtuous. Mencius is led, then, to think of moral emotions as things that *grow* as they are exercised, and realized in act, in due degree. Interesting additional material from the *Mengzi* can be brought in here to support this suggestion: for example, the puzzling short aphorism of 7A45 reveals its meaning when looked at in this light: "Those who feel the love of family toward their own kin will feel benevolence for all humans. Those who feel benevolence for all humans will be kind to all living creatures." This line is not a mere rhetorical jingle but restates something both Mencius and Yi Zhi assume in 3A5: I am naturally affectionate toward my parents, *and so* develop an effective benevolence toward all people, etc.[63]

And here is one last difference between Mencius and Aristotle: Mencius devotes no serious attention to the moral education of youth and places the full weight of responsibility for the moral development (as well as moral maintenance) of the real moral adult in that adult's own hands. There may be deep cultural factors behind this: perhaps it can be shown that Zhou Dynasty China, unlike classical Greece, simply did not have a *paideia* (although the lack, if there was one, was made good in a long literature of moral pedagogy in later dynasties). However, our discussion so far suggests some philosophical considerations that might lead Aristotle to be concerned with *paideia*, and Mencius not. Aristotle thinks that our morally neutral nature is shaped by habituation. By the onset of adulthood, habituation is almost complete. So seeing to it that children are properly cultivated is "very important, indeed all-important" (1985, 35, 1103b25). In contrast, Mencius thinks that our morally good nature provides any human (who has not become wholly "bestial") with the resources for moral growth. And since rulers and their ministers are the ones who have the most immediate opportunity to institute "benevolent government" (and since they are adults), Mencius focuses his attention on what we might call "adult education."

Kant

Skipping ahead more than a millennium for our next comparison, we see that Mencius stands Kant and his many later followers on their heads. In 7B24, Mencius suggests that moral acts are not good acts done out of a sense of duty, because "commanded" (*mìng* 命); one must come to want to do them, feel them as natural (*xìng* 性). In contrast, Kant argues that only what is morally commanded has genuine moral value:

> [L]ove out of inclination cannot be commanded; but kindness done from duty—although no inclination impels us, and even although natural and unconquerable disinclination stands in our way—is *practical*, and not *pathological*, love, residing in the will and not in the propensions of feeling, in principles of action and not of melting compassion; and it is this practical love alone which can be an object of command.[64] (1964, 67; Academy, 399)

James

William James, in contrast to Aristotle and Mencius, focuses not on the development or maintenance of character but on the function of the "will" in *particular* acts.[65] For James, acting morally, at least in tight cases, is something like starting an automobile. Worried about the free will problem, James held that the one thing we can *do* is focus our *attention* in the right direction — on the thing to be done, on the reasons why *it* rather than more tempting courses should be followed. Attention is normally *in*voluntary. Voluntary attending continues only for a few seconds and must be constantly renewed through "effort." If it catches, so to speak, involuntary attending takes over and appropriate action follows automatically. (This analysis leads James at one point to think of falling asleep as a kind of paradigm of intentional action. You start the process by counting sheep. . . .) But how do I *become* a person who *characteristically* "attends" in the ideal way? This was to be a vexing problem for later Mencian ethics (in sixteenth-century China).[66]

But there are already things in Mencius that point in a Jamesian direction. *Mengzi* 6A15, for example, argues that inner *attentiveness* to moral considerations and one's deeper moral dispositions, in the face of appeals to the senses, is the mark of the "great person" as against the "small person." He seems to be saying the same thing in 2A2.16 in the often quoted statement that "one must always be engaged" in the task of self-development, *never forgetting* it, though not forcing it. It is useful to point out that Mencius is concerned with my obligation to cultivate my *feelings*, and not with a Jamesian obligation and will to *believe* certain things — but with one exception: I have an obligation to be *self-attentive* (this is what the obligation in 6A15 really is) and so to obtain a correct *view* of my potential moral character. And this does appear to be a cognitive duty, which I can perform or shirk at will. But there is no "I will even have it so" about this. It *is* so, and if I look I will see.

So what is James' solution to the problem of becoming the sort of person who always attends? So far, I have found James always looking in other directions. There is the "soul well born" for whom there is no problem. Toward others James is hortatory, scornful, inspiring, but not instructive. He recognizes that some do achieve the change, but here he speaks unhelpfully of "the ripe fruits of religion."[67] I would suppose he thinks that understanding *clearly* how "attending" works is itself salutory.

And so in the end there is no solution to Ran Qiu's problem, in either China or the West. It remains essentially untouched, but over the course of millennia in two great civilizations it has served as a catalyst, bringing into dialogue ever new viewpoints, commitments, and interests, and as it does this provoking deeper and deeper search for self-understanding, and drawing out ever more of the richness and wonder of the human mind.

Philosophical Voluntarism in Fourth-Century China[1]

8.1 "What you don't get from 'words' . . . "

One of the half-dozen seminal texts for later Confucian self-cultivation philosophy is the short dialogue between Mencius and Gōngsūn Chǒu 公孫丑 in *Mèngzǐ* 孟子 2A2. It is chiefly here and in the first half of book 6 that Mencius discusses the problem of the relation of mind and will to passions and appetites, and it is in these two parts of the book only that Mencius mentions and argues against another moral philosopher named Gàozǐ 告子. Little, possibly nothing, is known of Gaozi otherwise. There is a chapter in the anonymous *Guǎnzǐ* 管子[2] which sketches a Confucian-like self-cultivation philosophy that may be partly Gaozi's; and the forty-eighth chapter of the *Mòzǐ* 墨子 (*Gōng mèng* 公孟), containing conversations that could have taken place early in the fourth century, records three incidents in which Mozi and a Gaozi, perhaps the same one, criticize each other.[3] But Gaozi's fame is in inverse ratio to the availability of details about him. Mencius held that human "nature" (*xìng* 性) is good—that we are predisposed to be moral. Gaozi countered that human "nature" is our animal appetites, without moral direction. To many Confucians of the next twenty-three hundred years—and that includes most Chinese intellectuals of any kind of the past seven hundred years—nothing has seemed more important than defending and not straying even implicitly from Mencius's position in this argument. The controversy has even drawn discussion in twentieth-century Communist writing, where we find philosopher Chén Bódá 陳伯達 coming down firmly on Gaozi's side.[4]

The controversy has been worked over again and again over centuries both in China and in the West, by involved philosophers and curious historians. Why, one will ask, yet another study of it? Because, I will argue, there is something more, of real interest, yet to be known about this famous collision of views. And if it is possible to know it, I would like to.

The most penetrating and insightful study of this particular subject known to me is Angus Graham's "The Background of the Mencian Theory of Human Nature" (1967, 7–66). Graham observes that Mencius tells us three basic facts about Gaozi:

(1) He attained an 'unmoved mind' (不動心) before Mencius himself (2A2).

(2) He held that 'there is neither good nor bad in our nature' 性無善無不善也 (6A6).

(3) He held that 'benevolence is internal, not external; duty is external not internal' 仁內也非外也義外也非內也 (6A4). (Graham 1967, 23)

Graham here omits—either as not to his purpose or as not being a "basic fact"—something else Mencius says about Gaozi. In *Mengzi* 2A1–2 Mencius and his disciple Gongsun Chou of Qí 齊 are engaged in a discussion about bravery, self-confidence, and moral steadiness. Mencius makes the statement about Gaozi's "unmoved mind," just quoted, and admits that he, too, has attained an "unmoved mind." His disciple then asks him to explain the difference between Gaozi's and Mencius's own methods of attaining this state (or, perhaps, the difference in their conception of it). Mencius begins his reply to this request by quoting one of Gaozi's maxims, as follows:

> What you do not get from "words," do not seek in the mind; what you do not get from the mind, do not seek in the vital energy (*qì* 氣).

The passage has always vexed commentators and translators, and even this bare rendering is tendentious. Gaozi's maxim is a bare sixteen syllables: "not get in words, don't seek in mind; not get in mind, don't seek in *qi*" (不得於言勿求於心不得於心勿求於氣). But recourse to basic English does not give a neutral translation, because, for example, the word I have rendered "get" (*dé* 得) can mean "understand." This is the way D. C. Lau takes it, and this translation can be made plausible by appropriate meaning-selections for other words, giving a completely different cast to the whole. Lau makes the whole passage into a piece of counsel for avoiding being worried or upset about what you do not understand (1970, 77).

Rambling through some other interpretations, one finds that Lau is close to the view of the Japanese commentator-translator Hattori Unoyoshi 服部宇之吉 (1922, 49). The late Han Dynasty commentator Zhào Qí 趙岐 ties Gaozi's words to the human nature controversy and has him saying that if you can't find goodness in a person's words you shouldn't pursue the matter by trying to find it in some sub-verbal level of his psyche. When the Song Dynasty commentator Zhū Xī 朱熹 makes a try at it, he seems to be guided by his own conception of the "investigation of things"; he supposes Gao to say "If there is something you don't understand in [some] words, then you should set the words aside and not insist on trying to get the principle (*lǐ* 理) from your mind. And if your mind is not at ease about something, you should forcefully control it and not seek help in the matter from your *qi*."[5] Dobson apparently takes Gaozi to be counseling distrust in one's ineffable insights, if any: "Do not seek in the mind for that which cannot be put into words. Do not seek in the physical realm, for that which is not in the mind" (1963, 85–86). James Legge's version is obscure to me.[6] J. R. Ware's translation is very close to the one I myself just offered, except that "words" becomes "your words" (1960, 64)—for which there is plenty of commentarial support; but what Ware's means, and for that matter what mine means, is yet to seek. Of the philosophers, interpreters, or translators who have thought carefully about the passage, the only person I know of who I suspect may have got it straight is the Ming Dynasty Confucian Wáng Yángmíng 王陽明. But the reason for this suspicion lies outside the scope of this paper.[7] In brief, one must wonder if anybody has really understood Gaozi's maxim, and this is embarrassing, for it appears to be introduced as a kind of pivot in an argument that, to judge from echoes and phrases in Song and Ming Dynasty philosophers, everybody learned verbatim at the age of six. Mencius has just affirmed that a good person, if confident that he or she is right, does not fear any adversary; and he goes on after quoting Gao to describe the will in relation to the animal energies as a kind of gentle commander, and then to make the famous claims that he himself understands "words," and knows how to nourish his "flood-like energy" (*hàorán zhī qì* 浩然之氣) but scarcely knows how to describe it; that this *qi* somehow connects him with the universe; that it is produced by "accumulated righteousness" (or "letting dutifulness accumulate," *jí yì* 集義) and "starves" without it; that Gaozi "never understood righteousness because he considered it external"; and, in a famous analogy, that one should not mismanage oneself, the way the silly farmer from the state of Sòng 宋 mistreated his crops, pulling up his grain stalks to make them grow faster. All of this subsequent discussion is drawn out of Mencius by Gongsun Chou apparently in qualification of Mencius's initial acceptance of the second injunction of Gao's maxim, "what you don't get from the mind [or "heart" *xīn* 心] don't seek in the vital energy." As to the first injunction, "what you don't get from words don't seek in the mind," Mencius rejects it out of hand, apparently with no further comment. Its meaning he must have supposed to be transparent. But that meaning now seems to have become opaque. Recently I have begun to think that I do understand it, and I will now try to persuade you. The matter is surprisingly deep.

8.2 Historical Assumptions

In proceeding, I shall make some assumptions that are controversial, without offering much argument. (Others have done enough of that.) Zhao Qi, writing about 160 A.D., says that he is working with a *Mengzi* text that came to him in eleven undivided books. He discarded four, divided the other seven in two halves each, and divided each half into sections as we now have them.[8] I take him at his word. Book 2, titled *Gongsun Chou*, begins with a dialogue, now in two sections, between that gentleman and Mencius (*Mengzi* 2A1–2). It is one single conversation, and I believe it to be a conscientious record. "Gongsun Chou" is not a posthumous name. That fact probably indicates, as Lau suggests (1970, 220), that Gongsun Chou was one of the disciples who edited the book we have in the generation after Mencius's death.[9] Following the dialogue that begins book 2 is a collection of long sayings of the master, which can be seen to bear on ideas in the dialogue. This in turn is followed by a collection of anecdotes and episodes of Mencius's brief official career in the state of Qi, including the events of 315–314 B.C. when King Xuān 宣王 invaded the state of Yān 燕. These too are commentarial, as the dialogue at the beginning and again toward the end discusses various famous officials and their attitudes toward their roles, and indeed it is in reference to such a role that the discussions of courage and the notion of the "unmoved mind" are introduced. Gongsun Chou was a native of Qi (so identified in the dialogue) and the dialogue begins with an evaluation of Guǎn Zhòng 管仲, famous seventh-century B.C. minister of Duke Huán 桓公 of Qi. The dialogue thus took place in Qi, and we may reasonably conjecture that it occurred not much before or after 315 B.C. I follow Lau (1970, 10) further in believing that Mencius at this time must have been close to seventy-five years of age or even older.[10] This means that his life span falls as much as two decades earlier than has usually been supposed: he was born, then, around 390 B.C.

Let us turn to Gaozi. There is nothing in book 6 to date the arguments that occur there, but I believe that any direct confrontation between Mencius and Gaozi occurred years earlier. In 315 B.C. Gao was probably already dead. Mencius refers to him in 2A2 in a way suggesting he was an older man ("He attained an unmoved mind at an earlier age than I did") and the arguments in book 6 read like the record of Mencius making his mark by successfully attacking well-known positions of an older, established philosopher. This is implied, also, by the fact that Mencius just takes it for granted that Gaozi's maxim, in book 2, can be quoted without any need for explanation. All of this makes it more reasonable to assume that the Gaozi who enters chapter 48 of the *Mozi* is the same man Mencius criticized. The dates of Mò Dí 墨翟 are of course uncertain and much debated.[11] I shall follow Qian (1956) and Mei (1934) in supposing that he probably lived until about 390—the approximate revised date of Mencius's birth. In chapter 48 of the *Mozi*, Gaozi appears as a renegade disciple of Mozi, brashly criticizing the master, who for his part seems almost benignly amused. The picture is easily that of a very young man trying his strength against a very old and respected one. This is important: it argues that we may hope to resolve obscurities in Gaozi by looking at assumptions in Mozi that could have impressed or puzzled a young follower trying to strike out for himself.

8.3 The Gongsun Chou Dialogue

I return now to Gaozi's problematic maxim in *Mengzi* 2A2. Remember, first of all, that Mencius in quoting it assumed he was answering Gongsun Chou's question about the difference between Mencius's and Gaozi's conceptions of absolute inner moral assurance and steadiness and how one obtains it. This would seem to rule out Zhao Qi's interpretation (that it merely restates Gao's position that goodness is not in our nature) and Dobson's (that it is a waste of time to hunt for unstatable intuitions in ourselves?). Lau's interpretation does make the maxim a kind of answer to the question, but in an implausibly trivial way (unflappable moral steadiness the result of learning not to be upset by what you don't understand?) and leaves incomprehensible the connection with the following discussion about the subtleties of moral self-cultivation (cultivating *qi* and letting dutifulness accumulate).[12] We have to do better.

In my attempt, I will (1) do what I can with the logic of the passage directly before us; but in doing this I shall need to (2) see what insight can be got from other things in the *Mengzi*, and then (3) I shall see what light may be thrown on the problem by other Warring States Period philosophical works.

First, the Gongsun Chou dialogue itself: the *question* asked was, "tell me about your, and Gao's, 'unmoved mind'." On its face, it is a question about methods and goals of self-cultivation, and Mencius's later cultivation analogy confirms this. Gao's maxim therefore must be understood by Mencius as indicating in some way how Gao would have people cultivate themselves. But Gao's maxim is not *about* "unmoved mind." That would not be coherent (do not "seek unmoved mind in mind"?), and further the maxim seems to be well known; and if it were simply about unmoved mind one wonders whether Gongsun Chou would have asked his question. It is more reasonable to take Gaozi's maxim given here as his general formula for *self-cultivation*, the *result* of which could be expected to be an "unmoved mind." (Notice that this is something he does *not* talk about in book 6. There, he is presented as defending certain theoretical statements about human nature, but not as applying this theory to the problem of managing and developing *oneself*.) Mencius appears to be understanding Gao to have believed in effect that there is something, or perhaps more than one thing, that one needs if one is to have an "unmoved mind"; and now there are perhaps two possibilities as to what Mencius thought Gao held:

(1) There is something you need that you can get only from "words," though some think you can get it from your mind. On the contrary, Gao implies, you have to put it there. There is something else you need that you can get only from your mind, though some think you can get it from your *qi*. On the contrary, Gao implies, you have to put it there.

Or (2) there is something you need that you can get only from words, not from your mind. On the contrary, Gao implies, you have to put it into your mind. If (after you try to do this) you find it's not in your mind, there's no point in hunting for it in your *qi*. On the contrary, Gao implies, once you've gotten it into your mind, you have to impose it on your *qi*.

There is a plausible and instructive argument for (1). If we need something we get from "words" these must be others' "words," hardly one's own. So this thing comes from *outside* us. What we get from our minds is already *inside* us. Now we know that in *Mengzi* 6A4 Gaozi says that *yì* 義 (dutifulness or rightness), is "outside" and *rén* 仁 (affection, kindness) is "inside." Perhaps he is talking about *yi* and *ren* here, and saying that we get *yi* from "words," and *ren* from our "mind" (or "heart").[13]

This could be right, but the second meaning seems to fit Mencius's following discussion better. Thus, Mencius accepts the second half of the maxim taken literally (if you find it is not in your mind, don't hunt for it in your *qi*) and proceeds to argue against what he supposes Gao to mean by it, and in doing so to talk about *yi*, not *ren*: do not be cruel to your *qi*, he says; your mind needs its support when it sets out to do something (thus becoming "will," *zhì* 志).[14] Let dutifulness (*yi*) accumulate around it and the *qi* will grow and strengthen you. But don't try to impose a shape on it. It is not something that *yi* can "raid and catch" (*fēi yì xí ér qǔ zhī yě* 非義襲而取之也). Perhaps this means, as is usually thought, that this nourishing is not accomplished just by forcing yourself to *do* something right regardless of how it feels, for Mencius next says again that the *qi* is starved if we do not *feel* satisfied when we act. But Gao (again) didn't understand *yi* because he thought it is "outside."

So, for Gao, the thing that we need for an "unmoved mind" is *yi*, dutifulness, rightness, on this analysis too; and Gao thought we get *yi* from "words," which are "outside." And this, of course, for Mencius, is dead wrong: *yi* comes from "inside."

The point here, that Gaozi's formula is his program for self-cultivation and that it is misdirected toward the "outside," is quickly confirmed when we look at some of Mencius's philosophical idioms and conceptions elsewhere in the book. In *Mengzi* 7A3 we find more talk of "seeking" (*qiú* 求) and "getting" (*de*):

> Mencius said, "'If you seek it you get it; if you neglect it you lose it.' In this case seeking is of use in getting, for it is a case of seeking within ourselves. 'For seeking it there is the Way; for getting it there is the Decree.' In this case seeking is of no use in getting, for it is a case of seeking something outside."

So, Mencius would have to say of Gao's program, if we need something in self-cultivation that we have to "get," if we get it at all, from "outside," i.e., from others' "words," then "seeking" will not help: this just isn't an area where the will (*zhi*) can operate with effect. And we can take Gaozi, for his part, as denying precisely this. Mencius's remark just quoted is usually taken as counseling a fatalistic attitude toward attaining wealth and rank, and I think it does, but this is not stated, and Mencius's argument may be a more general one that the satisfaction of *any* of our seekings for "external things" in the long run depends on fate ("Decree," *mìng* 命).

Mencius's description of the mind, the senses, and their objects in book 6 seems to bear this out. Each sense organ, he holds, has its natural ideal object (the eye, the beautiful, etc.). The mind (heart) is an inner sense with its own natural ideal object, i.e., morality (6A7). So, for Mencius and perhaps for all Chinese moralists, moral principles are grasped through a kind of perception, rather than being cognized intuitively like the truths of mathematics, as in most Western moralists. And so "thinking" (*sī* 思), which Mencius says is the mind's function (6A15), must be a kind of inner perception by our minds of ourselves.[15] But in exercising its function the mind differs from the other sense organs, whose objects are "things" (*wù* 物), outside of us: the operation of the physical senses is apparently governed by causal necessity; when a pleasing sense object appears, it is a matter of "a thing engaging a thing; the one simply attracts the other." But "the mind's function is to think; if it thinks it will get it [i.e., its object, morality]; if it does not think it will not get it" (6A15). Here we find more talk of "getting," and the same distinction between the outer as the sphere of necessity and the inner as the sphere of effective voluntary action— i.e., the action of thought.

But what, then (to return to book 2 and Gaozi's maxim), are "words"? Mencius has just said that he "understands words," and he now proceeds to elaborate: he sees in other people's words indication of shortcomings in their minds ("from biased words I can see wherein the speaker is blind," etc.) and he then adds some "words" of his own: "what arises in the mind will injure government; what appears in government will injure affairs." Mencius is talking, as Confucians often do, about the mind of a ruler or high officer, and that is appropriate enough to the encompassing subject of the whole dialogue, but it's not quite on target here: it *says* nothing about "words" at all. But then, Mencius did not compose it on the spur of the moment; we find the same maxim with minor differences stated by Mencius in 3B9.10—not by editorial accident, I think: this appears to be a maxim that Mencius often uttered and wished to be remembered by, for in both places he says of it that "a later sage will accept my words"—my *yán* 言. But should we be rendering this "words"? Perhaps better would be "word," "saying," "maxim"! That is, a verbal package (often, but not necessarily, a short maxim or epigram) presenting a *doctrine*. Mencius's *yan*, in sixteen characters, about mind (*xin*) closes a discussion that begins with Gaozi's *yan*, in sixteen characters, about "words" or statements of doctrine (*yan*). And in trying to discover what Gao meant by "words" we have been "hunting for a donkey while riding one."[16] Gaozi's position then is this: to achieve an "unmoved mind," we begin by a decision to take as ours a statement or statements of doctrine. We then implant the principle of right, the *yi*, in this doctrine into our minds (*xin*), and proceed then to regulate accordingly our *qi*, our emotional energies. But everything depends on the initial step of commitment to a doctrine.

Philology is hardly needed to confirm the crucial sense of *yan* here. One need merely recall that, e.g., Mencius just before reciting his maxim in 3B9 had complained that "the doctrines (*yan*) of Yang Zhu and Mo Di fill the world."[17] Or that the *Zuǒ zhuàn* 左傳 lists three ways to attain "immortality," one being "to establish one's words" (*lì yán* 立言).[18] Or that the famous Confucian "golden rule" is introduced in the *Analects* as a *yan*.[19] And so on: the usage was a general one.[20] And if I add another example, it is because it is particularly memorable. In the writings of Mozi, that most doctrinaire of philosophers, there is much talk of *yan*. There is, e.g., the well-known enumeration of three tests for a doctrine (*yan*) in the antifatalism chapter.[21] And there is Mozi's astounding statement about his own *yan*:

> My doctrine (*yan*) is sufficient. To abandon my doctrine and exercise thought is like abandoning the crop and trying to pick up grains. To refute my doctrine with one's own doctrine is like throwing an egg against a rock. All the eggs in the world would be exhausted without doing any harm to the rock.[22]

8.4 A Parallel in Zhuangzi

I shall now turn with greater care to some other Warring States Period philosophical works to see if they can throw more light on Gaozi's position here. Two philosophers will serve usefully to draw brackets around him. They are Zhuāngzǐ 莊子 and Mozi (just quoted).

Often a good way to see what a statement means is to identify what it denies. Gaozi of course denied the view of human nature that Mencius took up, but their opposition is not total; after all they were both moral self-cultivationists, and Mencius found it necessary to give qualified assent to half of Gao's maxim: one cannot get in *qi* what one doesn't get in mind. But in the *Zhuangzi* we find an explicit rejection in effect, without referring to him, of the whole of Gao's position, and its verbal packaging is almost as tight as his.

We find this in the fourth chapter of the *Zhuangzi*, "In the World of Men." That chapter, too, opens with a dialogue—a fictitious one—between a master and disciple on the kind of inner psychic self-management needed if a person is to cope adequately ("successfully" would be misleading) with an official position. I have even allowed myself to suspect that this dialogue may be a conscious and deliberate Daoist retort to the Gongsun Chou piece. The principals are Confucius—who here appears as a sort of slick Daoist sage—and his favorite disciple Yán Huí 顏回, who proposes to seek employment with the ruler of Wèi 衞, and asks for advice. Confucius puts him through a page or two of philosophical teasing, and then says "You must fast! . . . Fast with your mind!" And he continues:

> Make your will (*zhi*) one! Don't listen with your ears, listen with your mind (*xin*). No, don't listen with your mind, but listen with your *qi*. The ears stop with [ordinary] listening, the mind stops with tallying (*fú* 符),[23] but *qi* is empty and waits on all things.[24] It is only the Way (*dào* 道) that accumulates in emptiness. Emptiness is the fasting of the mind.[25]

More epigrammatically, we might imagine Zhuangzi putting it this way: "What you do not get in *qi*, do not seek in the mind; what you do not get in the mind, do not seek in words"—in what ears hear. So there *was* an idea that both Gao and Mencius would reject, that *is* denied in the words of the second half of Gao's maxim: what you do not get in the mind, do not seek in *qi*. But let us pause. The antithesis between Zhuang and Gao here is more than just formal antithesis. They are articulating antithetical goals. Zhuang's kind of unflappability is a total capacity to ride with the punch, we might say. Gao's may be just the opposite: getting so firmly planted that nothing can floor you. Zhuang's program depends on emptying oneself; Gao's, on filling oneself. So Zhuang's *qi* will have a mysterious, superordinary sense that Gao's surely didn't. Zhuang's *qi* is not, for example, just the energy in you that seems to get activated when you pant. (Contrast *Mengzi* 2A2.10.) And what one hears with the ear, for Zhuang, we should assume is just what people say, the literal meaning of statements commonly made and accepted, and not *yan* in any superordinary sense. But this contrast too could have been deliberate. Even minor touches here seem to be taunting counterpoints to the *Mengzi* dialogue: Mencius, too, advises a person to make his or her "will" one; but Zhuang's oneness of will is a negation of will in any ordinary sense. In Mencius's cultivation *yi*, dutifulness, "accumulates." In Zhuangzi, it is *dao*, the Daoist "Way," that "accumulates." In Mencius, our *qi* is "starved" (*něi* 餒) if this "accumulating" doesn't happen. Zhuangzi transvalues the image, making his cultivation itself a psychic "fast" (*zhāi* 齋).

Essentially the same idea Zhuangzi gives to Confucius in this dialogue is found much more richly expressed in chapter 49 of the *Guanzi* (*Nèi yè* 內業).[26] And in chapter 26 of the *Guanzi* (*Jiè* 戒), which contains a self-cultivation philosophy apparently like Gaozi's,[27] the "unmoved (unmoving) mind" idea has taken on a cosmic grandeur which may well be a fair representation of Mencius's concept. But is it Gao's? Perhaps it is closer to Daoism than he could have been. The ideal described is a completely effortless and totally effective self-control that is combined with totally effective action. In the meanest circumstances one's thoughts are unshaken; even if one is a king one has no pride or arrogance.

Heaven does not move, yet the four seasons revolve beneath it, and all things are transformed; the ruler does not move, yet edicts of government are promulgated beneath him, and all accomplishments are brought to completion; the mind [of the sage] does not move, yet it employs the four limbs, the ears, and the eyes, and all things realize [their true nature].[28]

8.5 Mohist Voluntarism and Gaozi

The *Mozi* provides a very different comparison. We must take seriously, I have argued, the possibility that Gaozi as a very young man was a disciple of Mozi. In one way, Mozi and Gaozi are obviously alike: if the *Mozi* is an indication, Mozi too denied that humans have any fixed moral nature—explicitly in the historically late third chapter,[29] but implicitly and more strongly in the historically early chapters on "Universal Love"[30] and "Identification with the Superior"; in the latter, it is assumed that in the state of nature each person has his or her own conception of right (*yì* 義), yet with suitable persuasions and constraints every person can be gotten to adopt any uniform standard one chooses.[31] In chapter 47, the cultivation of a person's character is likened to making a wall—an analogy not much different from Gaozi's "making cups out of willow wood."[32]

But in its original direction, I think, Mozi's philosophy is not self-cultivationist at all. Mozi has a conception of persuasion and of the relation between reason and emotions and belief that precludes this. (Hence his short patience with rites and music and his inability to see why Confucians valued them.)[33] Mozi appeared to think (the assumption is illustrated, I would argue, throughout the third chapter on universal love) that if you can get people to follow a properly constructed argument implying that it would be in their rational interest for them to have certain affections (and beliefs, for that matter), then they will conclude that they should have those affections, and can at that point if they will (and they are simply perverse if they don't) proceed to adopt them, just as they might decide, on persuasion, to move their limbs. It is usually said of Mozi's "universal love" (*jiān ài* 兼愛) that it is not "love" at all, but merely cold self-interest. This judgment, I suspect, is too quick. The individual who, in Mozi's schematic ideal world political order, adopts the ruler's standard of right (*yi*) on command really does adopt it, on Mozi's assumption, I think, and does not merely pretend to. The chapter on ghosts and spirits is a strange mixture of arguments designed to prove that they exist, and arguments designed to show that it would be useful for people to believe that they exist.[34] The strangeness abates if we suppose that Mozi assumed that our states of belief, too, are accessible to the control of the will. Mozi is surely not to be recommended as a philosopher with a deep understanding of love. But it is possible to read him as intending that his universal love really be an affection, and not just a stance.

Or perhaps the thing to say is that at this level of Mohist thinking there is not yet a sensitivity to distinctions that analysis makes for some of the rest of us: between (a) doing something as "right," i.e., identified by reason as useful and prudent; (b) doing something recognized as "really" right, i.e., dictated by morality (whether useful and prudent or not); and (c) doing it with the inner *feeling* that it just is the thing to do, a feeling that makes it the natural thing to do. Then a decision to do something under its first representation here would seem to carry along with it the appropriate disposition. Here we will find a comparison instructive. Mencius in 1A7 teaches King Xuan of Qi the distinction between not doing something and not being able to do it. The latter is exemplified by the impossible task of taking Mt. Tai under one's arm and jumping over the North Sea, the former by the quite possible task of ruling with kindness. The figure Mencius uses comes from Mozi's discussion of universal love.[35] Is universal love just impossible, like "carrying Mt. Tai and leaping over rivers"? Hardly. But Mencius carefully shows the king that he really has in himself all the time the disposition needed to be really kind. Mozi merely tells people like King Xuan, "you *can* practice universal love. The six Sage Kings did it." For him, all you have to do is make up your mind to do it, and there's no further problem.

Now, I suggest it may have been just this conception of the relation between reason, decision, and disposition that the young Gaozi absorbed. But Gaozi *was* a self-cultivation philosopher, albeit one with an exaggerated estimate of the power of the will over the dispositions and emotions, if I'm right about him. And so, too, was Mozi a self-cultivation philosopher, of at least a crude kind, as he appears—perhaps late in life—in the so called Mohist "analects" (*Mozi*, chapters 46–60). For there was a logical crevice in Mozi's doctrinaire consequentialism that pushed him in this direction. It was this: Mo Di believed, I think, that people can alter their dispositions if they conclude that it is the wise, i.e., advantageous, thing for them to do. But Mo did not give himself any reason to believe that people can be counted on to do this unless they reach this conclusion; and the matter becomes more precarious if the disposition demanded is a total commitment to a cause, to the total disregard of all personal comfort and advantage, even to the death. But this was exactly the commitment, to the Mohist ideal, that Mozi made himself, and that he demanded of his followers. Even Mencius said of Mozi that "if by rubbing the hair off his whole body from crown to heel he could have benefited the world, he would have done it" (*Mengzi* 7A26). Sooner or later the Mohist school must have had to accommodate and develop the idea of a person cultivating this needed kind of steadiness.

So it should not be surprising to find this a preoccupation of a Gaozi who began as a Mohist disciple and then went his own way. It is interesting that each of the three incidents involving Gaozi in the *Gong meng* chapter of the *Mozi* concerns the idea of self-strengthening and self-discipline aimed at making one's ideals effective in one's acts. In one, the brash disciple is reported criticizing Mozi for preaching righteousness (*yi*) and practicing unrighteousness. In another, Mozi tells Gaozi that he must learn to govern himself before he can hope to be an effective minister of state or be able to govern anything else. But one anecdote hints that Gaozi had adopted a bootstrap approach to himself that was too much even for Mozi. Some of Mo's disciples reported that Gaozi was zealous in practicing "humanity" (*ren*). Mozi sniffed. It won't last, he says, for "Gaozi practices humanity like people standing on tiptoe to make themselves tall, or spreading their elbows to make themselves broad."[36]

I take those to be ethical voluntarists who make either or both of two assumptions: (1) that we have no nature as humans; we create our nature by our commitments, our decisions, our historical acts; (2) that the good itself is created by our, or someone's, commitments, decisions, acts of choice. Marxism, at least in Stalinist forms, is voluntaristic in both senses. We have no way of knowing whether Gaozi was a voluntarist in the second sense—as Mozi was, perhaps, in the last analysis, even though the will that creates the good is the will of Heaven.[37] For Gao, conceivably, the good was absolute; it may even have been identical with the Confucian Way. But Gao was a voluntarist in the first sense. He assumes that he creates his character simply by resolving to act in a certain way; that he can add a cubit to his nature, nay, give it its form, simply by taking thought. This made even Mozi uneasy (though Mo implicitly thought the same thing). Many years later, Mencius tried to explain where the trouble lay. But Mencius himself had his voluntaristic residue. Perhaps all self-cultivation philosophers must have it, believing as they do that in some sense one can seek to become what one sees that one is not, at least not at the level of effective moral agency. We all have the "heart of compassion." King Xuan was not a good king. Not because he couldn't be, but because he wouldn't be. No Chinese religious philosopher was more a disciple in the spirit to Mencius than Wang Yangming. Wang went even beyond his mentor and held that good is not just a quality of our nature, but *is* that nature, really. Yet Wang, too, has his problem with getting his students *started* on the path to sagehood. To them we find him saying,

> The way of learning I am now talking about is the task of *creating something from nothing*. You gentlemen must believe me. All depends on *making up the mind*. (Chan, 1963, 72–73, no. 115; emphasis added)

Two Roots or One?[1]

My title has the grammatical form of a question. But I will make a promise at the outset. I am not going to try to answer the question. Instead, I shall use it as a stalking horse for taking some shots at problems that interest me. Let me clear away mystery by abstracting my "text."

It is found in the book called the *Mèngzǐ* 孟子, which is named after a Confucian moralist better known in English as "Mencius." Mencius lived approximately from the year 390 to 310 or 305 B.C. The location in the text is 3A5, which records an argument between Mencius and a man named Yí Zhī 夷之, who was a follower of the earlier (fifth-century) philosopher Mòzǐ 墨子. Mozi and his followers opposed the Confucians, and advocated many things the Confucians didn't like. In the present case, the argument involves two unwelcome Mohist tenets: (i) that religious rituals, in particular funeral rites, should be very simple, so as not to waste the people's productive energies and resources; and (ii) that the constant vendettas and intercity and interstate warfare of the times could be stopped if we would all "love one another impartially," without regard to family ties (or other, political ties).[2] The Confucians objected to both these doctrines as undermining our duties to our parents and respect for ancestors. Mozi in advocating these and other ideas talks as though attitudes like love, belief, and feeling obligated can be adopted at will, when one sees the material usefulness of having them. But by the time of this discussion this extreme voluntaristic aspect of the school has softened, as will be seen.

The story: Yi Zhi, the Mohist, desires to talk with Mencius. Mencius is difficult, won't even let him in; but an argument ensues, carried on through an intermediary. Mencius opens by criticizing Yi Zhi for burying his parents with elaborate rites, thereby doing something contrary to what he recommends, on Mohist principles, for all. Yi Zhi replies—but now I had better let him speak for himself:

> [Even] according to the Confucian Way (*dào* 道), among the ancients, [the right way to treat others was] "as if caring for an infant."[3] What does this maxim (*yán* 言) mean? I take it to mean that we are to love all without difference of degree. But the manifestation of love begins with our parents.

In other words, even Confucian authorities sanction our doctrine of universal love, Yi Zhi argues. The care-for-an-infant attitude is a universal one. But to love at all, we must first develop a capacity for loving.[4] And we do this by doing things—such as performing rich funeral rites for parents—which express and develop feelings of love toward close family members. Once we have the developed *emotional capacity* for love, then we can apply our *philosophical doctrines* and direct this capacity impartially toward all. So, my seemingly inconsistent conduct is merely a means toward my doctrinal end. So, in effect, Yi Zhi argues.

But Mencius sees that Yi Zhi is deceiving himself, rationalizing something he wants to do by twisting his own doctrines and Confucian ones as well. So he comes back at him:

> Does Yi Zhi really think that one's affection for one's brother's child is merely like one's affection for a neighbor's child? That [line he quoted] holds only in its intended application: if a baby crawling about is about to fall into a well this isn't its fault.[5] Moreover, Heaven has given birth to all creatures in such a way that they have *one root* (*yì běn* 一本), and Yi Zhi makes them have *two roots* (*èr běn* 二本). This is the cause [of his confusion].

What Mencius means by "one root" and "two roots" is not immediately evident; but he goes on: in the beginnings of human society, he says, sometimes people didn't bury their parents at all.

> When their parents died, they took them up and threw them into some water channel. Afterwards, when passing by them, [they saw] foxes and wildcats devouring them, and flies and gnats biting at them. There was perspiration on their foreheads and they looked away, unable to bear the sight. It was not on account of other people that this perspiration flowed. [The emotions of] their inmost hearts (*xīn* 心) extended to their faces and eyes; and we may suppose (*gài* 蓋) they went home and came back with baskets and spades and covered the bodies. If this was really right, then filial sons and good people in burying their parents must have a *dao*.[6]

So, Mencius argues, what we really want to do, and what we ought to do and can rightly recognize we ought to do, in the last analysis, both have their source in the human heart, the "one root." If you don't see this, you may suppose that the *heart* (*xin*) supplies emotional capacity, while a quite separate and quite possibly misguided philosophical *doctrine* (*yan*) tells you how the capacity ought to be used.[7] If you treat these—motivation and recognized obligation—as "two roots," you are likely to end not doing what you think you ought to do and then trying to make things right by deceiving yourself, making silly amendments to what was a bad doctrine to start with.

But what I want to emphasize here is not the difference between Mencius and his Mohist opponents, but their similarity.[8] What seems really odd to us about Yi Zhi is his notion that I have an *emotional* capacity—for love, e.g.— which I can then steer, focus, or spread out, this way or that, just by taking *thought*, in accordance with a doctrine that tells me I *ought* to. But when Mencius tells Yi Zhi that his trouble is that he has the wrong doctrine, which is wrong because it isn't derived from how we really feel, he leaves open a possibility that seems just as odd. For suppose I am freshly made aware of an obligation which from Mencius's point of view is a valid one; its "root" is the heart. Still, I have never thought of it (and so, a fortiori, haven't thought of it with any kind of emotional warmth). And it may now be an obligation that interferes with projects I am taken up in. Even if it is pointed out to me, and I come to see that I have feeling-capacities that are consistent with and would naturally be realized in the performance of this obligation, how can I, by taking thought, apply the motivation-capacity to the performance of the duty?

For reasons that will presently be evident, Mencius cannot take a stern Kantian line and say, "If it's your duty, do it! Forget about how you feel!"[9] Nor can he take another kind of line and argue that just recognizing a duty as a duty, if you really do, is motivation ("pro-attitude") enough.[10] He is going to have to argue that it is possible to take one's dispositions in hand and do something about them; and so, to the extent this may be necessary or desirable for acting rightly in the right way, that the management of one's dispositions falls within the range (in fact lies at the center) of one's moral responsibilities. "Motivation and Moral Action in Mencius" (chapter 7 in this volume) deals chiefly with the possibility of doing this in an effective way, and with the tasty question whether it doesn't lead to a "bootstrap" picture of action. In this paper, I want to look more carefully at the aspects of Mencius's concept of moral action that make a right cultivation of disposition *necessary*, and then to ask cautiously whether the picture makes any sense.

Mencius appears to be an unsystematic philosopher. The *Mengzi* (a rather short book) consists of conversations and memorable statements, often quite brief, and it is often difficult to see the reasons for the arrangement that the two-thousand-year-old editorial tradition has given to these things. A new kind of question about him requires a new arranging, and the relevance of part to part often has to be seen in the Chinese. But let me see what I can do toward extracting from him a simple theory of action.

In several places Mencius discourses interestingly on the relation between my sense-desires—for delicious foods, beautiful sights and sounds, etc.—and the part of me that thinks, decides, and chooses; and it is to the latter part that he assigns my moral "tastes." In one way, he assimilates the two parts of me: moral tastes are like other tastes; they are natural. Individuals differ a little. But (6A7) members of a species, and so of the human species, tend to be alike. It is just because this is so that a moral order has come into being that not only deserves our allegiance but also is something that we can and do tend to accept. Its authors were experts in the matter of the moral tastes of the heart; but this is no more mysterious than that in another realm of taste there have been persons whose cultivated sensibility has enabled them to be expert cooks.

But in some other ways, Mencius sharply distinguishes the sense appetites from the moral ones.

(1) The sense appetites are merely passive and reactive. They have their natural objects, and will be *automatically* drawn toward those objects when the objects are present, unless the heart-mind (*xin* means both) intervenes. It is the latter part of me that is autonomous and capable of choosing (6A15).

(2) This means, I think, that for him, in doing something intentionally[11] I am not just doing what I "want" most. Action in this sense is not just a cresting of the wave of desire, even including moral desire, but something *else*—though Mencius takes it for granted that I am more likely to choose to do, or will find it easier to choose to do, something that in some sense I want to do. So, sensibly, what I do when I choose to act contrary to some desire is to locate in myself some desire, perhaps a moral one within my heart, that supports the action and maneuver it into place, so to speak: "if you seek it you will find it" (6A6, 7A3).

(3) I could think of eating as something I do because I naturally want to, or as something I do because, given the way things are, I must. It is wise for me to take the latter attitude toward eating. On the other hand doing my duty is something I could think of in either way, but in this case it is wise for me to take the former attitude and school myself to think of it as something I do wanting to, rather than because I must (7B24).

This last point is very important to Mencius. He is a decent man. He thinks of morality as a good thing. And he thinks people ought to like good things, and not hate them. But if I do my duty just because I must, or worse, if I make myself or am made into a duty-doing person thinking of this as a change superimposed on natural inclinations, I am likely to come to hate morality, and this would be bad (6A1). But note that this seems to imply that I could conceivably do my duty just telling myself to, and not necessarily wanting to.

The picture requires a method and program for the cultivation of moral taste. Just as I might cultivate a taste for fine wine by some sensible and judicious drinking (my example!), so I heighten my moral sensibility and my readiness to act by doing right things, and savoring the feeling of satisfaction that follows. The feedback effect strengthens the disposition, so that next time I am able to do something that would have been too difficult for me to do before in the right way—that is, wanting to, and not simply ordering myself to (2A2.12–16, 4A27.2).

Moving from long-term strategy to particular cases, we see the picture in a different light. There is a well-known story of Mencius talking with King Xuān of Qí 齊宣王 (probably in 319 B.C.), trying to persuade him to lighten taxes and do other things that would make life less difficult for his people (1A7). The king sees this would be right; but he has "weaknesses" (*jí* 疾); he can't, he protests (1B3, 5). Mencius calls his attention to a recent trivial incident in which he displayed spontaneous compassion for an animal about to be sacrificed. It would be more appropriate, surely, for such compassion to be displayed toward your people. But, you see, you have the capacity for compassion. Just take it from *there* and apply it over *here*—"extend" (*tuī* 推) it—Mencius says.

The term he uses, "extend" (*tui*), and the idea behind the use, are from ancient Chinese logic.[12] *Tui*, "extending," was one of the four types of argument, defined by the Mohist logicians as "to propose to one's opponents something they don't accept that is the same as something they do accept," i.e., force them to "extend" their assent from this proposition to that one by showing that the two cases are relevantly similar.[13] Mencius extends the concept of "extending" from the logic of debate to my own management of my dispositions: seeing the similarity of this case, where I have an active feeling of compassion, to that, where I don't, I "extend" my compassion from this to that. Then I will be able to do—in the right way, wanting to—in that case what before I could see I should do but wouldn't, and—in the right way—couldn't.

Left here, Mencius sounds like Yi Zhi: how in the world can I just pick up this attitude here and apply it over there? As we see, Mencius has a program. But then, so did Yi Zhi. One wonders if either has a solution to the problem presented by an immediate need to act, even if one is not ready. If extending his compassion-capacity to the people were something the king is to do purely under the guidance of a principle, Mencius and Yi Zhi would be the same. But Mencius presumably could argue that if the king edges into it he will find increasing satisfaction in doing it. What about the (Confucian) philosophical *doctrine* (*yan*) that says this is what the king *should* do? That was discovered by the sages, those experts in moral taste, and we follow them for convenience. Presumably, exploring our own sensibilities as they explored theirs would lead us in the same direction. But right *now* steering my emotion-capacities in accordance with the sages' teachings looks much like what Yi Zhi was doing—only there is a guarantee that I won't get into Yi Zhi's trouble.

I want now to contrast Mencius with two of his late followers, Wáng Yángmíng 王陽明 and Dài Zhèn 戴震.[14] The object will be, in the end, to see more clearly what Mencius does say by seeing what he doesn't say. Both Wang and Dai think they are Mencians.

Mencius had a view with an implication I have barely noted: my natural taste for the good and the right can with a bit of strategy on my part *both* enable me to choose them happily *and also show me what they are*—because they are the things that will give me the feedback sense of pleasure or satisfaction and so lead me on. This is an idea that could be dangerous.

Wang Yangming fixes on this implication and transforms it. What is going on, he argues, is that there is latent in me all the time a perfect moral understanding-cum-disposition that, unobstructed, would let me just see in every situation what I should do, and would as part of that understanding involve my responding to the situation with just the right blend of attitude and action. The Mencian syncategorization of sense response and moral response is pushed further. I see a beautiful flower and like it. I do not first see its beauty and then decide to like it.[15] Sensing and valuing are inseparable, and valuing is already "the beginning of action." In another example of his treating evaluative response as a kind of sensing, we find him saying this:

> The eye has no substance of its own. Its substance consists of the colors of all things. The ear has no substance of its own. Its substance consists of the sounds of things. The nose has no substance of its own. Its substance consists of the smells of things. The mouth has no substance of its own. Its substance consists of the tastes of things. The mind has no substance of its own. Its substance consists of the right and wrong in the interaction of Heaven, Earth, and all things.[16]

Moral decision and action become, for Wang, a mode of *perception*: just open your moral eyes and *see*. And you *will* see, unless something interferes, some hang-up that prevents seeing, and "obscures" the "sunlight" of moral intuition (his metaphors).[17] This obscuring is caused by selfish impulses, which if they take hold will cause deviant action (or deviant nonaction). The "obscuring" in moral unfortunates may be lifelong; but it is thought of as abnormality nonetheless. For Wang, moral self-development takes the form of what he and others like him call *gōngfu* 功夫, a life of inner self-watching, to spot a "selfish thought" (*sī yì* 私意) as soon as it arises in the mind and immediately say "no" to it.[18]

Dai Zhen lived in a later and very different age. Mencius and Wang had both been charismatic guru types, with "disciples" hanging around and hanging on every word (unlikely as this may seem for a man of Mencius's personality). Dai was a lone bookworm—like me—who spent his life explicating ancient texts—like me again—but was somehow persistently interested in moral philosophy anyway—again like me. The resemblances go on. He was not a self-cultivationist; never a word about that. Instead, he wants to figure the thing out. And he worked at it, and worked at it, as a kind of half-secret sideline, to the embarrassment of his friends. He was one of those philosophers who spends his whole life writing the same book, compulsively, over and over. (I can't claim to that.) The book was a treatise supposedly on the ethics of Mencius, and Dai finished the fourth and last version of it in 1776—the last, we can be sure, only because he died unexpectedly the next year.

But Dai is still a moralist: in a sense, an intellectual life is a life of moral self-perfecting (though he never turns around and makes a personal application of this idea). If one could attain a perfect cognitive, intellectual understanding of moral norms, he thinks, one would have become a person of perfect virtue—and I think we can take my word in its Aristotelian sense here: a person who would always choose, and do, the right actions, and out of a fixed disposition of character. Just as food nourishes the growing body, Dai says, so knowledge nourishes the developing "virtuous nature" (*déxìng* 德性) (1777b, secs. 9, 26).

It works this way: there is no inherent opposition between desire and morality (between what I want and what I ought to do). Moral norms are refinements of desire. Dai quotes and leans on Mencius's view that our hearts have a natural pleasure in the right, but he means it differently. He does, like Mencius, speak about feelings of satisfaction we have in right action; but then he slides into a quite different idea. The refinement of a "natural" (*zìrán* 自然) desire I have into a norm that is "morally necessary" (*bìrán* 必然) consists in running it through a universalizability test, by applying to it Confucius's form of the Golden Rule, "Don't impose on others anything you would not accept yourself."[19] In a simple case, perhaps I want others to do something, or put up with something I do, in line with my interests. May I hold that they ought to? Well, would I accept this constraint as proper if I were in their situation? If so, I have arrived at an "unchanging standard" (*bú yì zhī zé* 不易之則), and this is "moral necessity" (*biran*).[20] To attain this result I have to be a desiring being twice over: first, to have a want to test, and second, to be capable of desiderative sympathy; so, doubly, norm is rooted in desire. Further, when I identify a norm I "approve" (*kě* 可) of it, and this sentiment of approval counts as the "pleasure" (*yuè* 悅) in the right that Mencius noticed.[21]

It seems clear now why Dai thinks perfect *knowledge* makes me perfectly virtuous. To the extent that a pro-attitude of pleasure secures my acting rightly, I maximize this attitude by perfecting my *intellectual* understanding of morality. He (like Wang) still talks about the "obscuring" effect of selfishness. But with Dai it is something that will interfere with my attaining understanding—not something that interferes with the functioning of a "knowledge" that in a deep sense I already (and always) have.

These two interesting and very different men, Wang and Dai, regarded and represented themselves as simply clarifying Mencius's moral philosophy. But on the matter I am looking at, they have turned him upside down.

Comparing them with him, I think we see two quite different ways of thinking of the relation between

(a) seeing that one ought to behave in a certain way

and

(b) actually behaving that way in a particular case.

First there is Wang, who says that if one really sees that one ought to act, in a situation where that action is an option, one just will. If something in you intervenes, a "selfish desire," which is abnormal, this negates the knowledge. Dai doesn't seem to raise the problem; but his concept of moral knowledge leads him to suppose there just couldn't be a problem: if you have it, you're virtuous. And there is Mencius, who says the sense desires are automatically, mindlessly (by definition) pulled toward their appropriate objects—the mouth toward pleasant tastes, the eye toward beauty, etc.—when those objects are present (and this may be good or bad). Nothing alters this situation unless the mind-heart *does* something.

On the first view, strictly speaking, action against knowledge is impossible. Acting intentionally, on this view, is in effect thought of as a sort of cresting of the wave of motivatedness. Intention and choice are not something other than a peaking of motivation, which is, in Wang, a perfect active "perceiving" of one's situation. For both Dai and Wang, seeing that you ought and being moved (two roots?) are the same thing: in the one being moved is assimilated to seeing; in the other it's the other way around. It then becomes a criterion of really knowing that one ought to do the thing, that one has sufficient motivatedness to crest into action at the right time. So, in acts or omissions that are wrong, the knowledge was imperfect: there was some residual "obscuring," or an intrusion of a selfish obscuring "I want this!" that neutralized knowledge at least momentarily.

On this view, *akrasia* is an interference with the functioning of a moral knowledge, which functioning would occur *of itself* if there were no interference.[22] So, relatively speaking and in a deep sense, *akrasia* is *doing* something, whether the result be wrong action or wrong nonaction.

Now, there is enough in Mencius that is like this to make it not puzzling how someone like Wang could think himself to be saying what Mencius was really saying. Mencius does say that those whose conduct is objectionable have "lost their original hearts" (6A10), and that if they would "just think" they would find their hearts again (in time) (6A15). Then, we are invited to suppose, all would be well. But the "thinking" itself is *doing* something. And the example of King Xuan and the ox (1A7) seems to show that even if (with help, perhaps) you do some "thinking" and find a right-favoring impulse in yourself, you may still just not apply it. So, in Mencius's picture, acting without regard to what you see you should do doesn't seem to require an explanation. It's just that, in the deepest sense of agency, you didn't do anything.

On this second view, then, *akrasia* is a failure to intervene in and steer the functioning of desires that would function of themselves in an unguided, mindless way if there were no intervention. So, relatively speaking, *akrasia* is *not* doing something, whether the result be wrong action or wrong nonaction. And so on this view acting intentionally, in a deep sense of agency, is *doing* something in addition to being moved, no matter how strongly one is moved and no matter how helpful the being moved might be. It may involve using, ordering, opposing one to another, focusing on or cultivating motives, focusing attention on what you know; but it is not just the causal effect of having certain motives and knowing or believing certain things.

So a performance criterion isn't logically imposed on knowing per se. If one doesn't act or lets oneself act wrongly, it may just be that one simply hasn't done the right thing:

> Here is a basketful of rice and a bowlful of soup. Getting them will mean life; not getting them will mean death. When these are given with abuse, . . . even a beggar will not accept them. Yet when it comes to [an income of] ten thousand bushels of grain, one accepts them without regard for propriety and right. . . . In the previous case, for the sake of one's own life one did not accept [what was offered]. In the current case, for the sake of a beautiful mansion . . . , for the obedience of a wife and concubine . . . , [and] in order to have poor acquaintances be indebted to oneself, one does it. Is there no way of stopping this too? (6A10)

It is the picture, again, of the heart-mind (*xin*) performing or failing to perform its function of reflecting and choosing, and so, if not acting, simply letting the material appetites go the way they will mindlessly, if unguided. So, even a failure to keep from doing something is represented as a passive failure to do something, rather than an active wrongdoing. This seems to me to be Mencius's characteristic way of thinking of the matter.

It is noteworthy that Mencius uses the paradigm of accepting an improper or compromising gift. He uses this paradigm over and over. In contrast, the favored paradigms of *akrasia* in Western literature—exercise of ravenous appetites, pursuit of what Aquinas delicately calls "the pleasures of touch"—go unexplored. The cultural reasons for his favoring this paradigm are deep, and interesting: gratitude is a compulsive psychic bond as subjectively experienced throughout this society, binding the beneficiary to open-ended and undefined obligations; accepting a gift, therefore, is dangerous, and giving one is a source of power, compelling approval. In accepting a gift, I am simply allowing an ongoing social activity to proceed, in which I as a morally weak person am in a passive situation.[23]

Where does "extending" fit into these pictures? In Wang Yangming, not at all. The problem is to get rid of the "clouds," and then the light of moral intuition (*liáng zhī* 良知) extends *itself*.[24] (In fact, it is sometimes defined in this school as being its own "extension.")[25] And in Dai Zhen, not at all: perfect intellectual grasp of oughts maximizes the moral-norm-favoring attitude of "approving" (*ke*), and this is the heart-mind's enjoyment of the right. Dai doesn't even conceive of there being a problem of action at this point.

The concept belongs to and is required by Mencius. I have noted its possible origin in ancient analyses of the logic of debate. But it is not just an imaginative transfer of a logical concept to moral psychology. It must arise as a problem when what I am doing is not just to get you to accept the truth of a proposition but trying to get you (or myself) to do something.

That, over there, is a white horse. Over here is a white horse with a person riding it. You grant in the first case "that is a horse," and you see the similarity of case (1) to case (2). So, you must grant in case (2) that "this is a horse." Thus, the person can not only be said to be riding a *white horse*, but can also be said to be riding a *horse* (simpliciter).[26]

In moral "extending" as in this case, the argument form is conceived as analogical. Here is a frightened animal. There are some desperate human beings—your subjects, oh king. In this case, you see that the creature is in a bad situation, pity it and spare it. So in that case, recognize the same fact, pity them, spare them, lighten their taxes, put an end to harsh punishments.

The difference is that, in "extending" in the case of extending an aggressive argument about truths of propositions, just getting your opponents to see the argument wins the day. But in the second example, just getting them to follow the argument doesn't guarantee they will do anything or change their attitude. (They may feel its force and feel an unpleasant tension between that force and their own nonaction, and say they "can't"—relieving the tension by deceiving themselves—to Mencius's great irritation.) More work is necessary. Now internalize the dialogue between Mencius and the king and think of it as a dialogue between me and myself, that leaves *me* with unfinished business. That unfinished business is "extending."

Succinctly, in a way of talking familiar to Western philosophers: in thinking out a practical syllogism, the akratic or potentially akratic person can be represented as doing the following.

First, the person thinks, "In S situations, one ought to do A acts"; and in thinking "ought," the person *feels*, as his or her imagination runs, "I should, and would want to, and would, do A in S."

Then the person notices, "This is a situation S that I am in now."

And he or she concludes, "So, I ought to do an A act now." So the person *thinks*; and the person may also notice that it would be appropriate for him or her to *feel* in this situation the way he or she did in the imagined one; indeed, that he or she ought to.

But the person doesn't *feel* this way. Seeing the connection in thought, and so *thinking*, "I ought to do an A act now" is, for that person (and for anyone), just a matter of consistency, of *thinking clearly*. But feeling doesn't work this way: we don't even have a use for the expression "feeling clearly." We might say that the person has drawn the cognitive conclusion, but he or she hasn't "drawn" the "feeling conclusion." Still, the person really does think that he or she ought to do an A act now. Right?

The strict "internalist," or the "prescriptivist," will say at this point, No: you can't think "ought" without being effectively disposed to do it.[27] It doesn't make any sense to say "I ought to, but I don't care"; if you *mean* "I ought to," you *do* care. And similarly with the universal premise: the question has already been begged in supposing there is a cognitive component and a separate dispositional component to the acceptance of a universal "ought" statement, such that a mental act of inferring could operate on the cognitive component only. If you *really* think, "In S situations, I ought always to do A acts," your *thinking* it will involve your being disposed to *do* A acts in every S situation to which you actually do, in inference, apply this premise. So, if in an appropriate situation you *don't* act, we must say that either you didn't really carry through the inference and draw the conclusion (you were just noticing what the premise would imply if one were to accept it, without taking into account that you do accept it); or you didn't really "have" the premise at all. In either case, "weakness of will" is an incoherent idea: there isn't any such thing.

One can say this, if one pays the price, which is fixed; one must add one of two things: (1) we never know whether we, or anyone, ever does accept a universal "ought" premise; because there could always be some unforeseen situation in which one would balk. But we don't talk this way about our moral understandings. What we do say is that when people balk, either they display weakness, or they are in the process of withdrawing their allegiance to a principle they had really held, even though as it turns out their allegiance to it didn't involve their being strongly motivated enough to do this, now.

Or one must say that (2) instantiating an "ought" premise requires more than just thinking something out in the ordinary way, noticing meanings, truth values, and logical relations. That's all very well for the "cats eat mice" kind of proposition; but the "one ought to keep one's promises" kind requires more: it requires that one have focused one's general disposition effectively on the particular case, before we can say an inference is made. And if internalists say this, I think they are just saying over again what I am saying (and seeing in Mencius) in other words.

Unless what they want to insist is that this richer kind of "inferring" is accomplished just by especially careful thinking, without requiring some additional kind of self-management. For whether thinking per se can have this kind of directive effect on one's disposition was what was at issue; and this issue seems to me to be not a philosophical question but one for empirical psychology. As amateur psychologist, whose material is mostly himself, I am inclined to say that thinking is often not enough. (But it could be that we are quite astonishingly different in this regard.)

To return to potentially akratic people: if they do find that careful thinking leaves them still in a bind, at this point, under the pressure of the impasse, they may, of course, review and reject their conclusion together with its basis, perhaps even having been led to see good reason for doing so (what Mencius ultimately led Yi Zhi to see). But if they maintain it, they have to choose one of three courses:

(1) They can do act A anyway, even though feeling negatively about A itself. They force themselves to do it, and the motive guiding them may now be just that they feel they must follow their rule. They act *encratically*, and in Mencius's terms "treat rightness as external" (2A2.15). But, according to Mencius, this is to do something other than an A action. Mencius is a kind of act-internalist: a moral act is related to the feeling it expresses in the same way that a smile is; and a forced smile, of course, isn't a smile. Furthermore, Mencius claims, doing the action in this way may actually hurt one's moral development (2A2.16).

(2) They can do nothing: this is full-fledged *akrasia*.

(3) They can take steps to "cultivate" the feeling-capacity elicited by hypothetical cases and "extend" it to the actual one they are in. This of course may take time, if they find a way to do it at all, and in that time the opportunity and need for action may threaten to pass—forcing a choice between (1) and (2). Life *can* be tragic; though Mencius, if he had noticed and pursued this, would have been loath to admit it.

The Mencian problem is unlike the "practical syllogism" formulation because he conceives moral reasoning as analogical: I ought to do, and feel like doing, that in that case. This case is like that one. So . . . Here the point of departure is a concrete case of focused disposition, which is *itself* and so *other* than the target case. It is not as if the point of departure were a commitment to a rule (*yan*) which "covers" the target case (the rule often lies buried, unanalyzed, in the intuition of similarity). So the problem of "moving this heart from here to there" is more obvious and urgent. But only more so: the problem is present in the practical syllogism too.

In the "practical analogy" (to adapt a phrase) the proximate case (the frightened animal) elicits both a recognition of fact (acceptance of a proposition) and a feeling of pity (with concomitant action). Just seeing the argument involves accepting a corresponding proposition in the target case (the downtrodden people). But the motivation component of an ideally complete "conclusion" isn't automatic: one has to do something. (In contrast, Wang Yangming says, look at a beautiful flower; you don't *first* see its beauty, and *then* admire it.)

One could just do something to or for the people, not to yourself. Mencius doesn't want it that way, for reasons already partly explained. The act should be done with a positive feeling about it (not "because" you have that feeling, either in the "for the reason that" sense of "because" or the other sense). And one could pursue this in a paradoxical direction for Mencius (doing something to yourself is doing something, and the same kind of analysis could apply: one could reason that one should; and perhaps one could just do it, but not necessarily in the right way). But what is of interest here is that the steps in the argument seem to be "action guiding" (must this expression mean "action causing"?)—but the conclusion turns out not to be. The motivational component is not something that just automatically is there when one sees the connection. One must take further measures with oneself. And, of course, one may fail.

Should this picture be counterintuitive? I want to try arguing that it is a quite natural one; and further, that it can plausibly be seen as applicable to reasoning of other kinds, not just to moral reasoning.

Here is an example that I find innocently amusing. Consider figure 9.1. Now, draw a freehand line intersecting each line segment exactly once. I begin this task in figure 9.2. Completing the line is left as an exercise for the reader.

But, of course, the task is impossible. I have several times in my life—for entertainment (when I should have been doing something else)—constructed simple proofs of its impossibility (and have forgotten them as many times, but I could produce one again easily). Furthermore, one can give an intuitive presentation of steps and premises—quite concretely: draw lines and figures that show you just can't do this or that—such that each has a "hat-doffing" obviousness, so that one would feel it ridiculous to do anything or start doing anything whose being done would be incompatible with those steps and premises. Yet, I could amuse myself for some time apparently (to myself) *trying* to draw *that* line. Here, an action-arresting sense of obviousness in the argument does not carry over to my acceptance of the conclusion "this is impossible."

This example both tempts and disturbs. You will immediately have said that I am not trying to do something I know to be impossible. One just *can't* do that. It wouldn't be, couldn't count as, *trying*. Alternatively, if it is trying, this just shows I'm not really thinking the thing impossible. I could duck this objection and save the example by saying that I'm *amusing myself* in a way one wouldn't expect for one so convinced of the arguments. (Or, trying to see how close I can come to doing what I know is impossible: again, inappropriate behavior, since one immediately finds one can get all but one of them.) And then one has to say, as I have, that here an action-arresting sense of obviousness in the reasoning does not automatically carry over to the *way* I accept the

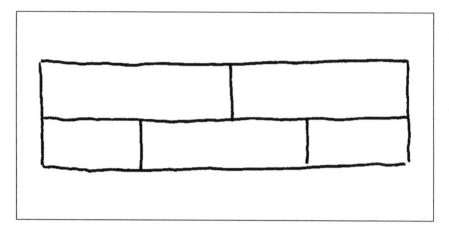

Figure 9.1

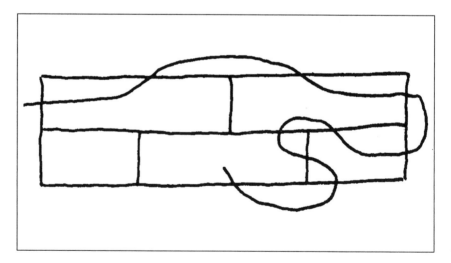

Figure 9.2

conclusion as applied to *this* case: *this* is impossible. I have to do something more than just think clearly.

The last part of this, at least, is right, I think. But let me bite the bullet. Whether or not this is a genuine example of attempting what one believes impossible, the example does seem to show a disturbing similarity between attempting what you think impossible (if possible) and doing what you believe you shouldn't. If trying to do something shows I don't really think I just can't, doesn't doing something show I don't really think I just oughtn't? And on the one hand I have as strong an intuition as most of you (this doesn't mean I'm convinced of it) that one can't attempt what one believes to be impossible. But on the other hand, I can't help but feel that the philosophers who think what the parallel would suggest—that freely and intentionally doing something one fully believes one shouldn't is an incoherent idea—are philosophers who are constructed psychologically very differently from the way I am.

One way to go at the matter might be to say that while one can go as far as one can toward doing the physically or mathematically impossible, and also can go as far as one can toward doing the morally or prudentially "impossible"—or impermissible-for-me—since the impermissible is often all too possible, "as far as one can" becomes vacuous; and since one knows this very well, one can, alas, intend the known-to-be-impermissible while one cannot intend the known-to-be-impossible.

But there is more than one way to compare attempting what I believe I can't do and doing what I believe I shouldn't do, and here I've let myself be tempted into one that is not to the present point. That point is better served by noticing that whatever I am doing with that silly line—trying or "trying"— the line is *silly*, and I know it. Yet I try (or "try") again. This is not *like* weakness of will; it *is* weakness of will. Why does it happen? But I'm flinching now: why don't I *stop* the silly business? I've already offered my answer.

Consider a modern ruler who is possibly like King Xuan of Qi. The ruler runs a fairly tight shop, and is now shopping for a new home. He or she might well be a perfectly decent person who would be upset and moved to intervene if he or she saw someone torturing an animal—the while bloodlessly aware that humans were being treated this way in the ruler's own prisons, and that the ruler could do something about it. But this would require an inconvenient reorganization of the ruler's time, projects, and sensibilities. It's easier to think of something more practical. The ruler does nothing.

This will serve to close with a reminder that the problems I've been teasing are not always as trivial as the little desk-blotter game I asked you to look at. But I will keep my promise, and will not try to answer my original question, "Two Roots or One?" Mencius's answer was, "One." And I take him to mean that *my right judgments about what I ought to do, if I probe, and how I really feel about such things, if I dig, both turn out to have their source or "root" in the "heart,"* which is at the same time for him the mind. This is not the problem that has interested me here. But there is a way of answering "one" that Mencius, I think, rejected implicitly (though some of his later followers, thinking they were following him, accepted it): Mencius would hold, I think, that my judgment that I ought to do something is not, in itself, a feeling moved toward doing it, still less a feeling moved in the right way. These matters do interest me very much.

Problems in the *Mengzi*: 6A3–5[1]

> My imagination had got started on the wrong scent, and that is always hopeless; one is sure, then, to go straight on misinterpreting everything, clear through to the end.
> —Mark Twain, *A Tramp Abroad*

Sections 6A3–5 of the *Mèngzǐ* 孟子 have always been among the knottiest for commentators and translators. They are intrinsically fascinating. Mencius and Gàozǐ 告子, and then two of their followers, are arguing about human nature and about moral virtues. Gaozi takes the offensive. He undertakes to compare sentences (or perhaps the logical structure of the facts they state) and tries to extract substantive moral conclusions from these comparisons. Mencius contents himself here with defense, although it is apparent what his positions are. The arguers (or the editors who report them to us) use, without amplification, terms that obviously carry a heavy load of meaning. They use logical moves obviously familiar to them, that may not be what we take them to be. A measure of the experienced difficulty is the fact that at two points in 6A4, the most problematic of these sections, various scholars (e.g., Yú Yuè 俞樾, Legge, Waley, Lau, and commentators in earlier centuries) have proposed emendations, or have at least supposed that the text cannot make sense as it stands.

I will offer here my translation of sections 3, 4, and 5. This translation will reject all proposed emendations and complaints about the text and will suppose that it is correct as we have it. My translation differs substantially from those of D. C. Lau and Angus Graham, the writers in English who have attended to these texts with the greatest care.[2]

The first emendation to set aside is the sectioning done by Zhào Qí 趙岐 in the second century A.D. Book 6A, at least, I consider to be a single unitary composition—at least in the sense that the order and arrangement of its parts are the work of an editor, who may have been Mencius, or someone able to consult Mencius. Sections 1 through 6 all develop, explicitly, Mencius's differences with Gaozi on human nature (*xìng* 性). The composition here is not seamless. There is an obvious change in the mode of argument from 6A2 to 6A3, and it is perhaps safe to start with 6A3. But seeing 6A3–4 as a unit will be important, and seeing 6A1–2 as leading into this unit will be relevant. (6A5, which I will discuss briefly, looks like an add-on to the group 6A3–4, and 6A6 is obviously added onto 6A1–5, and so on.)

Mengzi 6A1–2

Let me first, then, summarize what I think is going on in 6A1–2.[3] In 6A1 Gao argues that "to make morality out of human nature is like making cups and bowls out of willow wood."[4] This indicates that he thinks moral habits and dispositions are formed by education and discipline in a morally neutral human material. Under discussion here is the cause or origin of moral *dispositions*, not the particular occasional causes or promptings of particular moral *acts*. In this respect 6A2 is ambiguous. Gao shifts the analogy to rapidly moving water contained in some way.[5] "Give it an outlet in the east and it will flow east," etc. An outlet on this particular occasion, or a permanent channel? Mencius doesn't help resolve this ambiguity. While insisting this doesn't really show the nature of water, he grants that you can splash it over your head (producing behavior on a particular occasion) or dam it and keep it from flowing down (permanent or long-term modification of behavior). We can see from this that (1) one of the things that is going to be at issue in the subsequent arguments is the question, What is the *cause* of my morality—is it "inside" me or "outside" me? And (2) there is an initially unnoticed ambiguity about occasional causes and long-term causes, and so about morality as *act* and morality as *disposition*.

In proceeding, I shall use the standard numbering of Zhao Qi's subsections, alphabetically sub-subdividing for convenience of reference.[6] And since I shall be talking about what Gaozi and Mencius are saying about certain sentences, I shall have to indicate the latter separately; for this purpose I shall use capital letters.

Mengzi 6A3.1

Gaozi said,	告子曰
A *Shēng* is what is meant by "*xìng.*"	生之謂性

I agree with Lau and Yu Yue that the two crucial words here were in Mencius's time written alike and probably pronounced nearly alike, and so are in a sense "the same word."[7] What they mean we cannot yet say. *Sheng*, of course, can mean 'life', 'alive', 'produce', 'be born', and so it can easily yield a derivative meaning 'nature'. However that may be, Gao's statement would have come across to Mencius as

A' *Sheng*[ADJ] is what is meant by "*sheng*[P]."

We need the superscripts to keep track. Mencius didn't. I shall continue this usage.[8]

Mengzi 6A3.2a

Mencius said,"Is	孟子曰
A' *Sheng*[ADJ] is what is meant by '*sheng*[P]'	生之謂性也
like	猶
B White[ADJ] is what is meant by 'white[P]'?"	白之謂白與
[Gaozi] said, "Yes."	曰然

Bái 白 (literary reading *bó*) is the word for "white" here, but it is obviously not "white" in the same sense in both places. Here we have to read on to find out what is happening. But Gaozi didn't. He apparently recognized at once what must have been a standard way of talking among ancient Chinese logic-choppers. And Mencius evidently takes it for granted that Gao knows more of the game:

Mengzi 6A3.2b

白羽之白也猶白雪之白。白雪之

白猶白玉之白與。

曰然。

[Mencius said,] "Is a white[ADJ] feather's white[P] like white[ADJ]

snow's white[P],and white[ADJ] snow's white[P] like white[ADJ]

jade's white[P]?"

[Gaozi] said, "Yes."

My superscripts here are obviously a critical interpretive move. I am assuming that since, clearly, the problem word in sentence B and in, for example, "a white[ADJ] feather's white[P]" is in each case "white[P]," therefore "white[P]" in the one phrase can be identified with "white[P]" in the other; and similarly with "white[ADJ]." Mencius's immediate move to what he proposes in 6A3.2b suggests this, as does the fact that *bai*[ADJ] and *bai*[P] occur in the same order in both 6A3.2a and 6A3.2b. The text will presently reinforce this suggestion in its use of *sheng*[P]. But it is worth noting that one translator, Dobson (1963, 111), arrives at a momentarily coherent translation on a different assumption:

> Kao Tzu said, "What I mean by nature is the thing that gives life." Mencius asked, "Do you mean that in the sense that you would say that whiteness is the thing that whitens?"

My interpretation has the advantage of allowing the text before us to elucidate itself. We have, I take it, what Aristotle at the beginning of the *Categories* calls "paronymy": two words of different word-classes with the same root; and in English it is at least possible in the case of "white" for the two words to be even spelled the same.[9]

Notice, incidentally, that Mencius does not put forward his proposal in 6A3.2b as a consequence Gao ought to accept, having accepted what Mencius proposed in 6A3.2a (as, e.g., Dobson (1963) and Ware (1960) both suppose). The function of the first proposal was to prepare the way for the second in another sense: to license Mencius to draw out the implication of A' by talking about "white." In 6A3.2b Mencius offers another independent proposition about "white" that he thinks Gao *will* accept—as in fact he does. Mencius probably accepted it himself. (The question whether Mencius also accepts it is irrelevant to the argument considered purely as a piece of verbal swordplay.) But it *is* possible to take the view that the white of one kind of thing is not just like the white of another kind of thing, and Zhao Qi actually supposed this to be what Mencius thought. One must still distinguish this qualitative distinguishing of whites from Aristotle's notion of a "particular white"—the white that is Socrates' just because he is the individual he is.[10]

But I digress. We can now interpret B:

B When we speak of [the color] white[P], we are talking about the quality we ascribe to a thing when we speak of it as a white[ADJ] thing of some kind or other.

this in turn yields an interpretation for A (or A'):

A When we speak of the quality "live[P]," we are talking about the quality we ascribe to a thing when we speak of it as a live[ADJ] thing of some kind or other.

—and we would do this of a thing, in the intended sense of "live[ADJ]," if we simply identify that thing as an *animal* of some kind or other. Perhaps a white horse *is* a horse, but a dead horse is not.[11] So also with dogs, oxen, and people. Mencius continues:

Mengzi 6A3.3

然則犬之性猶牛之性。

牛之性猶人之性與。

"Then a [sc. *sheng*[ADJ]] dog's *sheng*[P] is like a [sc. *sheng*[ADJ]] ox's *sheng*[P], and a [sc. *sheng*[ADJ]] ox's *sheng*[P] is like a [sc. *sheng*[ADJ]] person's *sheng*[P], isn't it?"

But for Mencius, of course, *sheng*[P] will not do here for the word we now read *xing*. For him it is "nature," the nature of a living thing as a thing of its *kind*, what it is that distinguishes one kind of thing from other kinds.[12] Presumably

Mencius feels that Gao ought to be struck dumb at this point, and Zhao Qi, ending the section here, evidently thought he actually was. But for Gao, *xing* is not what distinguishes one species from another, but what distinguishes the living from the nonliving. And it is not unreasonable to suppose that he would have heartily approved the statement of Xúnzǐ 荀子 that things with desires and things without desires belong to two different categories, the categories of the living and the dead.[13] If the next section shows him continuing the dialogue, this is just what he says.

Mengzi 6A4.1

告子曰。食色性也。仁內也。非外也。

義外也。非內也。

Gaozi said, "Eating and sex are *sheng*ᵖ. *Ren* is internal, not external. *Yi* is external, not internal."

Perhaps for Gaozi "eating" and "sex" (*sè* 色, literally "color") are given here as examples of the sort of thing *sheng*ᵖ is, rather than as a definition of it. Perhaps "eating" will include or stand for all of the acquiring-and-consuming pleasures, and "sex" (maybe "color" is better after all) will stand for our being drawn toward any of the things (or persons) that we seem to relish seeing and contemplating.[14] The latter would then include the whole range of biologically and psychologically based affections for other persons; and so it will include *rén* 仁 (benevolence), which will be seen to be exemplified for Gaozi by affection for and care for persons in one's family.

Yi 義 is the major villain of the piece. The word, for Confucians and probably for Gaozi, means "right," "proper." But it can be a predicate of individual acts; or an act that is *yi*; or the kind of act that is *yi*; or the quality that *yi* acts have; or a predicate of persons (who regularly do *yi* acts); or the name of the quality or disposition or virtue that such persons have; or a verb, to do something that is *yi* to someone; or the esteem that someone enjoys in receiving such treatment; or a verb, to recognize people as and esteem them for being those who have the virtue *yi*; or the honor or esteem that this last kind of person enjoys. Gao and Mencius take for granted that *yi* involves such things as respect shown to elders.[15] Whether *yi* is just doing something, or has an important psychic overtone (and in whom), and what my vague word "involves" comes to, are things they are about to argue out. Mencius probes, and Gao expands:

Mengzi 6A4.2a

孟子曰。何以謂仁內義外也。

Mencius said, "Why do you say *ren* is internal and *yi* is external?"

Mengzi 6A4.2b

[Gao] said, "[In the following case,]   曰。

C He is *zhang*^{ADJ} and I *zhang*^{TV} him.   彼長而我長之。

D It is not that there is *zhang* in me."   非有長於我也。

Zhǎng^{ADJ} 長 is "older" (sc. than myself), and so, of course, in the case of a person, "elder" and to be respected. I use *zhang*^{TV} here for the verbal use of *zhang*: imputing, treating as, or causing to be older. It is not Gao's exhibition sentence (sentence C) but his comment (sentence D) that it is not the case that "there is *zhang* in me" (*yǒu zhǎng yú wǒ* 有長於我), that is the main problem here. I have left out the superscript of *zhang* in Gao's comment on his specimen sentence. The only nominal *zhang* available in terms of my analysis so far is *zhang*^P which presumably would be "the quality of being *zhang*^{ADJ}," i.e. "olderness," and so (at least among humans) "elderliness, seniority." This seems to make the line mean "it is not that I am older (sc. than he)," which is ridiculous. But there is a common idiom

     X *yǒu* Y *yú* Z

     X 有 Y 於 Z

meaning "in or for X there is Y in relation to Z," or more perspicuously, "X has Y from Z," "X is Y-ed by Z." So D can be

     D' It is not that [he] has *zhang*^P from me.

or

     D" It is not that [he] is *zhang*^{TV}-ed by me.

But, of course, he *is zhang*^{TV}-ed by me: ex hypothesi, "I *zhang*^{TV} him." At least, in one sense: I impute or recognize *zhang*^P in him, *see* him to be *zhang*^{ADJ}, perhaps even *treat* him appropriately as *zhang*^{ADJ}. So reading D" does not make sense in this context. On the other hand, I do not *cause* him to be *zhang*^{ADJ}, *give* him his quality *zhang*^P. Now, if I see him and treat him as *zhang*^{ADJ}, conceivably we can speak of my having at least the capacity, perhaps the disposition, in appropriate circumstances, to do so. Let us call this *zhang*^{DIS}. There are words that are usable in the idiom before us that seems to be like this, e.g., *chǒng* 寵, "favor," as in the *Zuǒ Zhuàn* 左傳:

子儀有寵於桓王。

Ziyi had favor with King Huan.

Ziyi was favored by King Huan.

For Ziyi there was favor in King Huan.[16]

Perhaps, in other words, Gao's language lures him into half thinking that in making the not-to-be-denied statement that

D' It is not the case that he gets elderliness from me.

he has nailed a quite different point. D' is, of course, in fact true: the elder just *is* older, and it is, we might say, an objective "institutional fact" (even, within the institutional context, a fact about the elder) that his juniors, including me, owe him respect for it.[17] But then the Chinese that goes into D' seems also to say

D''' It is not the case that there is a disposition or capacity in me to *zhang*[TV] him.

That is, it is not the case that there is in me any *zhang*[DIS] that accounts in any significant way for the fact that I *zhang*[TV] him now. And this may well be false.[18] Anyway, Mencius will certainly think that it is. But Gao will not regard D''' as problematic: it seems to slide into place from something he has said that has an obviously true interpretation, and he is not thinking here in terms of *dispositions*. The case seems to him to be like one of simple causal perception. There is something there now, that necessarily triggers my recognition.

And so, Gao continues:

Mengzi **6A4.2c**

"[This] is like	猶
E He is white[ADJ] and I white[TV] him	彼白而我白之
F following his white outside.	從其白於外也。
So I call it 'external.'"	故謂之外也。

Gao's comment (sentence F) is troublesome. *Yú wài* 於外 seems to be literally "in (on) the outside"; *wai*, "outside," is a nominal word, and comes to mean "external" either in the sense "located outside" or "related to the outside" in some significant sense (coming from it, caused by it, etc.). And what super-script am I to give "white" in my translation? The syntax of the comment,

F *cóng qí bái yú wài yě*
從其白於外也

is odd. Is something being said one would not ordinarily try to say or think of saying? "Following his whiteness being located outside," ought to be

> F* *cóng qí bái zài wài yě*
>
> 從其白在外也

If so, *bai* cannot be "white^P." And normal idiom decrees that "white^ADJ" in this context would give

> F' following his being whiter than outside.

which makes no sense here. *Bai* as a transitive verb, however, would give

> F" following his being *bai*-ed by [someone or something] outside.

and this might be usable: Gao might be saying that when I white^TV him, see him as white^ADJ, my doing so "follows" (is caused by, if I look at him at all) the fact that factors "outside" (i.e., independent of myself), also white^TV him. Specifically, these external factors white^TV him in the sense of making it the case that he is white^ADJ. In simplest terms, Gao would be·saying that I treat him as white because he just *is* white. An easier way to get this meaning, however—I think it must be the right one—is to read F as equivalent to F* after all: There was an old use of *yú* 於, obsolescent by Mencius's time, as a full verb, just meaning *zài* 在, "is located."[19]

The mischief in the ambiguity noted in 6A2 is now more visible. Is *yi*, on Gao's view, "external" because my disposition to, capacity for, *yi* behavior is caused by training rather than being latent within me? Or is it his view that it is external because my *yi* act now is prompted by something in front of me now, that is just "there," that does not depend on me for having the quality that prompts me now? Gao perhaps fails to notice that even seeing a white man as white is "internal" in one sense: his being-seeable-by-me-as-white is a quality he wouldn't have if I didn't have eyes. Nor, of course, does he reflect that I might have a disposition to respond to a certain color by going into an epileptic fit when I see it; such behavior he might well count as "internal," and yet the disposition might have an external cause, say, a head injury. But the need for another distinction draws Mencius's attention:

Mengzi 6A4.3a

曰。異於白馬之白也。無以
異於白人之白也。

[Mencius] said, "[The case of *zhang*^P] is not like [the standard example,] a white^ADJ horse's white^P. [This standard case] is not different from a white^ADJ person's white^P.

Mengzi 6A4.3b

不識長馬之長也無以異於
長人之長與。

[But] I wonder if a *zhang*[ADJ] horse's *zhang*[P] isn't different from a *zhang*[ADJ] person's *zhang*[P]?

My treatment of this passage differs from the consensus of translators. Others, following standard commentaries, insist the text is defective, and that either the opening words *yì yú* 異於 (here meaning "is not like") must be struck out, or something added.[20] They fail, I think, to ask, Why does Mencius start talking about horses? Presumably, because when one is talking about how in the normal case a predicate applies to a thing one does talk about a "white horse."[21] This must have been why Gōngsūn Lóng 公孫龍, to be maximally provocative, chose to deny the thesis that a white horse is a horse rather than, say, denying that a wooden bell is a bell.[22]

The second difference is my construing of the words *bái mǎ zhī bái* 白馬之 白, "white horse's white." Chai and Chai (1965), Couvreur (1910), Lau (1970), Legge (1970), Lyall (1932), and Wilhelm (1921) take this in effect as "to see-as-white a horse's white." Dobson (1963), Giles (1993), and Ware (1960) take the words as I do. But if, rejecting Zhao Qi's sectioning, one considers 6A4 as continuing on from 6A3, one simply cannot suppose an abrupt change of syntax in a word pattern that seems to be paradigmatic anyway. For, "a white horse's white," etc., here has just the same structure as "a white feather's white," etc., in 6A3.2b. Further, this interpretation is required in order to give point to Mencius's next remark:

Mengzi 6A4.3c

且謂長者義乎。長之者義乎。

Moreover, do you say that [his] being *zhang*[ADJ] is [what is] *yi*, or that [for me] to *zhang*[TV] him is [what is] *yi*?[23]

It is grammatically possible to render this, "Moreover, do you say that it is he who is *zhang*[ADJ] that is *yi*, or that he who *zhang*[TV]-s someone is *yi*?" Graham, Lau, and Ware take this to be the grammar of it, as do the commentary of Zhao Qi and the one ascribed to Sūn Shì 孫奭 (early Song Dynasty). It can easily be shown, however, that Mencius uses the form

... 者 ...，... 者 ...
... *zhě* ...，... *zhě* ...

as we might use italics, to pose alternatives.[24] And although Mencius does sometimes use *yi* as an adjective describing a person,[25] almost always it is a noun in his usage. The most reasonable assumption seems to me to be that Mencius is actually quoting words Gao had used in sentence C above. In any case, 6A4.3c shows that my analysis of 6A4.3a–b is right. There would be no point in Mencius here underlining "*zhang*^TV-ing him" (*or* "the one who *zhang*^TV-s him") if "*zhang*^TV-ing him," "white^TV-ing him," etc. were already the focus of attention.[26] But, one will ask, why labor the obvious? Was there any reason to suppose that someone might be tempted to think that it is being *zhang*^ADJ that is *yi*? Perhaps there was (as will be seen).

Mencius has just asked what seem to be two rhetorical questions, and Gao does not object, apparently. He continues his case, and I assume that he accepts both points: in talking about what *yi* is, we should be talking about X^TV-ing someone, not about his being X^ADJ; and it is only (at most) when it is a human being that is X^ADJ that my X^TV-ing him will be a case of *yi*. Still, the *yi* act, admittedly *my* X^TV-ing him, is "external," as Gao had said, if his being X^ADJ is not dependent on my X^TV-ing him but is a necessary condition for it. Gao now tries to show why it is reasonable to say this notwithstanding the fact that it is I who do it. The argument that he offers has caused much trouble. Most have despaired of making literal sense of it, and two, Lau and Graham, who are the ones who have given it the most careful attention in English, have felt it necessary, in effect, to emend the text.[27] I think that the text means exactly what it says, but finding out what that is is a nontrivial exercise. I will first try to give a neutral rendering:

Mengzi 6A4.4a

曰。吾弟則愛之。秦人之弟則不愛也。

[Gaozi] said, "If it is my younger brother, I love him; — [but] if it is a Qin person's younger brother, I don't.

Mengzi 6A4.4b

是以我爲悅者也。故謂之內。

This [is] take me as enjoy person. Therefore I call it internal.

Mengzi 6A4.4c

長楚人之長。亦長吾之長。

I *zhang*^TV the Chu people's *zhang*^ADJ [person]; — [and] I also *zhang*^TV my *zhang*^ADJ [person].

Mengzi 6A4.4d

是以長爲悅者也。故謂之外也。

This [is] take *zhang*? as enjoy person. Therefore I call it external."

In the first case, Gao picks an example of my X-ing someone which is for both himself and Mencius an example of *ren*, and "internal," part of my "nature": my affection for someone in my own family (someone younger, to isolate *ren* and exclude *yi*).[28] In the second case he naturally stays with the standard paradigm for *yi*, respect shown to elders.

Whatever else Gaozi may be saying, he seems at least to be developing his earlier point about "white": The white thing just is white, and I cannot look at it and, by my choice, see it as red, unless there is something wrong with me. So also with the *zhang*[ADJ] person; he or she just is *zhang*[ADJ], and if I "perceive" (interact with) this *zhang*[ADJ] person, I will *zhang*[TV] him or her, unless there is something "wrong" with me. But not so with a person who is *ai*, "loved," for it is my loving the person that makes the person loved (here possibly he thinks as do critics of the Mohists).[29] He sharpens the examples by locating them in Qin and Chu; the debate probably was in Qi.

There is an obvious point to be made about this. Gao has overlooked something. The point is that younger brotherhood and elderliness work logically the same way, and response in the one case is no more nor less selective than response in the other. For a younger brother to be the object of my affection he has to be younger brother *to me*; but just so, for an elder to be the object of my respect he must be older *than I*. Gao's trouble is that the word *zhang*[ADJ] in Chinese, like the word "elder" in English, is ambiguous. For me, it can mean someone who is older than I am—perhaps a child, if I too am a child; or it can mean a "senior citizen" in my community, even if he is younger than I am. So, in 6A4.4c, while I do respect my own elder, I do not (necessarily) respect "the Chu people's elder," in the sense of the expression that corresponds to "a Qin person's younger brother" in 6A4.4a.

I have had to resort to "basic English" to stay neutral in lines 6A4.4b and 6A4.4d; and it is just these lines that cause trouble. Lau and Graham propose taking the graph *yuè* 悅 (my "enjoy") as an equivalent for *shuō* 說, "explain" (I assume they have in mind the use of *shuo* as a term of art in the later Mohist logicians).[30] But while 說 is in many texts used for 悅 (regularly in the *Chūnqiū* 春秋 commentaries, where 悅 never occurs), I have not been able to find an instance of 悅 used for 說. I think we are stuck with *yue*, "enjoy," or some such meaning. What do we do with it?

First, notice a syntactic ambiguity in the lines. We can take *zhě* 者 as acting on and nominalizing the preceding verb phrase, or just the preceding word. Thus 6A4.4b,

是以我爲悅者也
Shì yǐ wǒ wéi yuè zhě yě.

can be parsed in two ways:

shi = ([yi wo wei yue] zhe)
"This [person] = one who takes *wo* (= self) as *yue*."

or,

shi = *(yi wo wei yue-zhe)*
"This [case] = taking *wo* (= me) as the one who *yue*-s."

And 6A4.4d,

是以長爲悅者也。
Shì yǐ zhǎng wéi yuè zhě yě.

can be parsed as either

shi = *([yi zhang wei yue] zhe)*
"This [person] = one who takes *zhang* as *yue*."

or

shi = *(yi zhang wei yue-zhe)*
"This [case] = taking the *zhang* as the one who *yue*-s."

Dobson seems to take the second option. He translates,

> I feel love for my younger brother, but I feel no love for the younger brother
> of a man of Ch'in. My brother provokes a feeling of pleasure within me, and so
> I say it is inherent. To a man from Ch'u who is my senior I pay the deference
> due to his seniority, just as I would pay deference to a senior of my own family.
> My doing so provokes a feeling of pleasure within my seniors. So accordingly
> I say that Justice is an external thing. (1963, 111–12)

Dobson seems to see Gao as saying this: *ren* is "in here," i.e., it is the warm
feeling in me when I love my brother. *Yi* is "out there," because there is a
pleasurable feeling in the elder when I show deference. One can't, along this
line, say that *ren* is my loving (rather than the pleasurable feeling I have), because then one would have to say that *yi* is *my* being deferent, and both of
them are mine, "in here." So this analysis has to have Gao saying that in so far
as *yi* is "external" it must *be* the pleasurable condition of being respected as
zhang, which is "in" the elder. On this way of talking, it really is the *zhang*
person that is *yi* and not the one who *zhang*s that person. (See 6A4.3c.)

I doubt that this is what Gaozi was thinking, but there is a way to make the
suggestion plausible (my suggestion; I doubt that Dobson thought it out).

Gao, one could argue, had in mind a conception that Mencius had also thought about. Mencius had, in a crucial particular, consciously rejected it; Gao had not. The conception is the way of thinking about *yi* that we find in "hedonists" of the fourth century B.C. such as Zǐhuàzǐ 子華子. For Zihuazi, *yi* does not mean doing what I ought, and so being "right," "rightness," but receiving what I am due, and so "honor." This ambivalence of the word *yi*, already pointed out (it could be documented at length) should not surprise us, for our word "honor" has the same double use. Persons of honor, we suppose, do what they ought to do, and would be ashamed not to. But also, one who is due respect and is duly respected enjoys honor, is honored, has honors; we may even address such people as "your honor." And Zihuazi explicitly says that "dishonor" is among the most distressing of things to have to endure, just as is having to see or hear what one most dislikes, or to eat rotten food. Zihuazi here is characterizing a "tormented life" as being one in which, instead of obtaining what we enjoy, we are forced to endure its opposite.[31] So, on this way of thinking, *yi* is something that is mine when you honor me, and it's something highly enjoyable when I can have it.

Gaozi, perhaps, is caught in a semantic confusion halfway between Zihuazi and Mencius. On the one hand he would say that *yi* is a moral standard that I cultivate or that can be trained into me; on the other hand he feels that the *yi* that I do when I treat you with the respect due your age is, qua something enjoyed, *yi* for you rather than in me.

Mencius, on the contrary, seems consciously to have turned Zihuazi's concept on its head. If *yi* were "honor" of the sorts the world bestows—noble rank, for example (6A16)—it could be given or taken away at the whim of others, and so would not be "real nobility" (*liáng guì* 良貴 6A17). The real honors are those bestowed on me by Heaven in giving me a "commission" (*mìng* 命) to be moral (7A1, cf. 6A16). These I can always find pleasure in, by seeking "within myself," no matter what happens "outside" (7A3); so for Mencius it is inconceivable that I could be forced to endure what is "not *yi*." But for Mencius too, *yi* is something enjoyable, just as pleasing objects of the physical senses are enjoyable; only it is the object of another sense, the sense of inner self-awareness. On this line of analysis, there was a point at stake genuinely needing the defense Mencius is attempting in his question in 6A4.3c: is it being an elder that is *yi*, or is it respecting an elder that is *yi*? Gaozi, we might suppose, really is taking the first alternative: *yi* is *where* the "enjoying" is.

But I have quoted Dobson, and have developed an analysis suggested to me by him, as a Socratic provocation. For some time, it even seemed right to me; and it may even be that the availability, in the background, of Zihuazi's way of thinking about *yi* is pulling at Gaozi here. But Mencius, or whoever wrote up 6A3–4 for him, cannot have been understanding Gaozi this way. The analysis depended on taking the locution

是以 X 爲悅者也

as

shi = (yi X wei yue-zhe)

i.e., "this is (a case of) taking X as the one who *yues*," which was the second syntactic option. But it is the first option,

shi = ([yi X wei yue] zhe)

i.e., "this (= such a person) is the one who takes X as *yue*" that is almost certainly right. We can see this through a consideration of a passage with parallel syntax: *Mengzi* 7A19 is a short section in which Mencius characterizes four types of persons of prominence. Lowest is the one (likely to be a flatterer) whose commitment is to a particular lord. Second is the officer whose loyalty is to his state (the "altars of land and grain"). Third, the person (who may not have any position) who is a subject of "Heaven," acting as effectively as possible for the benefit of the whole world. Fourth and highest is the one who simply aims at self-perfection, thereby exerting a transforming influence on everyone and everything. The second type is described as follows:

有安社稷臣者以安社稷爲悅者也
Yǒu ān shè jì chén zhě; yǐ ān shè jì wéi yuè zhě yě.

Literally, "There is the official who keeps safe the altars of land and grain; he is one who takes keeping safe the altars of land and grain as [his] pleasure." That is (as Zhao Qi says), "The loyal officer fixes his resolve on keeping safe the *she* and *ji*, and only then is he happy." The idiom used in the second half of this sentence in 7A19 seems to be the same as the one used in 6A4.4b and 6A4.4d, which must then mean,

(6A4.4d) This [such a person as I, in the hypothetical situation] is one who takes *zhang* as his pleasure [is concerned with what is *zhang*[ADJ], "out there," and acts accordingly, by *zhang*[TV]-ing as occasion requires].

It is even more obvious, now, that reading *yue* as *shuo* is not necessary, indeed, not possible. And one can put one's finger on the issue: What I "take pleasure in," i.e., what concerns me, in a response I make, is what causes the response. A response of mine is caused by a disposition *in me*, activated by an occasion *outside of me*. Gao and Mencius are agreed about *ren*, exemplified by loving: I won't show love unless I am disposed to, in virtue of the relation of the object to me. They disagree about *yi*, exemplified by behavior showing respect for elderliness, because Gao thinks of the occasional cause as the decisive one: It is what is "out there" that counts, every time, no matter where, including the applicable public standard.[32] (And if you point out to him that I must also have the appropriate disposition, if he grants this at all he will say, as he says in 6A1–2, that it was implanted in me.)

Mencius then finishes off, in 6A4, by selecting an example fitting the requirements of the Mohist "method of parallel": It is stated in a sentence of the same form as Gao's exhibit sentence 6A4.4c; namely:

> 長楚人之長亦長吾之長。
> *Zhăng Chú rén zhī zhăng yì zhăng wú zhī zhăng.*
> "I show respect for the Chu people's elders, and also show respect for my own elders."

Mencius now says:

Mengzi 6A4.5

> 耆秦人之炙無以異於耆吾[之]炙
> *Shì Qín rén zhī zhì wú yǐ yì yú shì wú [zhī] zhì.*
> "[I] relish the Qin people's roasts" just as "[I] relish our own roasts."

The conclusion (left unstated) would have to be, by parallel with 6A4.4d,

> 是以炙爲悅者也。故謂之外也。
> *Shì yǐ zhì wéi yuè zhě yě. Gù wèi zhī wài yě.*
> "This [such a person] is one who takes roasts as his pleasure; therefore I call it [savoring the roast] external."

Yet "eating" was for Gaozi (6A4.1) paradigmatically "internal." So also therefore (by the method of parallel) for *zhang*-ing.[33]

I see no language difficulties in 6A5, though the situations described are amusingly complex. The argument is again about the claimed "externality" of *yi*. The exchange is between Mèngjìzǐ 孟季子, a disciple of Gaozi, and Gōngdūzǐ 公都子, a disciple of Mencius:

Mengzi 6A5.1: Mengjizi asked Gongduzi, "Why do you say that *yi* is internal?"

Mengzi 6A5.2: [Gongduzi] said, "I am acting out my respect. Therefore I say it is internal."

Mengzi 6A5.3: [Mengjizi said,] "If a villager is a year older than your elder brother, which one do you respect?"

[Gongduzi] said, "I respect my elder brother."

[Mengjizi said,] "In a wine ceremony, which one do you serve first?"

[Gongduzi] said, "I serve the villager first."

[Mengjizi said,] "The one you respect is this one, but the one you treat as elder is that one. Obviously [the *yi* or *zhang*, the formal show of deference for elderliness] is on the outside, not from the inside."

Mengzi 6A5.4: Gongduzi was unable to reply, and told Mencius. Mencius said,

Say: "Do you respect your father's younger brother more, or your own younger brother?"

He will say: "I respect my father's younger brother more."

Say: "If your younger brother is a *shī* 尸 [impersonator of an ancestor in a ceremony], then whom do you respect more?"

He will say: "I respect my younger brother more."

Say: "Where is your respect for your father's younger brother?"

He will say: "The reason is that [my younger brother] was in a [special] role [on that particular occasion]."

You also say: "[So also in your example:] It was because [the villager] was in a [special] role. Ordinarily my [primary] respect is for my elder brother; my [primary] respect on this occasion was for the villager."

Mengzi 6A5.5: Mengjizi, hearing this, said, "When you respected your father's younger brother, that was respect; and when you respected your younger brother, that was respect. So actually the respect is in what's outside, and doesn't come from the inside."

Gongduzi said, "On winter days I drink hot water, and on summer days I drink cold water. So [on your argument] eating and drinking also are 'outside.'"

The language of analysis in this drama is frustratingly blunt-edged, but we can try to pick the action apart. In 6A5.3, Mengjizi had implicitly granted that *jìng* 敬, "respect," is "inside," but argued that it is distinct from *zhang*[TV], which both agree is *yi*. Notice that this is consistent with 6A4.2b, C, D: "He is *zhang* and I *zhang* him; it is not that there is *zhang* in me." And notice also that Gongduzi himself had not said that his respect (*jing*) had shifted to the villager in the ceremonial situation. But in 6A5.4, Mencius's strategy has kept the word *zhang* out of sight; every question-and-answer is (literally) about *jing*, "respect." So now (6A5.5) Mengjizi patterns his position on the 6A4.4c–d model; that model could have had an extra summary line:

長楚長則長亦長吾長則長。

Zhǎng Chǔ zhǎng zé zhǎng, yì zhǎng wú zhǎng zé zhǎng.

"When I *zhang* the *zhang* of Chu, I am *zhang*-ing, and also when I *zhang* my *zhang* I am *zhang*-ing."

Thus Mengjizi is implying,

是以敬爲悅者也故謂之外也。

Shì yǐ jìng wéi yuè zhě yě. Gù wèi zhī wài yě.

"This is one who takes *jing* as his pleasure; therefore I call it external."

This is senseless unless we understand *jing*, "respect," here as contrasted with *wo* (ego, as in *shi yi wo wei yue zhe*), i.e., Mengjizi is now conceiving "respect" as observable behavior according to public rules, objective not subjective, and so "outside." This is a significant shift in position; Mencius by coaching his disciple has set the opponent up for the kill.

In the context of *Mengzi* 6A3–4, we can see that, as before, the Mencius party looks at the dispositional cause, and the Gaozi party looks at the occasional cause: The latter insists that the disposition ("inside") counts only if it makes a difference in different situations; if it does not, then it must be that the occasion ("outside"), involving what is socially required, is the significant factor.

But of course, any instance of *yi* behavior needs both an adequate disposition ("inside") and an appropriate occasion ("outside"). The Mencius party, insisting on the priority of the former, and the Gaozi party, insisting on the priority of the latter, are both begging the question whether *yi* is "inside" or "outside." To throw a punch that connects, Gongduzi must, as did Mencius in 6A4, show a contradiction in his opponent's position. Eating, and so also drinking, are "nature" and "internal" for the Gao party; but though *how* we satisfy the "inner" disposition of thirst is determined by the (specious) occasion, winter vs. summer, satisfying it in some way is demanded by *my* being thirsty. Similarly with respect (Mencius hopes): the objects may differ in different situations, but respect is shown anyway, because *I* feel respectful.

One must wonder why—indeed whether—the punch hurt. If Gaozi had seen the argument about love as showing that *ài* 愛 is "internal" because I love my brother but not yours, Mengjizi could hold that his opponent's example shows that my desire for *hot* water is "internal" because I want it in winter but not in summer; and so, vice versa, for cold water; and this he need not deny. Gongduzi must then push him harder, by saying, "When you drink hot water you drink, and when you drink cold water you drink; in drinking as such you don't choose; you just have to.[34] So, by your logic, you are going to have to tell me that drinking itself is 'external,' and that my feeling that I do it because I'm thirsty is irrelevant. But you and Gaozi yourselves don't believe this."

Problems in the *Mengzi*: 7A17[1]

Mèngzǐ 孟子 7A17 is a very short text (of exactly seventeen words, it so happens), but it is worth close attention. A word-for-word "basic English" translation might go as follows:

無	爲	其	所	不	爲
wú	*wéi*	*qí*	*suǒ*	*bù*	*wéi*
do not	do	one's	what	not	do

無	欲	其	所	不	欲
wú	*yù*	*qí*	*suǒ*	*bú*	*yù*
do not	desire	one's	what	not	desire.

如	此	而	已	矣
rú	*cǐ*	*ér*	*yǐ*	*yǐ*
like	this	and	stop	[grammatical particle]

So understood, the lines could go over into smoother English possibly in this way:

(1) Do not do what you do not do.
(2) Do not desire what you do not desire.
(3) Simply be like this.

And thus the problem of our moral life is solved. In understanding this, presumably we must take the second "do not" in each of lines (1) and (2) as in "scouts do not tell lies." This normative use of an apparently straight statement is common also in Chinese—e.g. (*Analects* of Confucius), "If a person follows a different Dao, one does not take that person into counsel."[2] Thus the sense would be, "Do not do what (under the conventions of civilized life applying to a person such as oneself) one does not do." The alternative is to suppose the passage is directed to "you" individually, and appeals to individual normative autonomy: appearing in a classroom without a tie is something that *I* do not do, though in this case I do not think any the less of those who do. But my tie-wearing is, of course, just an evidence of my own nuttiness. There is no public pressure at all (or if there is, it is in the direction of the unbuttoned collar). Perhaps we should take Mencius as referring to my subjective "what I just don't do," but only when I am giving to myself, autonomously, a "rule" that coincides with a public standard.

There are matters of interpretation (and of ethics) connected with these issues that are of utmost importance: (1) if we understand Mencius to be talking just about "what isn't done"—what one *ought not* to do—it might be that his point is simply that *the* problem of human moral life is to keep certain kinds of *acts* from being done, accomplishing this straightening out of people's overt behavior by whatever means. If knowing the rules helps, learn them; if feeling them as rules helps, let us sharpen our moral senses; if neither helps, put people under constraint, but get the rules followed. Or (2) Mencius could be saying that we often do not act according to what we recognize to be, and accept as, the way we should act; and that *the* moral problem is just for us to see to it that we *do* as we *know* we should. In other words, that avoiding or overcoming *moral weakness* is the essential moral problem. I shall argue that Mencius is saying neither of these things here, exactly, but something that is connected strongly with the second.

There are two more interesting things to notice about this passage before going deeper into the problem of its exact interpretation: (1) Mencius seems to think it makes just as much sense for me to say to you "do not *desire* this thing," or "do not *desire* to do this," as for me to say "do not *take* this thing," or "do not *do* this." Most of us probably just assume without thinking about it that we can choose *what to do*, but cannot choose *how to feel*, or *what to want*.[3] Mencius seems just to assume here that we *can* as easily choose what to want as what to do. There are places where he is more sophisticated about this, but this is what he says here. (2) And there are places where he is more sophisticated about another thing that he seems to take for granted here: he seems to assume that the problem of "doing" (acting *or* feeling) is *simple*—"All you have to do is do *this*": no problem, then, of changing myself, cultivating myself so as to become the sort of person who will do and want the right. Here, he seems to say I can if I simply *will*. I will show that this direct voluntarism is indeed one of the faces of Mencius, and that one does not fully understand him as a moral philosopher unless one sees it and sees why it is there.[4]

Let us now look at the ways others have interpreted 7A17. I shall present a number of translations, followed by the commentary of Zhào Qí 趙岐, the commentary attributed to Sūn Shì 孫奭, and (later in my discussion) the commentary of Zhū Xī 朱熹.[5]

Chai and Chai: Master Meng said: "Do not do what you ought not to do; do not desire what you ought not to desire. That is all" (1965a, 163, no. 136).

Couvreur (French): Meng Tseu dit: "Ne faites pas ce que vous savez ne devoir pas faire; ne désirez pas ce que vous savez ne devoir pas désirer. Cela suffit" (1910, 614).

[Mencius said: "Do not do what you know you ought not to do; do not desire what you know you shouldn't desire. That is enough."]

Couvreur (Latin): Meng Tseu ait: "Ne agas quid ipse (naturali aequitatis sensu cognoscis) non esse agendum, ne cupias quod ipse (naturali aequitatis sensu cognoscis) non esse optandum. Ita *si facias*, jam satis erit" (loc. cit.).

[Mencius said: "Do not do what you yourself (know by your natural sense of right) is not to be done; do not desire what you yourself (know by your natural sense of right) is not to be desired. (If you act) thus, this already will suffice."]

Dobson: Mencius said, "Do not do what you should not do; do not wish for what you should not wish—there is nothing more to it than that" (1963, 190, no. 7.24).

Hattori (Japanese): Mencius said, "Let one not do what he does not do; let one not desire what he does not desire. It is simply like this" (1922, 252).[6]

Lau: Mencius said, "Do not do what others do not choose to do; do not desire what others do not desire. That is all" (1970, 185).

Legge: Mencius said, "Let a man not do what *his own sense of righteousness tells him* not to do, and let him not desire what his *sense of righteousness tells him not* to desire;—to act thus is all he has to do" (1970, 457).[7]

Lyall: Mencius said, "Do nothing they do not do, wish nothing they do not wish; that is all!" (1932, 208).[8]

Ware: "Do not have done what you yourself would not do; do not have desired what you yourself would not desire. It is as simple as that" (1960, 151).

Wilhelm: Meng Dsï sprach: "Tue nichts, was dir nicht entspricht zu tun; wünsche nichts, was dir nicht entspricht zu wünschen. Das ist es, worauf es allein ankommt" (1921, 160).

[Mencius said, "Do nothing it doesn't seem right to you to do; wish for nothing it doesn't seem right for you to wish for. This alone is what matters."][9]

Zhao Qi: Do not make others do what you yourself do not desire to do. Do not make others desire what you yourself do not desire. If everyone first makes himself 'be like this', then the Way of being a human will be complete.

Sun Shi: This section is saying, "What you yourself do not desire, do not do unto others." This is the Way of Confucius. Mencius is saying that people do not do what they do not do because they regard what they do not do as not righteous. They do not desire what they do not desire because they regard what they do not desire to do as not good. If people are capable of not doing what is not righteous, and also not desiring what they do not regard as good, the Way of being human is thereupon complete. Hence, he says, "Be like this."[10]

These ten translations and two commentaries range from the bizarre to the almost correct. Essentially they offer five different interpretations:

(1) Do not do what others do not do, etc.—Lau and Lyall, on the authority, perhaps, of Edmund Burke. (But Lau usually has a respectable reason for an unusual translation; his editors evidently crossed out most of his footnotes.)

(2) Do not make others do what you wouldn't do, etc.—Ware, evidently following Zhao Qi.

(3) Do not do what you shouldn't do, etc.—Chai and Chai, Dobson, and Hattori.

(4) Do not do what you know you shouldn't do, etc.—Couvreur's French.

(5) Do not do what your sense of what is right tells you not to do, etc.—Couvreur's Latin, Legge, and Wilhelm.

The first two interpretations here listed cannot be seriously considered. The motivation of both may well be a felt need to make the agents of the two doings different: why command *me* not to do something if *I* don't do it anyway? The difficulty disappears when we notice usages of the "one does not take them into counsel" sort.[11] The last three interpretations must be watched. But the very substantial differences between them involve just the major interpretive questions I have already pointed out: is the problem to eliminate behavior that is in *fact* wrong? or to bring one's behavior in line with one's moral *knowledge*? or to learn to attend to and obey one's moral *intuitions*?

Wilhelm says he is following Zhu Xi. It is time to see what Zhu had to say. His comment simply quotes his teacher Lǐ Tóng 李侗 (1093–1163):

Master Li said, "All people have the disposition [lit., the "heart," *xīn* 心] of having things they don't do or want. When selfish inclinations (*sī yì* 私意) once sprout, if we are not able to control them with propriety and right (*lǐ yì*

禮義), then we will often do 'what we don't do' and desire 'what we don't desire.' If we can restore this disposition, then we will, as [Mencius] said, 'expand and fill out our disposition to feel shame and dislike [at doing certain things],' and 'there will be more rightness (*yì* 義) than we can use.' And so he says 'Simply be like this.'"

This is probably the source of Legge's and Couvreur's (Latin) translation. But it says a good deal more than they do. The complete situation as Li apparently sees it is this: I have, for example, an intuitive aversion and dislike for telling lies—it is something "I do not do." This feeling is also completely in accord with *public* standards of morality, "propriety and right" (*li yi*, see 6A7). On a particular occasion I may be tempted to lie—have a "selfish inclination" (*si yi*) to do so. When this happens, something in me will, one hopes, identify the inclination as selfish, and I must then take myself by the scruff of the neck and make myself conform to the public standard, otherwise I will end by "doing what I don't do." Such discipline will enable me to avoid becoming inured to violating my instinctive aversions and help me to "restore this disposition." If I can do so, so that it always guides me in the matter of truth telling, then I will no longer need to worry about doing right. And so, also, for my other aversions and "dislikes."

Now, this dwelling on the need for stern self-discipline is a theme that belongs to Song and Ming Dynasty moral philosophy. The expression "selfish inclination" is not even a part of Mencius's vocabulary. Mencius's stress everywhere is on heightening moral *sensitivity*; and he even sometimes counsels *against* being severe with oneself (e.g., 2A2.16). So Li is distorting Mencius by here bringing to the fore his own anxieties about temptations to evil-doing.[12] Nevertheless, Li Tong knew his Mencius well; his short comment contains two quotations from other sections in Mencius, and both are highly relevant. The line "expand and fill out our disposition to feel shame and dislike" comes from 2A6 (the passage with the well-known example of the child about to crawl into a well), and is immediately followed by a line, "there will be more rightness than we can use," taken verbatim from 7B31.

I trust that everyone is familiar enough with 2A6. But 7B31 reads like a conscious comment on 7A17, and I must quote it in full:

> Mencius said, "People all have things they do not endure. Extending [this feeling] to what they do endure is Kindness (*rén* 仁). All people have things they do not do. Extending [this feeling] to what they do do is Rightness (*yi*).[13] If people can fully apply their disposition not to desire to injure others, their kindness will be more than they can use. If people can fully apply their dispositions not to bore through or jump over [a wall] their Rightness will be more than they can use. If they can fully develop the actuality[14] [in themselves] that refuses to accept 'thee' and 'thou' [when people address them], then whatever

they set out to do they will not do anything that is not right. If a gentleman speaks when he ought not to, this is toadying with speech. If he doesn't speak when he ought to, this is toadying with silence. Both are in the category of boring through or jumping over [walls]."

7A17 needed examples, and here they are. But what do they say? Two possibilities interest me:

(1) Mencius may think this: our moral intuitions exist at least in some small degree, however slight, whenever we are in a situation to which moral considerations really do apply. Acting morally is possible only if we both know what we should do and are "able" to do it, that is, have sufficient inner motivation to carry the act through. But we can always have this much motivation once we see the thing to be done (or avoided) as morally right (or wrong). The problem is to learn to recognize this disposition and use it. One can do this by noticing that there are relatively straightforward cases where our intuitions are obvious and insistent—I just *don't* jump over my neighbor's wall and steal my neighbor's daughter for a spouse.[15] I just *don't* desire to injure someone. This shows me that I am *capable* of being moral at least sometimes. But more: the same intuitions lurk in me in the less obvious cases (like flattering someone), and when I come to see the less obvious case as like the obvious one in some relevant sense, the latent intuition in the former will be recognizable to me, and in that case as well as in the paradigm case I will be able to avoid "doing what I do not do"—what, as my intuition *really* feels the matter, "isn't done."

(2) Or Mencius may think this: to begin with, we have natural moral impulses just in the straightforward cases. These may be thought of as manifestations of a sort of inner capacity, like the capacity to see things with my eyes, or to lift things with my arms (1A7.10). But this basic capacity can be used by me in various ways; just as I can *choose* to look at this or that, *choose* to pick up this thing or that, so I can *choose* to "extend" my capacity for moral motivatedness to this proposed act or that. And likewise for my capacity for shrinking from, being ashamed of, doing certain things, like digging through walls. I have "things I don't do," and I can, if I will, "extend" this feeling to "things I do." But I will not, of course, choose to "extend" it to every possible act, but only to those I recognize as being wrong ones.

Some might hope to find Mencius saying something else: that to *recognize* an act as right or wrong just *is* to be motivated to do it or not to do it. I may well be mistaken, but I do not think he says this anywhere. (And—but this is another story—*I* think he would have been wrong if he had said it.) Of the two views I have sketched, I do not know which one in the end he holds and I am not sure he knew either. If the first is his view, then Legge, Couvreur, and Wilhelm have translated 7A17 correctly, although we also must admit that Mencius has been extremely laconic. Here we would say that I really do have an intuition forbidding flattery, though it is less obvious to me than my intuition forbidding illicit sex, so that I could easily fail to attend to it and heed it, and then would in a sense be "doing what I do not do." And one might add, if this intuition can be disregarded at all, in principle it might be disregarded in any sort of case; so there would be point in telling me also not to do those things, like wall-vaulting, that I *just* "do not do."

If the second is Mencius's real view, then 7A17 is even more cryptic, and must be one of those maxims of a master that only the initiates can explain. It will mean, in effect, "extend to all occasions for morally objectionable behavior (or attitude) the capacity for moral shrinking back that exists in you when it's a question of doing or wanting something that for you is 'just wrong,' like stealing or wanting to hurt someone." Or more simply, "Do not do any 'what you don't do' *sorts* of things."

Strange though this last interpretation appears, there is a strong case for it, and there is much to be learned about Mencius by examining that case.[16]

On Translating Mencius[1]

The *Mèngzǐ* 孟子 (often called the *Mencius* in English) is a Chinese philosophical text of the late fourth or early third century B.C., containing the recorded conversations and sayings of Mèng Kē 孟軻, who probably lived from about 390 to about 305. What now exists (it may once have been longer) has been, since the Later Han Dynasty (A.D. 25–220), arranged in seven "books," divided into 260 sections. It has been translated many times, and it is hoped that someday it will be translated at least once more. This review of the present situation covers nine translators. In and out of print in English are translations by Legge (1861, 1893, 1895, and so on), Dobson (1963), the father and son team of Chai and Chai (1965a), and Lau (1970). Also available in most university libraries are Lyall (1932), the partial translation of Giles (1942), and Ware (1960). Among the translations in other Western languages I include two currently in print and widely used: Couvreur (French and Latin, 1895, 1910, and so on) and Wilhelm (German, 1913, 1921, and so on). There are, of course, a number of translations into Japanese and modern Chinese, some of which I shall refer to occasionally. I have found especially useful the translations by Hattori (1922), the Lanzhou University Chinese Language Department (1960), Uchino (1962), and Yang Yong (1970).

12.1 The Translators

The Western translators came to their task with a variety of backgrounds and experience:

James Legge (1815–1897) was a Scottish missionary with an academic and scholar's career, first in Malacca (from 1839), then in Hong Kong (from 1860), and later (from 1876) as a professor at Oxford. He published his translation of the "Four Books," including *Mencius*, in 1861 in Hong Kong. The following year he commenced a long association with the Chinese scholar and journalist Wáng Tāo 王韜 (1828–?), who assisted him with the remainder of his translation of the Classics (see Hummel, 1943–1944, 837). Even so, there are not many changes in the revised *Mencius* published in Oxford in 1893 and 1895. *The Chinese Classics* won for Legge the first awarding of the newly established Prix Stanislas-Julien in Paris in 1875.

Father Seraphin Couvreur (1835–1919), a Jesuit, was at the Catholic mission in Ho-chien-fu from 1870 onward. His work includes translations of the basic Confucian Classics into French and Latin, and the compiling of a number of dictionaries, notably the *Dictionnaire Classique de la Langue Chinoise* (1904, 1911, based on the compiler's *Dictionnaire Chinóis-Français*, 1890), still considered one of the best dictionaries of classical Chinese in any language. Couvreur received the Prix Stanislas-Julien four times.

Richard Wilhelm (1873–1930), author of more than a dozen important books and translations into German, including the *Zhuāngzǐ* 莊子, *Yìjīng* 易經, *Lǎozǐ* 老子, *Lǚshì chūnqiū* 呂氏春秋, and others, went to China in 1899 as an evangelical missionary, working in Qingdao.[2] (One of his books records the Japanese siege and occupation of the city, during World War I, to which he was witness.) In 1925 he founded and became first director of the China Institut at the Universität Frankfurt/Main.

Leonard A. Lyall (1867–?) has translated the *Zhōngyōng* 中庸 and the *Analects* of Confucius as well as the *Mengzi*, and also has written a book on China based on his long period of experience there. From 1886 he was in the China customs service, serving for forty-one years and becoming an accomplished sinologist. He was thus an eyewitness, with the perspective of the civil service, to the events of the fall of the Qing and the rise of the Republic.

Lionel Giles (1875–1958), son of the sinologist and lexicographer Herbert A. Giles, served for forty years in the British Museum, where he was Keeper of Oriental Printed Books and Manuscripts. He is the author of at least fifteen sinological works, including an English index to the Chinese encyclopedia *Túshū jíchéng* 圖書集成, and various translations published in the Wisdom of the East Series; these include partial or complete translations of *Zhuangzi*, the *Analects*, *Laozi*, *Lièzǐ* 列子, and *Sūnzǐ* 孫子.

James R. Ware was for many years Associate Professor of Chinese at Harvard University, with Mentor series translations of the *Analects* (1955) and *Zhuangzi* (1963) and a partial translation and study of Gé Hóng's *Bào pú zǐ* 葛洪, 抱朴子.[3]

W.A.C.H. Dobson was Professor of Chinese at the University of Toronto, with a series of four books on the grammar of early Chinese in different periods, beginning with Dobson (1959) and Dobson (1962). He also published Dobson (1974), a dictionary of Chinese particles.

Ch'u Chai and his son Winberg Chai were on the faculties of the New School of Social Research and of the City University of New York, respectively. The elder Chai had been a professor at National Taiwan University before being brought to the New School as a professor in 1955. The two have collaborated on a number of books and volumes of translation, including *A Treasury of Chinese Literature* (1965).

D. C. Lau taught in the School of Oriental and African Studies, University of London, from 1950 to 1978, when he returned to Hong Kong to take up the Chair of Chinese Language and Literature at the Chinese University of Hong Kong. He retired several years ago and is now Emeritus Professor at the same institution. With a B.A. from the University of Hong Kong, he received graduate training in philosophy at the University of Glasgow. His other translations include Lau (1963a) and Lau (1979), in the Penguin series.

These translators differ in readability, accuracy, supporting scholarship, and editorial conveniences. The touchstone here, of course, must be accuracy. With it, readability is a virtue; without it, a pleasingly written text is merely seductive. By supporting scholarship I refer both to accompanying analyses and to notes. By editorial conveniences I mean not just indices and glossaries but also the arrangement and organization of the text, the way in which notes are presented, and more.

Readability is a subjective (as well as ambiguous) value. To my taste Lau, Wilhelm, and Giles are especially well written, and Lyall, Dobson, and the Chais are usually acceptably well written. Ware's English is maddeningly disfigured by his personal translator's crotchets. Legge will impress many readers as old-fashioned and awkward; this is a consequence, in part, of the fact that this translation was the work of a missionary working more than a century ago. But in large measure it results from an extraordinary conscientiousness that refuses to smooth over a spot in the text where the translator feels the sense to be difficult to ascertain. Legge's awkwardness is therefore actually a virtue, and it is not his only virtue.

In the end readability is a matter which the reader must judge for him- or herself. I list below the translations here under review, with publication details, and descriptions of the supporting scholarship and editorial conveniences.[4] Following this I shall take up the all-important and often embarrassing problem of accuracy.

12.2 The Translations

Legge (1895): Text, translation, and notes appear together on the same page, section by section throughout the work. Legge has followed the standard ordering and sectioning of the text (due to Zhào Qí 趙岐 of the Later Han) and has numbered the sections, introducing numbered subsectioning when sections are long.[5] The notes are by far the fullest of any translation, and use Chinese characters freely, often quoting and translating or paraphrasing relevant Chinese commentaries. The long "Prolegomena" discusses the history of the text, and what is known or reported of the life of Mencius; there is a long and very perceptive treatment of Mencius's philosophy. Also included are translations (with Chinese text) of Xúnzǐ's 荀子 chapter on human nature, Hán Yù's 韓愈 essay on the same, parts of the Yáng Zhū 楊朱 chapter in *Liezi*, and the three versions of the chapter on "universal love" in the *Mòzǐ* 墨子. The long (seventy-page) third index of "characters and phrases" is especially useful.

A distinctive feature of the translation is Legge's use of the Biblical convention of indicating supplied words and phrases by using italics. Most of Legge's sources are listed in the "Prolegomena" to the first volume of *The Chinese Classics*. (A valuable critical bibliography of thirty-three works in Chinese is found in Legge [1971, 128–35].)

The 1895 edition has a few corrections in translation, text, and notes, and uses a slightly modified transcription system, and is the one usually cited. Among many photographic reprints in the Far East and the United States, two need to be noted. The Dover Paperback reprint of the 1895 edition, published in 1970, is easily obtainable. The entire *Chinese Classics* was reprinted by the Hong Kong University Press in 1960, and again by SMC Publishing of Taiwan in 1991. A distinctive feature of these editions is that each includes a reprint of Waley (1949). One more partial reprint must also be mentioned. Ballou (1939, 428–63) contains a section titled "The Works of Mencius (Meng-Tze)." This is obviously only a selection. The editors state that they are using a translation by a certain Charles A. Wong, "published in China without the imprint of a publisher or date." The "Wong" translation is actually taken from Legge's first edition and should be so credited if used; but because Legge did make some corrections in his 1895 edition, it is essential to use that edition. In any case Ballou (1939) does not use any section numbering, nor does it systematically indicate section breaks, or even divisions between half-books. One important text not included is 7A15 (see below, pages 179 and 195 f.). This book was used as a source on Mencius by Smart (1969, 155).

Couvreur (1910): Couvreur has text, transcriptions, and parallel French and Latin translations on the same page. Like Legge, he uses the standard organization of the text, without numbering subsections. There are no notes in the ordinary sense, but occasionally Chinese commentary is included in the text in small characters and translated, and sometimes explanatory comments are included in the translations in parentheses. For Couvreur's introductory remarks on what he is attempting, one must go to the first volume of *Les Quatre Livres*. There, Couvreur says that he has reproduced, as faithfully as possible, the interpretation given in Du (1779). (Du's work is described in Legge [1971, 129–30]; it was evidently also one of Legge's principal sources.) The few notes included by Couvreur that I have checked are usually close paraphrases of the commentary of Zhū Xī 朱熹. Couvreur warns that one attend to both his French and his Latin translation "because often one contains clarifications that are not in the other." In fact I have found a few minor discrepancies between the two translations and not so minor ones between the "clarifications"; for example, on p. 308, a note in the text explaining why King Huì of Liáng (Wèi) 梁 (魏) 惠王 identifies his state with defunct Jìn 晉 is transcribed in parentheses and is translated in Latin, but omitted in French. The French version, furthermore, is often much freer than the Latin, which I suspect Couvreur did first. As a whole, the translation (taking French and Latin together, as Couvreur intends), within the limits Couvreur has set for himself, is admirably careful.

Wilhelm (1921): In a short note on p. xviii of the general introduction (on Mencius's life, thought, and background) Wilhelm states that the best commentaries, and the ones he has chiefly used, are that of Jiāo Xún 焦循, and that of Ruǎn Yuán 阮元 (1764–1849) (that is, *Mèngzǐ jiàokānjì* 孟子校勘記), both found in the *Huáng Qīng jīngjiě* 皇清經解. The translation is distinguished by much fuller notes than most, and appears to me to be both careful and beautiful. It is available in Germany in paperback.

Lyall (1932): There are very few notes. The translator (intentionally I judge) uses an almost monosyllabic English, and usually to excellent effect. He states that he has used the Legge, Couvreur, and Wilhelm translations and acknowledges Chinese professional assistance, but otherwise does not discuss his sources. The text gives chapter numbers to each half-book.

Giles (1942): The translation (omitting 122 sections out of the total 260) is pleasing, with few errors. There are almost no notes. The standard order of the text is observed, and the standard sectioning is indicated, but the sections are not numbered—in an incomplete text, this is a great inconvenience, which must be rectified by hand if one is to use this translation carefully—and the reader is given no warning when the translator has left something out. Usually it is at least a whole section that is omitted and not a part thereof. Sometimes the omissions show shockingly bad judgment: for example, Giles has not given us 6A7 (see below, page 183 ff.), in which Mencius likens "what our hearts have [or approve] in common" to our shared preferences in taste, visible beauty, and so on, the most important source for the ethics of Dài Zhèn 戴震. Just as surprising is his omission of 7A15, on "What we know without having to think it out," the source of Wáng Yángmíng's 王陽明 concept of "pure knowing" (*liáng zhī* 良知) or moral intuition.[6] Giles' translation has recently been reprinted (Giles, 1993).

Ware (1960): The introduction contains Ware's translations of (1) the *Shǐ jì* 史記 biography of Mencius (pp. 10–11), (2) the "Robber Zhi" chapter of *Zhuangzi* (pp. 17–26), (3) the chapter "Confucius" from *Liezi* (which Ware accepts as a Zhou Dynasty text) (pp. 27–36), and (4) chapter 28 from *Xunzi* (pp. 37–42). The translation is without footnotes, but Ware has inserted in the text helpful cross-references to other parts of the book; and whenever Mencius refers to or quotes a poem from the *Shījīng* 詩經 (*Book of Poetry*, Legge 1991d), Ware inserts in brackets the Harvard-Yenching Concordance text number. (In at least two cases he quotes the whole poem: see 6B3, pp. 141–42.) Similarly where there are references to the *Shàng shū* 尚書 (*Book of History*, Legge, 1991e), Ware gives the chapter title; and he sticks in, gratis, references to the *Analects* of Confucius when he thinks them appropriate. As in his (1955) and (1963), Ware forces on his reader a number of bizarre pet translations. *Tiān* 天, "heaven" in most of the literature, is "Sky"; *rén* 仁 ("benevolence" for Legge, borrowing from Bishop Butler) becomes an etymological "manhood-at-its-best"; and *xīn* 心 is "heart-and-mind." Less defensible are "right procedure" (sometimes "Process," from Whitehead) for *dào* 道 ("Way"), and "Excellence" for *dé* 德 (no one likes "virtue," but I suspect it is here to stay). Worst of all, *jūnzǐ* 君子 and *xiǎorén* 小人 come out "Great Man" and "Petty Man," sans definite article (perhaps like "Everyman" in medieval morality plays). These annoyances and other quirks are at times almost unbearable. Nonetheless, Ware is a translator worth consulting on a tight problem. The face on the cover (ostensibly that of Mencius), is obviously a joke which has escaped me. (The face of Confucius, plainly labeled 孔子 on the cover of Ware's earlier Mentor Books translation of the *Analects*, is actually a caricature of Ware himself.)[7]

Dobson (1963): Dobson has rearranged the text (but without breaking up the sectioning of Zhao Qi) under the following headings: Mencius at various royal courts; public life; disciples; philosophical rivals; comments on the times; "teachings"; "maxims." One may notice the artificiality of this organization without denying its usefulness: "teachings" are not different from much of the matter incorporated into the sermons to royal patrons "at court"; while a "maxim" is obviously only a short "teaching." Still it is convenient, for example, to have all of the matter involving Gōngsūn Chǒu 公孫丑 brought together as Dobson does. However, users must not forget that the traditional ordering is not just accidental; book 6A, for example, shows evidence of subtle editorial organization, and this is lost in Dobson's presentation. Dobson's finding list is a two-way correlation of his section numbers with the Harvard-Yenching Concordance text numbers, enabling one to work easily with Dobson's translation. Each subsection in Dobson's text is prefaced with a short informative historical or analytical introduction. There are some footnotes throughout the text with obviously needed references to earlier classics, and so on. Bulkier notes are shunted to the additional-notes section at the end, apparently in the belief that the "general reader" ("that patient abstraction," as Chauncey Goodrich has called him) would be offended by too obvious a display of scholarship. The notes are often very good, even if not numerous enough. Whenever dating is a problem, Dobson follows (p. 208) Qian (1956) as a "system of reconstruction complete in itself." This leads him, like Lau (see below), to date Mencius's life-span about twenty years earlier (correctly, in my judgment—to circa 390–305 B.C.) than the dating traditionally accepted. (But it also leads him to date Xunzi far too early.) Obviously this is a book with virtues. The quality of the translation, which is smooth but sometimes too free, is more problematic, as will be seen.

Chai and Chai (1965): There are almost no notes. This translation, like Dobson's, rearranges the text according to the translators' intuitions ("The

Doctrine of Human Nature," "Political and Economic Measures," "Way of Life," "Comments of Mencius," with subsections), almost always keeping original sections intact, and giving the location according to traditional ordering in brackets at the end of each section. This is completely inadequate, since one wants to be able to find the Chais' translation of any text one is working on, and for this there is nothing else to do but create one's own finding list. Completing this task after several hours, I discovered that the Chais' translation has a number of misprints or mistakes in identification: "IV14" (no. 50) should be "IVA14"; "VB8" (no. 88) should be "VB9"; "LIIB7" (no. 163) should be "IIIB7"; "V5" (no. 166) should be "VB4"; "VIIA31" (no. 215) should be "VIIA30." Worse, six sections have been accidentally omitted entirely, namely, 4A9, 4A12, 4B4, 6B12, 7A11, and 7A15. (Note that if 4A9 and 4A12 occurred in the Chais' text they would be identified as 4A8 and 4A11; for the Chais, like Legge, Couvreur, Wilhelm, Lyall, and Lau, use a numbering in 4A that differs from the Harvard text, combining Harvard-Yenching 4A7–8 together as 4A7 and separating Harvard-Yenching 4A23 into two lines.) Some of the omitted sections are only one line in length, but the omission of 7A15 is particularly serious (see above, page 179 and below, 195 f.). (The Chais' text also omits the last paragraph of 1A7, intentionally, as it repeats almost exactly part of the text in 1A3.) The translation is often very close to Legge, and is good.

Lau (1970): The introduction alone in this valuable book must count as one of the best published studies of Mencius.[8] Chinese characters are not used except in the one page of textual notes and in appendix 5, which is a reprint of Lau (1963b). The other appendices, for example, "Early Traditions about Mencius," "Ancient History as Understood by Mencius," are useful; and the first, "The Dating of Events in the Life of Mencius" (pp. 205–13), though I would question some of its conclusions, is an important piece of scholarship. The translation is smooth, and often an improvement on earlier translations (though sometimes making new errors). Footnotes throughout are used far too sparingly; perhaps this was because of editorial policy, but Lau (1969), obviously a product of the research that went into the translation, was an opportunity to provide full and adequate notes, and although as far as it goes it is valuable, it does not do so. This lack is especially serious because Lau's translations are sometimes quite novel, as I will show, and the reasoning or authority that lies behind them (Lau never picks a meaning off the wall) needs to be made known. It should be added, however, that Lau probably thought of the rich material he provides in his introduction and appendices as taking the place of heavy footnoting, and thought it a better way of doing the same job. This in part is true.[9]

In addition to the aforementioned translations, Henri Cordier in *Bibliotheca Sinica* lists more than a dozen others between 1711 and 1904, in Latin, French, English, German, Dutch, Portuguese, and Russian.

12.3 Accuracy

There are many sections in the *Mengzi* that contain few problems and that most translators handle in a more-or-less acceptable way. To be fair to the art and to Mencius, I shall first examine several sections in the *Mengzi* that are both full of interest, and also technically easy enough to have made them favorite choices as elementary language texts.

Mengzi 2A2.16

In 2A2, which contains some very difficult material, there is the very simple story everyone knows, of the farmer in the state of Sòng 宋 who tried to get his shoots of grain to grow faster by pulling them a little. This is followed by a few lines in which Mencius briefly points out his moral: some people think it "of no use" to do anything for their "plants," and "neglect" them; others "help them grow" and actually hurt them. The language echoes 7A3 ("When you seek it you get it; when you neglect it you lose it; this is when seeking is of use in getting") and, roundabout, the quotation from Gàozǐ 告子 earlier in 2A2.9 ("What you do not get from 'words' do not seek in the heart . . .") showing that Lau (p. 77n. 3) is quite wrong in supposing 2A2 is actually two different sections joined together. We cannot expect any translator to point out such echoes; it will have to be enough if they get the translation right, and most do. The Chais' translation of 2A2 (pp. 148–49) has a wrenching misprint at the beginning: "Let us be like the man of Sung" (leaving out "not") and another, as absurd, toward the end: "they do not weaken their grain," where "weaken" is a typographical error for "weed." One should not be surprised to find that there are differences among commentators and translators on the precise sense of *máng-máng-rán* 芒芒然 (Legge, p. 191: "looking very stupid"), describing the farmer when he returns home. Lau has an outright error: *miáo* 苗, "young grain plant" (not specifying the kind) he renders "rice plant," which is not the meaning of the word *miao*. Anyway, the story assumes dry-land farming in which the young plants wither (*gǎo* 槁) when pulled up a little. In most other respects all the translators do well enough.

Mengzi 5A5

Longer but no more difficult is 5A5: the disciple Wàn Zhāng 萬章 asks how the emperor Shùn 舜 succeeded Yáo 堯; did Yao give the throne to him? No, only Heaven can do that; and Heaven did it by indicating its acceptance of Shun through the people's acceptance of him. Here and there one translator or another makes a questionable choice of words, but unvarnished errors are few. Lau is wrong (p. 143) in "Heaven does not speak but reveals itself through its acts and deeds." "Its" should be "people's" or should be omitted entirely, or we should have ". . . it revealed itself through his acts and deeds," as all other translators see. Dobson has four mistakes: (1, 2) After Yao's death and mourning, he has it (p. 65) that "Shun fled to the south of the Southern River to escape the sons of Yao." Here Dobson is probably thinking out what would have been the likely history behind the myth, if there had been any behind it. Often ugly political scraps get idealized; and Yao must have had more than one son, and obviously had not designated an heir, and primogeniture was a later development.[10] But it could not have seemed this way to Mencius, and Mencius is doing the talking; so Legge (p. 357), with "Shun withdrew from the son of Yao" (*Shùn bì Yáo zhī zǐ* 舜避堯之子), is right; in what follows, the people have an open alternative, whether to treat Shun as emperor—evidently he is not a fugitive—or *the* son of Yao. No one else translates "sons," but Ware, too, has "fled" for *bì* 避. (3) "The singers of songs sang not to the sons of Yao but to Shun." Singing ballads to a person does not mark him out as the world ruler, as does rendering homage to him or appealing to him as judge. The meaning is evidently "did not sing the praises of," or something of the sort, as in all other translations but the Chais'.[11] (4) "It was only after these things had happened that Shun returned to the central states, stood in the place of the Son of Heaven, and took up residence in Yao's palace. If he had begun by driving out the sons of Yao, it would have been pure usurpation." "Driving out" is too harsh for *bī* 逼 here; Legge's "applied pressure to" is what *bi* means if we suppose the possibility of Shun living together with Yao's son in Yao's palace. That is just the possibility imagined, and this requires making the sentence break after "stood in the place of the son of Heaven," continuing as Legge does: "If he [Shun] had, *before these things*, taken up his residence in the palace of Yao, and had applied pressure to the son of Yao, it would have been an act of usurpation, and not the gift of Heaven."[12] Ware makes this error too (as well as "fled" for *bì* 避), but all others have it right.

Mengzi 6A7

6A7 has Mencius arguing that if some people are sometimes morally wayward this is due to environmental influences, just as growing grain varies in quality with soil and climate; and that we all have basically similar moral sensibilities, just as we all have, as human beings, more or less similar preferences in food, music, and physical beauty. The ancient "sages" were, so to speak, connoisseurs in moral taste, and so we accept them as authorities, but our hearts (*xīn* 心) naturally prefer "order and right" (*lǐ yì* 理義) anyway, just as our eyes naturally delight in beauty. The argument is apparently adapted from the contemporary hedonist Zǐhuàzǐ 子華子 (as pointed out in Graham [1967, 37–38], but no translator notices this). Most translators have no trouble, but there are a few points on which they disagree, perhaps excusably. Contrast, at the beginning, Legge (p. 404) "In good years the children of the people are most of them good," with Lau (p. 164) "In good years the young men are mostly lazy." Legge (like Couvreur) follows both Zhao Qi and Zhu Xi. Lau follows Ruan Yuan, quoted approvingly by Jiao Xun, who takes *lài* 賴[13] as *lǎn* 嬾 "lazy," and argues that the young men's hearts can be "ensnared" by either plenty or want. Legge is probably right, but both views are respectable. Dobson's "amenable"[14] is also a plausible suggestion here (p. 114). In the grain analogy, *zhì yú rì zhì zhī shí* 至於日至之時 is sometimes rendered in the sense "When the full time (i.e., harvest time) is come" (so Legge, Wilhelm, Dobson, the Chais), and sometimes *rì zhì* 日至 is taken (I think correctly) in the sense "summer solstice," giving "by mid-summer" (so Couvreur, Ware, Lyall, Lau). In the phrase *xīn zhī suǒ tóng rán* 心之所同然, some follow what I take to be Zhao Qi's sense, taking *rán* 然 as "so," giving "the way in which our hearts are alike" (Lyall, Ware, Dobson, the Chais, Lau), and some follow Zhu Xi, taking *ran* as "to approve," giving "what all hearts alike approve" (Legge, Couvreur, perhaps Wilhelm). The loaded words *lǐ* 理 and *yì* 義 are, of course, translated variously. Couvreur follows the Zhu Xi tradition, and his translation here is heavily interpretative; Legge, likewise, with "principles *of our nature*" for *li*, with an additional note expanding on this in terms of Neo-Confucian metaphysical terminology, without seeing that he needs to warn his reader. Wilhelm has a note attempting to distinguish ancient and Neo-Confucian senses of the word—which, incidentally, Mencius uses nowhere else as a philosophical term of art.

Not excusable are the following outright mistakes. Regarding the fact that some young people become delinquent in hard times, Mencius comments, "It is not that the endowment," literally, material, *cái* 才, "that Heaven gives [them]," literally, sends down, *jiàng* 降, "is so different." Lau (p. 164) renders this "Heaven has not sent down men whose endowment differs so greatly," thereby missing a deliberate grammatical archaism. Mencius uses *tiān zhī jiàng cái* 天之降才 for *tiān suǒ jiàng zhī cái* 天所降之才. *Cai* can mean "people of such-and-such quality," but only in a very different context, for example, a court discussion on how to recruit "talent" into the bureaucracy. Dobson (p. 114) is out of line with "those who create these overwhelming conditions" for *qí suǒ yǐ xiàn nì qí xīn zhě* 其所以陷溺其心者, literally "that whereby they get their hearts sunk and drowned" (Lau: "what ensnares their hearts"). In the grain parable, the structure *suī yǒu bù tóng, zé dì yǒu féi qiāo . . . yě. Gù . . .* 雖有不同則地有肥磽 . . . 也故 is quite literally (italicizing translations of the functional words *suī* 雖, *zé* 則, *yě* 也, and *gù* 故) as follows: "*although* some of it is not the same, [if this is so] *then it is because* some soil is fertile and some stony. . . . *And so . . .* " Dobson is way off, with "*However*, differing circumstances do arise; some ground is rich, some is poor. . . . *Even so . . . ,*" thus taking *sui*, illegitimately, as *suī rán* 雖然; not seeing the conditional flavor of *ze*; not grasping the "X, Y *yě* 也" structure, where X is a clause, which here has (as very often) the force "X, because Y"; and finally finding himself driven to an absurd meaning for *gu*. Further on he slips again on the "X, Y ye" construction, with "Sandals resemble each other; men's feet are things of a kind." (Contrast Lau: "All shoes are alike because all feet are alike.") Further, his "All men relish flavourings in their food" won't do for *tóng shì* 同耆, which is literally "same preferences" (in taste), as Lau has it. Mencius says nothing at all about adding "flavourings" to food, and his point is lost when the operative word "same" is dropped. Ware has two careless errors in transcription ("Yi Wu" for "Yi Ya"; "Tu" for "Tzu Tu"). Lau carelessly omits "as to sounds" (or "music," *zhì yú shēng* 至於聲) before "The whole world looks to Shih K'uang." This section, as I noted, is not found in Giles.

Mengzi *3A4*

The first third of the long section 3A4—up to the famous "saying" Mencius quotes, "Some work with their physical strength, some with their hearts . . ."—is an account of the philosophical scene in Téng 滕. This leads into a conversation between Mencius and Chén Xiāng 陳相, a follower of Xǔ Xíng 許行, who thinks everyone, even a ruler, should grow his or her own food, and that a ruler who does otherwise is exploiting his people.[15] Mencius takes him apart fairly smoothly, but we encounter two problem spots: the word *shè* 舍 can (with Zhao Qi) be interpreted as "only" or "just" and taken with the following ("get everything he needs from his own house," Lau, p. 101) or it can with others be interpreted as "shop" and taken with what precedes ("operate a pottery or foundry," Ware, p. 85). The last seems wrong, but either interpretation gives the same sense.[16] Further on, there has been much argument about the word *lù* 路 in *shuài tiān xià ér lù* 率天下而路: either, if everyone has to make what he or she uses, this will "keep all the people running about on the roads" (Zhu Xi's sense, followed by Legge, Couvreur, Wilhelm, Lyall, and Giles); or "have everyone completely worn out" (Zhao Qi, seconded by Waley [1949, 102] and followed more or less by Ware, Dobson, the Chais, and Lau). I don't think the point is settled (see Jiao Xun's comment), but the overall sense is about the same.

There are other disagreements in translation where there should be none. A good ruler, Xu Xing says, "labors in the fields with his people and eats [the fruit of his labor]" (the Chais, p. 192, gloss in original) *yǔ mín bìng gēng ér shí* 與民並耕而食. Dobson (p. 116) misinterprets this as "should both plow and eat with his people," translating as if the particle *ér* 而 were not there. Ware's "Isn't the one who exchanges his grain for utensils exploiting the potter or the founder?" (p. 85) is wrong; in effect, Ware inserts a negative in the next clause to get this meaning. Ware is wrong again in understanding *hé Xǔzǐ zhī bú dàn fán* 何許子之不憚煩 as "Why doesn't Hsü hesitate before all the trouble he is causing?" The trouble is trouble to Xu himself, not to others. Dobson's handling of this line is even worse: "What can be said of Hsü Hsing's 'not involving himself in complications'?" *Bú dàn* 不憚 means "not avoiding" rather than "not involving himself in"; and the line is not a comment on an epithet. The idiom "*hé S zhī P?*" (何 S 之 P?) simply means "Why does S P so much?" So Dobson makes a double mistake here.

Dobson makes a double mistake again in a line farther on that has, surprisingly, caused all the translators trouble. The words *qiě yī rén zhī shēn ér bó gōng zhī suǒ wéi bèi*[17] 且一人之身而百工之所爲備 are translated correctly (if awkwardly) by Legge (p. 249). Mencius is emphasizing the beauty of the system of division of labor in our lives: high and low each have their proper work, "furthermore" (my translation) "in the case of each individual person even, all the various artisans' products are available [to him or her if needed]." There is what appears to be a slightly different interpretation which takes this as a statement of what is necessary if human needs are to be met, rendering *bèi* 備 ("available," "provided"), in effect, as "must be provided," that is, "are all necessary" (Couvreur, Wilhelm, Giles, the Chais, Lau); however, the sentence just does not say this, and obviously no one person needs *all* the kinds of things artisans can make.

To see how this mistake actually arises (and so, to see that it is not so minor) we must go to Couvreur's Latin, which is here defensively word-for-word: "Imo unius hominis persona est quam varii opifices faciunt instructam (rebus necessariis)" (p. 422). Literally, "Furthermore, the person of one human being is what the various artisans [make, i.e.] cause to be provided (with necessary things)" taking . . . *zhī suǒ wéi bèi* 之所爲備 as "What . . . cause to be provided," and so requiring something like "(with necessary things)" to complete the sense. Couvreur here ignores the grammatical function of *er* after *yī rén zhī shēn* 一人之身 ("unius hominis persona"). He evidently had a source in some commentary (not in Zhu Xi himself, who says nothing), for the grammatical error is cited and scotched by Jiao Xun (in loc.), who simply points out how Zhao Qi rearranged the syntax: *yī rén ér bèi bó gōng zhī suǒ zuò* 一人而備百工之所作 showing that *wéi* 爲 means *zuò* 作 here, and that *bei* is not part of the *suǒ* 所 construction. But Couvreur aims to give us Mencius as interpreted by Du (1779), and Du has this right (in loc.). So even if Couvreur had a source, he must be held accountable.

Ware ("A fulfillment takes place . . .") doesn't understand *bei* at all, and Dobson and Lyall miss the sense by trying to incorporate this sentence with the next as an extra conditional clause. Dobson's "in a single lifetime" for *yi ren zhi shen* is an additional mistake, apparently confusing *shēn* 身 here with its use in the idiom *zhōng shēn* 終身 "spend all one's life doing." Legge's meaning (he does not say so) is that of Zhao Qi; he is uneasy about it, and notes but rejects the meaning Couvreur and others adopted, which he identifies as from the *Rìjiǎng Sìshū yìjiě* 日講四書義解, an official publication of 1677 (which I have not been able to examine). Uchino has no difficulty with the line (p. 182), taking it properly as a separate sentence with the meaning I have given it.

There are a few more things to note: Ware's "sincere at being a prince of the highest caliber" (p. 84) is a daring attempt to give strict logical consistency to Chen Xiang's remarks; but the word *chéng* 誠 is not the verb in the sentence.[18] The Chais' "not," in "Why does he not carry on all this multifarious dealing . . ." (p. 193), I assume to be simply a lapse in editing. Their punctuation " 'Some toil with their minds, and some toil with their bodies.' Those who toil with their minds . . . ," limiting the "saying" to the first two phrases, and making what follows Mencius's comment on it, is a possible interpretation, but found nowhere else. I suppose it is inevitable that expressions like *shù shí* 數十 ("several tens," the number of Xu Xing's followers) will continue to be "translated" by inaccurate but more natural expressions in English such as "several scores" (the Chais, Lau) or "several dozen" (Wilhelm, Ware) when it does not seem to matter much (possibly justifiable, if one reflects that if Chinese had had a single word, say "X," for "dozen" and had not had a common phrase *shu shi*, Mencius probably would have said *shu X*).

These texts are, really, easy as well as enjoyable, and the translators' troubles, which I have thought it instructive to exhibit with care, are still relatively few compared to their difficulties in most parts of the book. In the texts so far, translators differ here and there, and here and there some of them trip, but usually not seriously. The sections are so rich anyway that readers get a lot for their reading time. If all of the *Mengzi* were like this, I perhaps would not need to go on.

Unfortunately all of the *Mengzi* is not like this. Much of the book is quite difficult. Often this is because Mencius is quoting earlier writings, or tagging and adroitly twisting earlier ideas (as in fact he was in 6A7), perhaps in ways his contemporaries recognized easily while we do not. Some of these difficult parts are very important for understanding Mencius's philosophy. Among them three are noteworthy: 2A2.9–10, 6A3–4, and 7A17, each of which I discuss at length in other essays in this volume.[19] 7A17 illustrates especially well the mutual importance of philology and philosophy, so I will touch on it here again.

This passage is a one-liner, only seventeen words in length: literally, "Do not do what [you] do not do . . ." I think it likely that no translator or Chinese commentator has understood it completely. Zhu Xi at least saw that 7B31 is an expansion of it, and no translator who fails to point this out in a note is doing his or her job. But this does not completely solve the problem. What is required here is that we reconstruct Mencius's entire philosophy of action (obviously a task for a substantial monograph), noticing that Mencius, as a Confucian moral self-cultivationist, had to believe that we *do* have moral responsibility for at least part of our structure of emotions and motivations, and that we *can* shape them. This is not a popular view in Western moral philosophy, and no doubt a subliminal feeling of charity has operated in the translators to steer them away from Mencius's real meaning, which I think was this: "You have an instinctive aversion to wrong acts of this or that kind in simple situations; *extend* (*tuī* 推) (you *can* do it! 1A7) that feeling to all not so simple situations of essentially the same kind." The thought is deep, and Mencius was right, but that is another story (and yet another essay).[20] But still, anything to avoid having Mencius say it: one translator (Lau) renders the line "Do not do what others do not choose to do . . ." giving no footnote; and another (Ware, apparently, though he does not tell us, following Zhao Qi), "Do not have done what you yourself would not do." I think it is clear that the difficulty here involves much more than the translator's ability to read Chinese.

There are many sticky passages like these in the *Mengzi*, often very important ones, whose interpretation is debatable. In some cases it is even true that how they are translated affects substantially how Mencius's philosophy as a whole is interpreted. Any translation that represents the *Mengzi* as smooth and unproblematic reading at these points is dangerously misleading. Even though I think I know how to handle these three passages (and there are others), I would have to respect a scholar who disagreed with me, and I could not, therefore, charge him or her with a blunder as a translator. In the case of 7A17, however, there is one criticism that must be made of the *translation* performance of Lau and Ware. Both recognized the text to be a problem. This is shown at once (to anyone checking the original Chinese) by the way they twist the original to get English that satisfies them as making sense. Any translator, for that matter, should be put on guard, at least, by the fact that Zhao Qi and Zhu Xi, the two best-known commentators, disagree so sharply as to what this section is all about. Yet, neither Lau nor Ware warns readers that they are looking at a problematic text; in fact, the only two translators being reviewed here who do (calling attention to different commentators' views) are Legge and Wilhelm.

I must pursue this issue further; and I shall not be impressed if I am told that the average reader does not want to be distracted by footnotes: readers too have their duties, and if they are not interested in being dealt with honestly they do not deserve our concern for them.

Mengzi *2B13*

Consider what happens as the translators confront 2B13.[21] Mencius, leaving Qí 齊 after failing to gain the serious attention of the king, is asked by a man accompanying him why he seems distressed, and is reminded that he himself has previously counseled that "The superior man does not murmur against Heaven" (Legge, p. 232). Mencius replies that a new king of all China should have appeared before now; Heaven must not wish it so; "If it wished this, who is there besides me to bring it about?" (that is, by converting a local ruler into a "true king"). Legge continues: "How could I be otherwise than dissatisfied?" A natural thing for Mencius to say, but unfortunately there is nothing in the Chinese corresponding to "otherwise than," and although Legge has a footnote, he does not mention this matter. Legge is followed by Wilhelm, Lyall, Ware, Dobson, and the Chais (Giles omits the section), none of whom footnote the difficulty. The last three, furthermore, did their work after the publication of Waley (1949), which points out that "Legge's 'otherwise than' is an arbitrary insertion" (p. 101). Lau does better, translating absolutely literally, leaving the reader to struggle with the apparent non sequitur.

What is amazing here is that the problem has been dealt with at length by Zhu Xi, who takes the text as it stands and argues that Mencius is indeed insisting he *is not* discontented, reassuring himself that if Heaven wished to act he would be Heaven's instrument. Zhu continues, "We see in this how the sage's grief for the world can coexist harmoniously with an honest delight in Heaven." (Zhao Qi argues similarly, but briefly.) Couvreur, who like Lau translates literally, gives us one of his rare in-text notes which paraphrases this resolution of Zhu's: "Although one mustn't resent Heaven, can't one be sad about Heaven's bidding?" Zhu may be right, though there is, if so, an undeniable lack of coherence in the section. But surely, only chaos can be the result if the principle is accepted that translators may supply or withhold a *negative* simply on the basis of their sense of the logic of a passage, without telling the reader what they are doing. Yet this is exactly what six of our nine translators have done. One begins to wonder if the translation of the *Mengzi* is out of control.

Mengzi *3B5.5*

Another example requires praise as well as blame. In 3B5 Mencius is moralizing on the Song state's difficulties in power politics, and has occasion to quote from a (now lost) *Shang shu* chapter dealing with the campaigns of King Wǔ 武王, founder of the Zhou Dynasty. King Wu marches eastward, "there being some who would not become the subjects" (sc. of Zhou). So Legge (p. 273), followed in substance by Couvreur, Wilhelm, Lyall, Ware, Dobson, and the Chais (Giles omits) and in agreement with commentators Zhao Qi, Zhu Xi, and Jiao Xun. In understanding the text, all take the word *yōu* 攸 in the line *yōu yōu bù wéi chén* 有攸不惟臣 as the early archaic equivalent of the preverbal pronoun *suǒ* 所 (literally, "There were [places] *where* [they] did not submit").[22] This is grammatically possible and makes good sense. Lau alone differs, translating (p. 110) "The state of Yu did not submit." Lau gives no note, no hint to readers that they will find this interpretation in no other translator, and probably in no commentator; nor any justification whatever for a radically new translation, taking what had been thought to be a pronoun as the name of a petty state.

Yet Lau's translation may very well be right, and impressive scholarship lies behind it. There *was* a feudal state of You in pre-Zhou China. It is mentioned repeatedly in late Shang oracle inscriptions concerning a royal campaign against eastern border peoples, and its location is known. It was less than a hundred miles east-southeast of the capital of the Song state of Mencius's day, where he probably was when this conversation took place, and so was also a territory King Wu would have had to march east to get to. Further, the Shang bone inscriptions indicate that it was a Shang frontier feudal dependency or a strong border supporting power. It would not be surprising if such an entity were to try to hold out after the main action of the conquest. There are probably references to the same entity, using variant graphs, in the *Zuǒ zhuàn* 左傳 and in early Zhou bronze inscriptions. The whole matter is dealt with in Chen (1956, 306), who himself cites *Mengzi* 3B5.[23] So, Lau knew what he was doing. Very good; but surely he should have told us.

Mengzi *1A1*

The reader needs a footnote when the translation calls for justification; but always, what is needed is correct translation. It is time to prick illusions about this matter, and one may as well begin at the beginning. *Mengzi* 1A1 gives us Mencius's initial interview with King Hui of Liang: "Aged sir, you have not thought a thousand *li* too far to come. . . ." The text is sometimes thought to be easy. (Dawson 1968, 12, 24–29, 80, uses it as his opening lesson.) It is hardly that, but the difficulties are ones we should expect a person publishing a translation of the *Mengzi* to be able to handle. Lau's translation (p. 49) is almost but not quite right; he errs in rendering *wáng yì yuē* 王亦曰 near the end as "perhaps you will now endorse what I have said," essentially following Legge, Ware, Lyall, and Wilhelm who take *yì* 亦 as "also"; others see that it is here, as at the beginning of the section, a particle reinforcing the final *ér yǐ yǐ* 而 已矣 "only" (see Waley 1949, 100). *Yì* at the beginning of Mencius's remarks is misinterpreted as "also" by Wilhelm and Lyall only.[24]

Lau (with Wilhelm, Couvreur, Lyall, and Giles) handles perfectly the idiom *zhě bì* 者必 halfway through: "When regicide is committed in a state of ten thousand chariots, it is certain to be by a vassal with a thousand chariots." Legge mysteriously (and inappropriately) uses the language of Biblical prophecy: "In the kingdom of ten thousand chariots, the murderer of his sovereign shall be *the chief of* a family of a thousand chariots." (Compare Isaiah 39.6: "Behold, the days come, that all that is in thine house . . . shall be carried to Babylon.") He is followed by the Chais (p. 109) who simply copy him, and in substance also by Ware. Dobson goes wild: "In a 'ten-thousand chariot state' [a major state] he who slew his prince might gain a 'thousand-chariot estate' [a large estate]," and so on (p. 26, glosses in original). He continues the error by translating a "thousand in ten thousand . . . is no small profit." (Contrast Lau's correct rendering: a "share of a thousand in ten thousand . . . is by no means insignificant.") Embarrassingly, Dawson follows Dobson at these points, in a model translation he provides for his beginning students (Dawson 1968, 80). Dobson should have recognized the *zhe bi* idiom as one that also occurs at the end of 6A1. (He translates 6A1 so loosely that I cannot tell whether he understood it there.)

We find several more difficulties in the rendering of this section. It will be noticed that Legge and Couvreur use the definite article before "kingdom of ten thousand chariots" ("le domaine qui"). This is acceptable, though not necessary; they do it following a tradition that only the Zhou king could have that many chariots. The Chais, copying and improving Legge without seeing what he was doing, also use the definite article in the next, parallel sentence: "In the kingdom of a thousand chariots . . . ," requiring us to give "the" a different sense ("the typical"). Returning to Dobson, we find more squeaks and rattles: *wèi yǒu rén ér yí qí qīn zhě yě* 未有仁而遺其親者也—what Lau has as "No benevolent man ever abandons his parents . . ."—Dobson inverts with "There has never been a Humane man abandoned by his kin." Dobson, of course, does not think that the Chinese has this meaning (he translates this sentence correctly in 1959, 119). He is just being very careless, as he is in 2B11 (p. 53) when having just translated "Duke Mu of Lu" he interpolates two references to him in the next three lines as "King." One more Dobson error is his rendering of the conditional particle *gǒu* 苟 (*gǒu wéi hòu yì ér xiān lì* 苟爲後義而先利) as "if indeed." *Gou* actually means "if at all" or "if . . . just . . ." (in Japanese: いやしくも). It is acceptable to render it simply "if" so long as the context shows Mencius's meaning, which is here that *just* making this *one* mistake (of putting "profit" before "right") is enough to ruin your state. But Dobson is convinced that *gou* is a synonym of *chéng* 誠 ("sincerely," "really," and so on), see Dobson (1959, 132), and so he roughs the sense here a bit. He repeats this error elsewhere, for example, in 2A6 (p. 132): "If, in fact, a ruler can . . ." should be "If a ruler can just . . . ," as the context here clearly shows.[25] Thus we find in 1A1 a disquieting parade of mistakes, in a very familiar section of only a dozen short sentences.

Henceforth I will take up either one-line sections or isolated points in longer ones to illustrate various kinds of problems. Sometimes the problem in a poor translation is not ignorance of language but ignorance (or ignoring) of a simple background fact.

Mengzi *1A7.4*

We find an example of this in Mencius's long conversation with King Xuān of Qí 齊宣王. Mencius repeats to the king an account another officer had given him of the king's having noticed an ox being led to sacrifice, taking pity on it, and ordering a sheep to be put in its place. The story begins, according to Lau (p. 54), with "The King was sitting in the upper part of the hall and someone led an ox through the lower part." In interpreting *guò táng xià* 過堂下 as "through the lower part," Lau stands with Couvreur, Giles, and Dobson, and in part Legge (who has "past the lower part"). It is an intriguing picture they seem to share. (How charmingly primitive these early royal courts must have been! Would there have been a flunky whose duty was to clean up the droppings? What would his title have been?) All have neglected two simple linguistic facts and one equally simple architectural fact: (1) *X xià* 下 can mean either "the lower part of X" or "below X," or even (if X is in a low position) "down in X"; (2) *guò* 過 can mean either "pass through" or "pass by"; and (3) important

Chinese buildings, such as royal audience halls, were in ancient and not so ancient times built with the main floor high off the ground and were approached by a broad stairway. So, from a purely grammatical standpoint, the line might have the meaning Lau gives it, or it might mean, as Lyall (Ware, the Chais, and Wilhelm are similar) translates: "The King was sitting in the hall above when a man passed below the hall dragging an ox." It is up to translators to notice these two possibilities, pick out the more likely one, and verify their choice with independent evidence if they can. In this case the independent evidence is plentiful, for we often find such expressions as *táng zhī shàng* 堂之上 ("up in the hall"), *xià táng* 下堂 ("descend from"—that is, go out of—"the hall"), and so on. For example, Zhuangzi tells of the sacred turtle shell of Chǔ 楚, which the king wrapped in a napkin and placed in a box, "keeping it in the ancestral temple" *cáng zhī miào táng zhī shàng* 藏之廟堂之上.[26] These are things translators ought simply to know—and be able to remember when they need to.

Some will have noticed that there is one translation problem I have been largely ignoring, and they may be puzzled. For example, Ware, whom I judged to have translated the foregoing text correctly, translates the word *niú* 牛 not as "ox" but as "buffalo." Is he right? One cannot fault him: *niu* is a generic term for bovid animals, and archaeology verifies that the water buffalo and other bovids already were domesticated in north China by Shang times. Perhaps ritual texts would pin down the zoological question here, but if so this would require a footnote, and not only a judicious use of English. It is even truer when accurate representation of the thought of a passage is at stake (which is not the case here) that at a problematic spot the translator has got to do more than just pick the "best" word. On the other hand, when nothing rests on the matter we tolerate patent inaccuracy. I will even forgive (as I often must in these translations) "mile" for *lǐ* 里 if it is clear what the translator is doing. But regarding "humanity" versus "benevolence" versus "love" versus "manhood-at-its-best" for *rén* 仁, although one may recognize degrees of appropriateness, even the best is not enough. This does not mean that pregnant Chinese philosophical terms like *ren* are in any paradoxical way not translatable, it simply means that the ongoing scholarship by which we continue to clarify these concepts is itself part of the process of translation. When translation really goes awry, the trouble, as in almost all the examples I am discussing, is usually a failure to grasp the structure of idioms and sentences, or the background or shape of thought in a whole paragraph or still larger context. For example, the *tang xia* problem is important for the thought, quite aside from the fact that mistranslation results in comic absurdity: Mencius, I suggest, builds his effect on the fact that the incident flowers out of a wandering of the king's attention (think of him as, so to speak, absent-mindedly looking out the window); and so he is able to say to the king more dramatically, "See? You can catch yourself doing it!"

Of course, it is possible for the translator to see perfectly well how the sentences are to be parsed, and still simply be wrong in his or her choice of some English word as the equivalent of a Chinese word in his text. Lau was just wrong in picking "rice plants" for *miao* in 2A2. Lau is probably persuaded that he has a reason for translating *bǎo* 保 in 1A7 and elsewhere repeatedly as "give peace to" rather than "protect" or "take care of," but I doubt that his reason can be adequate.[27] But the translator's most serious difficulties are likely to be structural confusions.

A telling reason for giving priority to such structural questions is that, with work, they can usually be settled with finality. They are "hard data" from which we can extend inferences into the less certain areas of the semantics of terms. Conversely, if the handling of idioms and syntactic structures goes wrong, everything is going to be nonsense.

Mengzi *4A15*

A methodologically very interesting instance is found in 4A15. Mencius is condemning ministers who devise and carry out "unbenevolent" policies for their princes—wars of aggrandizement, power diplomacy, and exploitation of the agricultural population. Consider, for example, Rǎn Qiú 冉求 ("Jan Ch'iu" in Wade-Giles), sometime disciple of Confucius, minister to the Jì 季 family ("Chi" in Wade-Giles), who was disowned by his teacher: "Ch'iu acted as chief officer to the head of the Chi family, whose *evil* ways he was unable to change, while he exacted from the people double the grain formerly paid" (Legge, 304–5; Wilhelm, Lyall, Giles, the Chais, and Lau have similar translations). Couvreur makes "Chi" the subject of "exacted," which is equally admissible; Ware's " . . . although he was unable to change their evil character, he did make the grain tax twice what it had been previously," mistakes the relationship between the clauses, but is otherwise acceptable. Now, the Chinese for Legge's "*evil* ways" (Ware: "evil character"), is *dé* 德, sometimes just the "character" of a thing or person, but almost always "good character," and the usual translation is "virtue." Dobson sticks to the normal meaning of *de* and misconstrues the line: "When Ch'iu was steward of the Chi family, upon whom Ch'iu's virtue exercised not the slightest effect, he even imposed, on their behalf, a double exaction of grain" (p. 126). Dobson uses the line (1959, 66) as an example, he supposes, of the passive use of a verb: *wú néng gǎi yú qí dé* 無能改於其德, "They would not be changed by his virtue." Dobson uses "would not" for *wú* 無 here, because one of his grammatical theories is that *wu* is a subjunctive negative (1959, 45). In (1963) he has apparently dropped this "subjunctive" theory of preverbal *wu*. He continues, however, to regard the construction as "passive," and so the "virtue" in question is for Dobson Ran Qiu's, and remains the sort of "virtue" that influences others for the better. However, in context we see that Mencius could not be ascribing this kind of "virtue" to Ran Qiu, for the whole point of the section is that (here, at least) Qiu is a scoundrel. Further, in this kind of situation, Ran Qiu's ideal role *would* be to improve and strengthen the *de* of his lord. A precise translation is "he [that is, Qiu] could change nothing in their [that is, the Ji's] character and [even, on their behalf,] imposed . . ." and not, as Dobson apparently supposes, "they [that is, the Ji's] were not capable in any respect of being changed by his [Qiu's] virtue, and he [i.e., Qiu, even] imposed [on their behalf] . . ." Notice that the correct interpretation smoothly keeps "Qiu" subject of the whole sentence, as subject of each of the succeeding phrases. In this instance, as often, error is avoided by arriving at an interpretation which best accommodates grammatical, rhetorical, situational, and semantic factors, and here the grammar, rhetoric, and situation force us to give *de* a very unusual but permissible (and quite interesting) meaning.

Mengzi 1A4

Another case is in 1A4, in which Mencius reproaches King Hui for seeing to it that "there is fat meat in your kitchen and there are well-fed horses in your stables" but so neglecting the people's welfare that in the countryside they drop dead of starvation. "This," says Mencius (Lau, p. 52), "is to show animals the way to devour men" *cǐ shuài shòu ér shí rén yě* 此率獸而食人也. The entire context shows that Mencius means this to be taken figuratively ("Is there any difference between killing [a man] with a knife and killing him with misrule?"), and in fact, as Dobson (p. 29n. 87) notes, Mencius is here using a (probably well-known) saying by the second-generation Confucian disciple Gōngmíng Yí 公明儀 (see *Mengzi* 3B9.9). Lau agrees with Legge's translation, as does almost everybody, and there really is no problem with the line (except that a few—for example, Giles [p. 24], "This is tempting beasts to devour men" and the Chais [p. 109], "This incites beasts to devour men"—are confused, supposing Mencius to be saying that animals will be tempted to eat the dead bodies). Dobson alone blunders, picking an inappropriate meaning for *shuài* 率 and matching it with a mistaken structural interpretation of the whole line: "This is a policy of 'governing animals and eating men'" (p. 29). He gives a note insisting on his interpretation, holding that the line is a deliberate paradox, a "reversal of the expected 'governing men and eating animals.'" Dobson repeats the mistake at 3B9 (p. 58), and at 4A15 (p. 126), already noticed, where, varying the metaphor, Mencius is condemning war as "showing the land the way to devour human flesh" (Lau, p. 124). Dobson has "governing property and living off human flesh." (But it is literally *shuài tǔ dì ér shí rén ròu* 率土地而食人肉,[28] "leading the land to eat human flesh"; would Dobson say "this is a reversal of the expected 'governing human flesh and eating land'?") Dobson has mechanically word-for-word-ed his way through a simple idiom, namely, "N_1 + V_1 + N_2 + ér 而 + V_2 + N_3," where the medial *er* with what follows is, so to speak, intentional only: "N_1 does V_1 to N_2, in order that N_1 (or N_2) shall do V_2 to N_3." Failing to see this, Dobson has chosen the wrong meaning for *shuai* (very often used in this idiom) which is not "govern" here, but "lead." It is only fair to add, however, that in other places Dobson handles this idiom quite correctly: for example, in 3A4.18 (p. 119), he translated *xiāng shuài ér wéi wèi* 相率而爲僞 as "men would be led on to swindle each other"; in 3A4.6, p. 117, he translates *shuài tiān xià ér lù* 率天下而路 as "would have everyone completely worn out"; in 6B3 (p. 79), he translates *yǒu rén yú cǐ, yuè rén guān gōng ér shí zhī*[29] 有人於此越人關弓而射之 as "Suppose a man is threatened by a Yüeh man drawing his bow." (The idiom occurs also at the end of 6A1 but here apparently Dobson, p. 110, does not understand it.) It should also be pointed out that although I have held up Lau as correct against Dobson's treatment of the "lead on animals" passages, Lau himself mistranslates the "intentional" *er* idiom in translating 6B3 (p. 173): "If a man from Yüeh bends his bow and takes a shot at him . . ." *Ér shí zhī* 而射之 here means "to shoot him" without implying that the shot is actually discharged, or if discharged, successful. (For examples of this usage, see Simon 1954, 32.) Giles omits the section, and all other translators get the phrase right.

If translators are making mistakes to this extent, sooner or later, we must find them misunderstanding sections that are philosophically quite important. Here are some revealing examples.

Mengzi *7A15*

I have already noted the importance of 7A15 (on *liáng zhī* 良知), a section which was omitted entirely by Giles and the Chais. I pursue the matter with hesitation, because this section of only sixty-two graphs contains some problems that I perhaps should classify as "monographic." We can note in passing the various translations of *liang zhi*, defined by Mencius as what one "knows without having to reflect on it" (Lau, p. 184): "intuitive knowledge" (Legge); "essential" ("eigentlich") knowledge (Wilhelm); what one knows *naturellement* (Couvreur); "true knowledge" (Lyall); "highest type of knowledge" (Ware); what one "truly knows" (Lau). Dobson's very free "endowment of good" is unfortunate only in being used for both *liang zhi* and *liáng néng* 良能.[30] Any of these attempts could be the beginning of explication and none is more than that. Mencius says simply that we have abilities that we do not have to learn and knowledge we do not have to think out; that these innately given things are a child's love for parents, which is "benevolence" (*ren*), and a maturing person's respect for elders, which is "rightness" (or perhaps "duty," *yi*). It is possible to argue whether Mencius says here that we are innately disposed in these ways, or simply that we have innate intuitions about how we ought to be disposed without necessarily feeling that way. (There are stubborn philosophers who will pronounce this last idea self-contradictory.) There is a fascinating discussion of this in Jiao Xun, who sternly argues (in effect separating moral "knowledge" and "action") that it was Mencius's view that to convert intuition into effective disposition requires education, and may well require the rod.

Here I am interested only in the following, final line. It reads, very simply, *Wú tuō, dá zhī tiān xià yě* 無他達之天下也, and may be rendered "There is nothing else [needed] but to extend these to [everyone in] the world." The commentators (Zhao Qi, Sūn Shì 孫奭, Zhu Xi, and Jiao Xun) would all accept my rendering, but only because my English is ambiguous. Does it mean that (1) morally "noble people" are to bring it about that all people in the world have the same (developed) moral feelings they have? Such, as I read him, is a possible view of Zhu Xi. Or does it mean that (2) such people are to direct toward and apply to all others (in appropriate ways and in due degree, we must suppose) their own moral-emotional capacities, which are in them naturally directed toward their parents and elders? Such is, explicitly, Zhao Qi's and Sun Shi's view of Mencius here. (It is also my view, and possibly Zhu Xi's.) Or does it mean that (3) moral teachers ("sages") have simply to spread, not their feelings (in some sense of "spreading"), but the "Way," the virtues of *ren* and *yi*, through the world, and that they are able to proceed with this moral educating because all people have moral-making intuitions toward love for parents and respect for elders, which are (potentially) *ren* and *yi*? This is Jiao Xun's view. The problem is one of the most important in the interpretation of Mencius. Lyall ("To spread these feelings . . . ," p. 208) may be taking either the first or the second view. Ware ("it only remains for us to spread these virtues through the world!" p. 148) seems to take the third. Wilhelm explicitly takes the second ("Es handelt sich um nichts anders, als diese Gefühle auszudehnen auf die ganze Welt," p. 160, citing Zhao Qi). Lau ("What is left to be done is simply the extension of these to the whole empire," p. 184) is as clever as I am, and can be read in any of the three ways. Legge, Couvreur, and Dobson have variations on a fourth interpretation, all taking *dá zhī tiān xià* 達之天下 somehow to mean (4) "they [these moral intuitions] are found throughout the world" (while they struggle with *wú tuō* 無他 in different ways). The translations of these last three must be rejected. They should have noticed the way Mencius uses the word *dá* 達 "to extend," in other passages, notably 7B31. Legge, in a footnote, bases his translation on phrases in Zhu Xi's commentary, which Legge also misinterprets. The same misinterpretation is found in Du (1779), and so Couvreur, aiming to give us Du's interpretation, must be excused. This fourth interpretation is also found in Uchino, p. 454.

Mengzi 7A45

Lau did well on 7A15. He does less well on 7A45. His translation:

> Mencius said, "A gentleman is sparing with things but shows no benevolence towards them; he shows benevolence towards the people but is not attached to them. He is attached to his parents but is merely benevolent towards the people; he is benevolent towards the people but is merely sparing with things."

A note on "sparing" (*ài* 愛) observes that Mencius is exploiting the fact that the word also means "to love."

There are two problems to be resolved here if this section is to be anything but sheer triviality. Lau gets his meanings "sparing" (for *ai*) and "things" (for *wù* 物) from Zhu Xi. But what could be the point? Who, in Mencius's time, would suppose the "gentleman" would ever be "benevolent" (*ren*) towards "things"? Wang Yangming might, indeed, say this; but this is not a point of view Mencius had to deal with. One has to notice that *wu*, "things," can also mean "animals"—a better completion of the series "parents, people (*min* 民) . . ."—and that "sparing" is not just another meaning for *ai*, completely different from and unrelated to the common meaning "love." *Ai*, even as "sparing," can be thought of as a limiting case of *caring*. Mencius seems to be saying that it is the kind of "love" appropriate only toward animate objects below the level of human beings. As other translators—Legge, Wilhelm, Dobson, and indirectly Lyall—note, this section is an attack on the Mohists (and so an endorsement of "graded love" against "universal love," *jiān ài* 兼愛).

However, its anti-Mohist message is subtler than this; and this is the second problem: what is the point of the last line? As Lau translates it, it merely repeats what has already been said, in a sort of empty jingle. Are we to suppose Mencius is merely mumbling here? Lau's "jingle" treatment of it is found in all the translators except Dobson and the Chais, who undoubtedly have it right. Dobson (p. 139): "He who feels the love of family towards his own kin will feel Humanity for all men. He who feels Humanity for all men will be kind to all living creatures." Some Mohists in Mencius's time seem to have admitted that their universal "love" would not be psychologically possible unless there were a natural developing ground for it, which presumably is family affection; but then, unlike the Confucians, went on to argue that one must spread it out flat, so to speak. This issue is argued out between Mencius and the Mohist Yí Zhī 夷之 in 3A5.[31] Lyall alone notes (p. 222) the relevance of 3A5, but misses the point, seeing Mencius as developing a primitive clan-centered morality. Mencius is actually arguing, as 7A45 now makes clear, that the family is a kind of nursery for our potential for a wider humanity (as 7A15, in another way, is also saying). This interpretation is stated succinctly by Zhao Qi (as Dobson should have footnoted) and indirectly but with more sophistication by Zhu Xi (who quotes 3A5 obliquely). The failure of seven translators to see it is hardly excusable.[32]

Mengzi 4A9.1

Turning to a specimen of Mencius's political thought, one finds 4A9 omitted by Giles, and again this does not mean that it is not important. Mencius says that the bad kings of old lost the world, and their thrones and lives, by losing the people's hearts, and that tyrants actually drive the people into the arms of more considerate rulers: "Thus the otter drives the fish to the deep . . ." (Lau, p. 122). But how does one "get" the people's hearts? There is a "Way," namely, *suǒ yù, yǔ zhī jù zhī; suǒ wù, wù shī ér yě* 所欲與之聚之 。所惡勿施爾也. Legge, p. 300, has rendered this, "it is simply to collect (*jù* 聚) for them (*yǔ zhī* 與之) what they like (*suǒ yù* 所欲), and not to lay on them (*wù shī* 勿施) what they dislike (*suǒ wù* 所惡)." In this he follows Zhu Xi and, with a minor difference, Zhao Qi also. Six later translators follow essentially the same interpretation. The Chais deviate slightly (for reasons not evident to me) but not significantly. Ware, evidently worried about "for them" for *yu zhi*, tries "give them (*yu zhi*), gather about them (*ju zhi*) the things that are desired (*suo yu*). Do not bestow upon them (*wu shi*) what they dislike (*suo wu*)."[33] *Ju*, here "gather about," must also be felt to be a problem; Zhao Qi interprets as if it came before *yu zhi* (as does Lyall), and Wilhelm just omits it. One may well wonder whether this picture of a good ruler as playing to his people's wishes is quite what Confucian benevolence implies. Perhaps Zhu Xi has this in mind in making the point of arguing that it is the basic desires of human life the king is to enable the people to satisfy.

Only one translator dissents. Dobson (p. 166) gives us this:

> There is a way to gain their sympathy. Share with them the accumulation of the things you wish for, and do not impose upon them the things you yourself dislike.

Dobson gets his translation simply by supplying "you" instead of "they" as subjects of the subjectless verbs *yù* 欲, "wish," and *wù* 惡, "dislike," and taking *yu zhi ju zhi* as "together with them [i.e., the people] accumulate them [i.e., the wished for things]," all perfectly possible. Unfortunately, he gives no note of justification or explanation for these choices. But Dobson is almost certainly right. And when one thinks out the reasons, one will wonder why no one else saw them.

The juxtaposition of the phrases *suo yu* and *wu shi* "What [you] wish . . . don't do to . . ." at once should suggest Confucius: *jǐ suǒ bú yù wù shī yú rén* 己所不欲勿施於人 "What you don't want done to yourself don't do to others."[34] From this much we don't *know* that this is what Mencius had in mind, but there's more. Consider 1B1 on King Xuan of Qi's fondness for music, concluding, "Now if you shared your enjoyment with the people, you would be a true King" (Lau, p. 61), or 1B2, on how King Wen shared his royal park with the people, or 1B4, to King Xuan, on whether good kings of old had palaces like his: "To speak ill of those in authority because one is not given a share in such enjoyment is, of course, wrong. But for one in authority over the people not to share his enjoyment with the people is equally wrong. The people will delight in the joy of him who delights in their joy . . ." (Lau, p. 63; see also 1A2); or 1B5, on the king's various "weaknesses": he is fond of wealth;

well then, let him govern in such a way that the people have wealth to enjoy too. He is fond of women; well then, let him "share this fondness with the people," seeing to it that men are able to find wives and women are able to have husbands. It has always been supposed that in this doctrine of governing by sympathy (notice Dobson's use of this word) Mencius had the Confucian "golden rule" in mind and was applying it to government. 4A9, as Dobson's translation reveals, proves that this is the case.

12.4 Judgments

Which is best? What can these translations be used for? What more do we need, and how can we get it? I am hardly in a position to submit a certified grade sheet. I have only presented a small sampling of translators' performances. To do enough of this to justify firm comparative judgments would require a book, containing all the work that would be needed for a really adequate retranslation of Mencius. I have not done this work, and if I had, the efficient way to present it would be to publish a new translation, with careful commentary.

Nonetheless, we can ask what the texts examined here show, if one chooses to treat them as a sample for making comparisons of competence. If you look back and count the errors I have noted and compared with others' performances, a plausible way of scoring them will show that Giles and Couvreur have very low counts of three errors. (Of course, Giles takes fewer risks: four of the sections discussed, including a third of the possibilities for error, are not translated by him.) The Chais have five errors; Lyall and Wilhelm, six each; Legge and Lau, seven and ten respectively; Ware is a bit higher, with about a dozen, and Dobson's score I leave to the reader. This does not take into account the important difference between the relatively minor error and the howler, and it rests in part on my doubtful distinction between passages that I call merely very difficult and those that I pronounce "problematic" (and so did not count). It also rests on a doubtful distinction between a minor error and a rendering that merely makes me uneasy. Still, the sampling has ranged over most of the subjects in the *Mengzi* and has included both easy and difficult sections.

So, some very tentative judgments are possible. In any case, it seems to me obvious that any translator who does as badly, *even once*, as does Dobson on 1A1 cannot ever be used with confidence. It appears equally obvious, that any translator who does as well in comparison with others, *even once*, as does Dobson on 7A45 and on 4A10 must always be consulted by the thorough scholar and must be read with respect. Dobson is perhaps the extreme case. To some degree the reader faces this dilemma with every translator. This isn't news, but it gets forgotten. Too often the translators are not giving us the real Mencius, who can be subtle and rich (and surprisingly systematic) behind a deceptive simplicity. The scholar or the student in an advanced seminar uses everything. In an introductory college course in Chinese philosophy I would use Lau (when he is in print) or Legge, or both. I'm not sure which translation is better or which book is better, all told, but the supporting material in Lau almost requires using him. Dobson's work, in spite of the "general reader" label, is more of a scholar's work than it seems.[35] However, Dobson's translation cannot be trusted enough to use at this level (I have tried it); and it is important to show the student what the book of Mencius actually looked like to the two millennia of Chinese who studied it. We have the same difficulty in the arrangement of the text with the Chais' translation, and the absence of a finding list (of the sort provided by Dobson) makes it virtually useless. This is unfortunate, for my study suggests that this translation is a rather good one, in spite of very sloppy editing. Giles, too, is relatively good and well written, but frequently out of print and with too much valuable material left out. Ware surely ought to be reserved to the user who can read him quite critically. Most American students no longer use French or German, unfortunately; but both Couvreur and Wilhelm seem to me to be very good, and I of course appreciate Wilhelm's commentarial conscientiousness. It should be pointed out, however, that Couvreur is not quite comparable to the others, since the task he attempted was not to translate Mencius himself but Mencius as interpreted in the Zhu Xi tradition. This was important to do, but is likely to have been an easier job, and the result less easily criticized. Whereas Mencius is often problematic, Zhu Xi and his followers are often much less so. Moreover, Couvreur's choice of Du (1779) as a standard was not the best; Du led him into error, and apparently did not enjoy the highest regard in China—for we do not find his work listed in the better bibliographies. It would be interesting, perhaps, to have a translation that presents Mencius strictly according to Zhao Qi.

But let us have a rest from new translations that are gotten out for no better reason than that a publisher of popular intellectual fare has his or her attention called to Mencius, discovers that he's interesting (he is), and thinks the books will sell. The basic uneasiness I have with such translations of Mencius is that inevitably conscience is going to be prostituted to readability. It is true that many parts of the *Mengzi* can be straightforwardly translated into an English that conveys Mencius's thought easily, and it is true that much of this material is so rich in philosophical and general human interest that it seems a shame not to make it available to people who are not specialists but are intellectually alive. Still it is also true that large parts of the *Mengzi* are very difficult to read, and true also that these difficult parts include texts that are crucial for a correct understanding of Mencius's moral philosophy.

Bad publications make it more difficult, and so even more expensive, to get really good books printed. The fact that this review leaves Legge's work, which came out more than a century ago, as still one of the best presentations available, should suggest how difficult it is going to be to do a really significantly better job. The research of the past century on Chinese history and society, and on Mencius's language, makes a much better job possible. But it will take a long time. And it will be better done, and more surely completed with due care, if done by several scholars in collaboration. Particularly interesting, it seems to me, would be a translation that attends not just to philological and historical problems in the text but also analyzes philosophical problems in it, and gives some space to the philosophical importance of this or that section at later points in the long tradition of Mencian ethics, among such very different thinkers as Zhu Xi, Wang Yangming, Dai Zhen, and Jiao Xun.

Mencius is surely worth this kind of attention and care.

Xunzi on
"Human Nature"

13

13.1 Prefatory Note

This essay came into being some time in 1975 or 1976, for a specific non-standard purpose. I was teaching a small innovative course for Stanford undergraduates, introducing to them the ideas of the major ancient Chinese philosophers and schools. I was also teaching courses in old Chinese, including a seminar reading philosophy. One of my language courses was an offbeat beginners' course, designed for students who had done no previous work in Chinese, i.e., for students who had not taken the standard route of doing two years of work in modern Chinese first. This approach to old Chinese was a success, although always resisted by the pedagogically conservative Stanford Department of Asian Languages. That Department reasoned (correctly) that students could not hope to become professionally serious in the use of old Chinese without being able to read contemporary scholarship in Chinese, and to communicate with contemporary scholars. I, located primarily in the Department of Philosophy, knew that there were not a few students who did not want to become "sinologists," but had reason to want to have some acquaintance with the old Chinese philosophers as part of a broader grasp of philosophy as a whole; and I also knew that they would in the end understand these old philosophers much better, and even avoid deep misunderstandings of them, if they had some acquaintance, even slight, with the language in which this philosophy had been written or thought out.

So I began to introduce a description of old Chinese into my course on ancient Chinese philosophy. This soon led to my experimenting with introducing the bare elements of reading the language into my philosophy course—enough, at least, so that the student could accustom his or her eye to distinguishing one graph from another, and could follow intelligently careful interlinear translations (which I provided) of a few pregnant and memorable texts. (This too was a success.)

For this purpose, Xúnzǐ 荀子 provided excellent material: he is a first-rate philosopher by any standard, and writes on problems that are immediately recognizable to the modern student as very important ones. And his language is both elegant and severely logical, while using a Spartan simplicity of vocabulary. He is, furthermore, challenging: the problems he deals with are problems he struggles with; they do not have obvious solutions.

The paper that follows was written for my students. I thought of it as a model for term papers, but also as a means of bringing out the philosophical interest of texts the students were reading in translation, and as providing a selection of texts that I could then use as exercises in the Chinese phase of the course. This is why there is so much quotation in the paper. I also intended the paper to be provocative; it was not intended to say all that could be said, but to point to ways in which analysis might continue.

Later, in 1979, I considered developing it into a presidential address for the Pacific Division of the American Philosophical Association; my late friend Monty Furth agreed that it had "possibilities"; but we both took for granted that one would wish to rework it. (In the end, I chose another subject, which continued what had been an invited paper for the 1977 meeting of the APA in San Francisco, the paper reduced from "Motivation and Moral Action in Mencius," exploring further the problem of weakness of will. Both this paper and the eventual presidential address, "Two Roots or One?" are included in this volume.)

Thus, "Xunzi on 'Human Nature'" was never conceived to be even my own "last word" on the subject. But I thought, and still think, that it makes an interesting, original, and valuable point. So here I offer it exactly as it was written (merely revising the romanization, and some of the translations; my editor has added some footnotes).

But let me preface it with two reflections that seem right to me now, and that in some cases were offered to my students in later classroom lectures.[1]

As I note below, Xunzi has been criticized as equivocating on the meaning of the word *kě* 可, "possible/permissible" (Lau 1953, 554n. 1). He would have had difficulty understanding this criticism. It was assumed in his kind of moral philosophy in old China that the kind of necessity that we subjectively perceive in binding moral rules is continuous, in the universal order of things, with the necessity of the regularities of the natural world. As Han Dynasty metaphysicians in the following century were to put it, the Way (*dào* 道) of the human world has its source in the Way of Heaven. As Xunzi does put it (in effect), the sages in creating the rites were simply discovering the only possible solution to the problem of optimizing civilized satisfaction while minimizing conflict. If I see this, I can come to see the natural (*zìrán* 自然) as the necessary (*bìrán* 必然), to use the language of Dài Zhèn 戴震 (if not quite his thought).

Much more could be said about this. Here I note only that the problem is continuous with another in Xunzi: even granting the foregoing, as I observe, I must sense a difficulty in being told by a sage that I am to adopt a rule as a *moral* rule because it is my only course for optimizing what I want. For the individual, the solution is gradual self-cultivation. But what about the sage himself? How did the traditional moral order get started? Xunzi does hint at the solution, and again it is gradualist: in "Human Nature Is Evil," we find him speaking of rites and norms (*lǐ yì* 禮義) as a gradual accumulation over a long time. Fully explicated, this idea would lead to a picture of the creation of civilization as a long process of piecemeal problem-solving, in which the creative sage may not realize that he is creating norms at all (nor will he think of himself as a sage). This was to be the insight of Dai Zhen's contemporary Zhāng Xuéchéng 章學誠.[2]

As Zhang puts it, the whole civilized moral order is the product of history, but the inevitable product of it. "Mankind had its Way in itself without realizing it." Here is another way of understanding Xunzi (although Zhang does not mention him) that reconciles his "ladder of souls" (discussed below, p. 206) with his sour judgment of human nature, without equating Xunzi's "ladder" picture (humans have a "sense of duty") with Mencius ("human nature is good"): in "Human Nature Is Evil," Xunzi is talking about how we are disposed as individuals. So is Mencius, and the two pictures conflict. In the "ladder" passage in "Regulations of a King," Xunzi is talking about humans as a species, making the point that as a species we tend to come to live in communities governed by moral rules, whereas horses do not. Mencius would agree with this, and would probably take it to be *implied by* his picture of humans as individuals. But we make a mistake if we suppose that Xunzi's picture of humans as a species *implies* Mencius's full picture of humans as individuals. At least, we have no right to insist that Xunzi ought to have supposed so.[3]

13.2 The Problem

The view of Xunzi on the relationship between human dispositions and morality would seem to be a subject by now so well explored that there should be nothing left to say about it, at least in a short paper.[4] But let that be a judgment made, if it is to be made, after I have made my attempt.

Any writer or lecturer who has tried to define and analyze the difference between Xunzi and Mencius (Mèngzǐ 孟子) on these matters has considered my problem at least indirectly. Mencius at some time or times in the later fourth century B.C. argued that "human nature is good" (*xìng shàn* 性善), a position he is represented as defending explicitly in *Mengzi* 6A6 and implicitly in the briefly recorded debate with Gàozǐ 告子 and his followers in 6A1–5.[5] Xunzi, some time in the middle of the third century B.C., wrote an essay, now chapter 23 of the eponymous *Xunzi*, titled "Human Nature Is Evil" (*xìng è* 性 惡), explicitly refuting Mencius. With such flag-waving statements we have the language of polemics, but not yet philosophy. There are long studies considering whether the term *xìng* 性 has the same meaning for the two philosophers, and whether "human nature" is a defensible translation of it.[6] I leave these controversies aside, for I think there is another way of getting at what they differed about, that as far as I am aware has never been noticed.

There is an apparent conflict within the *Xunzi* itself which any classroom teacher has to deal with. Xunzi's refrain at the end of each anti-Mencian argument in chapter 23 is "It is obvious from this, then, that man's nature is evil, and that his goodness is the result of conscious activity (*wèi* 僞)" (Watson 1963a, 157), or comes "only through acquired training" (Creel 1953, 121), or "is factitious" (Legge 1970, 79). We will try to see later just what Xunzi thinks he is saying here. But first, on its face, the words seem flatly to contradict something Xunzi has argued at some length in chapter 9, "The Regulations of a King":

> Water and fire have energy (*qì* 氣) but are without life. Grass and trees have life but are without consciousness (*zhī* 知). Birds and beasts have consciousness but are without a sense of duty (*yì* 義). Humans have energy, life, consciousness, and in addition, a sense of duty. Therefore they are the noblest beings on earth. They are not as strong as the ox, nor as swift as the horse, and yet they make the ox and the horse work for them. Why? I reply: humans are able to organize themselves in society and *they* are not able to organize themselves in society. How are humans able to organize themselves in society? I reply: by [hierarchical] divisions. And how are they able to set up [hierarchical] divisions? I reply: through the sense of duty. Thus, if they employ this sense of duty to set up [hierarchical] divisions, then there will be harmony. Where there is harmony there will be unity; where there is unity there will be strength; where there is much strength there will be power; where there is power then all things will be conquered.[7]

The trouble lies in Xunzi's picking out "sense of duty" (*yi*) as the differentiating property of human beings. For, doesn't this say in effect that it is human nature to feel that one ought to do what is (or what one sees to be) one's duty? And if one says this, then the statement "human nature is evil" has to be subject to such a major qualification as to make it, *tout court*, quite misleading if we are considering the relation between "human nature" and morality.

It is, of course, possible to say that Xunzi's two essays are not parts of a coherent position; or even that he did not write them both as they stand—and these things have been said about much of the *Xunzi*.[8] But analysis has the proper task of seeing whether coherent sense can be made of texts as they are received, unless there are obvious reasons to reject them. In what follows I will try to do this. The first attempt at reconciling these positions will fail, but will uncover important things that Xunzi did think. The second attempt, I believe, fares better.

13.3 First Hypothesis

Xunzi's apparent recognition of a moral sense in human beings, in the passage just quoted, is overbalanced by many others. There is a whole chapter elaborating the view that we are greedy and selfish, craving physical satisfaction, and that if we follow these tendencies without being restrained we will soon be fighting among ourselves, so that anything resembling decent civilized life will be impossible. This picture is Xunzi's own amplification of his contention that "human nature is evil," in the chapter on that theme. The same thought is expressed at the opening of his chapter "A Discussion of Rites":[9]

> What is the origin of the rites? I reply: humans are born with desires. If their desires are not satisfied, they cannot but seek [to satisfy them]. If they seek without rule and measure, divisions and restrictions, then they will be unable not to fight. From fighting comes disorder and from disorder comes impoverishment. The ancient kings hated people being in such disorder. Hence, they established rites and duties (*lǐ yì* 禮義) in order to provide [hierarchical] divisions for them, so as to nourish and train human desires and to provide the things they sought.

Xunzi concludes "This is the origin of rites."[10]

So now it appears that humans need civilized order for two reasons: to raise themselves above the level of the animals and subject animals to their use, and to protect themselves from one another. Perhaps this quality *yi*, "sense of duty," that distinguishes humans from the animals—who already have "intelligence," i.e., consciousness—is better thought of as *a superior kind of intelligent insight*, the ability, at least in the persons of certain wise "ancient kings," to appraise the overall human situation, the vision to see that a moral order is needed if a halfway decent life is to be possible, and then the intelligence needed to create that moral order in "rites and duties" (*lǐ yì*).

Not a little in the *Xunzi* supports this interpretation. Repeatedly in the chapter on human nature, as in the "Discussion of Rites," Xunzi insists that "rites and duties" were *created* by the "ancient kings" or the "ancient sages." We would expect him to stress the importance of authority, to get people to accept this order uniformly, and the value and importance of accepting authority if one is to become a properly civilized human being; and so he does—for example, in the chapter "Improving Yourself":

> The rites are the means by which to keep oneself correct; the teacher is the means by which the rites are kept correct. Without the rites, how can I keep myself correct? Without a teacher, how can I know that the rites [that I follow] are correct?[11]

And in "On the Correct Use of Terms" (*Zhèng míng* 正名) he argues strongly for the contention that the "ancient kings" both created norms and standards and then required their acceptance.

But it is in a nonauthoritarian phase of his thinking that I see the strongest support for the present interpretation[12] — as well as a consideration that in the end leads one to reject it. At the end of the last-mentioned chapter Xunzi presents a rudimentary philosophy of action, in which he seems to be trying to ground my acceptance of a moral "way of life" in a more basic nonmoral or prudential appraisal of my desires, needs, and limits:

> Desires do not await being satisfiable, but seeking [something to satisfy those desires] follows what is approved (*kě* 可). That desires do not await being satisfiable is what is received from Heaven. That seeking follows what is approved is received from the heart (*xīn* 心).[13]

Xunzi is considering how it is possible to have "good government" (of the self, and of society) given the fact that we have desires, and that our desires taken by themselves tend to lead us into conflict. That I first do have desires is something I "get from Heaven," i.e., from nature; but that I follow the best course I see is something I get from my "heart," i.e., my *mind*. Consequently a naturally given desire may be regulated by many considerations my mind brings to bear on the problem of satisfying it, so that what I actually do can hardly be said to be "gotten from Heaven." For example, Xunzi says, as much as people love life and hate death, they may accept death because they find this the only possible course.

Xunzi has been charged with equivocating here on the word "possible," *kě* 可 or *kě yǐ* 可以. *Ke* also means "good" or "acceptable" (and so, "judge to be good," "approve") (Lau 1953, 554n. 1). Perhaps he does; but probably he thinks of my love of life as capable of being outweighed by a combination of other values.[14] This removes the immediate difficulty, but it remains a problem how Xunzi can ground a morality that may call for accepting death—the termination of all satisfactions—in a psychology of desire-satisfaction.[15] (What combination of values *could* there be that would outweigh my aversion to foregoing all future satisfactions of desire?) In any case, it is clear that Xunzi thinks that my judgments about what is the best course—best on some ground—can modify the action that desire alone would determine.

> Thus, my desire may exceed [the limit of what is right] yet my action does not reach it, the reason being that my mind stops it. If what the mind approves hits the mark of good order (*lǐ* 理), then although one has many desires, what harm is this to good [self] government? My desire may not reach [the limit of what is right] yet my action goes beyond it, the reason being that my mind

causes it to do so. If what the mind approves misses the mark of good order, then even if desires are few, how will one desist from [inner] disorder? Thus, the difference between good government and disorder [in oneself] lies in what the mind approves of, not in what the emotions desire. If you do not seek for it where it is, but seek for it where it isn't, even though you say "I've got it," you've missed it. Our nature is what Heaven has given us; our emotions are the substance of our nature; our desires are the responses of our emotions. To seek it, when I consider what I desire to be obtainable, is something my emotions cannot avoid doing. To take it as my Way (*dào* 道) when I consider [a course] acceptable (*ke*) is what knowledge necessarily proceeds to do.[16]

Xunzi then observes that even a humble gatekeeper cannot avoid having desires: they are inherent in the emotions; and even the ruler of the world ("son of Heaven") cannot satisfy all his desires. But it is possible to regulate one's seeking, even if not to get rid of desires themselves; and it is possible to approach satisfaction, even if not to attain complete satisfaction. And so it is possible to make an overall choice of courses of action that optimizes satisfaction and minimizes disorder, danger, and anxiety. This is a choice for *the* "Way" of civilization:

> The Way is like this: advance along it and you approach complete satisfaction; withdraw along it and you regulate your seeking. In all the world there is nothing like it. Now in general people never fail to follow a course they approve and to reject what they disapprove. There has never been anyone who has failed to follow the Way when understanding that there is nothing to compare to it.[17]

In short, Xunzi seems to agree with Socrates that no one knowingly chooses less than the best. When in fact people choose ill, they are simply confused: in a sense they have failed to add and subtract, and take one immediate satisfaction in place of many long-term satisfactions.[18] One of the most important things to see is the value of an ordered life itself. Without it "the mind will be full of anxiety and terror" and no pleasure will be worth having; with it "the mind is calm and at ease," and even simple goods will be gratifying.[19]

Now, I must make two points about Xunzi's position here presented, and here I must simply state them without full argument: (1) although I am here urged to choose the Way because of its *consequences* in greater satisfaction, the consummation of my choosing is that I shall come to value the Way as *good in itself*, and shall do this so completely that accepting, cherishing, and acting according to the Way become a part of myself. In "Encouraging Learning" Xunzi says that the truly virtuous

> train their eyes so that they desire to see only what is right, their ears so that they desire to hear only what is right, their mouths so that they desire to say only what is right, their minds so that they desire to think only what is right.[20]

And in the same chapter, we read that this transformation of self is to be so total that "The learning of noble people enters their ears, clings to their minds, spreads through their limbs, and manifests itself in their actions."[21] In this state I will have chosen the Way as good in itself, made it mine so completely that I will be ready to die for it.

So, Xunzi is offering a *consequentialist* argument for "adopting" a *deontological* moral position.[22] And this leads to my second conclusion about his argument: (2) it does not make sense to take him as denying the possibility of acting against judgment in *particular cases*. For if so, Xunzi would be saying to me, "You want object X now; course C will get it for you, so choose C; but to be effective the choosing has to be choosing C as an end in itself, and not for its consequences." And obviously I might agree with this as a description of my situation, yet fail to act accordingly, for as a set of directions it is patently self-contradictory. So Xunzi is not quite as Socratic as he seemed. His denial that I can fail to choose what I judge best must concern a *meta-choice* that I make for the Way as a total way of life. Having made it, I must then take steps to educate myself, or be educated, so as to become the sort of person who can live that life by inner conviction.

If this is right, Xunzi's argument is something like that of Pascal (1966, 149–53), who would have me bet on Heaven by immersing myself in "masses and holy water," knowing that this will make me a decent believer fully qualified for salvation. But Xunzi's position seems to me not to have a difficulty that infects Pascal's. Pascal's believers can still remember how it was they came to their belief: and it is difficult to see how this knowledge can fail to undermine, forever, the belief itself. Xunzi's "gentleman" is more like a man who decides to marry a woman before he has come to love her, because he judges she will be a good wife, confident that in time affection will grow and ripen. When that time comes, he can look back at his decision as a fortunate one (and at the same time realize that his wife *is* a good wife), without in doing so loving her the less.

But in one important respect Xunzi and Pascal are subject to the same constraint. Pascal must suppose that his wagerer is *psychologically capable of becoming religious*. Similarly, Xunzi must assume that a person is capable of coming to regard obligations as genuine moral obligations and not just as what is to be done if certain of one's wants are to be satisfied. That is to say, constructing a consequentialist argument for morality is not tantamount to reducing the psychological capacity for entertaining and responding to a duty as a duty to the capacity to pursue a desired object out of self-interest. So Xunzi in the end must assume that humans just have a "sense of duty," though he need not suppose it has any particular content. This, I suggest, is just what he was saying in contrasting humans with the animals, who merely have "intelligence," or consciousness.

And if this is right, there is still a problem of reconciling this view with Xunzi's view that "human nature is evil."

13.4 The Solution

I shall be provocatively brief.

Let us consider what is the case when I "want" something. It would seem that both of the following are the case:

(1) There is something "out there" that I *lack*, that I could have that I don't, and I am, perhaps painfully, aware of this *lack*, or "want."

(2) There is *in me* an urge or impulse or *motivation* to get that thing, and to feel badly if I don't—i.e., to *desire*, or "want" it.

I submit that Xunzi takes this common-sense picture for granted (and that so do you).

Now, when I see a possible action as something it is my *duty* to do, something I *ought* to do, many philosophers will insist (or just assume) that in so seeing I have a positive disposition, to *some* degree, to do that act: it just doesn't add up for me to say, "I *ought* to but so what?" Short-circuiting much philosophical argument, let us accept this view.[23] Let us go even further, and think of this disposition as a kind of "want." What is the case when what I "want" is to do my duty? Apparently,

(1) There is something I am *not doing* that I could do, and I am, perhaps painfully, aware of this.

(2) There is *in me* an impulse to do that thing, and to feel badly, or *ashamed*, if I don't.

If one dwells on the second aspect of the situation one will say, with Mencius, "Aha! This shows that I have an innate moral sense. I am naturally moved to do what I sense to be my duty, and because I so sense it. So, I am good by *nature*."

But if I focus my attention on the first aspect I will be far less pleased with myself. Indeed, insofar as I am *aware* of an unperformed duty (rather than simply, without reflection, going ahead and doing it), my attention is likely to be directed to counter tendencies in myself that keep me from doing it. In this frame of mind I may well say—as Xunzi makes Shùn 舜 say to Yáo 堯—"Human emotions, human emotions—they are very unlovely things indeed!"[24] It will then be easy to go on, and identify this dissatisfaction and the positive impulse toward duty-doing, so that this impulse itself then seems to validate the insight that I am a creature who resists his duty unless steps are taken: as though I wouldn't have the want unless I lacked the object.

Perhaps it is just this that Xunzi is doing in arguing that "human nature is evil." Consider the following from the human nature chapter:

> All people who desire to do good do so precisely because their natures are evil. A person whose accomplishments are meager longs for greatness; an ugly person longs for beauty; a person in cramped quarters longs for spaciousness; an impoverished person longs for wealth; a lowly person longs for eminence. Whatever people lack in themselves they will seek outside. Thus, someone who is already rich will not long for wealth, and someone who is already eminent, will not long for greater power. What people already possess in themselves they will not bother to look for outside. From this we can see that people desire to do good precisely because their natures are evil. Now, human nature inherently lacks rites and duties. Thus, people force themselves to study and to seek to possess them. Human nature inherently lacks rites and duties. Therefore we exert ourselves in study, seeking to have them.[25]

I think I am on the right track in suggesting this passage as a key to the problem, but more is needed.

More is needed, because, obviously, a Mencian reply will be, in effect, "Yes, but notice that people who see this much are, you admit, distressed by their lack of developed moral qualities and try to change themselves. The feeling and the effort are after all part of *them*, and furthermore so is the capacity to be morally educated. So human nature is really good." Earlier in the same chapter Xunzi has briefly noted this Mencian position: Mencius states, he says, that the very fact that people learn requires the assumption that their natures are good. But this is a mistake:

> It indicates that he [i.e., Mencius] has not really understood human nature nor distinguished properly between human nature and conscious activity (*wei*). In general, the nature is that which is given by Heaven. You cannot learn it, you cannot acquire it by effort. Rites and duties [on the other hand] are created by sages; they are what humans are capable of through study, can complete through effort. That in us that cannot be learned or acquired by effort is called the nature. That in us that we are capable of through study, and can complete through effort is called conscious activity. This is the difference between nature and conscious activity.[26]

So, in the end, Xunzi resorts to linguistic legislation (or, I'm sure he would say, linguistic law-enforcement): people do have the capacity to understand their needs and to act intentionally and intelligently to meet those needs, but this capacity is not human "nature" (*xing*) but something else, which Xunzi calls "[conscious] activity" (*wei*).

To return to questions at the beginning of this paper, we may ask why Xunzi in "The Regulations of a King" did not make *wei*, "conscious activity," the differentiating property of humans as contrasted with "birds and beasts." But obviously it isn't: it probably seemed to Xunzi that intelligently directed action in some degree is already evidenced by the lower animals. What distinguishes humans in his view—if this analysis is right—is the capacity to give this intelligent action a moral shape. If so we can see why he resists thinking of *yi*, the (unfilled) "sense of duty," as an aspect of human *nature*. Rather, it must be for Xunzi part (and the really human part) of humans' capacity to become aware of their needs and to act intelligently to fill them. But then, humans "have" *yi* not just in being creatures who produce moral systems within which to live, but also in the sense that they are capable of feeling and thinking morally.

Part III
Recent Centuries

The Philosophy of Wang Yangming[1]

14.1 Preface

Certain things about Wáng Yángmíng 王陽明 I am not going to dwell on this evening. I am not going to talk about his life, except to note that he was born in 1472 and died in 1529; was an official and eventually a general, commanding several important campaigns against rebels in central and south China; and had, by 1520, become famous as a moral teacher. I'm not going to talk about his political philosophy, except to note that he was, like many late Confucians, a utopian who idealized a remote and imaginary past, when he thought human society was bound together in a unity of feeling and purpose like the parts of a single living body (142–43); and that he had a kind of Daoist anti-intellectual persuasion that civilization has come to place too high a value on knowledge (in the sense of mere information) and on literary art and writing, and that a truly good society would preserve just enough of both to meet what need there might be for it in educating people to be virtuous and unselfish, and would do away with the rest (11).

I will add that these elements of his thought disturb me, because I can feel very well the appeal of his utopia—which he describes with some passion—and (at the same time) know it to be essentially totalitarian; and being a twentieth-century American who is older than the generation now in college I know that beautiful ideas like this can become the basis of something quite horrible. His anti-intellectualism is saddening, if understandable. But it too is disturbing, because I can see in both this and the utopianism a connection with parts of his thinking that both attract and fascinate me, even if they do not always persuade, and it is possible that this connection is a necessary one. If it is, there is a conflict within myself that I would rather not have to deal with.

14.2 *Xin xue*

The Chinese have had their names for keeping things tidy, and the name they have used for Wang Yangming's kind of Confucian moral philosophy is *Xīn xué* (心學), which it is tempting to render "literally" as "philosophy of mind."

But that expression, of course, is one of *our* names for keeping things tidy, so caution is at once in order.

There are pages in Wang, sometimes, that could almost make acceptable brief notes in a contemporary philosophy journal like *Analysis*; but it would be misleading and unfair to him to focus on these and let the rest go. Wang, in writing and talking philosophy, is also practicing and teaching a *religion* at the same time, and only by remembering this can one see what is going on. As a philosopher he is concerned with many "standard problems"—the relation of mind to body, the mind's place in nature, the way the mind works, the relation between mental and overt acts, between thinking, perceiving, and valuing, and between perception and reality. (There is not, I think, any treatment in him of a true free will-determinism problem, and the reason for this, as we shall see below, is interesting.) He is intensely interested in what it means to know what is good or bad, and he is constantly engaging in a sort of inner phenomenological scrutiny of moral experience.

But he is not interested in these subjects as theoretical objects of investigation. He is always a moralist, interested in straightening out people and society, teaching people how to make themselves better persons. And this moral-committed philosophy is at the same time a religion, in several senses.

(i) We find in Wang a striking and total seriousness. He has a sense of mission that is almost messianic. He has come to see (he says "Heaven," *tiān* 天, has taught him this) through his own trying experiences how the worms in a person's heart can be got rid of, so that one is at peace with oneself and is confident and free of anxiety in all one's actions, and he just *sees* that if all people could be so redirected, their lives in society, which are now miserable and ugly, would be beautiful and happy. Seeing this he *must* (he almost cries out to himself) "save people from their distress and difficulty," even if this makes ordinary "gentlemen" laugh at him (181). But this drive to give himself totally to a life of "saving" he himself recognizes to be an expression of his own being, the component in his nature that he, with Mencius, sees as common to all humans. He does not, in choosing this course, see himself as rendering a duty to some "other" power.

(ii) We will see that Wang shares with philosophical Daoists, earlier Confucian moral mystics, and Buddhists of most kinds a familiar structure of thought. There is a transcendent and immanent higher reality that all people (perhaps even all things) somehow partake of, ordinarily without being aware of it. The necessary consequence of this ignorance is a life that is unsatisfactory in various ways for different forms of thought: shabby, or ineffective, or unhappy, or miserable. And conversely what counts as "knowledge" brings virtue, power, or bliss. For the genuinely religious forms of this kind of thought the value of the enlightened state is such that the temporal extent of it often seems to be irrelevant, and so survival after death unimportant. In any case, it is unimportant for Wang.

The desired *knowledge* is not a grasping or conceiving by a knower of a known, but a pulling away of a veil of confusion that separates subjectively the knower from the known. Putting this knowledge into propositional form seems to imply this separation, for the proposition is *about* something *other* than itself, and what one wants in "real" knowledge is the reality itself. So these philosophies are "mystical" in the further specific sense that the highest truth, perhaps *any* truths, are inexpressible in any literal way. Language is then seen as instrumental merely, not necessarily to be kept consistent; and we find in such thinkers a characteristic disconcerting tendency to fuse the predicates "true" and "real," which persons like me, with a compulsion to orderliness, like to keep distinct. The mystic in grasping truth is grasping reality; and indeed "grasping" is only an ill-behaving metaphor.

The kind of *Confucians*—and Wang is one—who have this pattern of thinking conceive themselves to be different, in that for them the ordinary socially sanctioned moral good is not rejected, as they conceive both Daoists and Buddhists do reject it: early Daoists, in viewing moral standards as conventions that warp innocent human nature; later Daoists, in the essentially selfish quietism of a personal philosophy directed toward the goal of eternal life; Buddhists, in seeing moral norms as forms of "attachment," merely not as distressing as other forms (e.g., lusts), trapping the individual in the misery of unenlightened existence. Wang Yangming obviously feels the pull of these ways of thinking, but essentially he is a Confucian, saying that *he* in contrast identifies the moral good as the highest type of knowledge—so that for him attaining enlightenment, embodying this moral truth (reality?), means becoming morally perfect, a "sage."

14.3 The Goal

So Wang's religion is not a theism of devotion and salvation but a religion of self-transformation. But it has a surprising quasi-devotional-soteric aspect. One does not reorient one's life totally in the way Wang and his "disciples" did unless one is powerfully drawn to *something*, and his reflective reader comes to realize that the goal state of being a "sage" is one that has just as much pull as any kind of religious conception of salvation in "Heaven."[2] Both Wang and his disciples describe it as a state in which one spontaneously dances in sheer wordless delight. One student freely using the language of Daoism pleads for his teacher to help him break out of his psychic entanglements so that he can "roam the universe with the Creator" (162).[3]

But does Wang's religion have anything like an object of devotion or trust, anything like a god? Indeed yes. Mind, the concept which identifies him as a philosopher, is the focus of his religion. As in some kinds of Buddhism, so for Wang, mind is one, individuated as mine or yours, yes, but *one*—"this mind," as he calls it, all the same. Mind—the *real*—is identical with the *true*, the "principle of nature (Heaven)," with all moral truth. Its manifestations in me include my desires and thought, even my confusions and selfish impulses, but also an infallible awareness of that confusion and selfishness, an inner "shining mind," master, teacher, that is both myself *and* other, at least in the sense that for me there can be no justified pride of possession, only the duty to listen, heed, trust, reverence, obey. This aspect of mind Wang found a name for, in the last years of his life. He called it *liáng zhī* 良知, "pure knowing" (the word and part of the idea are from *Mèngzǐ* 孟子 7A15). It is for Wang a "God within" *and* without. It is an object of faith. It is described by Wang and his students in poems which have to be read as hymns:

> Pure Knowing has nothing to do with hearing much;
> At the time of the mysterious union of our elements its root was planted;
> If we follow it in our likes and dislikes, that is the learning of the Sage.
> When we lean neither forward nor backward to accommodate things,
>   there is the Principle of Heaven. (219)

So writes one of his students. Wang himself closes a poem with these words:

> The thousand Sages are all passing shadows;
> It is Pure Knowing that is my teacher.[4]

All of Wang's philosophical theory and suggestive phenomenological description of inner mental workings are directed toward guiding the "student" in what he and they call "the task" (*gōngfu* 功夫 or 工夫)—a never-ending "effort" of self-monitoring and self-change which is to let this inner voice speak clearly and ensure that we will always follow it. It would not be entirely misleading to describe this life of "effort" as conceived by Wang as an active life of constant prayer.

14.4 Wang's World View

Attending to Wang as philosophical theorist requires caution. Sometimes he is carefully analytical and he has certain conceptions he is insistent people get straight. But he often seems to be playing a kind of music with concepts, using them for their effect on you rather than for exact explanations. This mode of expression itself is probably a conscious application of theory: *lǐ* 理, "principle," can't be separated from "things," and so can't be communicated by a teacher in always valid generalizations about what to do, e.g., in this or that *kind* of situation. So on the one hand the *student*, at a given time, has his or her particular problem situation, with an approach to it proper for him or her, in regard to which there can be no carry-over from earlier situations. On the other hand the *teacher* has his or her problem—this particular student with his or her problem and inner snarls, *now*. So the *teaching*, if it is right, has to be thought of as a kind of specific "dose."

Wang's sensitivity to this problem is revealed over and over in a reluctance to have his teachings published, even written down. His student, and brother-in-law, Xú Ài 徐愛, who died quite young (more than a decade before Wang) but did gather together the first collection of conversations with "The Teacher," does an amusing twist with this problem in one of his prefaces.[5] Another student, he says, heard that he had in mind printing Wang's words and objected that Wang had told *him* not even to copy down his remarks—his teachings, Wang had said, were "medicinal," intended only for the occasions that prompted them. Perhaps so, Xu muses—that is, perhaps Wang *did* utter such a "teaching" to the other student at some other time. But if I let myself *now* be bound by that teaching *then*, am I not doing just what my teacher *in* that teaching said I shouldn't do, that is, taking past occasional teaching as applicable to another occasion? With a little more reflection, Xu finds little difficulty in justifying his project—surely a happy precedent.

With this caveat, we can consider circumspectly what seem to be Wang's conceptions of how the world, humans, and mind are put together. It is not an entirely consistent set of ideas, but Wang never tried to offer one. It does have a general direction. Wang denies (or tends to deny) the duality of mind and body. If it weren't for the mind, which is the "true self," the eyes would see nothing, true; but this simply means that "if there is no true self there will be no body" (122). That is, if we think of mind as a sort of "ghost in a machine," we have also to turn the thought about and see the ghost as constituting the "machine." On another occasion he speaks more fully:

> The ears, the eyes, the mouth, the nose, and the four limbs are parts of the body. But how can they see, hear, speak, or act without the mind? On the other hand, without the ears, the eyes, the mouth, the nose, and the four limbs, the mind cannot see, hear, speak, or act when it wants to. Therefore, if there is no mind, there will be no body, and if there is no body, there will be no mind. As something occupying space it is called the body; as the master, it is called the mind. (201)

Perhaps this is a sort of "identity theory," but it is not a reduction of mind to matter. Mind and body seem rather to be equally appropriate ways of describing the same thing.

We see this reciprocality in Wang's conception of the relation of mind to world. There is, first, the matter of the relation of *my* mind to *my* world. Here

Wang is sometimes almost Berkeleyan. My "clear intelligence," Wang says, sustains all things, but also, "separated from these, there will not be my clear intelligence." But how can "heaven, earth," and all things cease to exist when I do? "Consider a dead person," Wang replies. "That person's spirit has drifted away and dispersed. Where are *that person's* heaven and earth and myriad things" (337)? Yet Wang can turn this directly about. We perceive things with our senses. We "perceive," i.e., respond to the needs, obligations-for-us, inherent in situations, with our "minds"—in the limited sense of "mind" as organ of thought. But the senses and the "mind" have no "substance" of their own: they take their objects as their substance (277). This last idea is linked to Wang's ideal of a properly functioning mind: it is totally and perfectly responsive to every aspect of the situation it confronts right now, like a perfect mirror (21). Nothing lingers from past "reflections" to mar this one, and after this one nothing stays on to mar the next.

Wang says something slightly (or perhaps more than slightly) different when he insists that mind and universe are "one body." This is true for Wang of "my" mind—for example, we have this account of why we sleep at night:

> It is a general law in the universe that when it gets dark, things rest. As night falls, heaven and earth become undifferentiated. Forms and colors all disappear. With humans also, the ears hear nothing, the eyes see nothing, and all the apertures are closed. This is the time when "pure knowing" is collected and concentrated. As heaven and earth open up again, all the myriad things reveal themselves and grow. With humans also, the eyes and ears now see and hear, and all apertures are open. This is the time when the wonderful functioning of "pure knowing" starts. From this we see that the human mind and heaven and earth form one body. (267)

But Wang does not really here make a statement about all minds, this one, that one. "It is only because of their physical forms and bodies that humans are separated," he says (337). In short, in respect to mind, we are one, and it is "this mind," not "our minds," that we must consider. "This mind" is the mind of the universe, just as "my mind" is the mind of my body, and in each case "mind" and "body" are interdependent for their existence, "share the same material force," "enter into one another." So "without the pure knowing that is inherent in humans, there cannot be plants and trees, tiles and stones" (274). The universal forces *yīn* 陰 and *yáng* 陽, the states of Quiescence (*jìng* 靜) and Activity (*dòng* 動), are manifest equally in the universe and in our minds, and when Wang shifts into this kind of language (e.g., 157) it is sometimes not possible to distinguish which—mind or universe—he is talking about. Wang's utopianism (see especially 142–43 and 179–80) is a direct inference from this conception of mind and universe, as is the enlightened person's concern to bring that utopia into being:

Man is the mind of the universe. . . . Is there any suffering or bitterness of the great masses that is not disease or pain in my own body? . . . If gentlemen of the world merely devote their effort to extending their pure knowing they will naturally . . . regard other people as their own persons, regard the people of other countries as their own family. . . . When this is done, even if we wanted the world to be without order, it would not be possible. (179)

14.5 Wang's Philosophical Psychology

In oneself, the universal processes operate in the following way (Wang, like all Neo-Confucians on this point, takes his conceptions and much of his language from the opening section of the *Zhōngyōng* 中庸, a work more commonly known by the title, *The Doctrine of the Mean*):[6]

(i) There is the mind *in-itself* (*tǐ* 體), pure potential mentality, we might say, in the state of "equilibrium" (*zhōng* 中) before capacities for feeling, emotion, desire, intention, thought, are manifest.[7] This is the aspect of "tranquillity" (*jìng*).

(ii) There is the mind *in function* (*yòng* 用), and if functioning ideally, in balance and rhythm, every emotion, intention, thought are exactly appropriate. Here the mind is said to be in the state of "harmony" (*hé* 和), the state "after the feelings are manifest."

For many Song and Ming Dynasty Confucians these are temporally separate "states," and the religious objective of knowing the mind is sought by quieting it, returning it to "itself." But of course this very effort would be a "function," as would be the desired self-knowing. Seeing this, Wang insists that the two states are not literally "before" or "after." Even sleep is a function (267). We can know and deal with the mind only in its functions. Yet all the time the mind "in itself" is there, and we see it in our "pure knowing," an effortless, incessant self-evaluation by the mind of its functions and of all its objects and projects.

This is not a description of the subjective mental experience of most of us most of the time. Its not being so is what evil is. What happens is not the infusion into mind of some alien principle. Evil is the mind itself functioning in a distorted way (228). Harmony is prevented by one mental activity preempting our attention: we become "attached" to it and what would have been an innocent natural impulse, intention, or thought (generically, a "desire") becomes then a "selfish desire." In letting this happen we "deceive ourselves"; *this* for us is the desire that has to be satisfied, and the possibility of a balanced and appropriate total response of mind to situation is lost. When this happens, the light of our pure knowing, though still there, is lost to us, "obscured" (*bi* 蔽) as the sun can be obscured by clouds. But "pure knowing" responds even to this inner situation if we can glimpse its dimmed light, knowing it to be wrong.

Why evil at all? I think Wang has no real answer. He offers us a kind of deterministic account. Some few of us (here he follows the *Doctrine of the Mean* again, chapter 20) are "born with understanding," but most of us are born heavily "obscured," and must go through a long process of self-improvement before we are straightened out. Wang also, like Mencius, says that we "become confused and troubled by things coming and going" (311)[8]—environment and the petty way of the world dull us over time. But Wang's determinism is muted. He is more strongly and explicitly voluntaristic than Mencius. He cannot be really determinist, either in the sense of seeing our choices as causally traceable back to physical events or as seeing our subjective life as an illusory epiphenomenon, because there is no world of sheer physical nature governed by causal necessity contrasting with ourselves. The universe is the body of "this mind," infused with mentality, and not "other" but "one body" with us.

But if Wang doesn't account for evil, he does not see it as inescapable. Even the evil person who has "lost his substance" still has it, and could find it again. If you *call* a thief a thief to his face, he will blush (207). Wang is not really interested in the *theory* of evil. His problem is to guide us out of it.

14.6 Wang's Thought as a "Way"

Wang's *religion* is one of self-transformation. The good state—total anxiety-free effectiveness, "pure knowing" illuminating every response, the mind like a mirror so that we "roam the universe with the Creator"—has to be reachable, and in some way other than throwing oneself on God and praying for grace. Wang's religion requires a program of self-cultivation.

And so does his ethics. It is meaningless to say that anything is really good or right and at the same time to say that all "norms" are completely situational, unless one is saying this: that in a particular problem-situation, any morally perfected person would "hear" the voice of inner knowing in essentially the same way. And Wang insists repeatedly on this. The response of action or judgment of two perfected persons would be as alike as two bamboos in one's garden (293)—which is not to say exactly alike, but alike enough. Each would be an "original," we might say, but each would be right.[9]

But this still doesn't make ethics practically interesting unless one can point out the difference between the morally perfect (perfectly perceptive) person and the morally "obscured," and be guided into a way of becoming perceptive if one isn't.

Wang's program of self-cultivation is built on more concepts that were common coin, but he finds it necessary to do a bit of repair work.

14.6.1 Self-Cultivation

Wang Yangming had before him a received opinion of several centuries' standing. Zhū Xī 朱熹 (1130–1200) fixed on a classical text (perhaps third century B.C.) that stated a brief enigmatic scheme for one who wished to make oneself both socially effective and morally perfect: outer effectiveness depends on inner perfection. Paraphrasing that text: One had to "cultivate one's person" (*xiū shēn* 脩身); to this end one had to "correct one's mind" (*zhèng xīn* 正心); to this end one had to "Make sincere one's thoughts" (*chéng yì* 誠意); to this end one had to "extend one's knowledge" (*zhì zhī* 致知), and this consists in "investigating things" (*gé wù* 格物).[10] Zhu believed this text to have been written by Confucius. It has entered into the basic idiom of Chinese philosophy.

The last phrase is a philologist's delight. No one will ever know what it really meant in its *locus classicus*. Zhu took it to mean that one must do much reading to "extend knowledge," i.e., attain in-depth knowledge of the moral rules and standards of society, and the teachings of the wise and good of the past. One could then proceed to the next step, and the next. Or so Wang understood Zhu to mean. As Wang Yangming represents the idea, Zhu was proposing that one first acquire wide knowledge of "principles" (*li*) (i.e., knowledge of a normative kind although conceived in effect as factual knowledge) by studying the world, what is other than oneself, and then engage in a mental exercise Zhu called "seriousness" (*jìng* 敬), to "make one's thoughts sincere," meaning to make one's thought "whole,"[11] to bring one's motivational structure completely into line with the objective moral order—to overcome the apparent otherness of objective norm and incorporate it into disposition; to close the gap, we might say, between obligation and motivation.

Wang pronounces this impossible (129), and reinterpreted the text (he too, like everyone, believed it to be from Confucius) so as to collapse all the steps into one:

First of all, "things" are not "out there," "other" with respect to oneself. A *thing* is something I am doing, involved in, the "locus of my thought" (6).

Next, some quick philology on the word *gé* 格, "to investigate." Wang Yangming chooses another possible meaning, "to straighten out," "correct," i.e., to examine what I am involved in, and my process of involvement, to sense how it ought to go (still "investigating" in a sense), recognize that I *have* that sense, and see that it does go that way and that I am effectively disposed toward it as I should be (7).

Finally, Wang moves in on the words "knowledge" and "thought." "Knowledge" he takes as "pure knowing" or innate moral sense—his *liang zhi* (as I noted earlier, an idea from *Mengzi* 7A15). To "extend" it is to follow out its implications, i.e., make it effective in one's acts (perhaps involving, also, finding out "things" in the ordinary sense). (We might say that Wang's "extending" of knowledge is more like extending one's arm than, say, extending one's vocabulary.)

And a "thought" (*yì* 意) he defines as any activation of potential mental functions, any "coming out of mind," emotive and cognitive. So for Wang Yangming, *thought* is identified from the start as *act*. *Liang zhi* itself is *yi*, "thought," sometimes a *kind* of it (perhaps a separate second-order monitoring function, though Wang does not tend to talk that way) but an aspect or basic "substance" of all "thought."

14.6.2 Knowledge

In spite of Wang's redefinition of these words, there is a sense in which *liang zhi* really is knowledge, and one does learn in something like the ordinary sense by "investigating," i.e., acting correctly or seeing to it that one's action (including *yi*) is correct (*zhèng* 正) and complete (*chéng* 誠).

Perhaps Wang thinks this way: consider what happens when I set out to make something—say, a bookcase; or maybe even a poem or an essay (21, 168). I have an initial intention (thought, *yi*), which begins to shape itself in the process of my working toward the finished object. As I do this, I see in greater and greater detail how it ought to go, and I cannot see this in advance. I can, of course, see part of it in advance, and in many sorts of such projects I have to find out as much as I can in advance, and that is what Wang's critics keep harping on. But Wang keeps his eye on the part of my "learning" that is essential to my "thing" being real. I work it out, find out about it, straighten it (and myself) out, investigate it and myself, and use this knowledge, all at the same time. But *what* do I "learn" in this way that could be useful later? Hardly something I can store away for "next time," Wang would have to say. What I learn is (gradually) how to keep my mind, effortlessly, totally open to the instructions of my "pure knowing," which tells me how to deal with the next situation that comes. My mind becomes a perfect mirror. Nothing sticks to it from past reflections, and after this episode nothing remains.

So although Wang Yangming *seems* simply to pull a philological trick and toss out the meaning "to investigate," he doesn't really do so. The *ge wu* process is still a process of *finding something out* as well as a process of moving out from the latent capacity of mind to overt intentional action, and so making and executing a *decision*.

In fact, Wang makes a seemingly exaggerated epistemological claim about *liang zhi*: it is all we need. It gives *all* knowledge of importance, and the *li* of all is in me.

His students object: don't we have to engage in some hard work acquiring information in the ordinary sense (e.g., about *how* to care for our parents, and what the *rules* are) in order to live responsible moral lives? Wang Yangming answers in various ways, some of them already indicated:

(1) Only your moral sense can tell you how it should go in this situation. (Sage King Shùn 舜 had no authorities or precedents [139].)[12]

(2) One doesn't simply go out and gather information. (This would be like eating a lot of food and having it just sit in one's stomach.) One has a concrete problem and proceeds to respond. That response may lead one to the library. Information-gathering, then, is simply an extension of the functioning of *liang zhi*, perhaps just like seeing, in making a bookcase, when one comes to a certain point in the process, that one has to stop and read the directions for mixing the glue.

(3) Turning this about, if one *is* gathering facts, one *selects*, i.e., makes judgments of value and appropriateness all the time, and this is *liang zhi* at work.

(4) Even if one is just perceiving and experiencing, *liang zhi* plays the lead role.

One doesn't just perceive *what* is there and then back off and "decide" what to make of it. The "what to make of it," the *shì-fēi* 是非 (approval/disapproval), is part of the "what," and is taken in simultaneously in a total perception which is both sensitive and evaluative. This is one way Wang has of putting his *zhī xíng héyī* 知行合一 ("the unity of knowledge and action"). Thus, a student comes to Wang and objects that,

> ". . . there are people who know that parents should be served with filial piety and elder brothers with respect but cannot put these things into practice. This shows that knowledge and action are clearly two different things."
>
> [Wang Yangming] said, "The knowledge and action you refer to are already separated by selfish desires and are no longer knowledge and action in their original substance. There have never been people who know but do not act. Those who are supposed to know but do not act simply do not yet know. When sages and worthies taught people about knowledge and action, it was precisely because they wanted them to restore the original substance, and not simply to do this or that and be satisfied. Therefore the *Great Learning* points to true knowledge and action for people to see, saying, they are 'like loving beautiful colors and hating bad odors.'[13] Seeing beautiful colors appertains to knowledge, while loving beautiful colors appertains to action. However, as soon as one sees that beautiful color, one has already loved it. It is not that one sees it first and then makes up one's mind to love it. Smelling a bad odor appertains to knowledge, while hating a bad odor appertains to action. However, as soon as one smells a bad odor, one has already hated it. It is not that one smells it first and then makes up one's mind to hate it. If one's nose is stuffed up, one does not smell the bad odor even if one sees a malodorous object before one, and so one does not hate it. This amounts to not knowing bad odor. Suppose we say that so-and-so knows filial piety and so-and-so knows brotherly respect. They must have actually practiced filial piety and brotherly respect before they can be said to know them. It will not do to say that they know filial

piety and brotherly respect simply because they show them in words. Or take one's knowledge of pain. Only after one has experienced pain can one know pain. The same is true of cold or hunger. How can knowledge and action be separated?" (5)

What we would call a person's act, conduct, etc., is just the visible part of a seamless knowing-doing process. Turning this about, we find Wang Yangming saying that the whole of engaged mental activity from the beginning of any episode of it has to be regarded as "action":

> I asked about the unity of knowledge and action. The Teacher said, "You need to understand the basic purpose of my doctrine. In their learning people of today separate knowledge and action into two different things. Therefore when a thought is aroused, although it is evil, they do not stop it because it has not been translated into action. I advocate the unity of knowledge and action precisely because I want people to understand that when a thought is aroused it is already action. If there is anything evil when the thought is aroused, one must overcome the evil thought. One must go to the root and go to the bottom and not allow that evil thought to lie latent in one's mind. This is the basic purpose of my doctrine." (226)

14.6.3 The "Task"

For Wang this means that the subtlest incipient movings of mind are extraordinarily important. If we take the ordinary view that our inner mental activity ("knowing") and our overt behavior are separate areas of our moral lives, then our inner dispositions will always be at war with the norms we and others set for ourselves in behavior. At best anxiety, indecision, ineffectiveness will be inevitable.

So self-cultivation, the "task" of self-attention and self-perfecting, (i) must be *incessant*, and (ii) must primarily be directed, not to learning rules, acquiring "wisdom" in the ordinary sense by reading and studying, but directed to the constant stirrings of mind just as it begins to "function" (234). Our "pure knowing," if we constantly attend to it, will tell us unerringly if a "thought" be "selfish"—excessive or deficient; and we are to correct it—thereby "investigating" the "thing" that engages us—*then and there.* For the beginner this is hard. For the perfected person it is easy and natural (although the "task" [*gongfu*] never ceases, even for such a one). For the perfected person, as soon as *liang zhi* identifies a "selfish desire" it is resolved. For the beginner, it is more difficult; at this point the "task" is literally one of "creating something out of nothing." There, "everything depends on making up the mind" (115), so that the strength of a total initial resolve will carry "effort" forward.

But how? (i) How does the student *carry out* this direction to "make up one's mind," and (ii) how does one learn to *recognize* the inner voice, even if one wants to follow it? How does a teacher teach one *these* things? There can be no formal answer. As to the first, all Wang can do, really, is scare his students, shock them. "You are having difficulty," Wang says to some of them; for "you have not really made up your minds to become sages." "But we *want* to make up our minds," they reply desperately. Wang responds:

> If you really have the mind to become a sage, your "pure knowing" should be extended to the utmost in everything. If in your "pure knowing" you retain the least trace of alien thought, that is not the mind determined to become a sage. (260)

The students perspire with fright—seeing, without seeing, that total commitment is required *for* total effort, yet that effort constitutes that commitment.

Often Wang simply offers his students a formula and tells them to have faith in it, not to jiggle it. (Watch my finger, the ophthalmologist tells me— not here, *here*.) One is to search for the roots of selfish desire for sex, fame, profit as they are beginning to stir in the mind, and wipe them out. "Is this not like cutting out flesh to patch up a sore?" one student cleverly asks. Wang is not amused: this teaching of mine is a good medicine for you. If you can't use it, don't spoil it for others. Someone among you is undermining me (279). Again, they are frightened, not seeing what Wang sees they are not yet ready to see, that the question does perceptively identify a real difficulty—that the intense desire for perfection that Wang has to arouse and exploit at the beginning does itself become an obsession that will block its own realization.

What *is* the "task," concretely—how does one recognize and apply or "extend" one's "pure knowing"? Wang's teaching taken *in toto* is paradoxical here. He *says*, over and over, that "effort" must be "concrete"—one must be "doing something," involved in some problem that matters. Yet almost always, when a student asks a question and Wang answers, question and answer are abstract—often, probing for the feeling-shape of formulaic passages in the *Mengzi* or the *Great Learning*. Wang once explicitly *says* that even his "pure knowing" concept is like the Chan (Zen) master's dust whisk—words used as gesture, because words *really* fail. The student must find the way for himself (280). Wang himself, before hitting on "pure knowing" (*liang zhi*) uses the words "this little bit" (of intuition in the mind), *zhè xiēzi* 這些子 (208).

In part, Wang's problem is like that of the piano teacher trying to "tell" a student how one's inner finger-wrist kinesthetic state should be if one is playing correctly (and how to *get* it that way). But the problem is deeper. In *gongfu*, the "task," there must be total seriousness; that is its essence. So, there can be no demonstration, no example, no use of paradigm case to explain (at most, rarely, to remind). To have an example, Wang has to catch a student with a real problem. A student is sick (215). The conversation is light and witty, yet serious:

sickness is hard to deal with (*ge*, investigate/do right)—"how does it seem?" "The task is difficult." "Be cheerful; that's your task now," i.e., just the way we're doing it. Another student receives word that his son is dangerously ill and is distressed. Wang moves in on his problem: watch yourself *now*. A father's concern for his son is commendable, but everything has its measure, and you are overdoing it. There is *your* task now (44). A student is prone to anger and criticism of others (245). *Your* task is to examine yourself, Wang warns him. "Whenever someone should be criticized or refuted"—even if he really should be—"*you* should immediately see in this your selfish desire to become a big fellow, and overcome it."

I can feel these examples, too, not in the way the people involved in them felt them, of course. Others are closer to me. I am a writer and teacher—those are my "things." And we have *our* problems. How does Wang talk about that? One student writes an essay and worries about what the exercise of thinking it out and finding the words does to him: "It lingers in my mind." It's all right to think as hard as you need to when writing, Wang says, but after it's done let go of it; don't hang on to it or be narcissistic about it (233). The man writes a poem on the occasion of a friend's departure, and shows it to Wang. Wang only *seems* to be abstract:

> Whenever one writes, one should do so within the limit of one's capacity. If one is too excessive in expression, then one will not be carefully employing words or really being sincere.

One writes, and as one writes one thinks of an expression, reaches for a phrase that might impress, one feels; but it isn't quite one's own: one overreaches, and there is an intuition of honesty that tells one this. This, too, I take it, is "pure knowing." And *I* know what this is. Am I getting it right *right now* as I try to convey to *you* my perception of Wang's thinking? Or am I saying something that tempts me because ever so slightly I felt it would impress, or bring a chuckle? I *do* know the difference, if I will let myself. I could be *confused*, of course, *about* Wang. But I knew—really—what I needed to *do* in order not to be, as I did my work.

I think I have once seen Wang himself engaged in *gongfu* (101). A student is weeding the flowers in his garden, and Wang is there with him. The student makes light conversation (you all know how we do it) cleverly fitting the serious and the trivial together: "How difficult it is in the world to cultivate good and remove evil!" We are back with Mencius and the farmer of Song (2A2.16), and the remark about the people who don't even bother to "weed" their minds. Wang's answer has a verse-capping tone of pleasantry—"Only because you do not really try." But it *is* an answer, and the student is entitled to suppose he means it. A little later Wang catches himself. His answer is not the answer *this* student, *now*, should have; it is too easy, and closes off too quickly a conversation that could become uncomfortably difficult for the teacher himself. Wang opens it up again, and things get serious. Your remark, he says in effect, shows that your excessive concern with "weeding" (with self-cultivation) is itself selfish. You should see that "the spirit of heaven and earth is the same in flowers and weeds. Where have they the distinction of good and evil," in any ultimate sense? And the conversation is at once shifted to the difficult question whether this "beyond good and evil" conception of humans does not make Wang a Buddhist. No, Wang tries to explain. It is liking and disliking that make a flower a "flower" and a weed a "weed," even in the garden of one's impulses. But even this kind of liking and disliking (approving and disapproving) can be natural, "following the principle of nature," or forced and anxious. Wang is thus led into the most difficult thing he can talk about, how it is that the mind can be simultaneously tranquil and active, in "equilibrium" and in "harmony." He, as teacher, saw that getting into this thicket was *his* task at that moment—that he must not close off the conversation with a smooth answer. We teachers are often in similar situations with our students—though *our* problems are not Wang's—and we know the difference, I think, between heeding and not heeding the voice that tells us what our job is.

14.7 Conclusion

Let me call your attention to what I think I have been doing in the last few minutes.

It is a strong temptation for anyone who has to get into philosophy through careful historical reconstruction—and when working on Chinese philosophy one is always doing that—to separate off the problem of description from the problem of criticism. I will find out *what* this person is saying, I tell myself. As to the question whether the person is *right* in saying it, there is always tomorrow or the day after tomorrow.

What would Wang Yangming say of one thus tempted to separate one's intellectual-historian self from one's philosophical self? I think it is clear what he would say: such a person would be treating "knowledge" and "action" as two separate things, and in the end, such a person is deceiving him- or herself.

I have closed this lecture with the cautious suggestion that Wang is on to something, and something important. I did not do this because I got his message and accepted it. I did it because (this is the irony) I found that the problem of interpreting him drove me to it. How does one interpret Wang's abstractions about *liang zhi* and *gongfu*? He answers, *bì yǒu shì yān* 必有事焉—you must test them out in your own problems—not in examples that he shows you or that are made up, but in your own.[14] The only fair thing to do is to try it. And now the irony is that just so far as I do this successfully, *do* succeed in getting a reasonable fit of what he says over something important to *me*, I seem to reveal to myself that Wang Yangming is right.

Moral Decision in Wang Yangming: The Problem of Chinese "Existentialism"[1]

15.1 Chinese "Existentialism"

In 1970, after several years of exacting editorial work, William Theodore de Bary's *Self and Society in Ming Thought*, a collection of papers by a dozen distinguished scholars from three continents, was published (De Bary 1970). With this event, the study of Ming Dynasty philosophy came of age. I read the book. I admired it. It happened that I was asked to review it. I did so, and I praised it quite honestly. I also found some things in it difficult to understand, and I confessed this frankly. I had particular difficulty with a paper by Professor Okada Takehiko 岡田武彥 of Kyushu University, concerning Wáng Yángmíng 王陽明 and certain of his followers, notably Wáng Jī 王畿 (1498–1583); his essay is provocatively titled "Wang Chi and the Rise of Existentialism" (Okada 1970). I wrote about what Okada had to say in it, in part, as follows:

> . . . I think he means by "existentialism" the thesis that if we wish to grasp what our mind is we have to observe what it is doing; that is, that the mind's "substance," typically in late Neo-Confucianism identified with a world-ordering "principle," is not something lying behind a person's play of mental act, emotion and moral effort, but that play itself. But I am not sure of this. I do not think this is quite what "existentialism" has meant to other people, but perhaps it implies at least some genuinely existentialist themes. The problem is worth much more study. (Nivison 1971, 1206)

What might have been a ritualistic way to close a review turned out to be a trap for its author. To find that a matter is important, and to see clearly that you do not understand it, and worse, to have flatly said so in print ought to be intolerable to any person of conscience, and I have set to work to do better.

One may be permitted to wonder whether or not the problem is a real one. Okada, I have learned (and half-perceived), used the word "existentialist" *faute de mieux* to translate the difficult term *xiànchéng* 現成, applied to Wang Ji and his thought; he might equally well have rendered it "realization" or something of the sort, and then perhaps my problem would not have occurred to me (De

Bary 1970, 21). But Theodore de Bary, as the editor and as a contributor to the volume, took the "existentialist" characterization quite seriously (18), and I do not think it absurd for me to do so. An idea may be valuable even if it occurs to us accidentally. Indeed, it may even be right.

But there is one other threshold problem. The Western term "existentialist" is not in ordinary use a term with precise meaning. In fact, at least two recent writers on existentialism, Alasdair MacIntyre and Frederick Olafson, give up, at the outset, any attempt to isolate a context-free sense for "existentialism" and settle for description of certain historically related philosophers who have by more or less common consent been called "existentialists"—for example, Kierkegaard, Heidegger, and Sartre.[2] The indicated idea here is that existentialism is not some essential idea that gets realized or expressed here and there in the history of philosophy. It just *is* those expressions. The appropriateness of this remark will soon be apparent, but in the meantime, it is not very satisfactory. I shall have to let my meaning for "existentialism" emerge as I talk about it and then try to pull it together. This finding that the essentials of existentialism as a thought-type are not (or not easily) abstractable from its particular Western history should not encourage us to see the concept as a useful comparative one. But Okada's discussion does, I think, help one to understand better some features of Wang Yangming and his school. Perhaps, then, it will be a small service if I make an attempt to point out what specific Western existentialist themes do, at least, seem to have counterparts in Wang and what themes obviously do not. And, surely, the diversity of application of the label "existentialist" in present practice makes it absurd to consider its application to a group of Chinese philosophers necessarily illegitimate.

Okada applies the term "existentialist" to the "left" school of Wang Yangming's followers. But he also allows that Wang Yangming himself "came to assert his own existentialist doctrine" on the basis of the theory of Lù Xiàngshān 陸象山 that "mind is principle" (*xīn* 心 is *lǐ* 理) (Okada 1970, 122). Apparently, Okada sees existentialism both in the "left" school of the sixteenth century and in that part of Wang Yangming's thought that this school developed. The root conception seems to be not just "mind is principle," but this denial of dualism together with another, the denial of the dualism of "substance" and "function" (*tǐ* 體, *yòng* 用).[3] The first denial alone could yield quietism and meditation, if one identifies the "real" mind with what is there when all disturbances in it are stilled, revealing residual, pure *lǐ*, "principle." The second denial amounts to identifying the mind "itself" with its own "dynamic life," treating the mind's "original substance" (*běntǐ* 本體) and moral "effort" (*gōngfu* 功夫 or 工夫) as "inseparable." "*Gōngfu*" apparently means both, in a straightforward sense, the good person's continual life of moral choice and action, of trying to do right, and also the mind's self-surveillance function of being "cautious and apprehensive" lest one's thoughts be tainted with selfishness. Wang Yangming makes this point explicitly, and it is of some interest, for at least one of his disciples (until Wang straightens him out) takes this to mean that the good person lives a life of constant anxiety or "sorrow" (Chan 1963, 218, no. 266). In talking about Wang Ji, Okada's characteristic way of putting all this is to say that when we attain this correct conception of our mental "substance" it becomes for us "existential then and there"—it just is its manifestations. Wang Yangming's disciple Wáng Gèn 王艮 makes the same point in arguing that when Wang Yangming spoke of "extending" *liáng zhī* 良知 ("intuitive knowledge of good"), he was not urging quietists to engage in moral effort but was telling them what *liang zhi is* (Okada 1970, 125). It *is* its own "extension," not some latent mental resource or essence that we can "realize." If this really could mean that the mind has no inherent direction other than the direction it gives itself in acting, we might have a genuine existentialist element in the Wang school.

There are several other elements in the thinking of Wang and his followers that are relevant here. There is, first, an immediate corollary to the foregoing, the notion that, since moral truth is just given in the mind and the mind just is its acts in particular situations, it always has to be asked whether a moral teaching of the Master's is a "teaching to suit a particular circumstance" (Okada 1970, 127). Wang's ethics thus seems to be in a radical sense a "situation ethics," and this notion of ethics is another recognizable existentialist element. In Wang it is strikingly illustrated by his uneasiness about having his own teachings written down.[4] Closely related to this, there is much curiously existentialist-like talk about "freedom" and "nothingness" between Wang Yangming and his students. Qián Déhóng 錢德洪, for example, in explaining the first of Wang Yangming's famous "Four Propositions" ("absence of good and evil is the mind's substance"), says that if one seeks the supreme good externally as a "definite principle or standard in things" and supposes that this "good" exists in the mind, this "obstructs the original vacuous and omnipotent substance of mind from working with complete freedom" (Okada 1970, 127). This smells (again) like Sartre's view (anticipated in Kierkegaard) that the self, as a "nothing," is for that reason totally free, there being no predisposition in it to bind its choices. In Wang Ji (but not in Wang Yangming, as we shall see) this is combined with rejection of any kind of cerebral or intellectual approach either to a particular moral decision or to the self-change whose form is making right decisions: one just "lets everything go." A wrong view of this matter, Wang Ji says, will cause us to "fall into intellectual understanding" (Okada 1970, 135–36). For him, apparently, the mind-substance, if one lets it be, *is liang zhi*, which is "nothing" (*wú* 無), which is to say, complete spontaneity and absence of selfish concern or attachment, opening up unlimited possibilities of effective action. It was Wang Yangming's ability to let himself function in this way that explains his ability to deal with the rebellion of Prince Níng 寧 in 1519, making right decision after right decision without hesitation, unconcerned about his own or his family's safety (Okada 1970, 129).[5]

15.2 Some Differences Identified

"Existence precedes essence." Not every thought-type that can be understood as embodying this idea need be called "existentialist." (Marjorie Grene's example [1970, 3] will suffice: For Aquinas, our knowledge of God's essence is dependent on our noticing certain phenomena in the realm of existence, yet we do not, for this reason, call St. Thomas an existentialist.) But if we ask what a self is, and say that it is not some inner essence or "nature" or bundle of tendencies that would be expressed or realized now, then, here, there, but that it just *is* what I do, think, feel, decide, or choose or "will" now, then, here, or there, then we do have an idea existentialists have owned, and this does seem to be what Wang Yangming and many of his followers have said. It looks as though we have another closely related existentialist idea, too, if we say that my being such a self implies that I am totally free. So say both Sartre and Kierkegaard, and so, seemingly, said Wang Ji and even Qian Dehong. Nothing, furthermore, turns one's thoughts more readily to Heidegger and Sartre than thoughts of Nothing.

But already there are differences. "Nothing" for Wang's disciples seems to mean an absence of preconception or selfish interest that could attach or bind us to things. For Western existentialists, consciousness is *"nothing"* because it must be other than its object, which "is": while the object so to speak just sits there, a thing "in itself," we are things "for ourselves," as it were, tipped into the world, concerned with open possibilities of dealing with it.[6] One could argue that this is the direct opposite of "nothing" as "nonattachment."

Further, for Qian and Wang Ji, freedom is spontaneity and is something they take for granted that we want to have; indeed *the* task of self-cultivation is to adjust our understanding of ourselves so that "obstructions" to spontaneity, all anxiety or hesitation, fall away. For both Kierkegaard and Sartre our freedom is a terrifying burden, its exercise painful, something we can never really escape, though we will hide it from ourselves if we can. Perhaps, then, the Chinese *Xīn xué* 心學 school's self is not, after all, the Western existentialist self, and its life of moral endeavor is not, after all, the existentialist self's life of free choice, "authenticity," and "resoluteness," nor its freedom their freedom.[7]

Let us look more carefully at the concept of the choosing, deciding, active mind, which seemingly just *is* "its" choosing, deciding, and acting. Wang Yangming's name for mind, viewed under this aspect, is "pure intuitive knowing," *liang zhi*. *Liang zhi* is always in us (and indeed in everything, but to pursue that here would take me off my subject).[8] On one occasion, Wang Yangming is asked by a student if *liang zhi* does not, after all, disappear (or become "unconscious") when we are asleep; Wang replies, "if it is unconscious, how is it that as soon as one is called one answers?"[9] What Wang Yangming is saying, in effect, is that for me to respond to a call with an awareness that I *ought* to be awake, I must in some deeper sense be awake already.

We have heard something like this before. In fact, Wang Yangming here reveals a form of thought that underlies problem after problem in philosophy. How can I see that I *ought* to believe in God and commit myself to Him unless I already *do*? (Then there is nothing I can do to save myself, for if I could do it I would already be saved.) The question gives us the classic problem that in some theologies is acknowledged in a theory of predestination—if I am ever saved it is because in a sense I always *was*—and that in most theologies, even (or perhaps especially) a theology denying predestination, is resolved in a Doctrine of Grace. How, asked Meno of Socrates, can I really learn anything? For, to learn I must be aware of what it is I am to learn, and this implies that I already know it. Responding to this puzzle, Socrates deduces his (or perhaps really Plato's) theory of recollection: that the soul is immortal, and that when a teacher elicits from a student a process of reasoning to a conclusion, the soul is really just "recalling" what in its inner being it already knows.[10]

"If we really wanted Goodness," sighed Confucius, "it would be right here at hand."[11] But—in exasperation at a flagging student—"One cannot carve rotten wood or trowel a wall of dried dung!"[12] Confucius' problem as a moral teacher is, in effect, this: the crucial element in being moral is, obviously, *wanting* to be. How then can one teach a person to be moral? For to respond to the lesson the student must see it as a lesson to be learned; and if the student sees that, he or she is already moral. This is not, for Confucius, merely a threshold problem: at each step on the moral path the problem implicitly confronts the teacher anew: "I have never seen one leave off practicing Goodness because one had not the *strength* to go on," said the Master.[13] Either the student *is* motivated to take the next step or not. If the student is not, there seems to be no help for him or her. If the student is motivated, he or she already, in effect, has the "strength" for that next step.[14]

Confucius did not solve this problem, but Mencius did (at least within the Confucian point of view), leaving his solution to the ages: we are all predisposed to morality, in our "child's heart" (*Mèngzǐ* 孟子 4B12). Basically the teacher's task is to *wake us up* and elicit from us this predisposition to the moral. Mencius's doctrine is not quite a doctrine of recollection: after all, he lacks anything like Plato's theory of metempsychosis. But as Bertrand Russell (1948, 212) pointed out, we might have memories or experiences we could not distinguish from memory, even if there were no past. Mencius's theory arguably does the same job as Plato's recollection.

The interest of all this is twofold: first, as we all know, "pure knowledge" or *liang zhi* is one of *Mencius's* names for this built-in disposition to the good that he thinks we have; it is what we know without even having to think (*Mengzi* 7A15), and Wang Yangming in appropriating it, and in changing it, has not changed it in one essential respect. It is still, for him, the mental and intentional activity wherein we identify and try to effect *the* good—not simply *a* "good" for us. Both our choice to *be* moral and our particular moral choices are free in the sense of being unforced, but they are not in the most radical sense free: as we will see, there is still, for Wang Yangming, something about us that will lead us all to choose the same moral ends unless there is something wrong with us.[15] It may not be possible to give a general characterization of "good," or of *liang zhi* either; perhaps we have to grasp both via "existence," by looking at particular cases and particular acts. And so in this sense we can never point to anything we are, over and above and behind the feelings we have, the strivings we engage in, the decisions we make—in short, our existence. But *liang zhi* is not capricious. It could not both function properly and lead us to choose evil as our good, as does Milton's Satan. Wang Yangming is still in the tradition of Mencius.

Second, the formally congruent Socratic problem resolved by Socrates (or Plato) in the theory of recollection stands in a precisely opposite relation to the Western existential tradition. Kierkegaard devotes the *Philosophical Fragments* to an examination of it. Kierkegaard's view—a view that persists in some form in most later existentialisms—is that the Socratic conception of humans as programmed to rationality produces a perversion that has corrupted philosophy (especially, for Kierkegaard, the rationalism of Hegel). What must be rejected is the view that there is an objective right that embodies rationality, knowable by humans and there to guide them because that is how their natures are disposed.[16]

15.3 Existential Distress

If we abstract from Kierkegaard's view its theological direction and attend just to his claim that there is nothing in the individual prior to the moment of choice that determines or inclines one to one's "decision for Christ," we can work out (not for all existentialists, surely, but for many of them) the ethical consequences of this claim as follows:

1. There is *no* human nature predisposed to rationality, or to an objectively definable "good" or "virtue."

2. Hence humans, in choosing and deciding, are not able to rest their judgments on some "good" revealed to reason. Humans have no essence which existential acts of will can express. One just is those acts.

3. Hence one is completely free in one's moral deciding; one really can "choose either way." In making a choice, to that extent one both makes one's nature and constitutes what is for oneself the right. One's ultimate choices cannot be reasoned from any self-evident principle. They are wholly one's own: one just chooses.

4. Hence, one is completely responsible for what one is and for what one's "good" is. This burden of responsibility is almost intolerable,

and produces anguish in us. Most of us try to avoid the anguish of it by trying to ignore it or evade it. We really never can, but we can be self-deceived.

5. To see this fact and accept the burden is to escape "bad faith" and be "authentic." The anxiety of total responsibility is therefore to be savored: just in so far as we feel it we know we are really facing life, being "genuine."

The classic example of existentialist anguish is Kierkegaard's: it is the distress of Abraham (Genesis 22), committed to doing something and seeing it as obedience to God, while knowing that the whole world will regard it as murder.

I do not represent this schema as any particular existentialist view; it is, admittedly, an overly simplified sketch of but one kind of existentialist view. But it will, perhaps, serve as a useful premise for comparative investigation.

The investigation must first deal with a possibility that there is an existentialist element in Wang and his school that we have overlooked, that may show his thought to be closer to this existentialist schema than we might suppose. It is arguable, and there are striking elements in Wang to sustain the argument, that there *is* an equivalent of existential angst in Wang's philosophy. If this is true, it would indicate that we need to reexamine his supposed enduring link with Mencius.

Rather dramatic statements are sometimes made about Wang suggesting an element of existential distress in his own life. Okada remarks that "Wang Yang-ming attained his doctrine of the innate knowledge only after experiencing indescribable agonies" (Okada 1970, 128). This suggests that we might think of Wang's enlightenment as a kind of total and final "decision," in effect, settling all future decisions, with the angst concentrated in the experience leading to it. But, of course, there is no reason to think of his "attaining" his doctrine of intuitive knowledge of good (*liang zhi*) as a "decision" at all for Wang Yangming. "Attaining doctrine" was arguably a decision for Kierkegaard; it may well have been for Mencius's rival, Gàozǐ 告子. Gaozi's concept of "unmoved mind" might be reconsidered with this point in view, and with this, that dark saying of Gaozi's—that "what you do not get from words you should not seek for in your mind"—a saying which I think no one has understood.[17] And it is often the case with self-cultivation philosophies—Stalinism (or Maoism), for example, which is a genuine decision-ethic—that the process leading to perfection is one of agonizing trial and self-struggle.[18] But Wang Yangming's enlightenment was clearly for him a discovery, an immeasurably exciting one.

There is, however, one apparent striking example of what I am tempted to call existential distress in Wang Yangming, when Wang momentarily sees himself choosing his own moral course, utterly alone. Wang, even at this moment, attributes his views on intuitive knowledge to "divine guidance." (Kierkegaard? Not quite.) Seeing the "people's degeneration and difficulties," he feels "pain in my heart." He must help them with his teaching. But "when people see me trying to do this, they join one another in criticizing, ridiculing, insulting, and cursing me, regarding me as insane. Alas!" Should he not be content to be an insensitive "gentleman" like others, or should he really try to be a "sage"? But Wang then notices that

> there are cases when people see their fathers, sons, or brothers falling into a deep abyss and drowning. They cry, crawl, go naked and bare-footed, stumble and fall. They hang onto dangerous cliffs and go down to save them. Some gentlemen who see them behave like this talk, laugh, and bow ceremoniously to others by their side. They consider them to be insane because they have discarded etiquette and taken off their clothing, and because they cry, stumble, and fall as they do.

But such "gentlemen" who have no feeling of pity are "no longer human beings." A father or brother of a person in danger "will surely feel an ache in his head and a pain in his heart" and desperately will try to save his relative.

> He even ignores the danger of drowning himself. How much more will he ignore being ridiculed as insane! And how much more will he fail to worry about whether people believe him or not! Alas! It is all right if people say that I am insane. The minds of all people are the same as mine. There are people who are insane. How can I not be so? There are people who have lost their minds. How can I not lose mine?[19]

But if this is existentialist in temper, it is completely the opposite in content. Wang Yangming, in the end, does not make an utterly lonely and unsustained decision, his alone, to be "insane." He makes this decision just because he sees that his motivation to radical compassion is a universal and valid one: "The minds of all people are the same as mine." Mencius could not have said it better.

I noted earlier that the "self-watching" function of mind is seen by Wang Yangming as a basic aspect of the mind-substance (or of *liang zhi*, as he also says), and that this might be seen as a view that a distressing anxiety about the constant possibility of a wrong turn in thought is a necessary part of life. Wang addresses himself to this point directly in response to a question by his student Lù Yuánjìng 陸原靜, who asks about the concept of true "joy," which sages such as Confucius and Yán Huí 顏回 are said always to have. Is it different from ordinary joy? If so, then "is it present when sages and worthies meet with great sorrow, great anger, great terror, and great fear? Furthermore, since the mind of the superior man is constantly occupied with caution and apprehension, he is in sorrow throughout life. How can he have joy?"[20]

True joy is "characteristic of the original substance of the mind," Wang replies; even ordinary people have it, "except that these people do not realize it though they have it." Wang holds that true "joy" lies in totally sincere self-understanding and can be copresent with the bitterest grief, and he chides his student in his anxiety about anxiety for "looking for a donkey while riding it." It seems clear that the notion of existential anxiety is actually incompatible with Wang Yangming's point of view.

I close this brief look at the problem of a quasi-existential "anxiety" in Wang Yangming with these reflections. Existentialism is so varied that one is likely to find in some works of writers who are identified as existentialist expressions of the involvement of the self in the world that resemble Wang's thought here, in part: for example, it may be that it is not the self but the universe that is seen as unstructured, unreasonable, "absurd," giving no support or even meaningful opposition to the self's decision to act. It goes without saying that this would not yet give a real analog to Wang. It might also be supposed that Wang's "unity of knowledge and action" gives us something "existentialist," in another sense:[21] we could try taking him as saying, "Don't just *talk*. Do it! Until you have made and executed the painful decision to *act*, you have not worked any change in yourself that can be claimed as knowledge. Action is the completion of knowledge." This would be the more tempting in that this is just the direction in which China-admiring revolutionary thought (the new leftist of the '60s throwing his first rock?) took the "unity of knowledge and action." Wang Yangming himself might well deal with this suggestion in the way that Mencius dealt with Gaozi—by retelling the story of the farmer of Song (*Mengzi* 2A2.16).

15.4 The Nature of Moral Decision in Wang Yangming

I have already noted an apparent existential element in Wang Ji's rejection of rationality and deliberation in moral choice (only apparent, since it, too, as I suggested earlier, actually precludes existentialist "anxiety").

But Wang Ji in rejecting rationality links it to "selfish desire," which he sees as obstructing the total and immediate "existential" manifestation of the mind-substance. Its rejection is linked with a cultivation of self by which, he thinks, "you can arrive at the place where you will not go astray, and whatever you grasp will be the Way" (Okada 1970, 136). Not the way for you, but the Way that everyone would grasp. Wang Ji, to this extent, like Wang Yangming, is also still in the tradition of Mencius (and, one might add, Zhuāngzǐ 莊子).

The connection between selfishness and reasoning (easily thought of as calculation of advantage) is, of course, also Mencian, and should remind us that although Mencius's theory of human goodness and Socrates' theory of

242   David S. Nivison

recollection are logically congruent ideas up to a point, they are not the same. Although Socrates is hunting for virtue (like Mencius), his theory is, in effect, a theory of innate human *rationality*. (The classic example is Socrates as teacher eliciting a geometric proof from an ignorant slave.) Mencius's is a theory of innate human *affection*, not rationality at all. So it is not surprising that the rejection of rationality by a Western and a Chinese existentialist will be different in meaning. Interpreters of the Western existentialists, furthermore, differ sharply on whether or not and in what sense they can be said to "reject reason." To deny that a human has an essence that enables him or her to see what is reasonable and right in an absolute moral order of things is not the same as holding (as perhaps Wang Ji does) that when one chooses one ideally does it "spontaneously," without sometimes having to think and puzzle carefully about it.

Wang Yangming does not, I believe, reject the idea of cautiously thinking things out in our approach to the problem of what we are to do. But this does not mean that our decisions, instead of being spontaneous, become agonizing choices. One reason for this is that although Wang does sometimes encourage careful thinking out of problems of decision, the point of spontaneity is maintained, if the mind is working correctly: the workings of the selfish ego are excluded and, so to speak, one *lets* the mind's workings be a "decision procedure," which one follows. (More of this later.) But also, and this really just articulates this idea, for Wang it must be stressed that our choices are not, in the existentialist sense, radically free. On the contrary, I shall now argue, what Wang Yangming does is to assimilate our evaluating, and so our choosing, deciding, and acting, to the notion of *sense perception*.

We can see this as follows:

1. Wang Yangming, like Mencius, sees the mind as like the senses: for Mencius, this means that each has its proper ideal object (the eye: the beautiful; the mind: the good). For Wang something more is meant: the senses, and also the mind, have no "substance" other than the objects which it is their function to grasp: "the eye has no substance of its own. Its substance consists of the colors of all things . . . the mind has no substance of its own. Its substance consists of the right or wrong of the influences and responses of Heaven, Earth, and all things." Wang is not, I think, saying here that the mind just is its existential states. He is stating, in a special form, his often maintained idealist position that the mind—he often uses the word in a sense that includes both perceiving and thinking—and the universe, which is its object, "heaven, earth, spiritual beings and the myriad things," are "one body" or "have the same substance" (*tóng tǐ* 同體).[22]

2. This implies that for Wang Yangming there is no effective difference between perceiving a sensible quality with a sense (for example, sight)

and "perceiving" a value-quality with the mind in the noninclusive sense of the mind that thinks and conceives. In neither case can I, by my own volition, perceive something that you and others do not, when our organs (including our "thought organ") are working normally. Having them work normally requires that they be kept "clean": "not a single idea (*niàn* 念) should be allowed to attach to the original substance of the mind (*xīn tǐ* 心體), just as not the least bit of dirt should be allowed to stick to the eye." And the trouble, he explicitly adds, is not that the "idea" might be evil, but rather that it "blinds," preventing the mind from taking the world in as it is (Chan 1963, 256–57, no. 336).

3. This inference is confirmed by his famous analysis of the unity of knowledge and action (*zhī xíng hé yī* 知行合一). When I see a beautiful color, I do not first *see* it with my eyes (a kind of "knowing"), with *liking* it (a kind of "action") coming afterwards as the result of a mental *decision* to like it (Chan 1963, 10, no. 5). My perception of a thing as having visible and value qualities is total and unitary. As Husserl might say, it seems to be one unitary "constituting" intentional act of consciousness—just as when I look at a tree I see not only a shape but a solid extended *object* with a front and a back side, so here I "see" an object with a visible and a "value side."[23]

4. This does not have to mean, I think, that a mental act of preferring or choosing has to be either thoughtless or instantaneous. (After all, when we are looking in dim light, it may take time and careful attention to make out the color or shape of a thing.) But it does mean that Wang Yangming cannot make the kind of distinction between knowing and doing made by such later existentialists as Heidegger and Sartre, knowing being for them the passive mode of attention to "things in themselves" that *are there*, and "doing" (valuing, choosing, deciding, willing) the active mode of attention to what *is not* there, the as-yet-unshaped still-open future ("nonbeing" or "Nothing," as the existentialists sometimes overdramatically put it), the former bound, the latter free (Olafson 1967, 68–71). For Wang Yangming, neither mode can be free, in this radical sense.

5. More evidence is found in Wang Yangming's conception of moral teaching. We constantly notice in Wang Yangming that, as a teacher, he tries to guide his students to think out moral problems afresh for themselves, feel out for themselves their inner moral responsiveness as persons, and does not point to established doctrine and say simply "accept this." He is even reluctant to have his students write down his own words for fear they will be taken as dead dicta by later students. What is the value of my learning to think for myself, then? That my

thinking might lead me and through me others to take a new direction, to *create* new realms of value? No: not this, nor even much less, simply *discovering* something that has not been seen before in some basic sense. The point for Wang Yangming of my learning to do my moral thinking for myself is the same as the point of my learning to see for myself (to the extent that it makes sense to think of this as something I could need to learn): If I do not learn this, I will not even be a minimally effective human being: "In learning it is necessary to have teachers and friends to point out and explain things. But it is not as good as to point out and understand them oneself, for then if one succeeds in one case, one will succeed in all cases. Otherwise there will be no end to other people's helping" (Chan 1963, 234, no. 298).

But what is to be seen is always essentially the same. As de Bary says of Wang, "for all his insistence on discovering right and wrong for oneself, it does not even occur to him that there could be any essential conflict between subjective and objective morality, or that genuine introspection could lead to anything other than the affirmation of clear and common moral standards" (De Bary 1970, 156).[24]

What this has to mean is that each human does, after all, have a nature or direction that we may as well call the "substance" of the mind, which is not reducible without remainder to whatever might actually happen to be one's mental and intentional acts. One ought to "perceive" the objective world accurately, including the world of objective value; and one does do so precisely when one is being true to oneself, that is, when one lets one's "substance" be that world, and does not let any element of prejudice or personal desire distort one's responding to it. This point could be safely admitted by Wang Yangming and all of his "left school" followers, providing we separate it from two other points, both of which they wish to deny:

A. They deny that there can be some *state* of the mind in which somehow its "substance" is isolated and all of its "functioning" quieted. Indeed, if there *were* such a state, it would have to be seen as just one more "function." This is precisely what Wang Yangming says of the state of the mind in sleep (Chan 1963, 219, no. 267).

B. They also deny, even granted that the mind "substance" is other than or more than its functions, that there can be any final *definition* of that substance, an inner *xìng* 性 or *li* such that I could tell you what it is, or even use it for my own guidance as a premise having context-free validity.

But what the Chinese "existentialist" can admit, the Western existentialist must deny: For the latter, in effect, the mind has no "substance"; it just is its acts (or the directionless process of acting). Western existentialists deduce from this their characteristic views about anxiety, freedom, total responsibility, the ambiguity or absurdity of life, etc. For Chinese "existentialists," on the contrary, freedom turns out to be a spontaneity that does have direction, not a voluntarism that does not; in place of anxiety, they see joy as normal for humans; and in place of absurdity, they see a successful and entirely possible life to be one in which "whatever you grasp will be the Way."

Ultimately the difference between Western and Chinese existentialisms is best revealed in the nature of decisive choices. I find irresistibly interesting a legend about Wang's behavior in 1507, when he was on his way to exile in Guìzhōu 貴州. His enemies at court were trying to assassinate him. He went into hiding and was warned that his enemies' anger might turn upon his father. In this extremity Wang Yangming had recourse to divination and was bidden to turn aside from his journey to his assigned post and return to his father.[25] Here legend pictures Wang as finding the conflict of obligations an impossible one, and his solution is a paradigm of Sartrean "bad faith": he resolves his distress by seeking an oracle, thus entrusting his decision to Heaven. The story calls to mind an account of Zhū Xī 朱熹, who also at the end of his life, with enemies at court capable of destroying him, was unable to decide whether to submit a memorial of criticism that might be his undoing. Zhu also consults the milfoil, and is instructed to desist.[26]

I can recall that as a young man, I myself once had a choice to make, which I saw at the time as a distressingly important one for me. As it happened, I was alone, and I had to make the choice almost within seconds. I remember picking up a quarter from my desk, flipping it onto the floor and saying to myself "Heads it's . . ." Which? Another choice! Deliberately picking up the coin without looking at it, I accepted the pain of my decision as my own. At least *I* made it.

We do not, of course, have the kind of confidence in coin-flipping that people like Wang and Zhu had in the *Yì jīng* 易經, but that is the point. Our world has come to be so stripped of background essences and truths to rest on that our lives are filled with the sorts of experiences that give existentialism its plausibility. Wang Yangming's Heaven-saturated world was otherwise. He lived in a world—both inner and outer, for his metaphysics in the end did not separate them—which was *friendly* to right (*really* right) decision, if one learns not to obstruct or resist it. The Western existentialist—at least the kind who now has the largest audience—lives in an outer world which is utterly indifferent to the "rightness" of one's decisions and an inner world which just is those decisions.

The story about Wang is a legend; as far as I have noticed he did not use divination as a decision procedure.[27] He did not have to. For the sort of impersonal tapping of the mind of Heaven divination is supposed to achieve had an adequate counterpart for Wang in the working of his *own* mind, when that mind works rightly, carefully, and honestly, free from "obstructions" of the self-centered ego. I am not being fanciful here: this is precisely what Wang says himself. Zhu Xi, one of his students noted, interpreted the *Yi jing* as a divination treatise; Chéng Yí 程頤 read it as a treatise on "principle" (*li*). Who was right? Wang replies, "Divination involves principle, and principle is a form of divination." And he draws conclusions: People who fail to understand this "don't know that questions and answers between teachers and friends, such as we are engaging in today, and studying extensively, inquiring accurately, thinking carefully, sifting clearly, practicing earnestly, and the like are all forms of divination." It is only when one doubts one's ability to let one's mind function completely unswayed by selfish impulses that one consults the *Yi jing*, to "give the mind divine intelligence" and "seek answers from Heaven"—the idea being that "Heaven alone leaves no room for falsehood" (Chan 1963, 211, no. 247).

So Wang seems to be in the last analysis an "intellectualist," not a "voluntarist" in ethics:[28] when I am trying to determine what I am to do in a situation, my problem is to identify something there to be known, and that something, further, really *is* known all the time, both by me and by Heaven. My problem is not simply to choose how I will throw my weight in that situation. But it is worth remembering again, since this study of "existentialist" tendencies in Wang has been somewhat negative, how pervasive is the complex of existentialist-seeming elements in Wang's thought. He insists that there are no *rules* revealed to the reasoning mind that I can steer by; and he makes this point again in another remark linking moral intuition and divination. To a student pleading that innate knowledge seems to have "neither spatial restriction nor physical form" and is "most difficult to grasp," Wang replied by quoting, as the student had done, the appended remarks in the *Yi jing*. Intuitive moral knowledge (*liang zhi*) is the same thing as "changes" (*yi* 易) he says: "As the Way, it changes frequently. It changes and moves without staying in one place, flowing about into any one of the six places of the hexagram. It ascends and descends without any consistency, and its elements of strength (*yáng* 陽) and weakness (*yīn* 陰) interchange. It cannot be considered as an invariable standard. It changes to suit the circumstances" (Chan 1963, 259–60, no. 341). To suppose that it can be "grasped" is absurd.[29]

Even so, the whole picture we have of Wang's life as a teacher shows him recognizing that my learning to identify what it is I "just know," both in particular situations and throughout my life, is a task that takes time, patience, and careful thought. This is what happens in "questions and answers between teachers and friends"; and here we have, I think, striking evidence that Wang's moral intuitionism does not reject what we would ordinarily call careful thinking and reasoning. What he has done, in effect, is to put the human mind all the way back into nature (as early Neo-Confucianism had begun to do in treating human social life as natural), while remaining, to a degree, in the Daoist-Zen orientation that in its anti-intellectual phases had excluded mind from nature. To understand this we must take Wang absolutely seriously when he says, "At bottom, Heaven, Earth, the myriad things, and humans form one body. The point at which this unity is manifested in its most refined and excellent form is the clear intelligence of the human mind" (Chan 1963, 221–22, no. 274). I should not, then, think of myself as making my decisions arbitrarily and by myself, then forcing them into the world. When I "think," "sift," "practice," in short, reason, decide, and act, I am *letting* my intuitive knowledge *guide* me, as I would use the *Yi jing* itself, in functioning as a part of the world, the "one body," of which I am and in which I live.

The Philosophy of Zhang Xuecheng[1]

Zhāng Xuéchéng 章學誠 was born in 1738, three years after the emperor Hónglì 弘曆 ascended the throne of China, and died in 1801, when this same emperor, who was one of the longest lived in Chinese history, was himself but two years dead. His life and thought thus span the famous Qiánlóng 乾隆 era of Qing Dynasty history, and provide an outstanding example of the intellectual and scholarly brilliance for which that age is remembered. Zhang was an essayist, and although not a poet, he was much interested in poetry; he was also a philosopher of considerable ability, as well as a historian and critic of historiography, in which he took a particular interest in local history. It is in fact for his historiographical criticism that he is chiefly known. But I intend to make him out in this essay, somewhat against the general opinion, as a highly philosophical literary critic. Zhang's best known writings are two, the *Wénshǐ tōngyì* 文史通義, a collection of critical and philosophical essays on literature and history; and the *Jiàochóu tōngyì* 校讎通義, a more technical book, but still of philosophical interest, on the history and method of bibliography.[2]

Zhang's thought and writing were relatively neglected in his own country for more than a century after his death; but since the late great scholar, Naito Torajiro 內藤虎次郎, took an interest in him about thirty-five years ago,[3] he has been much studied in both China and Japan. The appraisals of him are extremely varied: his thought and his importance have been characterized in almost as many ways as there have been characterizers. He has been, in Japan alone, compared to Hegel, Ranke, Pascal, and Bergson. A well-known French scholar likens him to Vico (Demiéville 1961, 184). This variety of estimations is so striking as to merit some attempt at explanation.

The process of "understanding" another thinker, I would suggest, must start by grasping a few essential points where our conceptual schemes seem to overlap, taking these viewpoints hypothetically as identical with our own, and building out from there, imagining ourselves in the shoes of our subject. We try to imagine how we would think, were we in his position with his point of view and initial commitments, and we check our growing hypothetical reconstruction of his thought as we go along against what we can observe of his behavior, what he says, what he writes. When we find that our construction jibes with what we notice in him, we call this construction of ours *his* thought, and we say we "understand" him.[4]

Now this is frankly what I feel myself to be doing with Zhang Xuecheng. But the danger in this procedure, inevitable though it may be, is obvious: Since our check on our reconstruction is through what we notice, and since what we notice is likely to be what our preconceptions lead us to expect, the constant danger is that we will project more of ourselves, or of our own more familiar notions, into our subject than we realize. And if we start with any expectation or hidden desire to find in our subject a companion or opponent, we are rather likely to do so. This danger is the greater in the case of a person like Zhang. This is true, first because the complexity of his thought and the range of his imagination are so great that there is little one cannot "notice" in him if one wishes; and second, because although his distance from the modern world is great, in tradition and frame of reference if not in time, his originality within his own tradition tempts us to conceive him in images familiar to us, but of questionable appropriateness in a Chinese milieu. I propose, then, without denying that they may sometimes be useful, to eschew European parallels, and to attempt rather to see Zhang in terms of the problems which his Chinese intellectual and social background presented to him.

Zhang himself, of course, is an essential part of the background of his own thought. He was born, as I said, in 1738, in Shàoxìng 紹興, Zhèjiāng 浙江 province—a city later to become the native place of a famous writer of our own time, the novelist Lǔ Xùn 魯迅. This area in Zhang's day was one of the richest and most populous in China, famous (as it remains) for its wine, and an area withal which supplied considerably more than its share of clerks and scholar officials for the government bureaucracy. Zhang's clan was numerous in the area, and had besides a large contingent settled in the north in Běijīng 北京. His immediate family seem to have been local government clerks, and his father succeeded in obtaining the highest official degree, the *jìnshì* 進士, later being appointed a local magistrate; but he was subsequently charged, rightly or wrongly, with mishandling the funds of his office, and was fined so heavily that the family was reduced to near poverty. Zhang's father thereafter supported himself by teaching in local academies and by writing local histories under the patronage of local officials; and this was the course which Zhang himself followed for most of his life, like his father constantly faced at best with economic uncertainty, and at times with actual privation. His father managed to give him a good education, however, and got him into the imperial academy, *Guózǐjiàn* 國子監, in Beijing, where, Zhang tells us, he always got the lowest marks. He seems to have had considerable difficulty with the ordinary course of studies which led to the official examinations—reading and memorizing the Classics, and learning to write the formal style of the "eight-legged" essay or *bāgǔ* 八股. As he was by temperament proud, he reacted with intellectual rebelliousness: the things he found difficult and distasteful, he felt, were scarcely worth doing; his own talent lay in another direction—in the study of history. And it was one's intellectual duty, he began to claim, to develop one's natural gifts, for it was from these that one's contribution to human knowledge and one's own attainment of understanding were meant to come.

Zhang eventually learned to write well enough to impress favorably the examination officials (and well enough, I might add, to impress his modern reader with a considerable beauty of style); he obtained the highest degree, after repeated failures on the way, in his forty-first year, but did not follow this success by getting an official position, for qualified scholars of the eighteenth century were so numerous that there were far too few appointments to go around.

Zhang thus remained, in a sense, on the outside of things throughout his life, and a feeling of being at outs pursued him constantly, accentuating his proud and intensely serious disposition. Intellectually also Zhang felt, and was, at odds with his times. He disliked the meticulous and often pedestrian classical text-criticism which was rated the most praiseworthy type of scholarship in his day. Like the course for the examinations, he felt, this fashion was a claim upon him which would fetter his imagination in an irrelevant and useless waste of energy. Zhang is in fact the type of the protesting philosopher—haughty, often heated, with a rapid and brilliant tongue. One contemporary has described him vividly, as he saw him (at about forty) in the circle of a teacher and patron under whom they were both studying. Zhang, we are told, "talked like a bubbling fountain," much to the enjoyment of his teacher, and "would joke in a manner quite unbecoming a disciple," so that onlookers were surprised. As Zhang became older, he became more of an oddity, yet he continued to retain the deep respect of those who knew him well. In 1797, four years before Zhang's death, another patron wrote a poem in his honor:

> Master Zhang is so endowed by nature
> That both in virtues and defects he is far from common.
>
> . . . .
>
> His appearance is quite unimposing,
> And he is always the object of popular amusement.

He has a red nose, the poet continues, a blotched face, is hard of hearing, and constantly suffers from headaches; yet

> Though his senses are only half existent,
> His intelligence is marvelously active.
> Whenever he essays to express himself in writing,
> In discussion of learning he goes straight to the truth.

And he goes on to praise Zhang's scholarly attainments, concluding,

> Thus, if you judge a man by his appearance
> You will mistake a phoenix for a pheasant. (Hu Shih 1929, 124, 127–28).[5]

What we are after now is this brilliance in Zhang which could prompt this sort of admiration. Here our difficulties return—for to appraise Zhang's ideas and see how they must have struck his contemporaries, we must have before us the background of thought and attitude which was shared by him and his contemporaries alike. This background is what is commonly called "Neo-Confucianism."

16.1 The Neo-Confucian Background

Neo-Confucianism, which took definite shape in China about a thousand years ago, was the work of an intellectual class which was a fragment of the broader class of landholders.[6] The institutional base of these literati was the local private school, and the official examination system by which they were drawn into the civil service. The Neo-Confucians, as Confucians always, were literary people concerned with a literary person's place in and contribution to the state— as distinct from that of the military person, or of another whose qualifications were not those of the pen. Consequently, the literati were concerned with political and economic policy; with learning to write, and distinguishing good writing from bad; and with the ancient canon of Confucian Classics, on which they based their literary and social thought. But what really distinguishes Confucians of the last millennium from their ancient counterparts in the centuries following Confucius himself was the long intervening experience of Buddhism in Chinese thought. What we find characteristically in the Neo-Confucians is a secular form of that desire which gripped people's minds in Buddhist China, the desire for a sort of personal salvation through enlightenment, or through moral self-perfection. In the heat of this desire, the Neo-Confucian's various interests—mastery of writing, service to society, understanding of classical truth—were fused, and tended to be seen as aspects of a single problem of self-cultivation.

Against the background of this view of life the most varied interests, occupations, and articulated philosophies are deployed. But of the intellectual issues which engrossed the literati of Neo-Confucian China we need take note of but one. The great personal quest of the intellectual was for understanding, both of truth about the world—characteristically the world of humans—and of truth about what is *good* for humans, what human nature is, what constitutes good action. And what people of learning wanted was not simply a knowledge of truths: they wanted this knowledge to be part of their own mental processes, their own nature; intellectually they sought "enlightenment"; morally, an utter self-perfection. Consequently, we find Neo-Confucianism—the Chinese name for which is *Dàoxué* 道學, "the study of the Way"—much less interested in distinguishing *what* is true from what isn't, than in what we might call the vertical dimension of epistemology, viz., in the intensity of knowledge—in distinguishing genuine, "real" knowledge from knowledge which is merely superficial or verbal pretense.

Now the controversy is this: what is this goal, this "real knowledge," and how does one reach it? We find among Confucians two opposing points of view, which reflect an older conflict which ran through Chinese Buddhism—at times taking a form roughly analogous to the conflict between faith and reason in medieval Christianity. One view held that truths are immutable and fixed, can be learned by exhaustive study, characteristically of the Classics, and are reducible to philosophical generalizations. Enlightenment was a mysterious result of long and arduous work in which one accumulated as much of this knowledge as possible. The opposite view was that truth is not of this sort: that the world is infinitely various, both from situation to situation and from time to time. In the most extreme form of this latter position there can be no statement of the true, no cognitive apprehension of truth from words at all, for words and concepts are static, fixed, and something other than actual things and processes. Consequently, the only kind of real knowledge, for a late Neo-Confucian like Wáng Yángmíng 王陽明 in the early sixteenth century, is that which is had intuitively from direct engagement in the world, either experiential or active. Wang's characterization of this situation is that "knowledge" is inseparable from "action" (in a rather broad sense of the word "action").

This is approximately the point of view we find in Zhang Xuecheng. One more bit of preliminary clarification is necessary before we can make out Zhang's adaptation of it, however. We may note that Wang Yangming's point of view seems to involve a dilemma, which I propose to call the "dilemma of the rational mystic." It is this: the later Neo-Confucians' point of view leads them to the conviction that words are either untrue or meaningless. They tend to hold as a philosophical position that any fixed, clearly conceived position, and certainly any articulation of it, is false or absurd. Palpably, their own position must be true only if untrue, meaningful only if without meaning. They can assert it only by admitting in principle that they should not have asserted it. This difficulty is probably inherent in all mysticism, and its proximate source in Neo-Confucianism is the mysticism of Chan Buddhism.[7] But the difficulty is intensified for Confucians, for their rationalistic tradition compels them to talk, to explain themselves, to try to make sense. One can, I think, plot a large part of subsequent Chinese thought as a reaction to this "dilemma of the rational mystic"; and in fact it could be argued that it still persists, even in current Communist ideology, in the form of the demand made of individual Communists that in their thinking they avoid both what the party calls "dogmatism" and what it calls "empiricism."[8]

16.2 Zhang as Neo-Confucian

The most enduring result of Wang Yangming's rather extreme philosophical position and the dilemma it involved was to bring under suspicion any and all abstract philosophical speculation, and to drive Confucians back with renewed intensity to a study of the Classics—this time avoiding any generalizations of a lofty nature and sticking to a kind of knowledge which seemed to be closer to earth, more comprehensible—e.g., how were the words in ancient poetry pronounced, and what exactly did they mean? what were the actual details of ancient rituals? and so on. This was "solid learning"—learning that dealt with "actual facts," learning that had "reality" to it: and this learning of "actual facts" was everywhere contrasted (and nowhere so insistently as by Zhang Xuecheng) with "empty words"—vague and unfounded statements.

But in Zhang, nonetheless, there is a sharp contrast with the prevailing philological interest of the seventeenth, eighteenth, and nineteenth centuries, and a contrast which he himself was acutely conscious of. The philologues, when they carried out their point of view fully, reacted to the "dilemma of the rational mystic," which made any articulation of philosophy seem blameworthy, in effect by discarding philosophy—by suspecting any interest they might have (or at least any impulse they might have to state it) in the overall relevance of what they were doing. Being persuaded that to extract eternal metaphysical and moral truths from the Classics in the old way was self-deception, they took another kind of interest in the Classics. Now Zhang likewise responds to the dilemma by taking another kind of interest in the Classics; but his mode of interest is as different from the philological as day from night. If the Classics cannot be viewed as repositories of eternal truth, so much the better for the Classics, says Zhang. This means simply that they are not "empty words"; and it is precisely for this reason that they are entitled to our respect. Zhang thinks of them not as books, deliberately written by sages to set forth doctrines, but as anonymous accretions, and as tangible vestiges of the actual historical experience of people in the perfect society of antiquity. One should study them, not for explicit instruction, but in order to grasp intuitively through them the ever-changing play and development of *dào* 道 in human history. The Classics, Zhang feels, are products of traditions stretching down through time to the present, and it is on these traditions that he fixes his attention. It is an intuitive grasp of the total pattern of these that should result from correct classical study; such a study, in short, results in a philosophy of history, in which people in the present properly orient themselves in relation to antiquity. But this is precisely the aim of historical study itself: in fact, Zhang holds, what are ordinarily called histories may be thought of equally well as continuations of the Classics. All of this is what Zhang means by his often quoted and usually misunderstood statement that "the Classics are all histories" (六經皆史).

We have seen that the Neo-Confucians' concern with the problem of how to spend their lives profitably, how to achieve the perfection and understanding they sought, led in the two centuries before Zhang Xuecheng to a dilemma. Enlightenment did not seem to be a state which could be attained by learning more and more about things; indeed verbally expressible knowledge *about* truth will inevitably lead you away from what you seek. When Zhang considers directly the problem of what is the good life of the mind, he has a characteristic solution, which turns out to be intimately related to his philosophy of history. Learning *about*—the mere acquisition of wide knowledge—is both a meaningless and a dishonest way for scholars to spend their energy. Rather, Zhang would conceive the life of learning as itself a form of experience and action. Not breadth, but intensity, genuineness, and touch with reality—in a sense Zhang is at pains to explain—will be the values. What Zhang recommends is specialization; and there are, he thinks, three areas among which people, recognizing both their limitations and their talents, must make a choice—though in making this choice they should not be oblivious to the value of what they neglect: these three are literary expression (*wéncí* 文辭 or *cízhāng* 辭章), philology (*zhìshù* 制數 or *kǎodìng* 考訂), and philosophy (*xìnglǐ* 性理 or *yìlǐ* 義理). In this we see perhaps a rationalization of Zhang's own temperament—his rebelliousness, during his education, at being obliged to spend his time on that for which he had no aptitude or interest. His own special gift, he felt, was in historical study; but it was the criticism of historical *writing* especially that fascinated him, and this interest quickly extended itself to all kinds of writing. Zhang was basically a literary critic, though of a sort for which our preconceptions are unprepared. There are indications throughout his writing that it was the general area of literary expression which he regarded as his own province.

But if literary expression in a very broad sense—"words"—are Zhang's province, this intensifies for him the urgency of the problem he inherits from Wang Yangming, the "dilemma of the rational mystic." He must discover some way in which "words" can have value—can be other than "empty." And this will necessarily be to overcome the gulf that seems to exist between "words" and the real world of experience and action, that is to say, the reality of human feeling and of history. This aim, in fact, shapes Zhang's criticism of belles lettres, and of any kind of scholarly or philosophical writing as well: good literature, poetry for example, he holds, gains its contact with reality by its genuineness— by springing spontaneously and unforced from the feelings of the writer, without being a conscious striving after art for its own sake. Other kinds of writing, and any kind of scholarly work, are praiseworthy if they are dictated both by a person's native bent, and by the particular problems presented to that person by his or her particular tradition and particular historical lot. One must have "one's own work to do," as Zhang puts it, one's own specialty, and concentrate upon it. In this way the writer, whether poet or scholar, escapes from the "dilemma of the rational mystic." One uses words, but not deliberately to air one's views or gain a reputation. One writes because one has to; and just because of this bond of necessity between one's words and the real world, one's words are part of that world. But if this is so, they have no absolute meaning taken by themselves; to understand and judge them, we as critics must always approach them in the context of their author's personality and the historical circumstances of their production.

16.3 Zhang's Theories of History

Now let us turn to Zhang's theories of history—that is, of the historical process. (And let me make it clear that I am saying nothing directly now of his many critical ideas and proposals about historical writing.) Zhang has a theory of the history of Chinese civilization—and this of course for him was simply Civilization—down to classical times, and this theory incorporates his view of the Classics. In the beginning of human society there was something he calls *dao*: "truth," we may translate it, but it seems to be for him a sort of inexpressible principle of social organization, which has only and just such form as society developing in history gives it. As human beings multiply, society becomes more complex; laws and moral standards evolve, likewise schools and land and family systems; gradually the familiar forms and power arrangements of classical feudal China take shape, each new development being an inevitable and natural solution to some problem presented by the growing complexity of the whole. Ultimately the problem of organization becomes so great that it becomes necessary to have one person at the top. Here begins the succession of sage-emperors which traditional Chinese legend describes. But these sages, while they have Heaven-given ability, owe their greatness and fame not to any deliberate *attempt* to bestow wisdom upon humanity. They simply solved each problem as it arose, devising new institutions, patterns of behavior, principles of right, and instructing their people as might be necessary. In this natural and necessary way, human knowledge developed, and because it was functional knowledge, serving the needs of society and state (note that in Zhang's conception the two are not separate), it grew in the form of specialized technical traditions—of divination, of history, of ritual, of poetry even—within government offices. Officials were teachers, and as Zhang puts it, there was a unity of "government" and "doctrine." The Classics are the vestiges or distillations of these official traditions which historical accident or the foresight of Confucius have preserved for posterity. Somehow—Zhang is unable to say quite how—this ancient perfect society reached a peak of perfection in the Western Zhou state, and then, just before the time of Confucius, it disintegrated. With its disintegration, officials ceased to be teachers and the various official traditions went their several private ways, in the form of the various philosophical schools and separate disciplines of learning and writing. And as they became separated from their roots in the reality of the ancient society-state, they inevitably deteriorated in worth.

Let us now note what Zhang has done in constructing this myth. His ancient golden age is rather plainly a realization in history of something we could call — not indeed in all of Wang Yangming's sense — a "unity of knowledge and action": officials were teachers; government and doctrine, the active and the cognitive aspects of society, were identical. In fact, I should not overstress Zhang's originality in these views, for Wang's idealization of ancient society as an integrated harmonious whole had been rather similar to Zhang's own. The status of learning, and consequently of any writing, in this society is in two respects as Zhang would have it in his own time: it is specialized, and it is the natural product of necessity. The sage-ruler likewise is a model for the person of letters: the sage produces, articulates knowledge, but only in response to concrete need. Zhang actually describes the process of the evolution of civilization through the agency of the sage, and the process of literary creation or the production of original scholarship, in exactly the same words: "There must first be some need," he writes, "and afterwards the filling of it, first some grief and then the venting of it, first some abuse and then the remedying of it; one must not simply make a show of fine-sounding words in order to make a name for oneself" (2.46). A show of fine-sounding words is emphatically what the Classics are not; and in the sort of writing the Classics are, Zhang has his example of writing at its best. What Zhang has done, obviously, is to project into the historical past, and into the Confucian Classics themselves, his ideals of *writing*, and these ideals in turn were his solution to a metaphysical and psychological problem he inherited from late Neo-Confucian thought. It is worth noting that although in describing his theory of ancient history I have ended with his conception of post-Confucian genres of learning and writing, in the development of his own thought, this was the point at which Zhang himself had started. It was in the history of genres of writing that he was first interested, and his first attempt at historical theory resulted from his reflections on the ideas of the court bibliographer Liú Xīn 劉歆 of the first century B.C., which are found in the treatise on bibliography in the "standard history" of the Former Han Dynasty, *Qián Hàn shū* 前漢書. It is this occupation we find Zhang engaged in in his own bibliographical work, the *Jiaochou tongyi*, which he finished in 1779.[9]

I have remarked that there is a difficulty in explaining why Zhang should have brought his evolutionary development of history to a climax, and to a close, with the age preceding Confucius. In one sense there is no puzzle, for such an apocalyptic view of history — to use Collingwood's term (1946, 50) — that is, a conception of history as reaching a decisive turning point, and this in early Zhou, was common enough in Chinese thought (Nivison 1966, 291). For Zhang to have accepted the common notion was natural. Nonetheless, if we examine his notion of historical evolution, there seems to be no reason why this evolution should ever have stopped; for Zhang's *dao*, which develops within the historical process, is not a preexistent formal absolute which unfolds within history. For Zhang to have thought this would have been to admit the existence of a "truth" apart from actual "things," a situation which clearly his philosophy could not tolerate. His *dao grows* in history, and in principle any new historical development should be a further stage in its growth. An outright theory of progress was impossible for Zhang, but he is sensitive to this implication of his thought, and as a result, perhaps, in his conception of post-classical history devolutionary and evolutionary ideas are mixed; actually his ideas about history since the fifth century B.C. are worked out to fit the immediate need in the course of what remains his major interest, the tracing out of the later traditions of writing.

But while Zhang has no single theory of later history which unifies all of his thought about it, he does have a theory which pretends at least to cover the entire expanse of that history. For its boldness and sophistication, as well as for the evidence it provides of how Zhang does his historical thinking, this theory merits our attention. In it, once again we find him applying to the broad canvas of history certain assumptions about the nature of creative thought and expression. In working out this theory—my reconstruction of it here is based on several of his essays and letters which were written from 1789 to 1791— Zhang starts with an analysis of the process of forming conceptions; in forming a conception, he argues, we suppose that a fragment of the real world has a certain character, a certain structure; this is an ad hoc, pragmatic supposition, and by its means we are able to deal with such problems as the world presents. But the real world (as anyone after Wang Yangming would have to feel) is in fact quite unstructured, without fixed character or form, and our conceptions of it are consequently forever inappropriate to it. After a certain lapse of time their inappropriateness is obvious, and we "correct" them. The specific example Zhang uses of this state of affairs is the development and revision of systems of astronomy. But in this pragmatic theory of conception Zhang does not arrive at a notion of hypothesis—that is, of an infinite perfectibility of knowledge. For what he fixes on in mental constructs is not their function as enabling us to deal with, to approach the world, but—again an almost inevitable Neo-Confucian attitude—upon their *otherness from* the world. The correction of a construct once its error has become manifest itself contains an error, which in due time will make itself equally apparent in an opposite quarter. Consequently there is no progress, only an endless sequence of conception and revision, with the revision becoming the new conception which in turn will have to be revised.

Now, it is Zhang's suggestion that there is a close analogy to this situation in the total movement of intellectual history since classical times; only here, instead of the clear-cut constructs of astronomy, we find total attitudes toward the world, emphases of interest which dominate the intellectual life of an age:

Zhang's word for them is *fēngqì* 風氣—tendencies or fashions. At first such a fashion seems to solve all of the intellectual needs of its age; but it is inescapably one-sided, and as time passes its inadequacies become painfully apparent; it is then succeeded by another. We may note that this situation was not typical of the classical golden age; but the reason it was not is precisely because then human knowledge was perfectly at one with the real world of social experience and action. With the disintegration of the golden state, when government and doctrine went their separate ways, people ceased to be able to maintain a total, perfectly balanced attitude perfectly appropriate to the whole of the human situation; they became necessarily one-sided in their views. Once human knowledge became separate from reality, the succession of intellectual fashions in history then followed from metaphysical necessity.

It remains for Zhang to say what these "fashions" are, and to specify the order of their succession. Here too we find him taking psychological facts involved in the creative process—and this time, those which as he sees it are involved particularly in historical writing—and projecting them onto the face of history itself. Zhang starts with two passages in earlier historiographical criticism which excited his imagination greatly. The ancient philosopher Mencius, commenting on the *Spring and Autumn Annals* (*Chūnqiū* 春秋, later supposed to be the work of Confucius himself), said of it that "its style (*wén* 文) is the historical, its subject-matter (*shì* 事) is the affairs of Duke Huán of Qí 齊桓公 and Duke Wén of Jìn 晉文公, and as for its meaning (*yì* 義) it was with this that the Master [Confucius] concerned himself" (5.155).[10] Historical writing then, said Zhang (and he might as well have said any kind of writing), has three dimensions: style, or form; content, or fact; and significance, or meaning. Zhang then turned to the famous Tang Dynasty historical critic Liú Zhījī 劉知幾. One of Liu's most quoted remarks had been an epigrammatic statement of the qualities that a good historian must have. These qualities, said Liu, are talent (*cái* 才)—which is to say, literary talent—learning (*xué* 學), and understanding (*shì* 識). This trichotomy, Zhang saw, could be nicely correlated with that of Mencius, in a set of three mutually interdependent pairs: talent and form, learning and fact, understanding and meaning. These three categories are accounted for by a deeper analysis—there are, Zhang suggests, in human nature three faculties, which fully developed become Liu Zhiji's qualities. These are, a faculty of expression (*zuòxìng* 作性), a faculty of memory (*jìxìng* 記性), and a faculty of intuition (*wùxìng* 悟性). Now, differently developed and expressed, these basic faculties account for three fundamental kinds of intellectual interest, respectively literary art, philology (that is, the study of facts), and philosophy. Here we are back to the three lines of emphasis from which, we recall, Zhang held the sensible person ought to make a choice and in one of which one ought to concentrate one's energy, if one's intellectual life is to be successful. It now turns out that it is just these three lines of interest which constitute the "fashions" which succeed each other in the larger history of the mind. The first to appear was philology, obviously the dominant interest of the Han. Then came literary art, in the Six Dynasties and Tang; following that, philosophy, in the Song, Yuan, and Ming, which were the ages of speculation. The Qing, Zhang suggested, had brought in a new age of philology. But already he found this going to excess: it was time to correct matters, he thought, by a shift of emphasis toward literary expression (without, in the process, abandoning the virtues of "solid learning"), and this he conceived as his own mission. Here is one more indication of the fundamental seriousness of Zhang's interest in literary criticism.

In taking this role for himself, Zhang shows once more his belief as to how the life of letters is justified. For in discussing his notion of intellectual "fashion" he stresses again and again that one must recognize the task that history sets one and do that: when a "fashion" is on the ascendent one should join and support it; when it is decaying, one should oppose it. But perhaps this conception is not for Zhang the noble call to duty it appears to be; for though it fits his solution of the dilemma of the rational mystic—that one's words are justifiable and valuable if one speaks from historical necessity—we can nonetheless detect a note of rationalization in the view; for Zhang, after all, did not *like* the classical philology of his day, and his antipathy to it is not only philosophical but deeply rooted in his early conditioning. In his theory of "fashions" he has found a comforting self-justification for his lonely note of protest.

Two Kinds of "Naturalism": Dai Zhen and Zhang Xuecheng[1]

17

17.1 Introduction

The philosophies of Dài Zhèn 戴震 (1723–1777) and of Zhāng Xuéchéng 章學誠 (1738–1801) can be briefly described for the purpose of this paper.

17.1.1 Dai and Zhang

Dai rejected the distinction the Song Dynasty philosophers made between "principle" (*lǐ* 理) and "matter" (*qì* 氣). *Li* is not a separate "thing" given by Heaven to man as his "nature" (*xìng* 性). And it is not a moral directedness antithetical to "desire" (*yù* 欲). On the contrary, man, as a part of the universal processes of nature (*tiān dì zhī huà* 天地之化, the *dào* 道 of Heaven which is good in itself), has both desire (*yu*) and intelligence (*jué* 覺). These are "the natural" (*zìrán* 自然) for man. When "the natural" is refined to the utmost degree (*jí zhì* 極致), so that nothing is "amiss" (*shī* 失), the result is an "unchanging standard" (*bú yì zhī zé* 不易之則) which Dai calls "the necessary" (*bìrán* 必然). This Dai identifies with "principle" (*li*). The sages have been able to do this, thereby discovering what *biran* is, and (as Mencius said in 6A7) "anticipating what our hearts have in common" (先得我心之所同然). Moral orientation is therefore not antithetical to human desire but is in some sense desire in its purest form. In other words, in denying the metaphysical distinction between "principle" and "matter" Dai is committing himself to a program of explaining "principle," standards of right and good, as aspects of the natural world, as, so to speak, "moral facts," explainable in terms of needs, desires, and emotions. But moral truth is only what *all* hearts have in common. Therefore an intuition or mere opinion (*yìjiàn* 意見) must not be identified with "principle." One must apply the Confucian principle of reciprocity (*shù* 恕) to make sure that what one thinks is right is what all would insist on. But, of course, this has already been done by the sages, whose perfect intelligence and perfection of "the natural" in themselves has led them to "the necessary," which they have put in writing in the Classics. The highest intellectual calling is that study which enables us to read the Classics and understand this *dao*. This is Classical philology, which enables us to understand the words in the Classics, thereby understanding the statements in them, thereby understanding the *dao*.

Dai was a classical philologist.

Zhang accepted the Song metaphysical dualism Dai rejected, characterized by him as the distinction between "principle" and "affairs and things" (*shì wù* 事物) and (for him as for the Chéng-Zhū 程朱 tradition) the equivalent distinction between *dao* and "embodiment" or "implement" (*qì* 器). However (again a common though not universal Cheng-Zhu position) Zhang insisted that these things are actually and conceptually "inseparable."[2] So, in a way, Zhang's naturalism is even more radical than Dai's: for him, if he is strict with himself, a moral "principle" may not even be abstracted conceptually or verbally from its matrix of "affairs and things." *Dao*, in some sense rooted in the nature of the universe ("Heaven," *tiān* 天), also is "in" man, manifesting itself in the social and historical development that results from man's effort to satisfy the concrete needs of life. But the inseparability of *dao* and its manifestations means that *dao* or *li* cannot be abstracted and reduced to written statements. The developing human moral and political order as civilization evolves is the manifestation of *dao*, not *dao* itself (可形其形而名其名者皆道之故而非道也). As the process goes on, leadership roles evolve, requiring the ablest in the world to fill them. So develops the distinction between "sage" (*shèngrén* 聖人) and "ordinary men" (*zhòngrén* 眾人), who take part in the evolving manifestation in different ways. First Zhang distinguishes the *dao* itself, which is the "why" (*suǒyǐrán* 所以然) of things and is "natural" or "so of itself" (*zìrán* 自然), from what men see and understand, which is the way things "should be" (*dāngrán* 當然). But the ordinary man is involved in life unreflectively; his so doing is the *ziran* of *dao*. The sage, with his overview of the historical needs of his time, sees what is necessary, i.e., what "must be" (*bù dé bù rán* 不得不然), and makes laws and institutions accordingly, thus moving the *dao*-manifestation onward. This process culminated with the world order of the Duke of Zhōu (周公), and the residual literary products of the process, the surviving documents of the government of the ancient sage kings, were edited for preservation by Confucius in the Classics. The Classics are therefore not "books recording the dao" (*zài dào zhī shū* 載道之書) but residues of the *dao*'s historical manifestation, through which the *dao* can be grasped only intuitively by someone reading them as "history." The highest intellectual calling is to understand the Classics in this way and to continue their representation of the working out of *dao* in human affairs by recording and writing history.

Zhang was a historian.

17.1.2 The Issues

And now, some problems: Zhang Xuecheng in various essays and letters praises Dai Zhen as a philosopher, specifically mentioning as important his "Yuán shàn" (原善) and his "Lùn xìng" (論性) essays ("Analysis of 'Good'" and "On Human Nature," respectively). But almost without exception whenever Zhang writes about *specific* ideas of Dai's, he is critical, and he is reacting to "non-philosophical" ideas, e.g., Dai's views about the writing of *dìfāng zhì* 地方志 (local histories) and his evaluation of the Song encyclopedist Zhèng Qiáo 鄭 樵, whom Zhang admired. Even when Zhang criticizes Dai for disrespect for Zhū Xī 朱熹, he does not identify philosophical theses of Zhu's that Dai should have accepted.

What, exactly, did Zhang think of Dai as a philosopher? Perhaps he merely admired Dai's *Yuan shan* "for the fact that it was a piece of philosophy by a philologist, and because it represented a side of Dai that, Zhang could tell himself, only he could appreciate" (Nivison 1966, 47). But in view of interesting similarities in their quite different philosophical viewpoints,[3] the first conjecture is not likely to be adequate: for it suggests that Zhang simply ignored the *content* of Dai's philosophy.

I will argue that Zhang was, on the contrary, very interested in Dai's ideas, that he read all of Dai's philosophical writings available to him, and that sometimes Dai's detailed arguments and even his phrasings are reflected in Zhang's essays. I will argue that Zhang identified, correctly, Dai's central philosophical problem, and recognized it as his own. That problem was this: how can we give a rational account of the human world of value—human norms and goals—in terms of an abstract picture of the world as a whole in which norms and "virtue" are not explicitly posited—in such a way as to explain and justify our study and veneration of the Confucian classics? And conversely, how can we give a plausible natural account of the origin and nature of the Classics such that, given the respect we have for them, they in turn justify the personal values and goals we do have? The second part of this problem each philosopher dealt with successfully from his own viewpoint. But I will argue that both philosophers failed to solve the first part of this problem, the justification of the Classics, and for the same reason, although their approaches were so different that this similarity can be uncovered only by careful analysis.

Accordingly, this study has two parts: one historical and one critical. The *historical* problem is to chronicle, exactly, Zhang's becoming acquainted with Dai's ideas either through conversations or reading, and his adaptation of those ideas in his own writing. The *critical* problem will be to analyze and consider the cogency of each man's attempted solution to the problems of value posed above. In Dai, we are concerned with a thesis that is expressed both in the *Yuan shan* and (more explicitly) in the *Mèngzǐ zìyì shùzhèng* (孟子字義疏證). In Zhang we are concerned with a thesis that is suffused through a very large part of his writing but is most fully and explicitly set forth in his essays "Yuán dào" (原道, "Analysis of '*Dao*'") and "Yuán xué" (原學, "Analysis of 'Learning'").[4]

After these perspectives are duly perspected, it will be appropriate to notice that both Dai and Zhang were human beings who had a very human problem we all have; and, finally, to notice how much of this study is and must be conjecture.

17.2 The Historical Problem

As Yü Ying-shih (1976, 69, 85) has happily put it, Dai and Zhang were hedge-hogs (acknowledgements to Archilochus and Isaiah Berlin). It is characteristic of a hedgehog not just that he "knows one big thing" but that this is the one idea he *must* think. Translated into his behavior as a writer, this means he spends the meaningful part of his life writing and rewriting the same book. Plato did it. Marx (as Robert Tucker [1972] has brilliantly shown) did it. Dai did it. Zhang did it. Dai's one book began with the original three "Yuan shan" essays (in which he tries cryptically to derive "goodness" from the metaphysical clouds by constructing what are virtually mandalas of abstract concepts), with two supporting essays on *xìng* 性 (human nature) in the 1750s. It continues with the recasting of the essays into a book, *Yuan shan*, in 1766 and the completion of the *Xù yán* (緒言) in 1772. This was apparently soon followed by another attempt, only recently published for the first time, *Mèngzǐ sīshú lù* (孟子私淑錄); these two both are and are not early drafts of his *Mengzi ziyi shuzheng*[5] (hereafter referred to as "MZZYSZ"). With the last Dai stopped (1776), only because he died the next year. Zhang's book began with the "Hezhou Gazetteer" ("Hézhōu zhì" 和州志, 1774), was written again in the treatise on library science philosophically considered (*Jiàochóu tōngyì* 校讎通義, 1779, reworked in 1788), and yet again in the explosion of essays from 1789 to 1792, the central vision being what he says in the "Yuan dao" and its elaboration "Yuan xue" in spring-summer, 1789.

17.2.1 Chronology

I give herewith my chronological account of important thoughts, writings, encounters, and publications of the two men from 1755 to 1792.[6]

1755 Dai's letter to Fāng Jǔ (方矩) on the relative value of Han and Song Dynasty learning, identifying philosophy, philology, and literary art (see below) as the three principal ways for the person of letters (Qian 1957, 317).

1757–1763 Dai's three *essays*, "Yuan shan" ("Analysis of 'Good'") written (Qian 1957, 327).

c. 1764 Zhang's letters to Zhēn Sōngnián (甄松年) discussing among other things the nature of the Classics, attempting to see them as archetypes of writing, but *not* conceiving them yet as products of the historical process (Nivison 1966, 29–30).

1766 Dai uses the three "Yuan shan" essays as opening essays in a three-*juàn*

卷 expanded *book* with the same title, *Yuan shan*, incorporating his two essays on human nature (Qian 1957, 326). Dai and Zhang meet in the Xiūníng 休寧 hostelry in Běijīng 北京, probably discussing the "three ways" idea (see above) and the *Yuan shan* (which Dai probably showed to Zhang) (Yu 1976, 11–12).

1769 Dai writes (quickly) the first draft of his *Xu yan*, openly critical of "Song Confucians" and their *li-qi* distinction (Qian 1957, 328).

1770 (or earlier) Zhang by this time is interested in the ideas of Liú Xīn 劉歆 about the evolution of schools of philosophy from the offices of the Zhou Dynasty state, as indicated in a poem by Zhū Yún (朱筠) addressed to Zhang (Nivison 1966, 42–43, note a).

1772 Dai writes his finished version of the *Xu yan* (Qian 1957, 329). The *Sìkù quánshū* 四庫全書 project is begun (see Nivison 1966, 7), probably with Zhang's ideas a factor.

1773 Encounters between Zhang and Dai at literary gatherings in Níngbō 寧波 and Hángzhōu 杭州, at which Dai and Zhang disagree about gazetteer-writing, and Dai displeases Zhang with unrestrained criticism of Zheng Qiao and Zhu Xi (Nivison 1966, 47–49).

1774 Zhang completes the (never fully published) "Hezhou Gazetteer," internal prefaces of which are statements of his speculative philosophy of history and literature.

1776 Dai finishes the MZZYSZ (about half of it anticipated in or taken from the *Xuyan*). The preface is dated 1776. In this book Dai explicitly criticizes Zhu Xi as well as other "Song Philosophers" for importing Buddhist-Daoist ideas into Confucian philosophy.

1777 Dai dies in the fifth month.[7] In the eighth month *Yuan shan* and probably also the MZZYSZ were printed.[8]

1778 Zhang obtains *jìnshì* 進士 degree (Nivison 1966, 8–9, 53).

1779 Zhang finishes the first version of the *Jiaochou tongyi*; the "Yuan dao" in the opening *juan* restates the thesis of the "Hezhou Gazetteer" and anticipates his later three-part essay "Yuan dao" (Nivison 1966, 56).

1788 Zhang revises the *Jiaochou tongyi*, and begins the *Shǐjí kǎo* (史籍考) project, guided by the idea that all writing is historical material.

1789 The most important essays of Zhang's *Wénshǐ tōngyì* (文史通義) are written, including the three-part "Yuan dao" and the three-part "Yuan xue," and probably also the "Zhu [and] Lu") (Nivison 1966, 103–5).

1790 Zhang meets Duàn Yùcái 段玉裁. Zhang's "Postscript to the Essay on Zhu and Lu" ("Shū Zhū Lù piān hòu," 書朱陸篇後, hereafter referred to as "Postscript") was probably written this year. In it Zhang says (a) that Dai's philosophical writings, various essays such as the "essays on human nature and 'Analysis of "Good"'" (論性原善諸篇) are really Dai's most important work, though nobody realizes this; (b) that Dai's *writing* about philosophy is good, but his *talk* about philosophy was too unrestrained and disrespectful of the Song philosophers (Nivison 1966, 107, 105n. o; Qian 1957, 387–88).

1792 Duan Yucai publishes his *wénjí* (文集, "literary collection") of Dai Zhen in 12 *juan*, a rearrangement and expansion of the 10 *juan wenji* published shortly after Dai's death by Kǒng Jìhán 孔繼涵; Duan's preface is dated 1792. The arrangement accords with Zhang's ideas about *wenji*.

17.2.2 Comments on the Chronology

What Did Zhang Learn from Dai?

Notice that Zhang's letters to Zhen Songnian (1763–1765) and the revealing remark in Zhu Yun's poem to Zhang (1770) give us the end points for the critical period of Zhang's thinking out his basic philosophical position. In the middle occurred the first encounter with Dai. In that meeting, if Yü Ying-shih is right, Dai showed Zhang (and perhaps allowed him to borrow and copy) his finished *Yuan shan*, and in discussing it gave his views about the relation between *yìlǐ* (義理, philosophy),[9] *zhìshù* (制數, philology), and *wénzhāng* (文章, literary art). Zhang must have seen that Dai's problem was his own—or at least almost. Dai identified himself as a Classical philologist. The justification for this calling is that the Classics are "books containing the *dao*," statements of the sages' perfect knowledge; and philology is necessary for understanding them. Zhang identified himself differently: his callings were history and (he was deep in *jǔyè* 舉業)[10] literary art. So, he had to ask, how are these things related to the Classics? Simply second-level didactic restatements of the *dao* stated by the sages in the Classics? Zhang couldn't think that; the justification of the things he was doing must be a *direct* connection with the *dao*. But one couldn't suppose them *statements* of anybody's wisdom. A long tradition of literary thought would persuade him that good writing *expresses* ultimate values, it does not *state*.[11] So these things must be direct *expressions*, not *statements*, of *dao*. But if this is the right account of what makes writing valuable, it must account for the value of the Classics too. They too must be expressions, and as such archetypical of all valuable writing. But how? Zhang would have seen that Dai's scheme in the *Yuan shan* too neatly explained, through an abstract picture of human knowledge and psychology, how the sages could be seen as grasping "necessity" and communicating, *stating* their knowledge in the Classics. It couldn't be like this; but Dai was right, in a way: somehow one must see how the *dao* of Heaven became the *dao* of mankind, if there is to be any point in what we all, severally, are doing.

Somewhere in the course of such pondering he must have recalled Liu

Xin's insights about the evolution of the ancient schools of philosophy from the functions of the state. *That* idea could, and should, be applied to the Classics too! But what would this mean? That the *dao* of Heaven becomes the *dao* of mankind not by way of timeless psychological realities leading the sages to perfect *knowledge*, but through the total human *historical experience*, which is the true revelation, of which the Classics are but residues, things: "the Classics are all history" 六經皆史.

I have made this up, of course. We cannot know how the process of creation worked in Zhang's mind. We can know that by 1770 he had found the key to his problem.

How Much of Dai's Work Had Zhang Read?

We can assume that after 1770, Zhang's reaction to Dai and his ideas is guided by (i) admiration for Dai as a philosopher, and, probably, deep reflection on his thought; and (ii) at the same time, an attempt to work out more fully an alternative, along the lines of the insight that Liu Xin suggested to him, to Dai's solution to the problem of the relation of the scholar's life and work to the Classics and to the *dao*. After 1773 is added another motif, (iii) criticism of Dai for his disrespect, as expressed in *oral* argument, of people Zhang thought highly of, notably Zheng Qiao and Zhu Xi. In the 1790 "Postscript," Zhang says explicitly and bitterly that Dai's prestige has made this kind of criticism of Zhu fashionable.

Zhang probably never saw the *Xu yan*. It was not published until long after his death. But Dai did finish it just before their encounter in 1773, and was probably talking freely about the ideas he develops in it.

As for the MZZYSZ, Qian (1957, 388) believes Zhang never saw it. At first I thought so too, and further inferred (as perhaps did Qian) from the "Postscript" that Zhang knew only of the first (1757–1763) version of the "Yuan shan" and "Lun Xing" essays, i.e., that Zhang had not even seen the finished *Yuan shan*. I am now sure that this view is wrong. I have concluded that Zhang by 1789 had read both the finished *Yuan shan* and the MZZYSZ (probably as soon as they were available). I have the following reasons:

(1) Given Dai's fame, and given the fact that Zhang was often in Beijing (the center of literary discussion, and of the book trade) during the decade following Dai's death, the two books must have been easily available to Zhang.

(2) If the books were thus easily available to Zhang, and if he respected Dai as a philosopher as much as he says he did, it is almost inconceivable that he wouldn't have read them at once. They are not long.

(3) There are several (nonconclusive) indications in Zhang's writings that he had read the MZZYSZ:

(3.a) Compare the following line from the opening paragraph of Zhang's essay "Zhu [and] Lu":

理譬則水也事物譬則器也

("'Principle' is like water; activities and things are like vessels.")

with the opening of MZZYSZ 1.2:

性譬則水也欲譬則水之流也

("The nature is like water; desires are like the flowing of water.")

Comparing metaphysical entities with water is common enough.[12] But the 譬則 for "is like" is unusual, and the contrast in the meaning of the two passages puts in a nutshell the difference between Dai's and Zhang's philosophies.

(The "Zhu Lu" is assigned by Hu Shih (1929, 71) to 1789; this dating is followed without argument by Nivison (1966, 105), which observes (n. o), however, that Qian (1957, 422) believes it to have been written before Dai's death. Actually Qian holds that the fact that the "Zhu Lu" does not mention Dai by name shows it to have been written before his death, and for this reason Qian (1957, 419) mentions the essay under the year 1777 (the year of Dai's death) in his chronology of Zhang's writings. Yu (1976, 54, 57) takes the essay definitely to have been written in 1777, without giving reasons. It is even possible that the essay was written still earlier, and that Dai had seen it and was echoing it in MZZYSZ 1.2. But I assume that Dai would not have paid this much attention to Zhang. Also, I assume that Zhang did not see the MZZYSZ until it was published, some months *after* Dai's death; and that he would have had good reason to avoid an explicit written criticism of Dai for some years thereafter anyway. Most of the people on whom he was dependent, or on whom he hoped to become dependent, were Dai's admirers.)

(3.b) In parts of Zhang's three-part "Yuan dao," he appears to be adopting, adapting, and modifying ideas, and even phrases, from Dai's preface to MZZYSZ. For example, the *Analects* says of Confucius, "We cannot hear of the Master's discussing 'nature' and 'the *dao* of Heaven'" (HY 5:13). Dai claims that one does find the Master's discussions of these things in the *Yì jīng* 易經 (parts of which were believed by Dai and his contemporaries to have been written by Confucius). Zhang deals with this same passage from the *Analects* in "Yuan dao" 3.3 (see also 2.2), claiming that Confucius realized that these matters cannot be discussed abstractly, but must be grasped in the actions of the early sage kings; so he assembled and edited the Classics, as his only possible means of showing what the *dao* is. Zhang would have seen this suggested in what immediately follows in the preface (probably also seeing that Dai, with his 載道之書 "books recording the *dao*" conception of the Classics, couldn't really see it):

> When the *dao* of the Zhou dynasty declined, the models of perfect government of Yáo, Shùn, Yǔ, Tāng, Wén, Wǔ, and the Duke of Zhōu (堯舜禹湯文武周公), as brilliantly expressed in writing, were discarded as old residues 陳迹 [of the past]. Confucius, since he did not obtain position 不得位, was not able to pass these things on in the form of institutions, rites, and music [i.e., official cultural forms]. Therefore he established correct texts of them, identifying their sources, enabling people [to understand] the causes of good order and disorder over hundreds and thousands of generations, and what was correct [and incorrect] in the changes over time in institutions, rites, and music, as exactly as they might determine relative weights on a scale, or verify the accuracy of squares, circles, level surfaces, and straight lines by using angles, compasses, levels, and marking lines; his words appear to be lofty and distant, but he could not but speak 不得不言. (MZZYSZ, Preface)

Zhang uses the "residue" 迹 concept with a quite different twist in "Yuan dao" 1.4; he explores the implications of Confucius's "not getting position" 不得位 in "Yuan dao" 2.1.[13] The "could not but speak" 不得不言 idea is pursued in "Yuan dao" 3.2. Note that Zhang could not have read this preface in Dai's *wenji* (even if we can imagine him reading the preface and not going on to read the book). The ten volume *wenji* published in Kong Jihan's series between 1777 and 1779 did not contain this preface, and the twelve volume *wenji* edited by Duan Yucai (which did have it) did not appear until 1792, three years after the "Yuan dao" was written.

In any case, there are other indications that Zhang read farther.

(3.c) Qian (1957, 353; vide Nivison 1966, 144n. c) has noticed that Dai and Zhang are alike in holding (but with different implications) that the *dao* is (was) revealed in the "daily functioning of human relationships" (*rénlún rìyòng* 人倫日用), and alike again (but again in different senses and with different implications) in seeing moral-political truth (as captured or represented in "the necessary")[14] as apprehended by the sage and in some way distilled by the sage from "the natural."[15] If Zhang were consciously adopting and reorienting Dai's "natural-necessary" dichotomy, he need not have read MZZYSZ, for it is already repeatedly stressed in the "Yuan shan" in even its earliest form. But the related *renlun riyong* expression is not in *Yuan shan*, and although Qian says correctly that something like this concept can be found there (e.g., *Yuan shan* 1.6: *rìyòng shìwéi* 日用事為), it would be extraordinary indeed if purely by coincidence Zhang, having noticed this idea in inchoate form in the early *Yuan shan*, had then gone on to develop it in exactly the same terms as Dai in his mature philosophy. The *renlun riyong* phrase and concept occurs in the very first short paragraph of Dai's *Xu yan*. But Dai uses the expression repeatedly in the sections on "*dao*" in the last book of MZZYSZ (3.32 to 3.35). And if Zhang thought (as I believe he did) of his own "Yuan dao" as, *inter alia*, a response to Dai's philosophical position in MZZYSZ, he would have read just these sections with particular care.

(4) Qian (1957, 383) believes that Zhang never saw the *Xu yan* or MZZYSZ. It is true as far as I know that he never mentions either, and it is reasonable to suppose that he never saw the former. Indeed, almost exclusively when he names philosophical writings of Dai's, it is the "Yuan shan" to which he refers; and usually he refers to it as *piān* 篇, suggesting that it is the early *essays* he has in mind. In the "Postscript" he does also refer to the "Lun xing" essays, i.e., "A Discussion of Human Nature on Reading the *Yi jing* Appendices" 讀易繫辭論性 and "A Discussion of Human Nature on Reading the *Mengzi*" 讀孟子論性, but this just confirms that he is thinking of the early essay stage of the *Yuan shan*, because in its final "book" form the work *includes* the "Lun xing" essays (as 1.3 and 2.4 respectively). Does not this prove that, even if Zhang at some time did see the MZZYSZ, at least he had *not* seen or even noticed it prior to 1790 (or whenever the "Postscript" was written)?

No. The point of Zhang's remarks in the "Postscript" about Dai's philosophical writing is not at all to catalog what he had read. He is merely *tagging* Dai's philosophical work by mentioning what he could expect would be the best known pieces, and the point of his remarks is to insist that Dai's admirers are blind in dismissing his most important work as worthless — while he, Zhang Xuecheng, alone has the penetration to see their significance and value; a claim made the more dramatic in that it is combined with stiff criticism of Dai on other matters. In writing this, Zhang wasn't looking at the philosophical essays at all. He was looking at Dai's *preface* to the finished *Yuan shan*, only a few sentences long, in which Dai concludes:

> Since present times are now far removed from the wisdom of the sages of old, no scholars who work on the Classics are able to have a comprehensive understanding of it; they are stuck in their own perspectives, and fashion "truth" of cumulative error; and so I am afraid my words will not be enough to shake these dangling ends. So I have stored this away in my family schoolroom, to await a capable person to bring it forth.

Reading this piece of hypocritical conceit—after having tried to get through Dai's provocatively (and deliberately) opaque first "Yuan shan" essay—I was just a bit angry. Zhang Xuecheng, with a different viewpoint, must have been flattered. He incessantly projects a self-image as a person who understands things no one else can grasp. Dai in his preface was patently bidding for *cognoscenti* support. Zhang in his "Postscript" was rising to the bait.

Zhang probably wrote the "Postscript" after talking with Duan Yucai in 1790 when they met in Wǔchāng 武昌. Duan was probably already working on, or thinking about, the editing of his revision of Dai's *wenji*, which in fact is organized somewhat on the line Zhang recommended for *wenji* (Nivison, 1966, 121–24), i.e., disregarding literary forms and attending chiefly to content: thus, *juan* eight, containing philosophical pieces, includes essays (*lùn* 論), prefaces (*xù* 序), and relevant letters (*shū* 書). Notably, this *juan* does contain the preface to the finished *Yuan shan* (as the Kong *wenji* does not), together with the early "Yuan shan" and "Lun xing" essays.

(5) And (this will close the circle) we can be almost certain that Zhang did *not* mention in the "Postscript" *all* of Dai's philosophical writings he had read, even if we disregard the MZZYSZ problem. For he does not mention Dai's "Essay on Models and Images" ("Fǎ xiàng lùn" 法象論) which occurs at the very beginning of the philosophical *juan* of Duan's *wenji*, and *also* in Kong's *wenji* immediately preceding the three "Yuan shan" essays. But Zhang surely had read this essay by 1789. Nivison (1966, 154) notes that Zhang expresses views in his essay "On Learning" ("Yuan xue") that "are curiously like [Dai Zhen's]" in the way in which here he marks the difference between the ordinary person and the sage as a difference in inner perfection (it being in this way that the sages are the source of our moral knowledge of "standards," rather than, as in "Yuan dao," through their historical vision and creativity). Heaven gives us an "image" of correctness in the "virtue" and "position" of the sage; we then take the sage as a "model." (This *xiang fa* language is from the *Yi jing*.) This is not Dai's thought (he is cosmological, deriving human norms and roles from celestial *xiang*; thus "the sun is the *xiang* of the ruler.") But it seems to be one more of Zhang's attempts to say in comprehensible human terms what Dai should have said. If so, it is confirmation as well that the "Yuan dao" too is an attempt by Zhang to say what Dai should have said. For, in his letter to Chén Jiàntíng 陳鑑亭 in the winter of 1789, Zhang states that he wrote the "Yuan xue" to develop certain ideas in the "Yuan dao" (Nivison, 1966, 154).

(6) One objection remains. Qian (1957, 333) points out that Zhang

distinguished between Dai's criticism of the Cheng brothers and Zhu Xi in verbal discussion and his criticisms in writing, accepting the latter, but objecting to the former as excessive, disrespectful, a case of "forgetting one's origins." And, Qian notes, Dai's *Xuyan* (finished in 1772) is "still not like this" (so even if Zhang had seen it he need not have been offended). But (Qian 1957, 353) the MZZYSZ makes direct attacks on Zhu's quasi-Buddhist-Daoist antithesis between *li* and "desire" (*yu*), as inducing people to take their own "opinions" (*yijian*) as *li*, thus "bringing calamity on the world" (Qian 1957, 349; MZZYSZ 3.40). Does not this show that Zhang could not have seen the MZZYSZ, at least until after writing the "Postscript"?

We need not suppose this. What we lack is anything like a transcript of any *oral* argument Dai engaged in. He may, as a talker, have been far more severe than he was at any point in the MZZYSZ. Furthermore, what Zhang objected to was not reasoned criticism of Zhu (he engages in this himself, e.g., at the end of the first "Yuan dao" essay as printed in early editions); what riled him was disparagement. Criticism should be combined with respect: Zhang praises Dai for taking this approach to Zhèng Xuán 鄭玄.[16]

In what follows, I will — experimentally — assume the case established, that Zhang's 1789 "Yuan dao" does not just present a philosophy interestingly different from Dai Zhen's but actually is intended to be read as a response to Dai's views as he finally stated them. It is of course more than this. And it is of course also true that Zhang's philosophy is diffused through many other writings of different kinds: this is the way he wrote. But I suspect that when we are tempted to compare and contrast this or that position in the "Yuan dao" with positions of Dai's, we are doing just what Zhang intended. This would resolve the paradox of Zhang seemingly both praising Dai as a philosopher and ignoring his philosophy. He did not ignore it, I suspect, but in fact paid it the ultimate respect of really serious criticism.

17.3 The Critical Problem

Let me try in a quite arbitrary way to set in a schematic order some (not all) possible and at various times held views of the place of morality in the universe.[17]

17.3.1 Six Alternatives

(1) **Divine Command Theory** There is a divine law-giver who has commanded us to do this and that. Morality is commands, and being moral is obeying explicit commands.[18]

(2) **Dissolved Theism** The identity of the commander is dissolved in the universe ("Heaven"), which not only commands but also produces humans whose nature enables them to obey and disposes (at least some of) them to "listen," to ascertain by intuition or conscience or special intelligence what the commands are. Being moral is perfecting one's "virtue" so as always to obey these commands.[19]

(3) **Teleological Naturalism** The universe (whether God-like or not) is not a giver of *explicit* commands; however, the universe is not morally neutral either. It has a sort of teleological structure; it produces humans disposed to formulate and follow moral rules—not just any rules, but the right ones—and thereby indirectly creates the moral order. Certain forms of this position may allow the universe to be moral in other ways as well: e.g., favoring humans when they behave morally, or itself exhibiting processes (e.g., "productiveness") which are felt to be structurally similar to human moral behavior (e.g., "benevolence").[20]

(4) **Constructivist Naturalism** The universe just *is*, devoid of anything like intention toward humans, who nonetheless are natural products of the causal processes of the universe. However, humans are so constituted, and so situated in relation to other things and animals, that they have needs (outer-economic or inner-psychological or both) which can only be satisfied by a social-moral order, which they therefore either evolve or invent (if the latter, somehow accepting for themselves the rules they invent not just as counsels of prudence but as moral obligations). But the difference between right and wrong, and good and bad, is still a real one. Moral statements have truth value for us insofar as what they enjoin is, at least for us and for now, necessary for any mode of life a person fully enlightened as to his or her own needs would choose. And although we are not predisposed toward any particular standards, we do have the capacity to conceive of and accept a requirement as a moral one.[21]

(5) **Existentialism** The universe just *is*, indifferent to humans, not only in not wanting anything of them but also in not having set them in a situation that tends in any way to make one course "right" for them and another "wrong." The one aspect of ourselves that is morally significant is that we make choices. In choosing this course over that, I create what is right for me, and as commitment this choice creates my "nature." I have total responsibility for what shall be my moral world.[22]

(6) **Non-Cognitivism** The facts are that we have desires, and that we have a stubborn tendency to say things like "this is good" or "that is right," and to think that we are saying something true, when in fact we are merely expressing our tastes or approval, and encouraging others to share them. Moral "statements" are not really statements at all.

I shall not apologize for the inadequacy of this list, as a taxonomy of either religious or moral views (though inadequate it is — try fitting Vedanta onto it). A generally adequate schema would have to be multi-dimensional, not linear. I want merely to find out more, if possible, about Dai and Zhang. Neither philosopher espouses anything like the Divine Command Theory of (1). And neither intends, I think, that his position be the Dissolved Theism of (2), though surely many people around them all the time accepted it quite unreflectively. And although Dai (in his last period especially, but really in the *Yuan shan* too) insistently grounds morality in human *desire*, he is not thinking of anything like the Non-Cognitivism of (6), or the Existentialism of (5); still less is Zhang, despite the similar importance he assigns to human *needs*.

If the list has a use in this context, we must be concerned with positions (3) and (4).

17.3.2 Xunzi

There is a notorious problem in positions of type (4), which is variously shaped and described as the "is-ought" problem, or the (supposed) "naturalistic fallacy" or the problem whether morality has an "independent bottom," etc.[23] In Xúnzǐ 荀子, who belongs essentially in (4), this problem takes two forms.

Xunzi appears to reason as follows: As enlightened philosopher I might see that my human situation makes it most *advantageous* for me to become a being whose motivations are genuinely *moral*. Humans are "evil"; they have unruly desires; so their actions must be curbed and ordered if any of these desires are to be satisfied. Therefore, I make a *consequentialist* decision to accept a *deontological* point of view.[24] Since the decision is a meta-decision, there is no contradiction in this. Once I have become socialized (or "moralized" perhaps) you cannot fairly challenge me to derive my morality from my presocialized picture of the universe. But it does look as though, in my original enlightened position, I do not really regard "morality" as morality. Morality is an illusion, really, in this point of view, though the world is such that human beings must, and should ("should" in a utilitarian sense) come to have it. Xunzi tries to resolve this difficulty (e.g., in the "Essay on Heaven") by rapt expansion on the cosmic beauty of the universal order that includes humans with their self-made morality — Heaven, Earth, the sage, ritual, in intercausal coexistence — thus trying to give enlightened philosophers a higher reason to love the *dao* that, rationally, they see as useful.[25] But one may still ask whether utility plus cosmic beauty account for morality as *moral* — whether, e.g., they can show me why I am doing something morally *wrong* if I fail to observe mourning for my parents.

Of course, it may be that this apparent difficulty in Xunzi simply shows that we must take his cosmic picture as a picture of a universe that is not just beautiful but *morally* good, even though Xunzi's "Heaven" is not a divine being that could care about humanity. In him, we could say, theism is not only dissolved but washed away; but it leaves behind a *moral curvature* to the whole, like the smile of the Cheshire cat. If so, Xunzi is to this extent in position (3), and we can say that since the actual moral order (as Xunzi would insist anyway) is *necessary* for a satisfying life, and since it is right that humans live such a life, this order is as a whole and in detail in fact morally obligatory for us. And, fortunately, I as a human being have the capacity to come to see it in this way: although I have an "evil" nature (of conflict-generating desires), I also have *yì* 義, by which I suggest Xunzi means an unfilled, open capacity to form the *concept* of an obligation as a *moral* one rather than just as a cause-effect problem of what I must do if I am to get what I want.[26]

But if Xunzi (given sufficient charity) escapes this form of the difficulty, he fails (or needs even more charity) on a second form: Even supposing that the "moral" order really is moral and that I can come to accept it as such, how could the moral order have come into being as a human possession at all— again, supposing that we want to give a plausible naturalistic account, and avoid simply assuming *ad hoc* that it was *given* to humans. Xunzi says the "sages" invented it, being very intelligent and having seen the need for it. Yet these sages, like everyone, had "evil" desiderative "natures." How could the sages, even supposing there were such beings of perfect *intelligence*, have invented morality, which was a *good* thing, before they themselves had been transformed by that morality? Well, Xunzi half says they did it bit by bit, by cumulative intelligent decisions and acts (*jī wèi* 積僞). Perhaps this points to a way out of the difficulty, but in Xunzi it remains a difficulty.

17.3.3 Mencius

If category (4) was designed for Xunzi, category (3) was designed for Mencius. Mencius gives himself more in initial assumptions and perhaps has an easier time of it. There is a benevolent Heaven which both decrees (*mìng* 命) morality—though not explicitly—and so makes it right; and creates us with a mental-emotional tendency to savor and relish it for itself. If over time as need be we give priority to the inclinations of our hearts (*xīn* 心) over our other desires (which we can really see, if we reflect, to be of lower order), we will both find out more exactly what morality is—what, exactly, would perfectly satisfy our moral sensibilities—and at the same time strengthen our taste for it. As with Xunzi (who followed Mencius in this) there were sages who have figured this out for us; but (like Xunzi again) they were human like us, and we could be sages too. Again like Xunzi, Mencius sometimes gives consequentialist arguments for being committed to morality for its own sake (and he can do this without contradiction, since this is a meta-choice).[27] And it is worth noting that Mencius is not a moral hedonist: The point about morality being enjoyable is that, in this benevolently ordered universe, we are so constituted that it is easy for us to be moral. But what does seem puzzling is why the "sages" are needed in this picture at all. Did they not do only what, ex hypothesi, we could do for ourselves?

Notice that, if we take Mencius and Xunzi together, they pose a dilemma: On one account it is difficult to see why we should see the sages as having any special authority for their discovery of morality. On the other account, in which they *invented* it and were necessary for its inception, and so have their authority, it seems impossible to explain how they could have done this. This dilemma was the ancient form of a similar dilemma in justifying the Classics, which are supposed to be the words of the sages. Either the Classics are unnecessary and without authority—unless in the last analysis we simply posit that authority—since we could arrive at the truth ourselves; or they do have authority and are indispensable to us—but then, if one assumes as everyone did that all people are alike "by nature," it becomes impossible to account for their origin in a natural and rational way. This was the problem Dai and Zhang had; and it becomes far from quaint and trivial when we notice that we could as well put "generally accepted moral order" for "Classics."

17.3.4 Dai on Meng and Xun

I have had a reason for giving more attention to Xunzi than to Mencius. Although Dai Zhen's last and major work was ostensibly an explanation and defence of Mencius's moral philosophy, most scholars have long realized that he is actually closer to Xunzi—though, I think, just how this is so has not been presented clearly enough. Dai, first of all, misread Xunzi. He argues[28] that Xunzi counterposed *xing* ("nature," the source of desire) to *lǐyì* 禮義 (morality) as the two "roots" of his system. In fact Xunzi argues (in the "The Essay on Rites," and elsewhere) that it is desirable that human desires (deriving from our "nature," *xing*) be satisfied, but that they can be only if one accepts social-moral restraints, an insight given us by our capacity for intelligent action (*wèi* 僞). *Desire* and *intelligence* are thus Xunzi's two "roots," that *together* result in morality. This is Dai's own view, expressed in various ways and places (e.g., *Yuan shan* 1.3; MZZYSZ 1.10), with an interesting development: Dai (e.g., MZZYSZ 1.2) argues that to find moral truth and distinguish this knowledge from mere opinion (*yijian*) we must apply the Confucian principle of reciprocity (*shu*), and ask whether what we propose to do to others is something we would accept if done to ourselves. Now, this is an exercise of *intelligence*; but *desire* is essential to it in two ways. Obviously, we are starting with something we *want*. But also the very exercise of imaginative *sympathy* would be impossible for us if we were not capable of having desires (MZZYSZ 1.10). In this way we arrive at "What all hearts have in common" (*xīn zhī suǒ tóng rán* 心之所同然); and this is moral "principle."

Here Dai is using *Mengzi* 6A7, where Mencius argues that our hearts "enjoy" (*yuè* 悅) morality in the same way that our senses enjoy their objects, and that the sages have grasped before us "what hearts have in common," i.e., what we all (really) "enjoy." Dai's originality in combining these ideas is truly admirable. But there are two things this word "enjoy" could mean, and I do not think Dai notices the difference. (a) It might mean that my heart, as something like a sense-organ, finds morality (both the contemplation of it in others and the doing of it myself) so-to-speak "delicious" in itself. (b) It might mean that I consider the ways people might act, and come to see that for us all to accept a code of orderly behavior so drawn that each person gets a share of goods that on the average (perhaps) is more than one could get otherwise, and without anxiety, is a course that is going to give me the most satisfying kind of life I could lead; so seeing, I *approve* of doing this; and so I have the sort of good or positive feeling about it that is involved in *approving*; and so I "enjoy" it. Mencius certainly had the first meaning in mind. Dai waffles: he says first the one thing, then the other in the next breath—that what hearts have in common is what they *approve*, i.e., judge *acceptable* (*kě* 可; MZZYSZ 1.8):

> The [sense] organs—ears, eyes, nose, mouth—[exemplify] the "way of the subject"; the organ [of judgment]—the heart—[exemplifies] the "way of the ruler." The "subject" supplies the potentiality, and the "ruler" judges what is acceptable. "Principle" (*lǐ* 理)[29] and "right" (*yì* 義) come to just this: when one judges appropriately whether something is acceptable, this is "principle" and "right."

And it is this interpretation that he is clearly using in his philosophy. The method of imaginative sympathy has precisely the point that it leads to my asking, "What if everybody did this?" and so eventuates in identifying a set of "oughts" as *restrictions* on desire-satisfaction that everyone would approve of, seeing it to be *necessary* if everyone's desires are to be satisfied as much as possible. I suggest that this is precisely why Dai calls the morality that sage-intelligence uncovers "the necessary," *biran*. If so, for all of his Mencian language, he is really grounding morality the way Xunzi does.

So, apparently, Dai understands Mencius's "enjoys" as meaning "on balance judges to be the only acceptable (*ke*) course," and so "approves" in the sense "accepts as obligatory." In so doing Dai seems to forget Mencius's distinction (7B24) between the *ming* attitude and the *xing* attitude. Perhaps it would be fairer to take Dai as meaning all of what he says—and he does say (MZZYSZ 1.5) that "whenever one does something in accord with 'principle and right,' one always has a feeling in one's heart of pleasure and satisfaction," etc. Further, he is Mencian (via the *Yi jing*) in seeing human "nature" as the "completion" of a good universe (the "virtue" of Heaven and Earth; *Yuan shan* 1.3); human "goodness" is a "continuation without break" (*jì chéng bù gé* 繼承不隔) of this universe. But if so I think we must see him as assuming that "judging acceptable" automatically entails "enjoying." In effect, then, he commits the same error (I think it to be an error) as the modern moral philosopher who thinks of the two sentences "I want to do X" and "I ought to do X" as both expressing one homogenous "pro-attitude."³⁰ This says something important about Dai's "intellectualist" temper, well summed up by Yü Ying-shih in his succinct conclusion that Dai "saw morality to be no more than a product of knowledge."³¹

The explanation of what has been called Qing "intellectualism" must of course be a broad historical one. But we have here the logical core of Dai's form of it. If there is no *motivational* difference between (a) *believing* that I *ought* to do X and (b) *feeling* that I *want* to do X, then any kind of moral weakness is inconceivable; if you think you have some kind of *cognitive* access to truths of the kind "I ought to do X," it follows that any further talk of cultivating the dispositional "moral nature" through "seriousness" becomes so much medieval-religious nonsense.

In any case there is no problem in Dai's kind of naturalism in accounting for human moral-directedness. But Dai wants more. He actually wants to *reduce* moral "principle" to human psychology. He proposes that what morality (*li*) amounts to, really, is "what neither exceeds nor falls short of our feelings" (無過情無不及情之謂理; MZZYSZ 1.3). Does Dai really mean it? If he does, he would have to be willing to say that if *everyone* were to agree that X is right, their agreeing would make it right. I do not think Dai sees this problem; but if he did see it he would have to say, no: the rightness of X depends on X, not on us. "Where there is a thing there is a standard" (*yŏu wù yŏu zé* 有物有則), he quotes *Mengzi* 6A6, which is quoting the *Shī jīng* 詩經 (Mao no. 260). Values are just *there*; they are objective: *li* are inherent in "things," i.e., ordinary human social and biological activities (MZZYSZ 1.3), and one should never try to find them by introspection, to suppose that *li* is a kind of "thing" in the heart, as Zhu Xi said. The punch at Zhu is pulled, in effect, when Dai considers how "principles" are known: the mind just has this capacity, just as a light illuminates an object (MZZYSZ 1.8).

Dai's objection to Zhu's *li* as a quasi-thing in the heart is that it makes access to moral "truth" so easy that ordinary people substitute their own beclouded (biased) opinion (*yijian*) for it. But Dai's system does no better, really: anyone can use the "reciprocity" (*shu*) method of moral reasoning; and anyway, who is to say that I don't have a valid intuition into moral truth? To let this question go unanswered would allow what Dai deplores, the possibility of someone simply doing some thinking, without even looking at the Classics, and arriving at the insights of the sages (Yu 1976, 112).

So Dai has to say that the mind can be correctly used to identify value only if that mind is "unbeclouded" (*wú bì* 無蔽). He waffles again on whether to say that it is unbeloudedness that qualifies one as a sage (implied in MZZYSZ 1.6), or that it is being a sage that qualifies one as unbeclouded (implied in MZZYSZ 1.5). The latter assumption is the one he requires to save the Classics (by definition produced by "sages"), and the one that in the end he uses. Furthermore, in saying that the sage alone is completely "unbeclouded," Dai is in effect implying again that there is an absolute moral value that we all in some degree have insight into, independent of us. The notion of beclouding requires the (contrasting) notion of a direct intuition into *real* value, which was what Zhu Xi's *li* in the heart was supposed to be.

In the end, Dai saves the position of the Classics by fiat. The Classics are authoritative because they *state* the highest moral truth. And we *know* they do because we recognize them to have been written by sages, who are by definition persons who had perfect knowledge of the truth.

17.3.5 Zhang on Meng and Xun

Did Zhang Xuecheng read the MZZYSZ, see the problems in it, and in "Yuan dao" try to work out a position that solved those problems? This can only be speculation, but it leads to valuable insights into what Zhang is saying in "Yuan dao."

Zhang, I think, must have seen that to try to solve the justification problem abstractly is hopeless. If the Classics are characterized solely by certain abstract *qualities* (containing certain kinds of eternally true statements) and are supposed to have been written by humans characterized abstractly as having certain abilities, it must always be conceivable that I, ignorant of the Classics, might sit down at my desk tomorrow and write something just as valuable (or more valuable, unless one add the usual *ad hoc* assumption that the Classics contain all moral truth). If the Classics are to have any necessary uniqueness, their existence must be built into their essence; their *history* must be part of their *identity*. This implies two things: (a) a picture of the natural world implying a justification of the Classics as classics must include human history in all its particularity; and (b) a Classic qua Classic, like a poem (to paraphrase MacLeish) must "not say but be": its value as a Classic must consist not in what it says but in what it is.[32] These two assumptions are the foundation of Zhang's "Yuan dao."

Zhang was not in any special sense a Mencian, even though perfunctorily he accepted the Mencian picture of human nature (in "Yuan xue" 1.1, e.g.) and even though "Yuan dao" begins with (unlabeled) quotations from Dǒng Zhòngshū 董仲舒 (a Han Dynasty Mencian) and from Mencius. The operative idea at the start is that what went on prior to human existence is unknowable, and that to figure things out we start with the bare realities of human life. That idea is Xunzi's. If Zhang saw Dai as a self-labeled Mencian actually thinking like Xunzi, it would not be surprising for him, replying to Dai, to develop a Xunzian point of view more openly. Xunzi's sages do not "anticipate what our hearts have in common." They create institutions and standards (*li* and *yi*). So do Zhang's sages; but he deviates from Xunzi in two ways. First, he makes a Mencian admission that in some sense from the start man "had his *dao* in himself," of which the institutional moral order is an expression. But Zhang's human nature is not a psychological abstraction; it is spread out in human history in the form of concrete human needs in the context of social existence. Second, the generation of the institutional moral order is explicitly historical and cumulative, the sage-creators' response to needs as they arise. (And Zhang's sages, too, are naturalized—they are the most able people around, thrust to the top in the social evolution process.) Xunzi himself had suggested something like this in speaking (in "Human Nature Is Evil") of *li* and *yi* as "the cumulative product of intelligent intentional action" (*ji wei*) of the sages. Here Zhang may be saying what he thought Xunzi meant, or should have meant. In time, after centuries, the process resulted in the Classics, without anyone in the process intending to write a "Classic" or even intending to write a book, or being aware that "Classics" were being written.

Suddenly we see the solution to the difficulty implicit in Xunzi: We see how human institutions and standards, and so, eventually, the Classics, could have come into being in a natural way. And we get a *new* vision of the Classics' value. They are not codes of moral truth, but residues of the long historical process of humans working out their values as civilization first took shape.

This, of course, is to use the word "values" in a way very different from the way I used it in arguing that Dai believed, in effect, that "values are just *there*." For Zhang, "concepts (*míng* 名) of benevolence, right, loyalty, and filiality" ("Yuan dao" 1.1) are historical products, things of which one can "name the name" (*míng qí míng* 名其名; "Yuan dao" 1.3) and not *dao* itself. So what is Zhang's naturalistic picture? That morality is an illusion, which we have and accept as morality, because, somehow, the processes of history determine that we shall do so? Zhang's world is a good world, of course: he quotes all the pregnant lines from the *Yi jing* appendices that Dai does; so the illusion would be for the best. But still, an illusion? Yes and no:

> *Dao* is the "why" (*suoyiran*) of all things. It is not the "ought" (*dangran*) of all things. What human beings are able to see is only the "ought." ("Yuan dao" 1.3)

We do not see *dao* itself, but only its "traces" (*jī* 迹) ("Yuan Dao" 1.4) in human institutions and standards. This seems to be a "thing-in-itself" vs. "appearance" distinction, the former a realm of causal necessity, the latter (within which we do all our seeing) of normative necessity. Yet the norms—though apparently we owe them the reverence due the *dao*—are not absolute, but products of time and need, and, conceivably, subject to change.

But what of the difficulty implicit in Mencius and unresolved by Dai—the other horn of the dilemma? What makes Zhang's Classics unique? It is not the case that anyone can write a Classic, surely. (Zhang says over and over—e.g., in "Yì Jiào" 易教—that the Classics "cannot be imitated.") But this is not because the "sages" were mysterious supermen. It is simply that they were "present at the Creation," and we are not.[33]

This, however, does not solve the justification problem. The Classics have the *value* they have because they are the traces of *dao* in history. Does not history go on? The part of it that Zhang depicts, to the time of the Duke of Zhou, is a *progress*, from simplest beginnings to a rich and complex civilization. If the Classics are to have the unique *value* they are supposed to have—if it is to be forever inconceivable that more, perhaps even more valuable, Classics might be produced in the future—Zhang must somehow stop this process at the time of the Classics' redaction by Confucius. This he does with his conception of pre-Confucian civilization as an integral whole, a *unity* having "government" (*zhì* 治) and "teaching" (*jiào* 教) as simply two different aspects of itself, so that truth (knowledge) is never abstracted from practice. Eventually, Zhang says, this unity disintegrated, and "truth" (now necessarily partial) became the personal property of this or that philosopher, school, or author; these, with their separate viewpoints, could never again see the whole of the reality of human life and value.

Zhang offers no explanation for this change (he even *says* it's inexplicable); and this is surprising, for it seems not hard to continue his plausible line of speculation farther. We see over and over again the phenomenon of a developing society reaching a point of richness, variety, and complexity in which tensions and pluralities develop which rend and destroy the togetherness of the human community forever. These matters are hard to measure and describe, but they are real, and easy enough to feel. We have had this in our own history. Why didn't Zhang say something like this?

He did not, I suspect, because paradoxically such a suggestion would have given him just what he needed: it would have guaranteed, with historical necessity, that the golden bowl once broken could never be put back together; and so that there never could be a resumption of the *dao*-manifestation process that had produced the Classics in the first place. But Zhang did not say this, and perhaps could not; it was, after all, part of the ideology of the Qing imperial order that the golden bowl *had* been put back together, that *zhi* and *jiao* were again one, under the modern intellectual sage-emperors Kāng Xī 康熙 and Qián Lóng 乾隆; and the ideal, implicitly, perennially recurs as an overtone of Confucian utopian thought.[34]

So Zhang guarantees the priority, or at least the unsurpassability, of the value of his Classics in another way. He says in "Yuan dao" 1.4 that by the time of the Duke of Zhou the *dao*-manifestation in civilization had reached a state of "great completeness" (*dà bèi* 大備). This seems like a trivial ornamental twirl on his tapestry; but it quite betrays the underlying metaphysics of his naturalism. If the *dao* can get *completely* expressed in history, then it is not, after all, inseparable from its "embodiment" but is preexistent and eternal. Or, to put the matter another way, in order to make the judgment "That's *it*" we have to "just know" what "it" is. In his own way, Zhang has saved the Classics with the same *ad hoc* assumption Dai Zhen made. They are authoritative because they *express* the best, and we *know* they do because we *assert* that what produced them as expressions of itself *was* best.

I do not want it thought that I am gleefully giving Dai and Zhang a drubbing. On the contrary my sympathy is deep. I do not know how to solve the problem I see to have tripped them—either their form of it or mine. And I am very much aware that this kind of stretching out of inferences from my speculative reconstruction of other peoples' thinking can get badly off track. One thing that must not be forgotten is that the problem I see in them may have been much less interesting to them than it is to us.

Notes

Chapter 1. Introduction

1. Interestingly, in this respect Nivison is like Zhāng Xuéchéng 章學誠, the subject of Nivison's doctoral dissertation and first book. See Nivison (1966, 107).

2. Of Mencius's four cardinal virtues—benevolence, righteousness, wisdom, and ritual propriety—only one, wisdom, corresponds even vaguely to anything in the Aristotelian list of virtues. For an overview of recent literature on "virtue ethics," see Yearley (1990b). For a comparison (which is indebted to Nivison) of Mencius and Western virtue ethics, see Yearley (1990a).

3. Nivison's views on *akrasia* have been especially influenced by the work of Donald Davidson (1982b), who was his colleague at Stanford. One of the classic Western discussions of *akrasia* may be found in Aristotle, *Nicomachean Ethics*, book 7, chapters 1–10. For philosophical discussions of *acedia*, also called "spiritual apathy," see Thomas Aquinas, *Summa Theologiae* II–II.35, and Heath (1972, 189–92). For one popular account of *acedia*, see Fairlie (1979, chapter 4).

4. On prescriptivism, see Hare (1963, passim), but contrast Davidson (1982b, 26–27). The term "internalism" is actually used in a variety of ways. For a good summary, see Brink (1986).

5. It seems to me that Wang's favorite example of the unity of knowledge and action is so vivid that it deserves to become part of the idiom of contemporary Western philosophy: "Therefore the *Great Learning* points to true knowledge and action for people to see, saying, they are 'like loving beautiful colors and hating bad odors.'... Smelling a bad odor appertains to knowledge, while hating a bad odor appertains to action. However, as soon as one smells a bad odor, he has already hated it. It is not that he smells it first and then makes up his mind to hate it. [However, a] person with his nose stuffed up does not smell the bad odor even if he sees a malodorous object before him." Chan (1963, 10, no. 5).

6. For an excellent discussion of Aristotle's views on moral education, see Burnyeat (1980).

7. Williams (1973) is a helpful discussion of the Kantian position which influenced Nivison's understanding of Kant. Other important discussions of the issues raised by the Kantian view of emotions include Stocker (1976) and Blum (1980).

8. This emphasis is also evident in the work of Kwong-loi Shun, who was one of Nivison's students. See, e.g., Shun (1991a, 1991b, 1991c).

9. Hence, the title of this volume, "The Ways of Confucianism." (More on this

later in this chapter.) Incidentally, this disagreement disproves the assumption, which one still occasionally encounters (e.g., Hansen [1992, passim]), that there is such a thing as *the* orthodox interpretation, which all commentators allegedly share.

10. This is one formulation of what philosophers refer to as "the principle of charity." As Quine (1960, 59) remarks, "The common sense behind the maxim [of charity] is that one's interlocutor's silliness, beyond a certain point, is less likely than bad translation. . . ." See also Nivison's comments in chapter 16 of this volume, pp. 249–50.

11. Cf. Lau (1970, 82).

12. I owe this anecdote to P. J. Ivanhoe.

13. Interestingly, Mencius himself formulated a similar holistic interpretive principle (see *Mengzi* 5A4.2). In addition to Nivison's work, other excellent examples of the application of these hermeneutic principles include Graham (1967) and Bodde (1978). There is also an informed discussion of hermeneutic methodology in Hansen (1983, chapter 1).

14. On the relationship between Xunzi and Daoism, see Yearley (1980) and Nivison (1991a).

15. This sea-change in Confucianism is also stressed by both A. C. Graham (1958, 1992) and Nivison's student, P. J. Ivanhoe (1990b, 1993). A good general introduction to Theravadan Buddhist philosophy is Rahula (1974). But the forms of Buddhism that had the greatest influence on Neo-Confucianism were the Mahayana schools of the Huá–yán 華嚴 and Chán 禪 (Zen). See Cook (1977), Yampolsky (1967), and Dumoulin (1994). Many selections from Chinese Buddhist texts are included in Fung (1952, vol. 2).

16. For an introduction to these oracle bones, see Keightley (1978).

17. Indeed, by the end of the classical period *de* sometimes clearly means precisely "virtue": "Wisdom, benevolence and courage—these three are the universal virtues (*de*) of the world." *Zhōngyōng* 中庸, chapter 20. Legge (1971, 407).

18. For an illustration of the extreme significance of gift-giving in another East Asian culture, see Seward (1983, 130–32).

19. For the distinction between consequentialist (also called "teleological") and deontological positions, see Frankena (1973, 14–17).

20. This second point is crucial, for Confucians hold that the sages are merely perfected humans. This is a point stressed in Munro (1969).

21. See "Weakness of Will in Ancient Chinese Philosophy," in this volume, p. 80.

22. Nivison discusses the differences between the Western and Chinese views of *akrasia* further in "Two Roots or One?" in this volume.

23. "Two Kinds of 'Naturalism': Dai Zhen and Zhang Xuecheng," in this volume, p. 263.

24. "Two Kinds of 'Naturalism': Dai Zhen and Zhang Xuecheng," in this volume, p. 276.

25. In two essays not included in this volume, Nivison (1953, 1956), Nivison shows how the themes and issues he emphasizes can be identified in other thinkers in the Qing Dynasty, as well as in early Chinese Republican and Communist thinkers.

26. The only chapter that required substantial rewriting was "Motivation and Moral Action in Mencius." (See below, pp. 293–94n. 1.)

Chapter 2. "Virtue" in Bone and Bronze

1. This chapter, which has not previously been published, was delivered as one of The Walter Y. Evans-Wentz Lectures in February of 1980 at Stanford University. Other important studies of the topic of *dé* 德 include Munro (1969, 185–97), Nivison (1978–1979), Yearley (1990a, 53–58), and Ivanhoe (1993, 1–7). [Editor.]

2. The standard introduction to such "oracle bones" is Keightley (1978). [Editor.]

3. Di Xin is also known as Zhòu 紂 or Zhou Xin. Nivison's most recent dates for Wu Ding are 1250/47–1189 B.C. (fifty-nine years, with an initial three years for completion of mourning for the predecessor-king). On the date of April 18, 1040 B.C. for the founding of the Zhou Dynasty, see Nivison (1982–1983, 1983). [Editor.]

4. The two are below identified as *zuǒ zǐ* 左子, perhaps "assisting princes" at court, in contrast to *yì zǐ* 邑子, who may be princes posted to towns.

5. *Shang shu, Zhōu shū, Jīn téng* 周書, 金縢. See Legge (1991e, 351–61).

6. See Legge (1991e, 409, 539, and 592).

7. Duke Xī 僖公, Year 4, in Legge (1991b, 141, Chinese 139). (Legge dates the fourth year of Duke Xi to 655 B.C. Legge's dates are almost always one year late; Nivison learned from Bruce Brooks that this is because Legge followed some bad advice from an English astronomer. [Editor.])

8. *Jīn* 金 409 (S320.2). On the grammar of this passage, compare *Zuo zhuan*, Duke Zhāo 昭公, Year 14, in Legge (1991b, 655, Chinese 654, column 11 from right). See also "Problems in the *Mengzi*: 6A3–5," in this volume, pp. 154–55. [Editor.]

9. What I have said is even more true, if possible, of Japan. (For an illustration, see Seward (1983, 130–32). [Editor.])

10. There are five examples of *jing de* in *Shang shu, Zhou shu, Zhào gào* 召誥. See Legge (1991e, 420–33).

11. See Legge (1991e, 431–32).

12. See above, n. 3.

13. I now believe that this date is probably March 24, 1031 B.C.

14. For other studies (and sometimes quite different interpretations), see especially Tang (1976), Ma (1976), Zhang (1976), and Carson (1978–1979).

15. The "X" stands for a character that has not yet been identified (my transcription at 12A, figure 2.3, is a mere guess). In the translation, the last two sentences in the king's address will surprise other scholars. The exclamation "Oh! Even though . . . , surely . . . !" is actually a rhetorical question, literally "Even though . . . , is there no supposing that . . . ?!" To understand *wang shi . . . zai*, 亡識 . . . 𢦏, compare *Mencius* 6A4 *bu shi . . . yu*, 不識 . . . 與, "we don't suppose . . . , do we?" Others take *wang shi* at 8G–H with what precedes, as describing the "junior princes," and meaning "without knowledge." Such a translation would impute to the young King Cheng a character

and personality utterly different from what I am assuming here. So also with what follows: The boxed sentence (my primary focus) reads *hui wang gong de, yu Tian shun wo bu min*. Others would punctuate after "Tian," "Heaven," making this sentence a reply by the young princes; perhaps: "May it be the king who upholds virtue and nourishes (谷 for *yu* 裕) Heaven, instructing us in our lack of earnestness." But the next phrase, *Wang xian gao* 王咸算, is a conventional "close quote" in inscription style (abbreviated at times simply to "*xian*" 咸); so the words must be the king's. The meaning "help" for *hui* 重 can be recovered from other inscriptions, e.g., Mao Gong *ding* lines 11–14, which show that "*hui* 重 . . . *yu* 俗 . . ." is one extended construction, "help . . . so that . . ." (taking 谷 or 俗 as 欲, literally "desiring [that]"). Throughout the text, characters may have nonstandard phonetics, or lack radicals; e.g., 覞 for 視, 弋 for 哉.

16. See *Shang shu, Zhou shu, Tài shì* 泰誓 and *Mù shì* 牧誓. See Legge (1991e, 281–305). (The version of the *Tai shi* that best illustrates these ideas is one of the spurious chapters added to the *Shang shu* during the Jin Dynasty.)

17. Wei Bo Xing Bell Set A. See Shanxi Zhou Yuan Kaogu Dui (1978, 6), 13, illus. no. 20.

18. Wei Bo Xing Bell Set C. See Shanxi Zhou Yuan Kaogu Dui (1978, 7), 12, illus. no. 18.

Chapter 3. The Paradox of 'Virtue'

1. This chapter, which has not previously been published, was delivered as one of The Walter Y. Evans-Wentz Lectures in February of 1980 at Stanford University. [Editor.]

2. This passage begins chapter 38, the first chapter in book 2, in the Wáng Bì 王弼 text. But Wang Bi's book 2 is book 1 in the Mǎwángduī 馬王堆 text. [Editor.]

3. *Shàng shū, Zhōu shū, Zhào gào* 尚書, 周書, 召誥. See Legge (1991e, 431–32).

4. See the inscription discussed in "'Virtue' in Bone and Bronze," in this volume, p. 27 ff.

5. *Analects* 2:1. Most translations from the *Analects* in this chapter follow Waley (1938), with some modifications. Sectioning, as always, follows HY.

6. *Analects*, HY 12:19. Waley renders *de* in this context as "essence."

7. *Xúnzi* 荀子, HY 26/9/21.

8. For more on Zou Yan and Five Phases theory, see Needham (1956, 232–44) and Graham (1986b, 70–92). [Editor.]

9. *Zuo zhuan*, Duke Xī 僖公, Year 24. See Legge (1991b, 192, right-hand column, Chinese 189, second and first columns from the left).

10. The idea is spelled out in the *Xīn shù shàng* 心術上 chapter of the early philosophical encyclopedia *Guǎnzi* 管子, of about 300 B.C.; and also in *Zhuāngzi* 莊子, chapter 12. See, respectively, Rickett (1965, 175) and *Zhuangzi*, HY 30/12/38, Watson (1968, 131). Hereafter, unless otherwise indicated, "*de*" refers to 德.

11. See, e.g., *Mèngzi* 孟子, HY 4A10. Note that this is 4A9 in Lau (1970) and Legge (1970).

12. See, e.g., *Mengzi* 6A10.7: 所識窮乏者得我與, "[Do I do this so] the poor and needy whom I know will *be indebted to* me?" (Cf. the use of 德 quoted from the *Zuo zhuan*, earlier in this chapter, p. 33.)

13. On these problems, see, e.g., *Mengzi* 6B16: "There are many methods of teaching. My disdain to teach people teaches them too." *Analects*, HY 15:16: "With those who are not saying, 'What is to be done? What is to be done?' what am I to do?" [Editor.]

14. See "'Virtue' in Bone and Bronze" in this volume, p. 23.

15. The "old duke" (Dǎn Fù 亶父) was later recognized as dynastic founder *honoris causa* and called Tài Wáng 太王, "great king."

16. *Analects*, HY 8:1.

17. See *Shǐ jì* 史記 (*Records of the Historian*), chapter 77, "Biography of the Lord of Xinling."

18. *Analects*, HY 5:10. See Waley (1938, 109, no. 9).

19. *Analects*, HY 6:12. See Waley (1938, 118, no. 10).

20. Plato, *Meno* 80d ff.

21. On *acedia* and *akrasia*, see the introduction to this volume, p. 2, and p. 283, n. 3. See also "Weakness of Will in Ancient Chinese Philosophy," "Two Roots or One?" and "Motivation and Moral Action in Mencius," in this volume. [Editor.]

22. See *Mozi*, chapter 16, translated in Watson (1963b, 39–49).

23. See *Mozi*, chapter 11, translated in Watson (1963b, 34–38).

24. See *Mengzi* 3A5, and "Two Roots or One?" in this volume.

25. See *Mengzi* 1A7, and "Motivation and Moral Action in Mencius," in this volume.

26. *Analects*, HY 9:24: "For those who approve but do not carry out, who are stirred, but do not change, I can do nothing at all."

27. See *Mengzi* 2A2, 4A27, and 7A17, and both "Philosophical Voluntarism in Fourth-Century China" and "Problems in the *Mengzi*: 7A17," in this volume.

28. Gaozi may have been a disciple of Mozi as a very young man; if so, Gaozi was much older than Mencius. This is, in fact, suggested by *Mengzi* 2A2. See "Philosophical Voluntarism in Fourth-Century China," in this volume.

29. *Mengzi* 6A7 represents this strand in Mencius's thought. [Editor.]

30. On the Mohist use of *tui*, see Graham (1978, 482–85). On *tui lei*, see Graham (1978, 349–51). For a discussion of the Mohist aspects of Mencius's thought, see "Motivation and Moral Action in Mencius," in this volume. [Editor.]

31. See *Mengzi* 2A6.4–5.

32. For more on Wang Yangming, see the next chapter, section 4.3.1.

33. On the notion of a "pro-attitude" see Davidson (1982a, 3–4). [Editor.]

Chapter 4. Can Virtue Be Self-Taught?

1. This chapter, which has not previously been published, was delivered as one of The Walter Y. Evans-Wentz Lectures in February of 1980 at Stanford University. [Editor.]

2. Late Professor Emeritus of Philosophy at Stanford. See Stanford Philosophy Department (1994). [Editor.]

3. On the notion of a "pro-attitude" see Davidson (1982a, 3–4). [Editor.]

4. See, e.g., *Mèngzǐ* 孟子 4A1. [Editor.]

5. *Mengzi* 5A4. See 7B3 and book 5A generally for similar examples. [Editor.]

6. For more on Xunzi, including more detailed argument for the interpretation sketched herein, see "Xunzi on 'Human Nature'," chapter 13 in this volume, and Nivison (1991a).

7. Adapted from Watson (1963a, 136); *Xunzi*, HY 82/21/82–83.

8. Adapted from Watson (1963a, 30); *Xunzi*, HY 5/2/37–38.

9. "Unfunded" in the sense that we do not, according to Xunzi, have innate dispositions toward certain moral actions or judgments. [Editor.]

10. Even though Xunzi calls this order *tian*, "Heaven"—both the cosmic order and the internal psychological order in the human being are so denoted—and even though his rules (*lǐ* 禮 "rites") include religious rituals, his system is completely atheistic. (For a discussion of Xunzi's views on *tian*, see Machle [1993]. [Editor.])

11. *Xunzi*, HY 86/22/78; Watson (1963a, 154).

12. *Xunzi*, HY 85/22/67; Watson (1963a, 152).

13. Watson (1963a, 20); *Xunzi*, HY 2/1/34.

14. Adapted from Watson (1963a, 20); *Xunzi*, HY 2/1/30–31.

15. Compare this to *Mengzi* 2A2.9 and *Zhuāngzǐ, Rén jiān shì* 莊子, 人閒世, discussed in "Philosophical Voluntarism in Fourth-Century China," in this volume, section 8.4. [Editor.]

16. See, e.g., "in learning nothing is more effective than to associate with those [who are learned], and of the paths to learning, none is quicker than to be fond of such people" (*Xunzi*, HY 3/1/35–36); "Humans inherently have the beginnings (*duān* 端) of these two emotions [i.e., joy and sorrow] from birth. If one can trim them, stretch them, broaden them, narrow them . . . so as to make the roots and branches, endings and beginnings never fail to be appropriate . . . , *this* is ritual. But one who is not a noble person of thorough cultivation and practice has never known how to do this" (73/19/74–75). See also Watson (1963a, 22–23).

17. Watson (1963a, 24); *Xunzi*, HY 3/2/1–2.

18. Adapted from Watson (1963a, 30); *Xunzi*, HY 5/2/38.

19. The *Zhōngyōng* 中庸 is a Han Dynasty text, commonly known in English by the title *Doctrine of the Mean*, although the title *Centrality and Commonality* would be more accurate. The *Zhongyong* was a chapter of the *Lǐjì* 禮記, *Record of Rites*, given the status of an independent "classic" as one of the *Four Books* (see below, n. 21). For a translation, see Legge (1971). For a critical discussion, see Tu (1989). [Editor.]

20. *Zhongyong*, chapter 28; in Legge (1971, 424).

21. The *Mengzi*, the *Analects* (*Lúnyǔ* 論語) of Confucius, the *Dàxué* 大學 (the *Great Learning*), and the *Zhongyong* became known as the *Four Books*. They, along with commentaries of Zhū Xī 朱熹, became the basis of the civil service examinations in A.D. 1313, and remained so until the examinations were abolished some six centuries

later. The *Daxue* and the *Zhongyong* were originally chapters in another Classic, the *Liji*. Zhu Xi significantly modified and reinterpreted the text of the *Daxue* (see Legge 1971, 24–25 and Gardner 1986); whatever the merits of these changes, it is now his version that is usually cited. For more on the *Zhongyong*, see above, n. 19. For a discussion of translations of the *Mengzi*, see "On Translating Mencius," chapter 12 in this volume. For textual issues regarding the *Analects*, see below, p. 290, n. 4. For more on Zhu Xi, see below, n. 28. [Editor.]

22. Buddhism arrived in China some time during the first century A.D. For a general introduction to Theravadan Buddhism, see Rahula (1974). The forms of Buddhism that had the greatest influence on Neo-Confucianism were the Mahayana schools of the Huá-yán 華嚴 and Chán 禪 (Zen). See Cook (1977), Yampolsky (1967), and Dumoulin (1994). For an introduction to some of the basic texts and doctrines of Chinese Buddhism, see Fung (1952, 2: chapters 7–9). [Editor.]

23. See, e.g., *Mengzi* 2A7, 6A16.

24. *Analects*, HY 7:23.

25. On the *Four Books*, see above, n. 21. For a translation of the "Great Appendix," see Legge (1969, 348–407). [Editor.]

26. On the tension between the examinations and moral cultivation, see Nivison (1960).

27. The phrase *shèn qí dú* 慎其獨 ("being watchful while alone") is found in both the *Daxue*, commentary, chapter 6 (Legge 1971, 367), and the *Zhongyong*, chapter 1, section 3 (Legge 1971, 384). On the appropriation of the notion by Chinese Communists, see Nivison (1956). [Editor.]

28. For more on Zhu Xi, see Ivanhoe (1993, chapter 4) and Gardner (1990). For more on Cheng Yi and his brother Chéng Hào 程顥, see Graham (1992). [Editor.]

29. For more on Wang Yangming, see Nivison (1953), Ivanhoe (1990b; 1993, chapter 5), and Nivison, "Two Roots or One?" "The Philosophy of Wang Yangming," and "Moral Decision in Wang Yangming; The Problem of Chinese 'Existentialism'," all in this volume. [Editor.]

30. For a discussion of how this change came about, see Nivison (1953).

31. But this brick-by-brick idea overlooks something that Zhāng Xuéchéng 章學誠 (see below) keeps insisting on: not only does one need the details to understand the whole, but also one must grasp the *dàtǐ* 大體 of the ancients if one is really to understand the details. It is for this reason that he keeps jeering at the philological "fashion" (*fēngqì* 風氣) of his times.

32. *Xunzi*, HY 88/23/51 ff.

33. For more on Zhang Xuecheng, see "The Philosophy of Zhang Xuecheng" and "Two Kinds of 'Naturalism': Dai Zhen and Zhang Xuecheng," chapters 16 and 17 in this volume. In the latter, Zhang's basic philosophical stance is shown to be a conscious criticism of Dai Zhen's position. Dai Zhen is further discussed in "Two Roots or One?" chapter 9 in this volume.

34. *Analects*, HY 15:24. For more on "reciprocity," see "Golden Rule Arguments in Chinese Moral Philosophy," chapter 5 in this volume.

35. Ewell (1990, 182); Dai (1777b, I.14). Cf. Fung (1952, 2:669).

36. On the "mana thesis," see Munro (1969, 102–8), and the references cited therein. See also Fingarette (1972, 3–11). [Editor.]

37. Xunzi has two "self-teaching" problems: (a) how did mankind become moral? and (b) how do I become moral? He has two (perhaps conflicting) answers: (a) the sages thought it out; and (b) I have to "do arithmetic" and see that I must study the sages, under a competent teacher, and then study them. Dai can be seen as developing the second answer, calling for the talent of the philologist; and Zhang Xuecheng, not otherwise obviously part of the dialogue, can be seen as making sense of the first answer: the sages' "thinking it out" must be redescribed as the slow evolution of human civilization—which is the business of the historian. On Dai and Zhang, see "Two Kinds of 'Naturalism': Dai Zhen and Zhang Xuecheng," chapter 17 in this volume. [This note was added by Nivison in 1995.]

Chapter 5. Golden Rule Arguments in Chinese Moral Philosophy

1. This chapter, which has not previously been published, was originally Nivison's Inaugural Lecture for the Walter Y. Evans-Wentz Professorship in Oriental Philosophies, Religions, and Ethics at Stanford University, delivered February 13, 1984. Some comments more appropriate for the context in which the lecture was originally delivered have been left out. Other essays on related topics include Fingarette (1980) and Ivanhoe (1990a). [Editor.]

2. See also Leviticus 19:18, 19:34; Luke 10:27; Mark 12:31.

3. A hypothetical imperative enjoins us to perform act A because it is the best *means* to achieve some goal G that we happen to have. A categorical imperative enjoins us to perform act A irrespective of what our goals happen to be (Kant, 1964, 82–84; Academy, 414–417). Kant thinks there is only one categorical imperative, but he thinks it has several formulations, one of which is, "Act only on that maxim through which you can at the same time will that it should become a universal law" (Kant 1964, 88; Academy, 421). [Editor.]

4. Following the unpublished work of Bruce and Taeko Brooks (1985), I take book 4 to be the oldest, dating from 479–477 B.C., and book 5 to be only a little later. (For published discussions on the dating of the *Analects*, see Eno (1990, 80–81 and 239–42 nn. 2–6) and Van Zoeren (1991, 19–28 and passim). [Editor.])

5. Or, ". . . desire that it not be done to others."

6. "Si" is the personal name of Zigong.

7. *Analects* 5:12. All citations of the *Analects* in this chapter are to the sectioning in HY.

8. Again I follow the Brooks on dating.

9. *Analects* 15:24. The difference between the negatives *wú* 無 and *wù* 勿 will be important later. See section 5.5 of this chapter.

10. Cited in Alton (1966, 50).

11. For more on the *Zhongyong*, see above, p. 288, n. 19.

12. *Zhongyong*, chapter 13, in Legge (1971, 394).
13. "Shen" is the personal name of Zengzi.
14. Still I follow the Brooks (1985).
15. For more on the *Daxue*, see above, pp. 288–89n. 21.
16. *Daxue*, Commentary, chapter 10, in Legge (1971, 373–74).
17. Quoted in Ching (1978, 169).
18. The immediately preceding section is usually taken up in connection with this one. *Analects* 12:1 has Yán Huí 顏回 asking Confucius about *ren*. Confucius replies, "If you can fully satisfy the requirements of ritual as they apply to yourself (*kè jǐ fù lǐ* 克己復禮), this is benevolence." The dominant tradition of commentary—that of Zhū Xī 朱熹, who accepts Mencius's view that "human nature" is "good," but also believes (with Xúnzǐ 荀子) that our appetitive and desirous nature constantly threatens to lead us into wickedness—takes this formula as two phrases, "to overcome the self (*ke jí*) and return to ritual (*fu li*)." Thus Zhu's morality is characteristically a matter of self-discipline. For more on Zhu Xi, see section 5.5 of this chapter.
19. *Xunzi*, HY 104/29/8–14. (Confucius does not explicitly use the word *zhong* here, but it is referred to earlier in the chapter (HY 104/29/5–6). [Editor.])
20. But see below, p. 292, n. 40.
21. See Kant (1964, 97n; Academy, 430n). On the Categorical Imperative, see above, p. 290, n. 3.
22. *Zhèng méng* 正蒙, chapter 2, section 8, in *Zhāngzǐ quánshū* 張子全書 (SBBY).
23. *Xunzi*, HY 106/30/14–16.
24. See, e.g., Fung (1953, 43).
25. Legge's translation of the last line in *Analects* 4:15 reflects Zhu Xi's reading: "The doctrine of our master is to be true to the principles of our nature and the benevolent exercise of them to others—this and nothing more" (1971, 170). [Editor.]
26. On the distinction between *ti* and *yong*, see Graham (1992, 39–40 and passim). It is easiest to understand the concepts via examples: the eye is substance, seeing is function. [Editor.]
27. "*Encratic*" is a term from Aristotelian ethics. Aristotle is concerned with virtuous knowledge, desire, and action. One who is *encratic* has base desires, but knows what is virtuous, and makes him- or herself do the right thing. The *encratic* person is contrasted, on the one hand, with the *akratic* person, who also knows what is virtuous, but *fails* to make him- or herself do what is right, and, on the other hand, with the fully virtuous person (who has the virtue of *sōphrosunē*), who knows what is virtuous, desires what is virtuous, and does what is virtuous. [Editor.]
28. "That there not be," occurring in 5:12, literally ". . . I desire that there not be a doing of it to others."
29. "Do not," in the rule ". . . do not do to others."
30. Cheng Hao's comment is quoted in Graham (1992, 98–99).
31. See Chan (1963, 272).
32. His life and work have been ably described in a book by Professor John Wang (1972, 45–47).
33. For more on Zhang Xuecheng, see "The Philosophy of Zhang Xuecheng" and

"Two Kinds of 'Naturalism': Dai Zhen and Zhang Xuecheng," chapters 16 and 17 in this volume, as well as Nivison (1966).

34. For more detailed discussion and argument regarding Dai, see "Two Kinds of 'Naturalism': Dai Zhen and Zhang Xuecheng," and "Two Roots or One?" chapters 17 and 9, respectively, in this volume.

35. I myself have pointed out this complexity in essays such as Nivison (1953).

36. *Mengzi* 7A4.

37. Duke Xiāng 襄公, Year 23, in Legge (1991b, 504, Chinese 500). (Legge gives the twenty-third year of Xiang as 549 B.C., but see above, p. 285, n. 7. [Editor.])

38. Interestingly, the verbs have the expected directional aspect: one "serves" (*shì* 事) superiors, but "deals with" (*shī* 施) inferiors; so this example confirms my suggestion that *shu* normally applies downward—as, indeed, in ordinary idiom: *shù zuì* 恕罪, "forgive a fault," where the one forgiving is in a position to punish the one forgiven.

39. Not to notice the difference would be to make the same kind of mistake made by the scholar examining ancient Chinese logic, who marvels at the logical sophistication of the ancient Chinese when he or she finds some actual argument that requires an intricate use of quantification or set theory to reduce to canonical form.

40. I was for this reason tempted to call *shu* a "supererogatory virtue." But that might have been misleading: It does not necessarily direct one toward action that would be beyond the ordinary person's capacity for courage or sacrifice; whereas *zhong* sometimes does just this.

Chapter 6. Weakness of Will
in Ancient Chinese Philosophy

1. This paper, which has not previously been published, was presented at Haverford College in April of 1973, and in July of the same year at the International Congress of Orientalists in Paris. [Editor.]

2. For an introduction to the study of Chinese oracle bones, see Keightley (1973). [Editor.]

3. *Jīn* 金 409 (S320.2). On the grammar of this passage, compare *Zuǒ zhuàn* 左傳, Duke Zhāo 昭公, Year 14, in Legge (1991b, 655, Chinese 654, column 11 from right). See also Nivison (1978–1979) and chapter 2, pp. 25–26, in this volume.

4. For an interesting discussion and illustration of the implications of gift-giving in Japanese society, see Seward (1983, 130–32). [Editor.]

5. For the identification of this character, see Nivison (1978–1979). [Editor.]

6. On the date of the founding of the Zhou Dynasty, see Nivison (1982–1983, 1983).

7. Plato, *Meno* 80d ff.

8. See Waley (1938, 129, no. 29); HY 13/7/30; Lau (1979, 90, no. 30). Translations of the *Analects* in this chapter follow Waley with some modifications.

9. See Waley (1938, 143, no. 23); HY 17/9/24; Lau (1979, 99, no. 24).

10. See Waley (1938, 101, no. 26); HY 5/3/26; Lau (1979, 71, no. 26).

11. See Waley (1938, 100, no. 22); HY 5/3/22; Lau (1979, 70–71, no. 22).

12. See Waley (1938, 93, no. 24); HY 4/2/24; Lau (1979, 66, no. 24).
13. See Waley (1938, 94, no. 3); HY 4/3/3; Lau (1979, 67, no. 3).
14. See Waley (1938, 101, no. 26); HY 5/3/26; Lau (1979, 71, no. 26).
15. See Waley (1938, 88, no. 4); HY 2/2/4; Lau (1979, 63, no. 4).
16. See Waley (1938, 124, no. 8); HY 12/7/8; Lau (1979, 86, no. 8).
17. See Waley (1938, 109, no. 9); HY 8/5/10; Lau (1979, 77, no. 10).
18. See Waley (1938, 118, no. 10); HY 10/6/12; Lau (1979, 82–83, no. 12).
19. *Mozi*, chapters 14–16. See Watson (1963b, 39–49).
20. "Mo Di" is the full name of Mozi.
21. *Mozi*, chapters 11–13. See Watson (1963b, 34–38).
22. *Mozi* in HY 24/15/30, 26/16/46–47. See also Watson (1963b, 44). For more on Mengzi 1A7 and its Mohist aspects, see "Motivation and Moral Action in Mencius," chapter 7 in this volume.
23. *Mozi*, in HY 25/16/21–22, 26/16/34–35, 27/16/71–72. See also Watson (1963b, 39–49, passim).
24. I ordinarily do not say "you *ought* to do this" unless I assume that you *can* do it. But also, there is no point in my saying "you *can* do it" unless there is an imaginable possibility that you *might* just *not* do it. So "ought" seems to *imply* "might not." The possibility of weakness of will seems to be implied by the moral point of view itself.
25. I.e., when the physical sense organ perceives the sense object.
26. I.e., what it seeks, which we know to be morality.
27. On the notion of a "pro-attitude" see Davidson (1982a, 3–4). [Editor.]
28. For more on Xunzi, see "Xunzi on 'Human Nature,'" chapter 13 in this volume, and Nivison (1991a). [Editor.]
29. HY 89/23/69–90/23/75. See also Watson (1963a, 167–68).
30. Cf. HY 86/22/74–78, and Watson (1963a, 153–54).
31. HY 85/22/67. Cf. Watson (1963a, 152).
32. On *si*, see Waley (1938, 44–46) and Van Norden (1992, 169, 170 n. 34). [Editor.]
33. For more on these issues, see the introduction to this volume, p. 2 ff. [Editor.]
34. Translation slightly modified. [Editor.]
35. For more on Mengzi 2A2, see "Philosophical Voluntarism in Fourth-Century China," chapter 8 in this volume.
36. For more on Wang Yangming, see the references in the bibliography to this volume.
37. *Daxue*, commentary, chapter 6, section 1, in Legge (1971, 366).
38. Han Yu A.

Chapter 7. Motivation and Moral Action in Mencius

1. The original "Motivation and Moral Action in Mencius" was written in August of 1975. Versions were submitted to the Berkeley Regional Seminar in Confucian Studies in November of the same year, and the Pacific Division Meeting of the American Philosophical Association, in Berkeley, California, in March of 1976. "Motivation and Moral Action in Mencius: A Comment for the Workshop on Classical Chinese

Thought," notes modifications of the paper as it was prepared for the Harvard Workshop on Classical Chinese Thought, in August of 1976. In addition, a supplement, "Problems for Revision," was appended for the Berkeley and Harvard seminars. Finally, a much-edited version of this paper was published as Nivison (1980a). This chapter is a synthesis (prepared by the editor of this volume) of the earlier, unpublished papers. It has been reviewed and approved by Dr. Nivison himself. Other works influenced by the earlier versions of this chapter include Shun (1989), Van Norden (1991), and Wong (1991). [Editor.]

2. On *akrasia* and *acedia*, see the introduction to this volume, p. 2, and p. 283, n. 3.

3. One must distinguish between the following, though: (a) failing to perform a *particular* (possible) act one judges best; and (b) failing to pursue a *course* or adopt a policy or "way," or fill a *role* one judges best. Chinese discussions and examples of action failure are usually of the latter sort of failure. Perhaps for this reason the Chinese moralists do not puzzle in the Socratic way about how one could knowingly fail to do what one sees to be best, asking (with Aristotle, Davidson, etc.) "How is weakness of will possible?" Rather, they tend to ask, "How can one be moral?"—i.e., how can I adopt and pursue a way or fill a role I see to be right for me, and do so wholly, "sincerely," effectively, without backsliding?

4. As I note in "Two Roots or One?" in this volume (p. 141), the favorite example of moral weakness in Western philosophy is succumbing to illicit sexual desire (clearly an instance of *akrasia*). In contrast, improperly accepting an inappropriate gift is a favorite Confucian paradigm of moral weakness. When offered a gift I am initially in a passive state, the object of someone else's action, and the temptation to be avoided is remaining passive—being unable to summon the moral stamina to refuse the gift—an instance of *acedia*.

5. Compare Davidson (1982b, 27–28).

6. This passage is numbered 4A10 in Lau (1970) and Legge (1970). [Editor.]

7. *Analects*, HY 6:12. Translations in this chapter largely follow Waley (1938) and Lau (1970) with some modifications. Sectioning follows HY.

8. The latter passage is numbered 4A14 in Lau (1970) and Legge (1970). [Editor.]

9. See Graham (1978, 448–50).

10. See later in this chapter, p. 97.

11. Watson (1963b, 44); *Mozi*, chapter 16, "Universal Love."

12. *Ji* has a range of meanings, including "quickness" (it may be cognate with *ji* 急 "anxious," "hurried"), "feverishness," "haste," etc. Is Xuan then suggesting, not a "weakness" (Lau 1970) or an "infirmity" (Legge 1970), but "a tendency to get excited over X and lose my head"? Compare the distinction between the two forms of *akrasia* in Aristotle (1985, 192, 1150b19–30).

13. Mencius's argument here should be read in the light of 1B1, which argues that one enjoys such things as music more if one shares them with others.

14. See Watson (1964b, 73–79).

15. *Mengzi* 1A7.10. Lau (1970) mistranslates the last sentence as "Hence your

failure to become a true King is due to a refusal to act, not to an inability to act." Legge (1970) gets it right.

16. The tension between general tenets and particular feelings is discussed in Yang (1959, especially 146–56). Observe, also, the formal similarity here to Aristotle's wrinkle, that virtue is, sometimes, vice combined with *akrasia* (1985, 176, 1146a15–31). The point contrasts nicely with Davidson's proper observation (1982b, 30 and 30–31 n.14) that *akrasia* is not necessarily a victory of temptation over virtue but may be a victory of "virtue" over "temptation." Perhaps also related is R. M. Hare's observation in *The Language of Morals* (1952, 65) that we simultaneously discipline our actions by our principles and test (or refine) our principles by evaluating the decisions to act that the principles would imply—for this allows that it is sometimes *wrong* to follow a principle stubbornly, and *right* to be "acratic" with respect to a badly fitting principle.

17. *Mengzi* 1A7.12.

18. "Names and Objects" 11. See Graham (1978, 482–85).

19. Here and below, it should be kept in mind that the Mohists were not concerned with formal logic, as understood in the West. Rather, they were concerned with the broader notion of "dialectic." [Editor.]

20. See Graham (1978, 487–89).

21. *Mengzi* 2A9.

22. I am here interested only in this text as another explicit reference to "extending" (*tui*), overlooking for the present the fact (perhaps embarrassing) that Mencius here finds Bo Yi's "extending" to be something he must criticize as going too far.

23. On the notion of a "pro-attitude" see Davidson (1982a, 3–4). [Editor.]

24. On *tui lei*, see Graham (1978, 349–51).

25. For an extended use of linguistic metaphors to understand the philosophies of Mencius and Xúnzǐ 荀子, see Ivanhoe (1994). [Editor.]

26. One must not, however, suppose Mencius to think that any simple "extending" of a basic moral-making disposition is going to result always in good action. One can fall short, or—like Bo Yi (2A9)—go too far. (Notice that Bo Yi's *wu e zhi xin* looks like Mencius's "sprout" of "rightness," *xiū wù zhī xīn* 羞惡之心, in 2A6.) Does this mean that Mencius requires two "roots" after all, (1) the basic "heart," and (2) a standard of correct proportion? One possibility (I owe the suggestion to Paul Kjellberg) is that one must judiciously "weigh" (*quán* 權) and "estimate" (*duò* 度) the root disposition (see 1A7.13), to get to a satisfactory "surface structure." But the "weighing" metaphor implies a standard of weight; so Mencius does begin to look like Xunzi (see later in this chapter, section 7.6.1).

27. This passage is discussed in more detail in "Two Roots or One?" in this volume.

28. Here Yi Zhi quotes one of the Confucian Classics, in which this is recommended as an attitude for a king to have toward his people. (See Legge [1991e, 389], *Shàng shū, Zhōu shū, Kāng gào* 尚書, 周書, 康誥.)

29. I have had to render the same word, *qīn* 親, "those who are close to you," in one case as "parents" and in another case "family," and again below as "feel close to,"

i.e., "love," in a sense; but the identity must be kept in mind to see the point of the argument.

30. "Names and Objects" 12. See Graham (1978, 482–85).

31. This passage is discussed in more detail in "Philosophical Voluntarism in Fourth-Century China," chapter 8 in this volume.

32. *Mengzi* 2A2.9.

33. Contrast the notion of "fasting the mind" and "listening with the *qi*" in the fictitious dialogue between Confucius, represented there as a kind of slick Daoist sage, and his disciple Yán Huí 顔回, in *Zhuāngzǐ* 莊子, chapter 4. (This passage is discussed in "Philosophical Voluntarism in Fourth-Century China," section 8.4 in this volume.)

34. Actually a common enough meaning of *yan*. For examples, see "Philosophical Voluntarism in Fourth-Century China," in this volume, p. 128 f.

35. This argument is carefully analyzed in Lau (1963b), Shun (1991a), and "Problems in the *Mengzi*: 6A3–5," in this volume. [Editor.]

36. See Chan (1963, 86, 175), and "The Philosophy of Wang Yangming," chapter 14 in this volume.

37. For more on Zihuazi, see "On Translating Mencius," in this volume, p. 183.

38. My interpretation of 4A27 follows Zhū Xī 朱熹, Legge (1970), and most other translators. Lau (1970) differs, following Zhào Qí 趙岐, without saying so.

39. See *Mengzi* 4B19, translated earlier in this chapter, p. 99.

40. For the distinction between consequentialist (also called "teleological") and deontological positions, see Frankena (1973, 14–17). [Editor.]

41. Note that the difficulty developed obtains also for (4) (Doing A from motive C) from motive O, where O is the bare motive to do what I ought. O can be (perhaps) my motive for cultivating myself, but not my motive for a particular moral act (and so, not my motive for the individual things I do in cultivating myself) without contamination of C.

42. For more on 2A2 and the notion of "voluntarism," see "Philosophical Voluntarism in Fourth-Century China," chapter 8 in this volume.

43. The moral life can be far more distressing than this, even. We do have to make choices where there is *no* "really" right course to take. But this won't do for Mencius. I think that Fingarette (1972, chapter 2) is basically right in arguing that Confucianism is innocent of the notion of basic existential moral choice. I discuss this more in "Moral Decision in Wang Yangming: The Problem of Chinese 'Existentialism'," chapter 15 in this volume.

44. Quoted in Goldman (1976, 449).

45. Does this criticism apply to Confucians generally? Probably not, but I am not sure. Zhāng Xuéchéng 章學誠, an eighteenth-century Confucian, e.g., insists repeatedly that one should recognize one's limitations of ability; but he is talking about the activity of the writer and scholar, and not addressing the question whether it might sometimes be morally right to choose for oneself what one sees to be a less than *morally* ideal course of action. To be sure, for Neo-Confucians like Zhu Xi and Wang Yangming,

it is a metaphysical fact that I always have available to me (at any given moment) the ability to recognize (and the motivation to perform) the right action. All I need do to succeed is to attend to my true self. So, in a way, the problem of insufficient motivation is metaphysically ruled out by Neo-Confucianism. Yet a related problem is there anyway. Consider Wang Yangming, and his students who want to "make up their minds" to become "sages" but can't. (See Chan, 1963, 216, no. 260). Still, no one even thinks of settling for a lower objective.

46. See later in this chapter, section 7.6.1.

47. See the discussion later in this chapter, section 7.6.2.

48. See the discussion later in this chapter, section 7.6.2.

49. Mencius also thinks that I and everyone have basic dispositions that such reflection can bring into play. In the present example I can be described as attending more closely to attitudes I already have, and to their implications; but where those attitudes came from is a separate question.

50. On internalism, see the introduction to this volume, p. 3, and above, p. 283, n. 4. [Editor.]

51. See, e.g., Butler (1983, 15, preface). See also Legge (1970, 56–57, 60–64). [Editor.]

52. See Chan (1963, 224, no. 280).

53. See Chan (1963, 224, no. 280), for the dust whisk example.

54. Watson (1964a, 68): *Zhuangzi*, chapter 5.

55. Watson (1964a, 75): *Zhuangzi*, Chapter 6.

56. See Fung (1952, 1: 140–41).

57. For more on Xunzi, see Nivison (1991a) and "Xunzi on 'Human Nature'," chapter 13 in this volume.

58. *Xunzi*, HY 96/27/21.

59. *Xunzi*, HY 85/22/67. Cf. Watson (1963a, 152).

60. See Watson (1963a, 154); *Xunzi*, HY 86/22/78.

61. See *Xunzi*, chapter 21; Watson (1963a, 121–38).

62. For more on the Chinese and Aristotelian notions of 'virtue', see "The Paradox of 'Virtue'," chapter 3 in this volume. I do not plan to enter here into the complicated debate over the extent of overlap between the Greek *phusis* and the Chinese *xìng* 性. I assume only that there is enough overlap in the concepts to make my comparison here fruitful. (For more discussion of this issue, see Graham (1967), Ames (1991), and Bloom (1994). [Editor.])

63. Mencius would insist, of course, that Yi Zhi was muddled about the true nature of "loving" and "caring." For more on 7A45, see "On Translating Mencius," in this volume, p. 196f.

64. Kant's point of view also seems nicely set out in Williams (1973).

65. I draw chiefly on "Attention and Will," in James (1969, 72–102).

66. See, e.g., "The Philosophy of Wang Yangming," chapter 14 in this volume.

67. See "Saintliness" in James (1969, 233–72).

Chapter 8. Philosophical Voluntarism in Fourth-Century China

1. This paper, which has not previously been published, was originally delivered at the twenty-fifth annual meeting of the Association for Asian Studies, Chicago, March 30, 1973. Other important studies of *Mengzi* 2A2 include Riegel (1980), Shun (1991b), and Van Norden (1997) (all of which were influenced by Nivison's work). The reader may wish to scan one or two translations of *Mengzi* 2A2.1–17 before proceeding to Nivison's detailed exegesis. [Editor.]

2. A collection of essays on philosophy, economics, etc., perhaps deriving from the philosophers of the Jìxià 稷下 academy under the patronage of the kings of the state of Qí 齊 in the late fourth and early third centuries B.C. For partial translations, see Rickett (1965, 1985). [Editor.]

3. These passages are discussed later in this chapter.

4. For more on Chen Boda, see Nivison (1956).

5. "Investigation of things" is the standard translation of *gé wù* 格物, a much-disputed phrase that occurs in the Confucian classic, the *Great Learning* (*Dàxué* 大學). For the locus classicus, see Legge (1971, 358, verses 4–5). For discussions, see Lau (1967), Graham (1992, 74–82), Ivanhoe (1990b, 81–82, 107–8), Gardner (1986, 53–59), and "The Philosophy of Wang Yangming," in this volume, p. 225 ff. On the *Daxue* itself, see above, p. 288–85, n. 21. [Editor.]

6. "What is not attained in words is not to be sought for in the mind; what produces dissatisfaction in the mind, is not to be helped by passion-effort" (Legge 1970, 188).

7. See, e.g., Chan (1963, 53–54, no. 81; 153–55, no. 170; 174–75, no. 187; 220–21, no. 272). Wang Yangming is also mentioned again later in this chapter (p. 132). [Editor.]

8. See Zhao's *Tící* 題辭 (the preface to his commentary).

9. For a contrasting view, see Riegel (1980, 450n. 4). [Editor.])

10. See also "The Dating of Events in the Life of Mencius" (Lau 1970, 205–13).

11. "Mo Di" is the full name of Mozi.

12. Indeed, Lau suggests that what we have in *Mengzi* 2A2 are two separate conversations that were spliced together. See Lau (1970, 77n.3).

13. Compare Eno (1990, 260n. 56). For additional discussion of *Mengzi* 6A4, see the essay "Problems in the *Mengzi*: 6A3–5," in this volume. [Editor.]

14. For a discussion of whether it is appropriate to render *zhi* as "will," see Van Norden (1992, 172–73). [Editor.]

15. On *si*, see Waley (1938, 44–46) and Van Norden (1992, 169, 170n. 34). [Editor.]

16. The image is from Wang Yangming. See Chan (1963, 148, no. 166).

17. Yáng Zhū 楊朱 was a philosopher of the fourth century B.C. For speculation about Yang Zhu's views, see Graham (1978, 15–18; 1989, 53–64), and Eno (1990, 257–58n. 41). [Editor.]

18. Duke Xiāng 襄公, Year 24. Legge (1991b, 507, Chinese 505, fourth column from right).

19. HY 32/15/24. Lau (1979, 135, no. 24).

20. There is also an interesting use of *yan* in *Mengzi* 3A5, which I discuss in "Two Roots or One?" in this volume, p. 133.

21. See Watson (1963b, 117–18), where *yan* is rendered both as "words" and as "theory." See also HY 56/35/5–57/35/10.

22. Translation adapted from Mei (1973, 229). HY 84/17/53–55.

23. I take *tīng zhǐ yú ěr* 聽止於耳 as *ěr zhǐ yú tīng* 耳止於聽, parallel with the following phrases. What the text seems to be saying is that listening in the ordinary sense of the word, i.e., with the ears, only enables you to apprehend what knowledge you can pick up from what others tell you. "Listening" with the mind gets you further, cutting out the mediation of other people and letting you interpret "signs" (*fú*), i.e., letting you apprehend directly the meaning of what you see. (Compare the *Zhuangzi* chapter title *Dé chōng fú* 德充符, "the [validating] signs of the completeness of Virtue.")

24. That is, it is like a mirror, responding exactly to what comes, but "accumulating" no impressions that would distort the next response.

25. HY 9/4/26–28. Translation modified from Watson (1964a, 54). Compare Graham (1986a, 68).

26. For a translation, see Rickett (1965). For an alternative translation and discussion, see Graham (1989, 100–105). [Editor.]

27. In which we have *yi* coming from "outside" and *ren* from "inside." See Graham (1967, 24–25), Rickett (1985, 379).

28. The exact meaning of the last phrase is doubtful (and the text may be corrupt), but the general sense is probably close to that of *Zhōngyōng* 中庸, chapter 22. Compare Rickett (1985, 379).

29. See especially HY 3/3/12.

30. HY 27/16/72–28/16/81. See Watson (1963b, 47–49).

31. HY 14/11/1–15/11/5. See Watson (1963b, 34).

32. See *Mozi*, HY 83/47/29–30, Mei (1973, 225–26), and *Mengzi* 6A1, respectively.

33. See, e.g., "Moderation in Funerals," "Against Music," and "Against Confucians" in Watson (1963b): *Mozi*, chapters 25, 32, and 39.

34. *Mozi*, chapter 31, "Explaining Ghosts." See Watson (1963b, 94–109).

35. *Mozi*, chapter 16. See Watson (1963b, 44), Mei (1973, 92).

36. For these incidents, see HY 88/48/81–87, Mei (1973, 241–42).

37. See especially HY 40/26/17–41/26/19, and Watson (1963b, 80).

Chapter 9. Two Roots or One?

1. Versions of this paper were delivered as the Presidential Address to the Pacific Division of the American Philosophical Association (San Francisco, California, March

28, 1980), and published as Nivison (1980c). This reprinting omits text at the beginning and elsewhere that was appropriate only in its presentation as his presidential address. Much of the vocabulary and the concepts employed in this paper come from Davidson (1982b). However, if I read him correctly, Nivison argues that Mencius would reject Davidson's principle P2: "If an agent judges that it would be better to do x than to do y, then he wants to do x more than he wants to do y" (1982b, 23). Other important studies of *Mengzi* 3A5 include Wong (1989) and Shun (1991c). [Editor.]

2. For the Mohist discussions of these issues, see Watson (1963b), "Moderation in Funerals" (pp. 65–77) and "Universal Love" (pp. 39–49) (*Mozi*, chapters 25 and 14–16 [respectively]).

3. Here Yi Zhi quotes one of the Confucian Classics, in which this is recommended as an attitude for a king to have toward his people. See Legge (1991e, 389), *Shàng shū, Zhōu shū, Kāng gào* 尙書, 周書, 康誥.

4. For this idea, compare *Mengzi* 7A45 in Dobson (1963, 139). See also the discussion of this passage in "On Translating Mencius," in this volume, pp. 196–97.

5. And so, Mencius implies—compare *Mengzi* 2A6—we would naturally want to prevent the accident; likewise, a king ought not to let his people suffer if they have done nothing amiss; as for the care-for-an-infant attitude, considered in itself it is not naturally directed with equal intensity toward all infants.

6. I.e., act according to a valid moral rule.

7. This was the mistake of Gàozǐ 告子—possibly a former Mohist—as criticized by Mencius in 2A2. See my discussion in "Philosophical Voluntarism in Fourth-Century China," chapter 8 in this volume.

8. I further discuss the similarities between Mencians and Mohists in "Motivation and Moral Action in Mencius," chapter 7 in this volume. (For a discussion of some of the issues that divide Confucians and Mohists, see Wong [1989]. [Editor.])

9. See Kant (1964, 67; Academy, 399). There is an immense amount of recent literature, which cannot be summarized here, discussing and critiquing Kantian notions of the relationship between duty and the emotions, but a few of the seminal works are Williams (1973), Stocker (1976), and Blum (1980). [Editor.]

10. The notion that to recognize a duty is to be motivated in a certain way is referred to as "internalism" or "prescriptivism." On prescriptivism, see the introduction to this volume, p. 3, and p. 283, n. 4. On the notion of a "pro-attitude" see Davidson (1982a, 3–4). [Editor.]

11. "Doing something intentionally" in a strong sense of agency. Of course, in reaching for that orange, knowing that it's that one and not this one, I act intentionally. But I have in mind intentional action in the sense that involves a serious choice of one value over another. (Cf. Charles Taylor's notion of "strong evaluation" [1985]. [Editor.])

12. This is not formal logic, which was not discovered in ancient China, but "logic" in the sense of rhetoric or dialectics. [Editor.]

13. See Graham (1978, 482–85, no. 11, D). HY 77/45/5–6. See also Nivison, "Motivation and Moral Action in Mencius," chapter 7 in this volume.

14. See the annotated reference list. [Editor.]

15. See Chan (1963, 9–12, no. 5).

16. Translation modified from Chan (1963, 223, no. 277).

17. See, e.g., Chan (1963, 193–94, no. 207; 228–29, nos. 289, 290).

18. Wang uses the phrase *sī yì* seventeen times in the *Chuán xí lù* 傳習錄, and uses the related phrases *sī xīn* 私心 ("selfish heart") eight times, *sī yù* 私欲 ("selfish desire") twenty-one times, and *sī niàn* 私念 ("selfish notion") twice (Ivanhoe 1990b, 160 n. 26). For a representative passage on "selfishness," see Chan (1963, 35–36, no. 39). Wang also uses the term *gōngfu* 功夫 (also written 工夫) frequently. For a representative passage, see Chan (1963, 173–74, no. 186), where the term is rendered "task." [Editor.]

19. On the universalizability test, see Dai (1777b, secs. 2 and 5); *Analects*, HY 32/15/24; Lau (1979, 135, no. 24); *Dàxué* 大學, commentary, chapter 10, sec. 2, in Legge (1971, 373–74) and "Golden Rule Arguments in Chinese Moral Philosophy," chapter 5 in this volume. On the "natural" and the "necessary," see Dai (1777b, sec. 13; 1766, I.5–6).

20. On the "unchanging standard," see Dai (1777b, secs. 4–5).

21. On the pleasure resulting from moral approval, see Dai (1777b, sec. 8).

22. On *akrasia* see the introduction to this volume, p. 2, and p. 283 n. 3.

23. I discuss these matters further in " 'Virtue' in Bone and Bronze" and "The Paradox of 'Virtue'," in this volume. (For an interesting discussion and illustration of the implications of gift-giving in Japanese society, see Seward (1983, 130–32). [Editor.])

24. The locus classicus for the notion of *liang zhi* is *Mengzi* 7A15, but Wang uses the notion in a very different way. For representative passages, see Chan (1963, 193–96, nos. 206–12), where the phrase is translated "innate knowledge." [Editor.]

25. See Nivison, "Moral Decision in Wang Yangming: The Problem of Chinese 'Existentialism'," chapter 15 in this volume.

26. Nivison is using examples from Mohist dialectics. For further discussion, see Lau (1952–1953) and Graham (1978, sec. 2/5). [Editor.]

27. On "prescriptivism" and "internalism," see above, n. 10. One might distinguish two cases in which one thinks one ought to do A, yet fails to do A: (1) One is motivated to do A, but insufficiently to overcome competing motivations. (2) One is not motivated to do A at all. The latter is, perhaps, more conceptually puzzling. [Editor.]

Chapter 10. Problems in the *Mengzi*: 6A3–5

1. This paper, which has not previously been published, was originally written in 1975 and revised in 1995. In addition to Lau (1963b) and Graham (1967), another important study of *Mengzi* 6A3–5 is Shun (1991a). [Editor.]

2. Lau (1963b, especially 241–43 and 250–55), and Graham (1967, especially 45–49).

3. Discussed at length by Lau (1963b, 236–41). (I do not follow Lau entirely, but will stay close to his translation.) See also Graham (1967, 43–45).

4. "Morality" is *rén-yì* 仁義, but Gao from the first is talking about *yì* 義; of this, more later in this chapter.

5. The text has *tuān shuǐ* 湍水, usually translated (Legge, Lau) as "whirling water," following Zhao Qi and Zhū Xī 朱熹 (Legge 1970, 395). But one would expect the word *tuān* to be cognate with *duān* 端, which I understand in *Mengzi* 2A6 as "sprout" (the root graph, 耑, depicts a sprouting plant), Mencius's metaphor for the four morality-generating dispositions in human nature. This points to the meaning "sprouting water" (i.e., spouting water), e.g., water bubbling up out of a spring. Compare *Mengzi* 4B18, where Mencius uses a similar "bubbling spring" metaphor for the moral energy in human nature.

6. See *Mengzi* in the annotated references in this volume. [Editor.]

7. Lau (1963b, 241n).

8. The superscripts have been chosen as mnemonics. Thus, "ADJ" stands for adjective, "P" for property, "TV" for transitive verb, and "DIS" for disposition. (Nivison originally used a similar notation.) [Editor.]

9. See Aristotle, *Categories*, chapter 1, 1a12 ff. and chapter 8, 10a27 ff.

10. Aristotle, *Categories*, chapter 2, 1a23 ff. (See also the discussion by Ackrill in Aristotle [1966, 74–75]. [Editor.])

11. Compare Aristotle, *Metaphysics* 7.10, 1035b24–25.

12. See Lau (1970, 21).

13. *Xunzi* HY 85/22/56–57; Watson (1963a, 150).

14. Compare Aquinas' use of the concept "the pleasures of touch."

15. Indeed this is often a sort of paradigm case of it, as Lau shows (1963b, 252).

16. Duke Huan, Year 18, in Legge (1991b, 71, Chinese 70).

17. On the notion of "institutional facts," see Searle (1969, especially 50–53, 184 ff.). [Editor.]

18. To summarize, the Chinese sentence D is ambiguous between D', D'' and D'''. D'' cannot be what is meant, as it amounts to a denial of what Gao has just said in C. D' is trivially true. D''' is, at least, controversial. [Editor.]

19. The use here is in an embedded sentence; verbal *yu* survived in certain embedded clause idioms.

20. Lau (1970, 264n. 14) suggests emending the text to *yì yú bái, bái mǎ zhī bái* 異於白。白馬之白 . . . , and translates, "The case of rightness is different from that of whiteness. 'Treating as white' is the same whether one is treating a horse as white or a man as white." Legge (1970, 398n. 3) proposes deleting the *yì yú* 異於, and translates "There is no difference between our pronouncing a white horse to be white and our pronouncing a white man to be white." Without explaining his rationale, Giles (1993, 93) translates, "Certainly there is no difference between the whiteness of a white horse and the whiteness of a white man." [Editor.]

21. See, for example, the very first example of inference in the *Mòzǐ, Xiǎo qǔ* 墨子, 小取. HY 77/45/12. See also Graham (1978, 217–18, 485–87).

22. See Graham (1990, 125–215) for a discussion of Gongsun Long's "white horse paradox." [Editor.]

23. Amounting, it would seem, to "Moreover, do you say that his *zhang*ᴰ is what is *yi* . . . ?"

24. See, for example, 1A7.11: 不爲者與不能者之形何以異 ("What is the difference in form between *not doing* and *not being able*?"). Legge takes this option: "The fact of a man's being old? Or the fact of our giving honor to his age?" (Legge 1970, 398.)

25. 4A20 and 4B5 both have 君義莫不義.

26. In other words, if the *bai* of *bai ma zhi bai* (6A4.3a) were a transitive verb (as Legge, Lau, et al. suppose), there would be no need to draw attention to the transitive use of *zhang* here. [Editor.]

27. Lau (1970, 264n. 15; 1969, 78–79); Graham (1967, 48n. 116).

28. Xunzi, like Gaozi in important ways, later points out that this is a disposition humans share with all creatures "which have blood and breath." *Xunzi*, HY 74/19/97–98. Watson (1963a, 106).

29. The Mohists advocate universal (hence, nonselective) "love" of others.

30. It is interesting that the Mohist logicians, whose techniques Mencius and Gaozi are using, have dealt explicitly with the problem of the location of *yi* (as D. C. Lau has noted [1963b, 258–59]. See also Graham [1978, 450–51]). In one passage Mencius's position appears to be defended: *ren* and *yi* are both "internal," because both are identified with my doing something, and not with the one to whom I do it. Here *yi* is defined as "to benefit" (a definition that would have appalled Mencius). Another definition goes as follows:

"*Canon*: The *yi* of Yao arises in the present but is located in the past. Yet these are different times. The explanation is found under 'what we *yi*.' They are two."
"*Explanation of the Canon*: The *yi* of Yao—this is reputation, in the present. The reality that we *yi* is located in the past." (*Mozi*, HY 66/41/9–10 and 73/43/60–61. I am not sure of the translation, which does not follow the Sun commentary [1987, 292, 345], or Graham [1978, 421–23].)

Here *yi* cannot be "benefit" (or "to benefit"), and I take it to be "commendation" (or "to commend") "for his benefiting," i.e., "honor," in the sense of what one has or enjoys when one is "honored" by others.

31. "In a tormented life, none of the six desires gets what suits it, all receive what they utterly despise: subjection is this sort of thing, disgrace is this sort of thing. No disgrace is greater than dishonor (*bú yì* 不義). Hence, dishonor is a tormented life, although not only dishonor is a tormented life." *Lǚshì chūnqiū, Guì shēng* 2.2 呂氏春秋, 貴生 (SBBY 4b–5a; also cited in Feng [1993, 175]; for a different translation, see Graham [1967, 36] or Graham [1989, 63–64].) See also above, n. 30, on "the *yi* of Yao." [Editor.]

32. Against the proposed interpretation is the difficulty of really making plausible sense of 6A4.4b this way: "This [person, i.e., I] is one who takes *wǒ* 我 as his pleasure." To make this interpretation work we have to suppose Gaozi to be holding that *ren* (exemplified in loving a younger brother) is really a kind of "ego-trip," or at least in some sense a self-directed or self-serving attitude.

33. Cf. *Mengzi* 6A7.8: "Hence, good order and righteousness please my heart just as grass-fed and grain-fed animals please my mouth."
34. Mencius himself says something that sounds much like this; see 7B24.

Chapter 11. Problems in the *Mengzi*: 7A17

1. This chapter, which has not previously been published, was originally written in May of 1975.
2. HY 33/15/40. See Lau (1979, 137, no. 40) for a looser translation.
3. Aristotle did think about it, and said this explicitly. (Kant would also disagree with Mencius. See Kant [1964, 67; Academy, 399]. There is an immense amount of recent literature discussing and critiquing Kantian notions of the relationship between duty and the emotions which cannot be summarized here. I merely direct the reader to a few of the seminal sources: Williams [1973], Stocker [1976], Blum [1980]. [Editor.])
4. On "voluntarism," see "Philosophical Voluntarism in Fourth-Century China," chapter 8 in this volume.
5. For a detailed discussion of various translations of the *Mengzi*, see "On Translating Mencius," chapter 12 in this volume.
6. Hattori's translation is "direct," that is, it simply applies rules for converting classical Chinese into an artificial literary Japanese. Hattori gives his interpretation in a note: "If in whatever situation you are in you avoid doing or desiring what is not right, then wherever you go everything will be right; and so by this the Way of man is satisfied." This is a paraphrase of part of the commentary attributed to Sun Shi.
7. Legge, following the editorial practice of the King James Bible, uses italics to indicate what he supplies that is not in the original text. He has a note summarizing: "A man has but to obey the law in himself"—and partly translating (and rejecting) Zhao Qi's commentary: "'Let a man not make another do what he does not do himself,' &c."
8. Lyall adds a footnote: "Cf. Burke, 'Let us identify, let us incorporate ourselves with the people.'"
9. Wilhelm has a brief comment approving of Zhu Xi's interpretation and rejecting that of Zhao Qi.
10. The "Sun Shi" commentary taken as a whole actually seems to agree with Zhao Qi, and supposes Mencius here to be stating an implication of Confucius' "golden rule," as stated in the *Analects*, HY 32/15/24, Lau (1979, 135, no. 24). See "Golden Rule Arguments in Chinese Moral Philosophy," chapter 5 in this volume.
11. See above, n. 2.
12. On the differences between the views of Mencius and those of his Song and Ming Dynasty interpreters, see Graham (1992), and Ivanhoe (1990b, 1993). [Editor.]
13. Zhu Xi comments, "Humans all have the hearts of compassion and disdain.

Hence, no one does not have things that he will not bear, and will not do. These are the sprouts of benevolence and righteousness." [Editor.]

14. Compare *Mengzi* 4A27 on this use of *shí* 實 in the sense of "actuality" or "core reaction." [Editor.]

15. Compare *Mengzi* 3B3, 6B1. (But also see Lau (1979, 145, no. 12), *Analects* HY 17:10, which suggests that Mencius has in mind burglars who bore through or jump over walls. [Editor.])

16. See "Motivation and Moral Action in Mencius," chapter 7 in this volume.

Chapter 12. On Translating Mencius

1. A version of this paper was published as Nivison (1980b). For some works referred to in passing in this survey, complete bibliographical information has not been provided. [Editor.]

2. We owe to the German influence on Qingdao the presence of an excellent brewery there.

3. For more on Ge Hong and his work, see Hsiao (1979, 644–56), and Eliade (1987, 8:359–60). [Editor.]

4. Additional information is provided in the references to this volume.

5. Legge's subsections apparently correspond to the places in the text where Zhū Xī 朱熹 inserts commentary. [Editor.]

6. For more on Wang Yangming and Dai Zhen, see the annotated references to this volume.

7. I originally wrote this paragraph in 1980. After almost two decades of further reflection, I am now convinced that Ware intended the picture of Mencius to be an amiable representation of the once chairman of Harvard's Department of Far Eastern Languages, Serge Elisséeff.

8. Others of especially high quality include Lau (1953; 1963b) and Graham (1967). (Another excellent study of Mencius that has been published since Nivison wrote this review is Ivanhoe [1990b]. [Editor.])

9. Lau (1984) is a revised translation of the *Mengzi*, with English and Chinese on facing pages. This work incorporates some, but not all, of Nivison's suggested corrections. Unfortunately, it is not widely available in the U.S. [Editor.]

10. My present view, suggested in Nivison and Pang (1990, 93) and Nivison (1990, 172n. 13), is that the Yao-Shun legends are a mythicization, ca. 425 B.C. or earlier, of two quite real "rulers" (in some sense of the word) in the first half of the twentieth century B.C., and that in the fifty-eighth year of the one who now is called "Yao," the so-called "Shun" imprisoned "Yao" for the rest of his life and actually banished his son. If this is right, the "idealization" of ugly fact was far more radical than is suggested by Dobson.

11. In Chinese the words for "son of Yao" are the direct object of the word for "sang songs" or "balladed," with no mediating preposition.

12. (1) This observes, properly, the parallelism of the two clauses *jū Yáo zhī gōng* 居堯之宮 and *bī Yáo zhī zǐ* 逼堯之子. (2) Recall my earlier observation about Legge's use of italics, p. 178.

13. For Legge *(zì) lài* 自賴 "(self-) relying," hence "good," contrasting with *bào* 暴 "(self-) abandoned," in the next line.

14. Similarly contrasting nicely with *bao* as "violent."

15. For a discussion of the intellectual movement represented by Chen Xiang, see "The Nung-chia 'School of the Tillers' and the Origins of Peasant Utopianism in China," in Graham (1990, 67–110). [Editor.]

16. Perhaps a third view, offered in Lanzhou (1960, 132, 397), is right, taking *she* as a particle meaning "whatever [kind of thing is needed]."

17. *Bó* is the literary pronunciation of *bǎi* 百.

18. Still the intuition is right: Chen is, in effect, suggesting that the Duke's intentions, at least, are good; he *is* a *xián* 賢 ruler, but he cannot *do* what is *xian* in the way he is proceeding.

19. See "Philosophical Voluntarism in Fourth-Century China," "Problems in the *Mengzi*: 6A3–5," and "Problems in the *Mengzi*: 7A17," chapters 8, 10, 11, respectively, in this volume.

20. See, for example, "Motivation and Moral Action in Mencius," chapter 7 in this volume.

21. This passage is discussed at length in Ivanhoe (1988). [Editor.]

22. It does not affect the point here, but there is a textual variant of this key line: 有攸不為臣. [Editor.]

23. Incidentally, some would want Lau to render *yǒu Yōu* 有攸 as "the ruler of You"; but Lau is correct here. See Nivison (1977).

24. Waley's very first note in (1949) criticizes Legge for just this mistake. Legge does make the error in the 1861 edition, but corrects it in the Oxford edition of 1895, which Waley unwisely did not use.

25. To see the difference, ask yourself what "in fact" and "just" *deny* as well as what they *say*.

26. *Zhuangzi*, HY 45/17/82; Watson (1964a, 109).

27. Lau is not absolutely consistent about this; for example, in 2A6, *bao* becomes "protection."

28. *Rù* is the literary pronunciation of *ròu* 肉.

29. *Shí* is the literary reading of *shè* 射.

30. Incidentally, there is an error in Dobson's "finding list": his section number for 7A15 is not 6.14 as given there, but 6.42.

31. See "Two Roots or One?" chapter 9 in this volume.

32. Kanaya, in vol. 2, p. 290 misses this, but Lanzhou on p. 322, Uchino on p. 481, and Yang Yung on p. 347, also get it exactly right, and Uchino further appears to notice its connection with Mencius's concept of "extending" (*tuī* 推) moral feelings: その心を推して民を仁し, 民を仁して後, 物を愛すべきである。 With その心

を推して that is, *tuī shì xīn* 推是心, compare, for example, *Mengzi* 2A9.1, *tuī wù è zhī xīn* 推惡惡之心 and 1A7.12, *tuī ēn* 推恩.

33. Note that Ware numbers this passage 4A10.

34. *Analects*, HY 32/15/24. Lau (1979, 135, no. 24).

35. And it can be relatively good: compare Dobson p. 205 (5.1, note 1) on Zhāng Yí 張儀 and Gōngsūn Yǎn 公孫衍, to Lau, p. 107, who renders 3B2 as though these men were already dead (perhaps true: Zhang Yi died in 309 B.C.), with no note.

Chapter 13. Xunzi on "Human Nature"

1. I should also say that this paper was presented at the Paul Desjardins Memorial Seminar on Classical Texts, in Jay, New York, in August of 1992, and that I am grateful for ideas that emerged there in our discussions.

2. For more on Dai Zhen and Zhang Xuecheng, see the references list in this volume.

3. This prefatory note was added by Nivison in 1994.

4. Nivison has in mind works such as Lau (1953; 1970, 19–22), and Dubs (1965). Other important studies of Xunzi that have been published since Nivison wrote this essay include Yearley (1980), Schwartz (1985, 291–302), Graham (1989, 244–55), Nivison (1991a), Ivanhoe (1991), Van Norden (1992), Ivanhoe (1993, 35–47), and Machle (1993). [Editor.]

5. See the essay, "Problems in the *Mengzi*: 6A3–5," chapter 10 in this volume.

6. See, for example, Graham (1967), Ames (1991), and Bloom (1994). [Editor.]

7. *Xunzi*, HY 28/9/69–29/9/72. I have in general used or adapted translations from Watson (1963a), in this case from pp. 45–46. In some cases the adaptation has had to be extensive; and in other cases it probably should have gone further for complete accuracy. In addition, in this text I have translated *zhi*, normally "knowledge" or "intelligence," as "consciousness." Compare *Mòzǐ* 墨子, HY 49/31/16, arguing that the dead "have *zhi*." (Some would prefer "awareness" for *zhi* here.)

8. For textual discussions of the *Xunzi*, see Kanaya (1951) and Knoblock (1988–1994). [Editor.]

9. Note that for Xunzi, as for all Confucian moralists, "rites" (*lǐ* 禮) include not just, or even primarily, religious rituals, "rites of passage," funeral ceremonies, etc., but all of the customary and legally correct forms of behavior. (For discussions of the concept of "rites," see Fingarette [1972] and Shun [1993]. [Editor.])

10. *Xunzi*, HY 70/19/1–3. Cf. Watson (1963a, 89).

11. *Xunzi*, HY 5/2/37–38. Cf. Watson (1963a, 30).

12. That is, the interpretation of *yi*, "sense of duty," as being for Xunzi in this context a superior kind of *zhi*, "intelligence."

13. *Xunzi*, HY 85/22/57–58. Cf. Watson (1963a, 150–51).

14. In which case I could see death as "the only possible course," in the sense of being the course I have to take if I am to optimize the realization of what I value.

15. Contrast Mencius on this problem (*Mengzi* 6A10). (For a discussion that explicitly compares these passages, see Van Norden [1992]. [Editor.])

16. *Xunzi*, HY 85/22/60–64. Cf. Watson (1963a, 151–52).

17. *Xunzi*, HY 85/22/66–67. Cf. Watson (1963a, 152).

18. Cf. *Xunzi*, HY 86/22/74–78. Watson (1963a, 153–54).

19. *Xunzi*, HY 86/22/80, 86/22/84–85. Watson (1963a, 154, 155).

20. *Xunzi*, HY 3/1/47–48. Cf. Watson (1963a, 22).

21. *Xunzi*, HY 2/1/30–31. Cf. Watson (1963a, 20).

22. On the distinction between "consequentialist" theories (also called "teleological" theories), and "deontological" theories, see Frankena (1973, 14–17). [Editor.]

23. This view is referred to as "internalism." See the introduction to this volume, p. 3, and p. 283n. 4. [Editor.]

24. *Xunzi*, HY 90/23/77. Cf. Watson (1963a, 168).

25. *Xunzi*, HY 88/23/32–35. Cf. Watson (1963a, 161–62).

26. *Xunzi*, HY 87/23/10–13. Cf. Watson (1963a, 158–59). At the opening of this chapter, Xunzi offers a series of definitions of "unfilled" and "filled" senses of key words, including the word *wei*: "When the emotions are thus and so, and the mind makes a selection [as to which to satisfy], we call this ratiocination. When the mind engages in ratiocination and our ability is accordingly active, we call this *wei* [in sense (1): 'conscious activity,' or 'intentional activity']. When ratiocination accumulates in [the matter at hand] and ability is accustomed to it, so that then [the project of creation or self-shaping] is brought to completion, we call this *wei* [in sense (2): the result of 'conscious activity,' i.e., something 'made' or 'done']." (*Xunzi* HY 83/22/3–4. Cf. Watson, 1963a, 139–40.) The next to the last occurrence of "conscious activity" in the quotation in the body of this paper seems to evidence a sense midway between the definitions: here *wei* is the capacity of our *wei* in the first sense (i.e., doing things) to result in *wei* in the second sense (i.e., specific things done).

Chapter 14. The Philosophy of Wang Yangming

1. Versions of this chapter, which has not previously been published, were delivered as talks at San Jose State University (March 9, 1973) and Haverford College (April of the same year). Since this talk is about Wang Yangming, who was suspicious of the educational value of the written word, Nivison prefers to leave this chapter in the informal, conversational style in which it was originally delivered. Consequently, it should be noted that all footnotes in this chapter are additions by the editor. All parenthetical references in this chapter are to the sections in Chan (1963). Translations are those of Chan (with occasional modifications). [Editor.]

2. Although the Chinese term *tiān* 天 is normally translated "Heaven," Wang does not use it to refer to a place where the souls of the "saved" reside after death. (Some Chinese Buddhists did have such a conception, though.) [Editor.]

3. Cf. *Zhuāngzǐ* 莊子, HY 93/33/67. [Editor.]

4. Wang (1933: section 20, 133.) [Editor.]

5. For a translation, see Ivanhoe (1990b, 115–16). [Editor.]

6. See Legge (1971, especially 383–85). See also above, p. 288n. 19. [Editor.]

7. On the distinction between *tǐ* 體 (usually rendered "substance") and *yòng* 用 (see the next paragraph in the chapter), see Graham (1992, 39–40 and passim). [Editor.]

8. Cf. *Mengzi* 6A8. [Editor.]

9. These issues are discussed further in "Moral Decision in Wang Yangming: The Problem of Chinese 'Existentialism'," chapter 15 in this volume.

10. The *Great Learning*, *Dàxué* 大學, Text. See Legge (1971, 357–58). For other discussions of this passage, see Lau (1967), Graham (1992, 74–82), and Ivanhoe (1990b, 81–82 and 107–8). For more on the *Daxue* in general, see above, p. 288–89n. 21. [Editor.]

11. Note that the characters *chéng* 誠 ("sincere") and *chéng* 成 ("whole, complete") are etymologically related, and are also regarded as conceptually related in the Confucian tradition. Thus, in *Zhongyong*, chapter 25, we find, "Sincerity is that whereby self-completion is effected." (Translation by Legge [1971, 418].) [Editor.]

12. Wang is referring to *Mengzi* 5A2, and may also have in mind 7A16. [Editor.]

13. The *Great Learning*, commentary, chapter 6. Legge (1971, 366). [Editor.]

14. The expression *bì yǒu shì yān* 必有事焉 originally comes from *Mengzi* 2A2.16. For a discussion of its meaning for Mencius and Wang Yangming, see Ivanhoe (1990b, 83–84). [Editor.]

Chapter 15. Moral Decision in Wang Yangming: The Problem of Chinese "Existentialism"

1. This essay was originally published as Nivison (1973).

2. MacIntyre (1971, 2–3) makes this move explicitly. Olafson argues that existentialism must be understood as the product of a particular philosophical history, the chief ingredient being Western ethical voluntarism, and simultaneously as a modern reaction against what he calls ethical "intellectualism" (the thesis that what a thing is is determined by its "nature," not by "mere will"), seen again as a specifically Western tradition. See Olafson (1967, 3): "Existentialism is, in fact, a reactive movement of thought which becomes fully comprehensible only when the philosophical positions against which it is reacting are identified and understood." (See also pp. 3–17 and 235–41, passim.) While Olafson does, of course, seek to extract a characterization of a kind of existentialism, a historical accounting is essential to his idiom of description.

3. On the distinction between "substance" and "function" see Graham (1992, 39–40 and passim). [Editor.]

4. For Wang's reluctance to have his ideas committed to a fixed written text, see Chan (1963, 271). See also the story told by Xú Aì 徐愛, a disciple of Wang's who recorded many of Wang's sayings. Xu reports that, on one occasion, Wang objected to a disciple recording conversations with himself on the ground that what he said to a student was always adapted to that student's needs at the time he asked his questions. Did this mean, Xu asked himself, that Wang's teachings should not be printed? Xu

rejects this suggestion on the ground that Wang's objections must themselves be regarded as teachings to suit a particular occasion. (For a translation of this anecdote, see Ivanhoe (1990b, 115–16). For a discussion of Wang's philosophy, see chapter 14 in this volume. [Editor.])

5. Wang Yangming himself discusses this matter in Chan (1963, 238–39, no. 312).

6. See Olafson (1967, 69 ff.), Plantinga (1958, 250 ff.), and Sartre (1966, 178–80).

7. On *Xin xue*, see "The Philosophy of Wang Yangming," chapter 14 in this volume, pp. 217–18.

8. See Chan (1963, 221, no. 274; 255, no. 331).

9. See Chan (1963, 218–19, no. 267).

10. Plato, *Meno* 80: "And how will you inquire, Socrates, into that which you do not know? What will you put forth as the subject of inquiry? And if you find what you want, how will you ever know that this is the thing which you did not know?" (trans. Jowett). The theory of recollection follows in Stephanus page 81. Cf. Henke (1916, 32), for an example of this learning paradox in a conversation between Wang and a disciple.

11. *Analects*, HY 7:30. (I have used throughout this essay, with some deviations, the translation of the *Analects* of Arthur Waley [1938].)

12. *Analects*, HY 5:10.

13. *Analects*, HY 4:6. Cf. also 9:19 and 15:16.

14. For more discussion of this issue, see "Weakness of Will in Ancient Chinese Philosophy," chapter 6 in this volume.

15. Of course, Wang is often quite explicit in saying people are "naturally good." See, for example, Chan (1963, 256, no. 335).

16. This appears to me to be Alasdair MacIntyre's appraisal of Kierkegaard's thought at this point, though as he points out, Kierkegaard (consistently) leaves the reader to choose between the two views of knowledge that he offers (MacIntyre 1971, 5). Kierkegaard, in the *Philosophical Fragments*, if I understand them, has a theological interest and is addressing the theological form of the problem already tagged—he insists that the individual turning to God at the decisive moment of conversion cannot be seen as a kind of Socratic "recollection"—that on the contrary God at this moment gives to the individual the needed "condition" for his or her choice.

17. See *Mengzi* 2A2.9 and "Philosophical Voluntarism in Fourth-Century China," chapter 8 in this volume.

18. The amount of literature on this point is great. See, for example, such differing studies as Lifton (1961), Meyer (1961, especially 80–85, "Psychosurgery," and 133–42, "The Cadre Crisis"), and Nivison (1956).

19. See Chan (1963, 168–69, no. 181); De Bary (1970, 159–60).

20. See Chan (1963, 147–48, no. 166; see also 230, no. 292).

21. On the "unity of knowledge and action," see later in this chapter, p. 243.

22. See *Mengzi* 6A7 and Chan (1963, 223, no. 277; 258, no. 337).

23. Other affinities between Wang and Husserl are explored by Yol (1965). On the

"perception" of value, two passages quoted by Olafson from Husserl's *Ideen* are instructive: "without further effort on my part, I find the things before me furnished not only with the qualities that befit their positive nature, but with value characters such as beautiful and ugly, pleasant and unpleasant and so forth." And "these values and practicalities belong to the constitution of the actually present objects as such, irrespective of any turning or not turning to consider them or indeed any other objects" (Olafson 1967, 64).

24. Perhaps de Bary has overstated the matter. For example, in Chan (1963, 254, no. 326), Wang holds that differences abound when people merely *talk* about "nature." The differences disappear when they *realize* "nature." This shows that the problem *does* occur to Wang but having seen it he immediately rejects the possibility that such conflicts could be "essential." See also Chan (1963, 230, no. 293), where differences in interpreting the *Yi jing* 易經 are compared to the (nonessential and nonsignificant) differences in the growth of bamboos in a garden.

25. See Henke (1916, 12). Chan (1972, 65) identifies the factual and legendary elements in this event. (See the surprisingly similar anecdote reported by Sartre (1993, 42–45), who derives a very different lesson. [Editor.])

26. See Schirokauer (1962, 185). (Milfoil stalks were used with the *Yi jing* in divination. [Editor.])

27. Tu Wei-ming has told me that he has found evidence that Wang did use the *Yi jing* at times. But it seems to me that he did not have to use it—given the structure of his philosophy—as a *decision procedure* (that is, for deciding what to do, given one's knowledge of the facts, such as it is, as distinct from, so to speak, asking the universe what is the case or what is going to happen—quite another use of divination).

28. On these terms, see the reference to Olafson, above, p. 309, n. 2.

29. We have had occasion in this investigation to refer to arguments in Plato's *Meno*. It is perhaps worth noting that Plato at the close of that dialogue has Socrates arguing (provisionally, for the inquiry is not complete in the *Meno*) that since the virtue of the statesman seems to be unteachable, it cannot be "grounded in knowledge"; that, on the contrary, "statesmen must have guided states by right opinion, which is in politics what divination is in religion; for diviners and also prophets say many things truly, but they know not what they say" (*Meno* 99). This apparent partial coincidence invites further study, but I shall not pursue the matter here.

Chapter 16. The Philosophy of Zhang Xuecheng

1. This essay was originally delivered as an address to the Kansai Asiatic Society, and published as Nivison (1955b). For other important studies of Zhang, see the references section of this volume, under "Zhang Xuechang."

2. The titles of these works might be rendered, "General Principles of Literature and History" and "General Principles of Bibliography." For more discussion, see Nivison (1966, 2 and 41–43). [Editor.]

3. Recall that this paper was originally published in 1955. [Editor.]

4. Nivison reports that this paragraph was inspired by a lecture he heard W. V. O. Quine give at Harvard in 1953, on how we understand language. [Editor.]

5. See also Nivison (1966, 257).

6. Other helpful introductions to major Neo-Confucian thinkers include Graham (1992), Ivanhoe (1990b, 1993), Gardner (1986, 1990), and "The Philosophy of Wang Yangming," chapter 14 in this volume. [Editor.]

7. Chan Buddhism is better known in the West by its Japanese name, "Zen." For more on it see Yampolsky (1967) and Dumoulin (1994). [Editor.]

8. See also Nivison (1956).

9. The *Jiaochou tongyi* manuscript was stolen, reconstituted in part from copies in the hands of friends, and completely revised a decade later. It is this rewriting that made it into a distinct "book." [Note added by Nivison, 1995.]

10. Cf. *Mengzi* 4B21, and Nivison (1966, 230).

Chapter 17. Two Kinds of "Naturalism": Dai Zhen and Zhang Xuecheng

1. This paper, which has not previously been published, was prepared for the "Asilomar Conference on Early Ch'ing Thought" in June of 1977. For more on issues discussed in this paper, see Yü (1996) [Editor.]

2. "Cheng-Zhu" refers to the intellectual tradition that derives from the thought of the Cheng brothers, Chéng Yí 程頤 and Chéng Hào 程顥, and of Zhū Xī 朱熹. For discussions of these thinkers, see Graham (1992), Ivanhoe (1993, chapter 4), and Gardner (1990). [Editor.]

3. Pointed out, briefly, in Nivison (1966, 142–54, passim).

4. There are three essays by Zhang that bear the title "Yuan dao." The first is part of the preface to the Hezhou Gazetteer (Nivison, 1966, 58), the second is part of the *Jiàochóu tōngyì* 校讎通義 (Nivison, 1966, 59–64), and the third and most important is a three-part essay written in 1789 (Nivison, 1966, 140 ff.). [Editor.]

5. A pseudo-philological title, "commentary and evidence on the meaning of terms in the *Mengzi*."

6. Most of this follows Qian (1957), but I also make reference to Yu (1976) and Nivison (1966).

7. Duàn Yùcái 段玉裁. *Niánpǔ* 年譜.

8. Both are numbered 9 in the *Dàishì yíshū* (戴氏遺書) printed by Kǒng Jìhán (孔繼涵), and the *Yuan shan* is dated to the month.

9. Such as the *Yuan shan*, thought of by Dai as a component of his *Qī jīng xiǎo jì* 七經小記. (Dai, like Zhang, was thinking of all his writings as components of one vast book, for which this was his name. In Zhang's case, the title was *Wenshi tongyi*, conceived by him as not just the essays now included in the book so titled, but as including all his writings, of whatever sort. It's the ultimate "hedgehog" point of view.)

10. *Juye* is the study of writing compositions in civil service examinations. [Editor.]

11. For more on this, see Nivison (1966, chapters 5, 8) and (1953).

12. See, for example, Han (A): 氣水也; 言浮物也 ("Energy is water; words are floating objects").

13. According to Zhang, Confucius in being a "transmitter but not creator" (*Analects* 7:1) was doing all he could do: "he had virtue but not position, and this meant that he lacked the authority to create institutions; and at the same time he couldn't use empty words to teach people."

14. For Dai, *bìrán* 必然; for Zhang, *bù dé bù rán* 不得不然.

15. For Dai, the *zìrán* 自然 of human nature; for Zhang, the *ziran* of *dao* itself, identified with the *bù zhī qí rán ér rán* 不知其然而然, the "unselfconscious activity" of ordinary people.

16. Commenting on Dai's "Zhèngxuézhāi jì" 鄭學齋記. See Nivison (1966, 201). Dai's essay is found in both *wenji*.

17. The reader may wish now to review the introduction of this paper (sec. 17.1).

18. For a discussion of Divine Command Theories, see Frankena (1973, 28–30). [Editor.]

19. Stoicism is a version of Dissolved Theism. The Mohist essay "The Will of Heaven" seems to advocate either a version of this position or of the Divine Command Theory. [Editor.]

20. Both classic Aristotelianism and (as we shall see) Mencianism are instances of this type. [Editor.]

21. In the West, the philosophy of Thomas Hobbes is an instance of Constructivist Naturalism. [Editor.]

22. For more on Existentialism, see "Moral Decision in Wang Yangming: The Problem of Chinese 'Existentialism'," in this volume. [Editor.]

23. For an introduction to these issues, see Frankena (1973, 96–102). [Editor.]

24. For the distinction between consequentialist (also called "teleological") and deontological positions, see Frankena (1973, 14–17). [Editor.]

25. For a detailed discussion of Xunzi's "Essay on Heaven," see Machle (1993). [Editor.]

26. For more discussion of what Xunzi means by *yi*, see "Xunzi on 'Human Nature'," chapter 13 in this volume.

27. Though with some logical oddity, e.g., when Mencius says (in effect, but plainly enough) to a king, "It is not useful to value utility" (1A1).

28. *Xu yan* 3.9; apparently none of the third (last) *juan* is duplicated in MZZYSZ. See also *Yuan shan* 2.4; Qian (1957, 345).

29. In Mencius this would have to be rendered "good order."

30. On the notion of a "pro-attitude" see Davidson (1982a, 3–4). [Editor.]

31. Professor Yü made this point in his presentation to the 1977 conference at which this paper was originally read.

32. For the phrase from MacLeish, see his "Ars Poetica."

33. The full quotation, "Had I been present at the Creation, I would have given some useful hints for the better ordering of the universe," was allegedly made by Alfonso the Wise, King of Castile (1221–1284) (after studying the Ptolemaic system). [Editor.]

34. See, e.g., the discussion of Lǐ Guāngdì 李光地 in Nivison (1953).

Annotated References

Alton, Bruce Scott. 1966. "An Examination of the Golden Rule." Doctoral Thesis, Philosophy, Stanford University. (University Microfilms International Order Number 674315.)

Ames, Roger. 1991. "The Mencian Conception of *Ren xing* 人性: Does It Mean 'Human Nature'?" In *Chinese Texts and Philosophical Contexts*, ed. Henry Rosemont, Jr. La Salle, Ill.: Open Court.

Aristotle. 1966. *Categories and De Interpretatione*. Translated by J. L. Ackrill. New York: Oxford University Press.

——. 1985. *Nicomachean Ethics*. Translated by Terence Irwin. Indianapolis: Hackett Publishing Company.

Ballou, Robert O., Friedrich Spiegelberg, and Horace L. Fries, eds. 1939. *The Bible of the World*. New York: Viking Press.

Bloom, Irene. 1994. "Mencian Arguments on Human Nature (*Jen-hsing*)." *Philosophy East and West* 44:1 (January): 19–53. (This is a response to Ames [1991].)

Blum, Lawrence A. 1980. *Friendship, Altruism and Morality*. Boston: Routledge and Kegan Paul.

Bodde, Derk. 1978. "Marshes in *Mencius* and Elsewhere: A Lexicographic Note." In *Ancient China: Studies in Early Civilization*, ed. David T. Roy and Tsuen-hsuin Tsien, 157–66. Hong Kong: The Chinese University Press. (Bodde's article is an excellent brief example of good hermeneutic technique!)

Brink, David O. 1986. "Externalist Moral Realism." In *Spindel Conference 1986: Moral Realism*, ed. Norman Gillespie, 23–41. Supplement to *The Southern Journal of Philosophy* 24.

Brooks, E. Bruce and A. Taeko Brooks. 1985. *Studies in Warring States Text Chronology: 1: Confucian Beginnings: The Nature and Evolution of the* Analects. Unpublished manuscript. 71 pp.

Burnyeat, M.F. 1980. "Aristotle on Learning to Be Good." In *Essays on Aristotle's Ethics*, ed. A. O. Rorty, 69–92. Berkeley: University of California Press.

Butler, Joseph. 1983. *Five Sermons*. Indianapolis: Hackett Publishing Company.

Carson, Michael F. 1978–1979. "Some Grammatical and Graphical Problems in the *Ho Tsun* Inscription." *Early China* 4: 41–44.

Chai, Ch'u and Winberg Chai. 1965a. *The Sacred Book of Confucius, and Other Confucian Classics*. New York: University Books. ("Mencius," pp. 91–220; glossary [with

Chinese characters], pp. 369–73; index, pp. 375–84. For a discussion of this translation, see "On Translating Mencius," in this volume.)

——. 1965b. *The Humanist Way in Ancient China*. New York: Bantam Books. (This is apparently a paperback reprint of Chai (1965a), with one or two typographical errors corrected. This edition has the same pagination as the other, but does not include an index.)

Chan, Wing-tsit. 1972. "Wang Yang-ming: A Biography." *Philosophy East and West* 22:1 (January): 63–74.

Chan, Wing-tsit, trans. [1963]. *Instructions for Practical Living and Other Neo-Confucian Writings* by Wang Yang-ming. New York: Columbia University Press. (See Nivison [1964] for a review of this translation.)

Chang Yü-ch'üan. 1939–1940. "Wang Shou-jen as a Statesman." *Chinese Social and Political Science Review* 23: 30–99, 155–257, 319–75, 473–517. (A valuable, but often overlooked, series of articles. Discussed in Nivison [1964].)

Chén Mèngjiā 陳夢家. 1956. *Yīnxū búcí zòngshù* 殷虛卜辭綜述 Beijing: Kexue chuban she.

Cheng Chung-ying. 1971. *An Inquiry into Goodness*. Honolulu: East-West Center Press. (A translation of Dai [1777a].)

Ching, Julia. 1978. "Chinese Ethics and Kant." *Philosophy East and West* 28:2 (April): 161–72.

Collingwood, R.G. 1946. *The Idea of History*. Oxford: Oxford University Press.

Cook, Francis H. 1977. *Hua–yen Buddhism*. University Park, Pa.: Pennsylvania State University Press.

Couvreur, Seraphin. 1910. *Oeuvres de Meng Tzeu*. Vol. 4 of *Les Quartre Livres*. 1895. Reprint, Ho Kien Fou. (For a discussion of this translation, see "On Translating Mencius," in this volume.)

Creel, Herrlee G. 1953. *Chinese Thought from Confucius to Mao Tse-tung*. Chicago: University of Chicago Press.

Dài Zhèn 戴震 (1724–1777). For discussions of Dai Zhen's thought in general, see "Can Virtue Be Self-Taught?" "Two Roots or One?" and "Two Kinds of 'Naturalism': Dai Zhen and Zhang Xuecheng," chapters 4, 9, and 17, respectively, in this volume, as well as Freeman (1933), and Ivanhoe (1993, chapter 6).

——. 1772. *Xù yán* 緒言 (*Prolegomena*).

——. 1777a. *Yuán shàn* 原善 (*The Origin of Goodness*). (For a discussion of this work and of the translation by Cheng [1971], see Ivanhoe [1993: 84–85].)

——. 1777b. *Mèngzǐ zìyì shùzhèng* 孟子字義疏證 (*An Evidential Commentary on the Meaning of Terms in the* Mengzi. The best English translation is Ewell (1990). Lodén (1988) is also good. For a discussion of some difficulties in translating this work, see Van Norden [1993].)

Davidson, Donald. 1982a. "Actions, Reasons, and Causes." In *Essays on Actions & Events*, 3–19. New York: Oxford University Press.

——. 1982b. "How Is Weakness of the Will Possible?" In *Essays on Actions & Events*, 21–42. New York: Oxford University Press.

Dawson, Raymond. 1968. *An Introduction to Classical Chinese*. Oxford: Clarendon Press.

De Bary, William Theodore. 1953. "A Reappraisal of Neo-Confucianism." In *Studies in Chinese Thought*, ed. Arthur F. Wright, 81–111. Chicago: University of Chicago Press.

———, ed. 1970. *Self and Society in Ming Thought*. New York: Columbia University Press. (Reviewed by Nivison [1971].)

Demiéville, Paul. 1961. "Chang Hsüeh-ch'eng and His Historiography." In *Historians of China and Japan*, ed. W. G. Beasley and E. G. Pulleyblank, 167–85. London: Oxford University Press. (Nivison has praised this article as the best general study of Zhāng Xuéchéng 章學誠 in any language.)

Dobson, W. A. C. H. 1959. *Late Archaic Chinese: a Grammatical Study*. Toronto: University of Toronto Press. (Index on pp. 237–54.)

———. 1962. *Early Archaic Chinese*. Toronto: University of Toronto Press.

———. 1963. *Mencius: A New Translation Arranged and Annotated for the General Reader*. Toronto: University of Toronto Press. (Introduction, pp. xi–xviii; translation, pp. 3–190; additional notes, pp. 193–207; finding list, pp. 209–15. For a discussion of this translation, see "On Translating Mencius," chapter 12 in this volume.)

———. 1974. *A Dictionary of the Chinese Particles*. Toronto: University of Toronto Press.

Donagan, Alan. 1977. *The Theory of Morality*. Chicago: University of Chicago Press.

Dù Dìngjī 杜定基. 1779. *Sìshū bǔzhù fùkǎo bèizhǐ* 四書補註附考備旨. (This work is an introductory-level commentary on the *Four Books*, based on an earlier work by the Ming Dynasty scholar Dèng Lín 鄧林.)

Dubs, Homer H. 1965. "Mencius and Sun-dz on Human Nature." *Philosophy East and West* 6: 213–22.

Dumoulin, Heinrich. 1994. *Zen Buddhism: A History*. Vol. 1. New York: Macmillan Publishing Company.

Eliade, Mircea, ed. 1987. *The Encyclopedia of Religion*. New York: Macmillan.

Eno, Robert. 1990. *The Confucian Creation of Heaven: Philosophy and the Defense of Ritual Mastery*. Albany, N.Y.: SUNY Press. (Reviewed in Shun [1992].)

Ewell, John. 1990. *Re-inventing the Way: Dai Zhen's Evidential Commentary on the Meaning of Terms in Mencius (1777)*. Ph.D. dissertation, History, University of California at Berkeley. (University Microfilms International Order Number 9126550. Perhaps the best translation of Dai [1777b].)

Fairlie, Henry. 1979. *The Seven Deadly Sins Today*. Notre Dame, Ind.: University of Notre Dame Press.

Féng Yǒulán 馮友蘭. 1993. *Zhōngguó zhéxué shǐ* 中國哲學史. 2 vols. 1944. Reprint, Taibei, Taiwan: Taiwan shangwu. (Translated as Fung [1952].)

Fingarette, Herbert. 1972. *Confucius—The Secular as Sacred*. New York: Harper Torchbooks. (For an insightful critique of Fingarette, see Schwartz [1985: 67–85].)

———. 1980. "Following the 'One Thread' of the *Analects*." *Journal of the American Academy of Religion* 47:3, Thematic Issue S (September): 373–403. (See also Ivanhoe [1990a].)

Frankena, William F. 1973. *Ethics*. 2d ed. Englewood Cliffs, N.J.: Prentice-Hall.

Freeman, Mansfield. 1926. "Yen Hsi Chai, a Seventeenth-Century Philosopher." *Journal of the North China Branch of the Royal Asiatic Society* 57.

———. 1933. "The Philosophy of Tai Tung-yuan." *Journal of the North China Branch of the Royal Asiatic Society* 64: 50–71.

Fung Yu-lan. 1952. *A History of Chinese Philosophy*. 2d ed. 2 vols. Translated by Derk Bodde. Princeton: Princeton University Press. (A classic, but now somewhat dated, history of Chinese philosophy. Reprinted numerous times.)

———. 1953. *A Short History of Chinese Philosophy*. Translated by Derk Bodde. New York: The Macmillan Co.

Gardner, Daniel K. 1986. *Chu Hsi and the* Ta–hsueh. Cambridge, Mass: Harvard University Press.

Gardner, Daniel K. trans. 1990. *Learning to be a Sage: Selections from the* Conversations of Master Chu, Arranged Topically. Los Angeles: University of California Press.

Giles, Lionel. 1942. *The Book of Mencius (abridged)*. London: John Murray. (For a discussion of this translation, see "On Translating Mencius," chapter 12 in this volume.)

———. 1993. *The Book of Mencius (abridged)*. Reprint, Rutland, Vt.: Charles E. Tuttle Company. (Facsimile edition of Giles [1942].)

Goldman, Holly. 1976. "Dated Rightness and Moral Imperfections." *The Philosophical Review* 85:4 (October): 449–87.

Graham, Angus C. 1958. *Two Chinese Philosophers: Ch'eng Ming-tao and Ch'eng Yi-ch'uan*. London: Lund Humphries. (Still one of the best works on Neo-Confucianism! Reprinted as Graham [1992].)

———. 1967. "The Background of the Mencian Theory of Human Nature." *Tsing Hua Journal of Chinese Studies* 6 (December): 215–71. (This is a paradigm of sophisticated research on Chinese philosophy! It was reprinted in Graham [1990]. All references are to the pagination in the reprint.)

———. 1978. *Later Mohist Logic, Ethics and Science*. London: School of Oriental and African Studies.

———. 1985. *Divisions in Mohism Reflected in the Core Chapters of* Mo-tzu. Singapore: Institute of East Asian Philosophies.

———. 1986a. *Chuang-Tzŭ: The Inner Chapters*. London: George Allen and Unwin, 1981. Reprint, Winchester, Mass.: Unwin Hyman.

———. 1986b. *Yin-Yang and the Nature of Correlative Thinking*. Institute for East Asian Philosophies Occasional Paper and Monograph Series No. 6. Singapore.

———. 1989. *Disputers of the Tao: Philosophical Argument in Ancient China*. La Salle, Ill.: Open Court. (One of the best introductions to early Chinese thought. See also Schwartz [1985].)

———. 1990. *Studies in Chinese Philosophy and Philosophical Literature*. Singapore: Institute of East Asian Philosophies, 1986. Reprint, Albany, N.Y.: SUNY Press.

———. 1992. *Two Chinese Philosophers: The Metaphysics of the Brothers Ch'êng*. La Salle,

Ill.: Open Court. (Reprint of Graham [1958], with a new foreword by Irene Bloom, and an index by P. J. Ivanhoe and Jon W. Schofer.)

Grene, Marjorie. 1970. *Introduction to Existentialism*. Chicago: The University of Chicago Press. O.p. *Dreadful Freedom*. Chicago: University of Chicago Press, 1948.

Gù Yánwǔ 顧炎武 (1613–1682). *Rìzhī lù* 日知錄. (Guangzhou shugutang ed. "A Record of [what I have come to] Know Day by Day." This book was highly esteemed in the middle and later Qing Dynasty as a model of scholarship; it is Gu's very careful notes on the Classics, history, and geography. For more, see Hummel (1943–1944, 424).)

Hán Yù 韓愈 (A.D. 768–824). A. *Dá Lǐ Yì shū* 答李翊書 (*Response to a Letter from Li Yì*).

———. B. *Yuán dào* 原道 (*The Origin of the Way*).

Hansen, Chad. 1983. *Language and Logic in Ancient China*. Ann Arbor: University of Michigan Press. (For a review, see Ivanhoe [1987].)

———. 1992. *A Daoist Theory of Chinese Thought*. New York: Oxford University Press. (Reviewed in Van Norden ([1995].)

Hare, R. M. 1952. *The Language of Morals*. Oxford: Clarendon Press.

———. 1963. *Freedom and Reason*. New York: Oxford University Press.

Hattori Unoyoshi 服部宇之吉. 1922. *Kokuyaku Mōshi* 國譯孟子. Vol. 1 of *Kokuyaku Kambun Taisei*. Tokyo: Kokumin Bunko Kankō Kai. ("Japanese Translation of the *Mengzi*" in "Grand Collection of Chinese Literature in Japanese Translation." Translation (literary) with notes at bottom of each page, followed by Chinese text, section by section [sections unnumbered].)

Heath, Thomas R., trans. 1972. Thomas Aquinas, *Consequences of Charity*. Vol. 35 of *Summa Theologiae*. New York: McGraw-Hill Book Co.

Henke, Frederick G. 1916. *The Philosophy of Wang Yang-ming*. La Salle, Ill.: Open Court. (This is a translation of Wang's *Chuán xí lù* 傳習錄, *Dàxué wèn* 大學問, and some of his letters. Henke was, apparently unknown to himself, translating part of a book which was itself only a selection, with some cutting, of important writings in Wang's complete collection. This translation is reviewed and critically compared with Chan [1963] in Nivison [1964].)

Hsiao, Kung-chuan. 1979. *A History of Chinese Political Thought*. 2 vols. Translated by F. W. Mote. Princeton: Princeton University Press.

Hú Shì 胡適 (Hu Shih). 1929. *Zhāng Shízhāi niánpǔ* 章實齋年譜. 1922. Reprint, Shanghai: Commercial Press. Revised by Yáo Míngdá 姚名達. (This is a chronology of events in the life of Zhāng Xuéchéng 章學誠.)

Hume, David. 1978. *A Treatise of Human Nature*. 2d. ed. Edited by L. A. Selby-Bigge and P. H. Nidditch. New York: Oxford University Press.

Hummel, Arthur, ed. 1943–1944. *Eminent Chinese of the Ch'ing Period (1644–1911)*. 2 vols. Washington, D.C.: United States Printing Office, Library of Congress.

HY: This is a reference to the Chinese text in the appropriate volume of the *Harvard-Yenching Institute Sinological Index Series*.

Ivanhoe, Philip J. 1987. "One View of the Language-Thought Debate: A Review of

'Language and Logic in Ancient China.'" *Chinese Literature: Essays, Articles and Reviews* 9: 115–23.

——. 1988. "A Question of Faith: A New Interpretation of *Mencius* 2B.13." *Early China* 13: 153–65.

——. 1990a. "Reweaving the 'One Thread' of the *Analects*." *Philosophy East and West* 40:1 (January): 17–33. (See also Fingarette [1980].)

——. 1990b. *Ethics in the Confucian Tradition: The Thought of Mencius and Wang Yang-ming*. Atlanta: Scholars Press.

——. 1991. "A Happy Symmetry: Xunzi's Ethical Philosophy." *Journal of the American Academy of Religion* 59:2 (Summer): 309–22.

——. 1993. *Confucian Moral Self Cultivation*. New York: Peter Lang. (This is an introduction to a number of major Confucian thinkers, stressing the variety within the tradition.)

——. 1994. "Human Nature and Moral Understanding in Xunzi." *International Philosophical Quarterly* 34:2 (June): 167–75.

——. 1996. "'Existentialism,' in the School of Wang Yangming." In *Chinese Language, Thought, and Culture*, ed. Philip J. Ivanhoe. Chicago and La Salle, Ill.: Open Court.

Ivanhoe, Philip J., ed. 1996. *Chinese Language, Thought, and Culture: Nivison and His Critics*. Chicago and La Salle, Ill.: Open Court.

James, William. 1969. *The Moral Philosophy of William James*. Edited by John K. Roth. New York: Thomas Y. Crowell Co.

Jiāo Xún 焦循 (A.D. 1763–1820). *Mèngzǐ zhèngyì* 孟子正義 (SBBY, *The Correct Meaning of the* Mengzi.)

Kanaya Osamu 金谷治. 1951. "'Junshi' no bunkengaku teki kenkyū" 荀子の文獻學的研究. *Nihon gakushiin kiyō* 日本學士院紀要 9:1 (March): 9–33. ("A Philological Study of the *Xunzi*.")

——. 1955. *Mōshi* 孟子 (*Mengzi*). 2 vols. Tokyo: Asahi Shimbun Sha. (Sections are numbered consecutively from 1 to 260, not beginning over in each half-book; long sections are broken into smaller units for translation [literary] and comment. Includes an index in volume 2.)

Kant, Immanuel. 1964. *Groundwork of the Metaphysics of Morals*. Translated by H. J. Paton. New York: Harper and Row. (References are of the form "Kant [1964, X; Academy, Y]," meaning page X in the Paton translation and page Y in the Royal Prussian Academy edition of Kant's works.)

Keightley, David N. 1978. *Sources of Shang History*. Berkeley: University of California Press. (This is the standard introduction to the study of Chinese "oracle bones" and their inscriptions.)

Knoblock, John. 1988–1994. *Xunzi: A Translation and Study of the Complete Works*. 3 vols. Stanford: Stanford University Press.

Lánzhōu dàxué Zhōngwénxì 蘭州大學中文系. 1960. *Mèngzǐ Yìzhù Xiǎozǔ: Mèngzǐ Yìzhù* 孟子譯注小組孟子譯注. 2 vols. Beijing: Zhonghua shuju. ("Lanzhou University Department of Chinese Literature, Mencius Translation and Annotation Section: Translation and Annotation of the *Mengzi*." Numbers books as does

Lyall [1932] [numbering each half-book]. Includes text, modern Chinese translation, and notes, presented section by section. Index on pp. 346–483.)

Lau, D. C. 1952–1953. "Some Logical Problems in Ancient China." *Proceedings of the
Aristotelian Society* 53: 189–204.

———. 1953. "Theories of Human Nature in *Mencius* and *Shyuntzyy*." *Bulletin of the
School of Oriental and African Studies* 15: 541–65. (An excellent, but often overlooked, study.)

———. 1963a. *Lao Tzu: Tao Te Ching*. New York: Penguin Books.

———. 1963b. "On Mencius' Use of the Method of Analogy in Argument." *Asia Major*, n.s., 10: 173–94. (This essay was reprinted in Lau [1970]. All page references
are to the reprint.)

———. 1967. "A Note on *ko-wu*." *Bulletin of the School of Oriental and African Studies*
30: 535–37.

———. 1969. "Some Notes on the *Mencius*." *Asia Major*, n.s., 15 (Part 1): 62–81.

———. 1970. *Mencius*. New York: Penguin Books. (Introduction, pp. 7–46; translation, pp. 49–204; appendices, pp. 205–63; textual notes, p. 264; glossary of personal and place names (actually an index), pp. 265–80. See also Lau [1984] and
the discussion of this translation in "On Translating Mencius," chapter 12 in this
volume.)

———. 1979. *Confucius: The Analects*. New York: Penguin Books.

———. 1984. *Mencius*. 2 vols. Hong Kong: Chinese University Press. (This is a revised
translation of the *Mencius*, taking into account some, but not all, of Nivison's
objections; Chinese and English on facing pages; not widely available in the U.S.)

Legge, James. 1861. *The Works of Mencius*. Hong Kong.

———. 1865–1895. *The Chinese Classics; with a translation, critical and exegetical notes,
prolegomena and copious indexes*. 5 vols. Oxford: Clarendon Press. (Monumental
translation [with Chinese text and explanatory notes] of the *Four Books* and three
of the *Five Classics*. Reprinted [in whole or part] numerous times.)

———. 1895. *The Works of Mencius*. 2d ed. (1st ed. 1861 [Hong Kong] and 1875
[Oxford].) Vol. 2 of Legge (1865–1895). (Includes "Prolegomena," pp. 1–123;
Chinese text, translation, and notes, pp. 125–502; index of subjects, pp. 503–9;
index of proper names, pp. 510–13; index of Chinese characters and phrases, pp.
514–86. For a discussion of this translation, see "On Translating Mencius," chapter
12 in this volume.)

———. 1960. *The Chinese Classics*. 1865–1895. Reprint, Hong Kong: Hong Kong
University Press.

———. 1969. *I Ching: Books of Changes*. 1899. Reprint, New York: Bantam Books.

———. 1970. *The Works of Mencius*. 1895. Reprint, New York: Dover Publications.

———. 1971. *Confucius: Confucian Analects, The Great Learning, and The Doctrine of
the Mean*. 1893. Reprint, New York: Dover Publications.

———. 1991a. *The Chinese Classics*. 1865–1895. Reprint, Taipei, Taiwan: SMC Publishing.

———. 1991b. *The Ch'un Ts'ew with The Tso Chuen*. Vol. 5 of *The Chinese Classics*.
Taipei, Taiwan: SMC Publishing. (References to this work are of the form "Legge

[1991b, X, Chinese Y]," meaning that the English text may be found on page X, while the Chinese text will be found on page Y.)

———. 1991c. *Confucian Analects, The Great Learning, and The Doctrine of the Mean.* Vol. 1 of *The Chinese Classics.* Taipei, Taiwan: SMC Publishing.

———. 1991d. *The She King, or The Book of Poetry.* Vol. 4 of *The Chinese Classics.* Taipei, Taiwan: SMC Publishing.

———. 1991e. *The Shoo King, or The Book of Historical Documents.* Vol. 3 of *The Chinese Classics.* Taipei, Taiwan: SMC Publishing.

———. 1991f. *The Works of Mencius.* Vol. 2 of *The Chinese Classics.* Taipei, Taiwan: SMC Publishing.

Lifton, Robert. 1961. *Thought Reform and The Psychology of Totalism.* New York: W.W. Norton.

Lǐjì 禮記. (SBCK, "Record of Rites.")

Lodén, Torbjön. 1988. "Dai Zhen's Evidential Commentary on the Meaning of the Words of Mencius." *Bulletin of the Museum of Far Eastern Antiquities* (Stockholm) 60: 165–313. (A good translation of Dai [1777b].)

Lowe, Scott. 1992. *Mo Tzu's Religious Blueprint for a Chinese Utopia.* Lewiston, United Kingdom: Edwin Mellen Press.

Lyall, Leonard A. 1932. *Mencius.* London: Longmans, Green and Co. (Index of subjects, pp. 243–60; index of names, pp. 261–77; analytical table of contents, pp. vii–xvi. For a discussion of this translation, see "On Translating Mencius," chapter 12 in this volume.)

Mǎ Chéngyuán 馬承源. 1976. *Hé zūn míngwén chū shì* 何尊銘文初釋. *Wenwu* 1: 64–65, 93.

Machle, Edward J. 1993. *Nature and Heaven in the* Xunzi. Albany, N.Y.: SUNY Press.

MacIntyre, Alasdair. 1971. "Existentialism." In *Sartre, A Collection of Critical Essays,* ed. Mary Warnock. Garden City, N.Y.: Anchor Books.

———. 1988. *Whose Justice? Which Rationality?* Notre Dame, Ind.: University of Notre Dame Press.

———. 1990. *Three Rival Versions of Moral Enquiry.* Notre Dame, Ind.: University of Notre Dame Press.

———. 1991. "Incommensurability, Truth, and the Conversation between Confucians and Aristotelians about the Virtues." In *Culture and Modernity: East-West Philosophic Perspectives,* ed. Eliot Deutsch, 104–22. Honolulu: University of Hawaii Press.

Mann, Susan. 1996. "Women in the Life and Thought of Zhang Xuecheng." In *Chinese Language, Thought, and Culture,* ed. Philip J. Ivanhoe. Chicago and La Salle, Ill.: Open Court.

Mei, Yi-pao. 1934. *Motse, the Neglected Rival of Confucius.* London: Probsthain.

———. 1973. *The Ethical and Political Works of Motse.* 1929. Reprint, Westport, Conn.: Hyperion Press.

Mèngzǐ 孟子. Sectioning in this volume follows HY unless otherwise noted. Subsectioning follows that in Legge (1970). (Incidentally, Legge subdivides according to the points at which Zhū Xī 朱熹 inserts commentary.) The translations of Chai and Chai, Legge, Couvreur, Wilhelm, Lyall, and Lau use a numbering in book 4A of the *Mengzi* that differs from the Harvard-Yenching text (HY), combining 4A7–8 together as 4A7 and separating Harvard-Yenching 4A23 into two lines. A critical discussion of the text of the *Mengzi* may be found in Lau (1970: 220–22). A number of translations are critiqued in "On Translating Mencius," chapter 12 in this volume.

Meyer, Frank S. 1961. *The Moulding of Communists*. New York: Harcourt, Brace.

Miào Tiānshòu 繆天綬, ed. *Míng rú xué àn* 明儒學案 (*Record of the Ming Confucians*). Xuesheng guoxue congshu ed.

Mòzǐ 墨子. This book is actually a collection of a variety of writings from various periods and factions in the Mohist school. It includes the "synoptic chapters" (chapters 8–39; see Graham [1985] for a discussion), works on rhetoric, philosophy of language, and natural science (chapters 40–45; see Graham [1978] for a discussion), the "Mohist analects" (chapters 46–50), and military essays (chapters 52–71; see Yates [1980] for a discussion). For translations of different portions, see Watson (1963b), Graham (1978), and Mei (1973). For a general study of early Mohist thought, see Lowe (1992). For a brief, readable introduction to Mozi and Mohism, see the relevant chapters in Graham (1989).

Munro, Donald. 1969. *The Concept of Man in Early China*. Stanford: Stanford University Press.

Murdoch, Iris. 1962. *The Bell*. 1958. Reprint, New York: Penguin Books.

Needham, Joseph. 1956. *History of Scientific Thought*. Vol. 2 of *Science and Civilisation in China*. London: Cambridge University Press.

Nivison, David S. 1953. "The Problem of 'Knowledge' and 'Action' in Chinese Thought since Wang Yang-ming." In *Studies in Chinese Thought*, ed. Arthur F. Wright. Chicago: University of Chicago Press.

———. 1954. "Communist Ethics and Chinese Tradition." Center for International Studies, MIT. Mimeographed. 83 pp. (A shortened version of this paper was published as Nivison [1956].)

———. 1955a. Review of *Chinese Thought: from Confucius to Mao Tse-tung*, by Herrlee G. Creel. *Far Eastern Quarterly* 14: 574–75.

———. 1955b. "The Philosophy of Chang Hsüeh-Ch'eng." *Occasional Papers* 3 (August 10). Kyoto, Japan: Kansai Asiatic Society: 22–34.

———. 1956. "Communist Ethics and Chinese Tradition." *Journal of Asian Studies* 16:1 (November): 51–74. (This is a shortened version of Nivison [1954]. This essay was also reprinted in *Thirtieth Anniversary Commemorative Series: Enduring Scholarship Selected from the Far Eastern Quarterly—the Journal of Asian Studies, 1941–1972* [Tucson: University of Arizona Press, 1972].)

———. 1959a. "Ho-Shen and His Accusers: Ideology and Political Behavior in the Eighteenth Century." In *Confucianism in Action*, ed. David S. Nivison and Arthur F. Wright, 209–43. Stanford: Stanford University Press. (There is a small error in the notes to this essay, pp. 358–59: There are two persons named "George Staunton," father and son. The author of the account of the embassy, published

1797, was the father, George Leonard Staunton, 1737–1801. The translator of the Qing law code published in 1810 was the son, George Thomas Staunton, 1781–1859. Both of them are "Sir.")

——. 1959b. Introduction to *Confucianism in Action*, ed. David S. Nivison and Arthur F. Wright, 3–24. Stanford: Stanford University Press.

——. 1960. "Protest Against Conventions and Conventions of Protest." In *The Confucian Persuasion*, ed. Arthur F. Wright, 177–201. Stanford: Stanford University Press. (This paper should be required reading for graduate students, for the problems that concern the Chinese intellectuals Nivison discusses are problems for everyone who hopes to lead a virtuous life in an academic context.)

——. 1964. Review of *Instructions for Practical Living and other Neo-Confucian Writings*, by W. T. Chan, and *The Philosophy of Wang Yang-ming*, by Frederick Henke. *Journal of the American Oriental Society* 84 (4): 436–42. (The manuscript Nivison submitted to *JAOS* included a table in which items in the left-hand column [i.e., sections in Chan's translation] were correlated with items in the same row in the right-hand column [i.e., sections in Henke's translation]. The editor of *JAOS* misunderstood, and hence incorrectly transcribed, Nivison's table. Consequently, in the table on p. 439 of the published review, items in the left-hand column correspond to the items in the right-hand column one row above them. Thus, p. 3 in Chan corresponds to p. 47 in Henke, p. 25 in Chan corresponds to p. 73 in Henke, and so on.)

——. 1966. *The Life and Thought of Chang Hsüeh-ch'eng (1738–1801)*. Stanford: Stanford University Press.

——. 1971. Review of *Self and Society in Ming Thought* by William Theodore de Bary. *American Historical Review* 76:4 (October).

——. 1973. "Moral Decision in Wang Yang-ming: The Problem of Chinese 'Existentialism.'" *Philosophy East and West* 23 (January/April): 121–37.

——. 1977. "The Pronominal Use of the Verb *Yu* . . . in Early Archaic Chinese." *Early China* 3 (Fall): 1–17. (On this topic, see also Nivison, "Reply to Professor Takashima," *Early China* 4 [1978–1979]: 30–36.)

——. 1978–1979. "Royal 'Virtue' in Shang Oracle Inscriptions." *Early China* 4: 52–55.

——. 1980a. "Mencius and Motivation." *Journal of the American Academy of Religion* 47:3, Thematic Issue S (September): 417–32.

——. 1980b. "On Translating Mencius." *Philosophy East and West* 30: 93–122.

——. 1980c. "Two Roots or One?" *Proceedings and Addresses of the American Philosophical Association* 53(6): 739–61. (The previously published version of "Two Roots or One?" suffers from sloppy typesetting. The version in this volume has been corrected.)

——. 1982. "Emperor of China Studies." Review of *Chinabound: A Fifty-Year Memoir*, by John King Fairbank. *New York Review of Books*, 13 May.

——. 1982–1983. "1040 as the Date of the Chou Conquest." *Early China* 8: 76–78.

——. 1983. "The Dates of Western Chou." *Harvard Journal of Asiatic Studies* 43(2): 481–580.

——. 1985. "D. C. Lau, *Mencius*: Comments and Corrections." 4 pp. Photocopy.

(This is a handout that was used in Nivison's introductory Chinese philosophy course. See also Nivison, Ivanhoe, and Van Norden.)

———. 1987a. "Chang Hsüeh-ch'eng." In *The Encyclopedia of Religion*, ed. Mircea Eliade, 3: 197–98. New York: Macmillan.

———. 1987b. "Chinese Philosophy." In *The Encyclopedia of Religion*, ed. Mircea Eliade, 3: 245–57. New York: Macmillan.

———. 1987c. "Hsin." In *The Encyclopedia of Religion*, ed. Mircea Eliade, 6: 477–78. New York: Macmillan.

———. 1987d. "Jen and I." In *The Encyclopedia of Religion*, ed. Mircea Eliade, 7: 566–67. New York: Macmillan.

———. 1987e. "Li." In *The Encyclopedia of Religion*, ed. Mircea Eliade, 8: 535–36. New York: Macmillan.

———. 1987f. "Meng-tzu." In *The Encyclopedia of Religion*, ed. Mircea Eliade, 9: 373–76. New York: Macmillan.

———. 1987g. "Tao and Te." In *The Encyclopedia of Religion*, ed. Mircea Eliade, 14: 283–86. New York: Macmillan.

———. 1988. Review of *The World of Thought in Ancient China*, by Benjamin I. Schwartz. *Philosophy East and West* 38 (October): 411–20.

———. 1990. "Response." *Early China* 15. (This essay accompanies Nivison and Pang [1990].)

———. 1991a. "Hsun Tzu and Chuang Tzu." In *Chinese Texts and Philosophical Contexts*, ed. Henry Rosemont, Jr. La Salle, Ill.: Open Court. (This paper was originally written in 1984 and revised in 1985. There is a typographical error affecting the sense on page 140 of the published version: in the nineteenth line from the top of the page, "but like the Taoist" should read "but unlike the Taoist.")

———. 1991b. "Qingming Day 1040." Unpublished paper, delivered as a talk to the Western Branch of the American Oriental Society in Eugene, Oregon (October).

Nivison, David S. and K. D. Pang. 1990. "Astronomical Evidence for the *Bamboo Annals'* Chronicle of Early Xia." *Early China* 15.

Nivison, David S. and Arthur F. Wright, eds. 1959. *Confucianism in Action*. Stanford: Stanford University Press.

Nivison, David S., Philip J. Ivanhoe, and Bryan W. Van Norden. "Comments and Corrections to D. C. Lau's *Mencius*." Photocopy. (This is an expanded version of Nivison [1985]. Various versions have been circulated.)

Nussbaum, Martha C. 1988. "Non-Relative Virtues: An Aristotelian Approach." In *Midwest Studies in Philosophy XIII: Ethical Theory: Character and Virtue*, ed. Peter A. French, Theodore E. Uehling, Jr., and Howard K. Wettstein, 32–53. Notre Dame: University of Notre Dame Press. (An excellent study of the technique of comparative philosophy.)

———. 1990. *Love's Knowledge: Essays on Philosophy and Literature*. New York: Oxford University Press.

———. 1993. "Comparing Virtues." *Journal of Religious Ethics* 21 (Fall): 345–67. (This is a critical discussion of Yearley [1990a].)

Okada Takehiko. 1970. "Wang Chi and the Rise of Existentialism." In *Self and Society in Ming Thought*, ed. William Theodore de Bary, 121–44. (This essay is discussed at length in "Moral Decision in Wang Yangming: The Problem of Chinese 'Existentialism'," chapter 15 in this volume.)

Olafson, Frederick A. 1967. *Principles and Persons: An Ethical Interpretation of Existentialism*. Baltimore, Md.: The Johns Hopkins Press.

Pascal, Blaise. 1966. *Pensées*. Translated with an introduction by A. J. Krailsheimer. New York: Penguin Books.

Plantinga, Alvin. 1958. "An Existentialist's Ethics." *The Review of Metaphysics* 12:2 (December).

Qián Mù 錢穆. 1956. *Xiān-Qín zhūzǐ xìnián* 先秦諸子繫年 (*A Chronology of the Pre-Qin Philosophers*). Hong Kong: Hong Kong University Press.

———. 1957. *Zhōngguó jìn sānbǎi nián xuéshù shǐ* 中國近三百年學術史 (*A History of Chinese Learning in the Last Three Hundred Years*). 2 vols. 1937. Reprint, Taiwan: Commercial Press.

Quine, Willard Van Orman. 1950. *Methods of Logic*. New York: Holt. (Revised numerous times. 4th ed., Cambridge, Mass.: Harvard University Press, 1982.)

———. 1960. *Word and Object*. Cambridge, Mass.: MIT Press.

Rahula, Walpola. 1974. *What the Buddha Taught*. Revised and enlarged ed. New York: Grove Weidenfeld. (A good, basic introduction to Buddhist philosophy.)

Rickett, W. Allyn. 1965. *Kuan-tzu, a Repository of Early Chinese Thought*. Hong Kong: Hong Kong University Press. (This contains some chapters not translated in Rickett [1985], including *Nèi yè* 內業, *Xīn shù shàng* 心術上, and *Xīn shù xià* 心術下.)

———. 1985. *Guanzi: Political, Economic, and Philosophical Essays from Early China*. Vol. 1. Princeton: Princeton University Press.

Riegel, Jeffrey. 1980. "Reflections on an Unmoved Mind: An Analysis of *Mencius* 2A2." *Journal of the American Academy of Religion* 47:3, Thematic Issue S (September): 433–57.

Rosemont, Henry, Jr., ed. 1980. *Journal of the American Academy of Religion* 47:3 (September), Thematic Issue S. (Note that "Thematic Issue S" is a special volume of this journal, a supplement to volume 47, no. 3.)

———. 1991. *Chinese Texts and Philosophical Contexts: Essays Dedicated to Angus C. Graham*. La Salle, Ill.: Open Court.

Russell, Bertrand. 1948. *Human Knowledge: Its Scope and Limits*. New York: Simon and Schuster.

Sartre, Jean P. 1966. "Being and Doing: Freedom." In *Free Will and Determinism*, ed. Bernard Berofsky, 174–95. New York: Harper and Row.

———. 1993. "The Humanism of Existentialism." In *Essays in Existentialism*, 31–62. New York: Carol Publishing Group. (O.p. 1965 as *The Philosophy of Existentialism*.)

SBBY: This is a reference to the appropriate volume of the *Sìbù bèiyào* 四部備要

SBCK: This is a reference to the appropriate volume of the *Sìbù cóngkān* 四部叢刊.

Schirokauer, Conrad M. 1962. "Chu Hsi's Political Career." In *Confucian Personalities*, ed. A. F. Wright and Denis Twitchett. Stanford: Stanford University Press.

Schwartz, Benjamin. 1985. *The World of Thought in Ancient China*. Cambridge, Mass.:

Belknap Press. (One of the best introductions to early Chinese thought. See also Graham [1989].)

Searle, John R. 1969. *Speech Acts: An Essay in the Philosophy of Language.* New York: Cambridge University Press.

Seward, Jack. 1983. *Japanese in Action.* 2d ed. New York: Weatherhill. (An entertainingly irreverent introduction to Japanese language and culture.)

Shǎnxī Zhōu Yuán Kǎogǔ Duì 陝西周原考古隊. 1978. "Shǎnxī Fúfēng Zhuāngbái yíhào Xī Zhōu qīngtóngqì jiàocáng fājué jiǎnbào." 陝西扶風庄白一號西周青銅器窖藏發掘簡報 *Wenwu* 3: 1–18.

Shima Kunio 島邦男. 1971. *Inkyo bokuji sōrui* 殷墟卜辭綜類. 2d rev. ed. Tokyo. O.p. 1967. (This is a concordance for a large number of published collections of "oracle bone" inscriptions. For more on "oracle bones," see Keightley [1978].)

Shun, Kwong-loi. 1989. "Moral Reasons in Confucian Ethics." *Journal of Chinese Philosophy* 16 (September/December): 317–43. (See also Van Norden [1991] and Wong [1991].)

———. 1991a. "Mencius and the Mind-Dependence of Morality: An Analysis of *Meng Tzu* 6A:4–5." *Journal of Chinese Philosophy* 18 (June): 169–93.

———. 1991b. "Mencius and the Mind-Inherence of Morality: Mencius' Rejection of Kao Tzu's Maxim in *Meng Tzu* 2A:2." *Journal of Chinese Philosophy* 18 (December): 371–86.

———. 1991c. "Mencius' Criticism of Mohism: An Analysis of *Meng Tzu* 3A:5." *Philosophy East and West* 41 (April): 203–14.

———. 1992. Review of *The Confucian Creation of Heaven* by Robert Eno. *Harvard Journal of Asiatic Studies* 52:2 (December): 739–56.

———. 1993. "*Jen* and *Li* in the *Analects*." *Philosophy East and West* 43:3 (July): 457–79.

Sīmǎ Qiān 司馬遷 (145–86 B.C.). 1894. *Shǐjì* 史記. Shanghai: Tongwen shuju, photolithographic reprint. ("Records of the Historian.")

Simon, Walter. 1954. "Functions and Meanings of *Erh* IV." *Asia Major*, n.s., 4.

Smart, Ninian. 1969. *The Religious Experience of Mankind.* New York: Charles Scribners.

Stanford Philosophy Department. 1994. Memorial notice for John Goheen. *Proceedings and Addresses of the American Philosophical Association* 68:2 (November): 73–74.

Stocker, Michael. 1976. "The Schizophrenia of Modern Ethical Theories." *Journal of Philosophy* 73 (August): 453–66.

Sūn Shì 孫奭 (A.D. 962–1033). *Mèngzǐ zhùshù.* 孟子注疏. (SBBY, "Commentary and Subcommentary on the *Mengzi*." Although this commentary is attributed to Sun Shi, it probably is not actually by him. See Legge [1970, 7–8].)

Sūn Yíràng 孫詒讓. 1987. *Mòzǐ jiàngǔ* 墨子閒詁 (*The Mozi Parsed and Annotated*). 1894. Reprint, Taibei, Taiwan: Huazheng shuju.

Táng Lán 唐蘭. 1976. "Hé zūn míngwén jiě shì" 何尊銘文解釋. *Wenwu* 1: 60–63.

Taylor, Charles. 1985. "What Is Human Agency?" In *Human Agency and Language*, 15–44. Vol. 1 of *Philosophical Papers*. New York: Cambridge University Press.

Tu Wei-ming. 1989. *Centrality and Commonality: An Essay on Confucian Religiousness.* Revised and enlarged ed. Albany, N.Y.: SUNY Press.

Tucker, Robert. 1972. *Philosophy and Myth in Karl Marx*. 2d ed. New York: Cambridge University Press.

Uchino Kumaichiro 內野熊一郎. 1962. *Mōshi* 孟子. Vol. 4 of Shinshaku Kambun Taikei. Tokyo: Meiji Shoin. ("*Mengzi*" in "Grand Collection of Chinese Literature, Newly Interpreted." Sections have conventional numbering; Chinese text with literal literary translation beneath, followed by free interpretive translation in modern Japanese, and comment; index, pp. 515–58.)

Van Norden, Bryan W. 1991. "Kwong-loi Shun on Moral Reasons in Mencius." *Journal of Chinese Philosophy* 18:4 (December): 353–70.

——. 1992. "Mengzi and Xunzi: Two Views of Human Agency." *International Philosophical Quarterly* 32 (June): 161–84.

——. 1993. Review of *Tai Chen on Mencius* by Ann-ping Chin and Mansfield Freeman. *Journal of Chinese Religions*: 148–50.

——. 1995. Review of *A Daoist Theory of Chinese Thought* by Chad Hansen. *Ethics* 105:2 (January): 433–35.

——. 1996. "What Should Western Philosophy Learn from Chinese Philosophy." In *Chinese Language, Thought, and Culture*, ed. Philip J. Ivanhoe. Chicago and La Salle, Ill.: Open Court. (This is an overview of the secondary literature on Chinese philosophy in English.)

——. 1997. "Mencius on Courage." In *Midwest Studies in Philosophy XXI: The Philosophy of Religion*, ed. Peter A. French, Theodore E. Uehling, Jr., and Howard K. Wettstein. Notre Dame: University of Notre Dame Press.

Van Zoeren, Steven. 1991. *Poetry and Personality*. Stanford: Stanford University Press.

Waley, Arthur. 1938. *The Analects of Confucius*. New York: Random House, Vintage Books.

——. 1949. "Notes on *Mencius*." *Asia Major*, n.s., 1: 99–108. (This is reprinted in pp. vii–xiv of volume 2 of Legge [1960] and Legge [1991f]. The original article was based on Legge [1861]. In the reprints, the page numbers have been changed to accord with Legge [1895].)

——. 1958. *The Way and Its Power*. New York: Grove Press. (First published in 1934.)

Wang, John Ching-yu. 1972. *Chin Sheng-tan*. New York: Twayne Publishers.

Wáng Yángmíng 王陽明 (1472–1529). References in the present volume are to either Chan (1963), Henke (1916), or Wang (1933). For those who like that sort of thing, Ivanhoe (1990b, appendix III) includes a finding list correlating Chan's sectioning to passages in the SBCK. Nivison (1964) evaluates the translations of Chan and Henke. For discussions of the thought of Wang Yangming, see "Can Virtue Be Self-Taught?" "Two Roots or One?" "The Philosophy of Wang Yangming," and "Moral Decision in Wang Yangming: The Problem of Chinese 'Existentialism,'" in this volume, and also Chang (1939–1940), Nivison (1953), and Ivanhoe (1990b; 1993, chapter 5).

——. 1933. *Wáng Wénchéng Gōng quánshū* 王文成公全書 Commercial Press. (Wan-you Wenku ed. References are by *juàn* 卷, followed by page number.)

Ware, James R. 1955. *The Sayings of Confucius*. New York: Mentor Books.

———. 1960. *The Sayings of Mencius*. New York: Mentor Books. (Introduction, pp. 7–43; translation, pp. 44–165; index, pp. 169–73. For a discussion of this translation, see "On Translating Mencius," chapter 12 in this volume.)

———. 1963. *The Sayings of Chuang Chou*. New York: Mentor Books.

Watson, Burton. 1963a. *Hsün Tzu: Basic Writings*. New York: Columbia University Press.

———. 1963b. *Mo Tzu: Basic Writings*. New York: Columbia University Press.

———. 1964a. *Chuang Tzu: Basic Writings*. New York: Columbia University Press.

———. 1964b. *Han Fei Tzu: Basic Writings*. New York: Columbia University Press.

———. 1968. *The Complete Works of Chuang Tzu*. New York: Columbia University Press.

Wilhelm, Richard. 1921. *Mong Dsi (Mong Ko)*. Jena: Eugen Diederichs Verlag. (Index, pp. 185–207. Previously published 1913 and 1916. For a discussion of this translation, see "On Translating Mencius," chapter 12 in this volume.)

Williams, Bernard. 1973. "Morality and the Emotions." In *Problems of the Self*. New York: Cambridge University Press.

Wong, David. 1989. "Universalism vs. Love with Distinctions: An Ancient Debate Revived." *Journal of Chinese Philosophy* 16 (September/December): 251–72.

———. 1991. "Is There a Distinction between Reason and Emotion in Mencius?" *Philosophy East and West* 41 (January): 31–44. (This is a discussion of Shun [1989].)

Wright, Arthur F., ed. 1953. *Studies in Chinese Thought*. Chicago: University of Chicago Press.

Xú Gàn 徐幹 (A.D. 171–218). *Zhōng lùn* 中論. (SBCK.)

Yampolsky, Philip B., trans. 1967. *The Platform Sutra of the Sixth Patriarch*. New York: Columbia University Press.

Yang, C. K. 1959. "Some Characteristics of Chinese Bureaucratic Behavior." In *Confucianism in Action*, ed. David S. Nivison and Arthur F. Wright, 134–64. Stanford: Stanford University Press.

Yáng Yǒng 楊勇. 1970. *Mèngzǐ yìjiě* 孟子譯解 (*Mencius Translated and Explained*). Hong Kong: Dazhong shuju. (Includes text, notes, and modern Chinese translation, section by section [sections not numbered]. No index; end has Zhao Qi's *Tí cí* 題辭, and so on, untranslated.)

Yates, Robin D. S. 1980. "The Mohists on Warfare: Technology, Technique, and Justification." *Journal of the American Academy of Religion* 47:3, Thematic Issue S (September): 549–603.

Yearley, Lee H. 1980. "Hsün Tzu on the Mind: His Attempted Synthesis of Confucianism and Taoism." *Journal of Asian Studies* 39:3 (May): 465–80.

———. 1990a. *Mencius and Aquinas: Theories of Virtue and Conceptions of Courage*. Albany, N.Y.: SUNY Press. (An outstanding example of comparative philosophy. See also Nussbaum [1993].)

———. 1990b. "Recent Work on Virtue." *Religious Studies Review* 16:1 (January): 1–9.

Yol, Jung Hua. 1965. "Wang Yang-ming and Existential Phenomenology." *International Philosophical Quarterly* 5: 612–36.

Yú Yīngshí 余英時 (Yü Ying-shih). 1976. *Lùn Dài Zhèn yǔ Zhāng Xuéchéng* 論戴震與章學誠. (*On Dai Zhen and Zhang Xuecheng*). Hong Kong: Longmen shudian.

Yü Ying-shih. 1996. "Zhang Xuecheng Versus Dai Zhen," In *Chinese Language, Thought, and Culture*, ed. Philip J. Ivanhoe. Chicago and La Salle, Ill.: Open Court.

Yú Yuè 俞樾 (1821–1907). *Mèngzǐ píngyì* 孟子平議 (A Balanced Account of Mencius). (This work appears to be part of Yu's *Qún jīng píngyì* 群經平議, 1867. For more, see Hummel [1943–1944, 945].)

Zhāng Bǐngquán 張秉權. 1957–1972. *Xiǎotún dìèrběn: Yīnxū wénzì: Bǐng biān* 小屯第二本: 殷虛文字: 丙編. Taibei, Taiwan. (This work, which was published in a series of installments, is the publication of a large cache of inscribed "oracle bones" found at the Xiaotun village site in Anyang: plates, transcriptions, and analysis. Its great value is not only the large quantity of material, but also the fact that the material can be dated to the last part of the reign of Wǔ Dīng 武丁 [Nivison's date for his death is 1189 B.C.], and was a controlled excavation. For more on "oracle bones," see Keightley [1978].)

Zhāng Xuéchéng 章學誠 (A.D. 1738–1801). *Zhāngshì yíshū* 章氏遺書. (Jiaye tang ed. "The Posthumous Writings of Mr. Zhang." On the thought of Zhang Xuecheng, see Demiéville [1961], Nivison [1953, 1966], Yü [1996], Mann [1996], as well as "The Philosophy of Zhang Xuecheng," and "Two Kinds of 'Naturalism': Dai Zhen and Zhang Xuecheng," chapters 16 and 17 in this volume.)

Zhāng Zhènglǎng 張政烺. 1976. "Hé zūn míngwén jiě shì bǔyí" 何尊銘文解釋補遺. *Wenwu* 1: 66.

Zhào Qí 趙岐 (A.D. 108–201). *Mèngzǐ zhù* 孟子注. (SBBY, "Commentary on the *Mengzi*." All references to Zhao Qi are to this work. This work has never been translated into English.)

Zhū Xī 朱熹 (A.D. 1130–1200). *Sìshū jízhù* 四書集注 (SBBY, "Collected Commentaries on the *Four Books*." Unless otherwise noted, all references to Zhu Xi are to this work. This work has never been translated into English. For more on Zhu Xi, see Ivanhoe [1993, chapter 4] and Gardner [1990].)

Index of Names and Subjects

Index Locorum

Mengzi

Lun yu (Analects)

Zhongyong (Centrality and Commonality)

Daxue (The Great Learning)